The Frasers of Philorth, Volume 1

Alexander Fraser Saltoun

Nabu Public Domain Reprints:

You are holding a reproduction of an original work published before 1923 that is in the public domain in the United States of America, and possibly other countries. You may freely copy and distribute this work as no entity (individual or corporate) has a copyright on the body of the work. This book may contain prior copyright references, and library stamps (as most of these works were scanned from library copies). These have been scanned and retained as part of the historical artifact.

This book may have occasional imperfections such as missing or blurred pages, poor pictures, errant marks, etc. that were either part of the original artifact, or were introduced by the scanning process. We believe this work is culturally important, and despite the imperfections, have elected to bring it back into print as part of our continuing commitment to the preservation of printed works worldwide. We appreciate your understanding of the imperfections in the preservation process, and hope you enjoy this valuable book.

SIR ALEXANDER FRASER OF PHILORTH
BORN CIRCA 1537. DIED 1623
FOUNDER OF FRASERBURGH.

THE

FRASERS OF PHILORTH

BY

ALEXANDER FRASER
OF PHILORTH
SEVENTEENTH LORD SALTOUN

IN THREE VOLUMES: VOLUME I.

EDINBURGH—MDCCCLXXIX.

IMPRESSION:

ONE HUNDRED AND FIFTY COPIES.

PRINTED FOR PRIVATE CIRCULATION.

No. 139

Presented to The Lord Polwarth.

Contents of Volume First.

	PAGE
TITLE-PAGE.	
GENERAL TABLE OF CONTENTS, ...	i-iv
PREFACE, ...	v
PEDIGREE OF THE FRASERS OF PHILORTH, LORDS SALTOUN, ...	xiii
DESCENTS FROM HON. WILLIAM FRASER OF FRASERFIELD, SECOND SON; AND HON. JAMES FRASER OF LONMAY, THIRD SON OF WILLIAM, ELEVENTH LORD SALTOUN,	xvi
PEDIGREE OF THE ABERNETHIES, LORDS SALTOUN, .	xvii
INTRODUCTION, ...	1
THE FRASERS IN EAST LOTHIAN, ...	12
THE FRASERS OF TOUCH-FRASER, ETC., AND COWIE, .	33
THE FRASERS OF COWIE, DURRIS, AND PHILORTH, .	92
THE FRASERS OF PHILORTH, LORDS SALTOUN, . .	169

CONTENTS.

ILLUSTRATIONS IN VOLUME FIRST.

I.—PORTRAITS.

	PAGE
SIR ALEXANDER FRASER, EIGHTH OF PHILORTH, FOUNDER OF FRASERBURGH,	*Frontispiece.*
ALEXANDER FRASER, NINTH OF PHILORTH,	*between* 166 *and* 167
ALEXANDER FRASER, TENTH OF PHILORTH, AND TENTH LORD SALTOUN,	168 *and* 169
CHARLES KER, SECOND EARL OF ANCRUM,	180 *and* 181
ALEXANDER FRASER, MASTER OF SALTOUN,	186 *and* 187
ALEXANDER FRASER, ELDER SON OF THE MASTER OF SALTOUN,	188 *and* 189
WILLIAM FRASER, ELEVENTH OF PHILORTH, AND ELEVENTH LORD SALTOUN,	*to face page* 193
JAMES SHARPE, ARCHBISHOP OF ST. ANDREWS,	*between* 194 *and* 195
ALEXANDER FRASER, TWELFTH OF PHILORTH, AND TWELFTH LORD SALTOUN,	198 *and* 199
ALEXANDER FRASER, THIRTEENTH OF PHILORTH AND THIRTEENTH LORD SALTOUN,	202 *and* 203
GEORGE FRASER, FOURTEENTH OF PHILORTH AND FOURTEENTH LORD SALTOUN,	204 *and* 205
ALEXANDER FRASER, FIFTEENTH OF PHILORTH AND FIFTEENTH LORD SALTOUN,	206 *and* 207
MARJORY FRASER, LADY SALTOUN, HIS WIFE,	206 *and* 207
SIMON FRASER, ESQ. OF NESS CASTLE,	210 *and* 211
LIEUT.-GEN. ALEXANDER GEORGE FRASER, K.T., G.C.B., G.C.H., SIXTEENTH OF PHILORTH AND SIXTEENTH LORD SALTOUN,	226 *and* 227

CONTENTS. iii

ILLUSTRATIONS IN VOLUME FIRST—PORTRAITS—*continued.*

	PAGE
THE HON. SIMON FRASER, SECOND SON OF ALEXANDER, FIFTEENTH LORD SALTOUN,	*between* 234 *and* 235
THE HON. WILLIAM FRASER, THIRD SON OF ALEXANDER, FIFTEENTH LORD SALTOUN,	312 *and* 313

II.—CHARTERS, BUILDINGS, ETC.

Charter by Earl Waldeve to the Monks of Melrose, of pasture on Lammermuir, *ante* 1182,	12 *and* 13
Cairnbulg Castle, or Old Manor-House of Philorth,	114 *and* 115
Keep of Fraserburgh Castle, Wine Tower, etc. (1850),	154 *and* 155
Letters Patent by King Charles the Second in favour of Alexander Fraser of Philorth, of the title and dignity of Lord Abernethy of Saltoun, 1670,	184 *and* 185
Armorial Bearings,	192 *and* 193
Town Hall and Market Cross, Fraserburgh,	304 *and* 305

III.—ARMORIAL SEALS. *Woodcuts of*—

Richard Fraser, *ante* 1276,	40
Sir Richard Fraser, 1297,	40
Sir Andrew Fraser, 1297,	48
Sir Alexander Fraser, the Chamberlain, 1320,	76
Margaret Fraser, 1392,	89
Euphemia, Countess of Ross, 1381,	121
Hugh de Ross, Lord of Philorth, 1365,	121
Alexander Fraser, Master of Saltoun, 1676,	188

CONTENTS.

ILLUSTRATIONS IN VOLUME FIRST—*continued.*

IV.—SIGNATURES. *Woodcuts of—*

	PAGE
James, Earl of Morton, Regent, 1575,	157
King James the Sixth, 1588, 1596, and 1602,	158, 160, 161
James, First Duke of Hamilton, 1648,	176
John, Second Earl of Lauderdale, 1648,	176
James, First Earl of Calander, 1648,	176
John, First Earl of Traquair, 1648,	176
William, Earl of Lanrick, 1648,	176
John, Earl of Crawford and Lindsay, 1648,	176
King Charles the Second, 1651,	178
Alexander Fraser, Master of Saltoun, 1676,	188

PREFACE.

SOME years ago I was induced to investigate the history of the family to which I belong, and at first I sought information from the various accounts of the Frasers, both manuscript and printed, that have appeared from time to time; but I found them so contradictory of one another, and in many respects so far at variance with indubitable facts, that I came to the conclusion that dependence upon any of them would only lead me into error, and that I must search for myself among old records in order to arrive at any approximation to the truth.

In pursuing these investigations, I determined to rely on the four kinds of evidence, which are placed below in the order of their respective degrees of value :—

First. Charter evidence, or the mention of individuals in various degrees of relationship to other persons in charters, royal mandates, or other important legal or official documents. Although these are not always conclusive as to the possession of the lands they assume to grant, or the performance of the acts they order to be done, they are, with scarcely an exception, trustworthy as regards the relationship of individuals when it is noticed in them.

Second. Evidence from succession to property by persons of the same surname, combined with due attention to dates, to the positions in which those persons are found, and to evidence of relationship with other persons, of whose existence and position there is certain record.

Third. Evidence from the mention of persons by trustworthy contemporary, or nearly contemporary historians, and other authors; consideration being given to the circumstances in which their names appear.

Fourth. Evidence from tradition, or writings of genealogists, when nothing adverse to the statements is gathered from other and more trustworthy sources.

When the above-mentioned four kinds of evidence have failed me, I mention that it is so, sometimes offering a suggestion.

Although naturally my researches have been directed more especially to that line of the family which I represent, yet they have led me to investigate the origin of the principal other branches, and if I had found evidence that any of them was senior to my own line, I would at once have acknowledged it, for there can be no dishonour in the accident of birth; but since, on the contrary, I have found full proof that the line I represent is the senior line of all now surviving, and is descended from Sir Alexander Fraser, Chamberlain of Scotland, who was head of the family in the time of King Robert Bruce, I have no hesitation in asserting my own position as the head of the family at the present day.

Some remarks upon the subject of the Highland Clan Fraser will explain their position; for their great influence in the Highlands of Scotland during comparatively modern times, and their possessions in those districts, have created the belief that all of the name must necessarily be members of that Clan, and some have supposed that the family had a Highland or Celtic origin, a supposition in some degree countenanced by one or two writers on the subject; especially by one who styles the town of Fraserburgh "strange offspring of a Highland Clan."

But the fact is, that the origin, or formation, of the Highland Clan Fraser cannot be dated further back than the fifteenth century, for although the surname appears in the Lowlands of Scotland as early as the middle of the twelfth century, none of its members acquired any permanent settlement in the Highlands until the fourteenth century, at which time a branch, which also held lands in Forfarshire, obtained large possessions in the districts around Inverness, and eventually becoming very numerous, originated or formed the Highland Clan of the name.

But the senior line, which continued to have their principal seat in the Lowlands, and those of the surname who remained in that section of Scotland, where Teutonic institutions prevailed, and whence the patriarchal system of Clans and Clanships had long been banished, had nothing to do with the origin or formation of the Highland Clan, and never belonged to it.

I have noticed, p. 130 vol. i. and p. 170 vol. ii., the extreme probability, indeed almost certainty, that the representatives of the respective lines of Philorth and Lovat were nearest of kin to each other in 1464, with the exception of the six sons of the Philorth of that date; and such has been the extinction of male descendants in the various branches of the line of Philorth, that at the present time, with the exception of my own two sons, my two brothers, and their four sons, numbering eight persons in all, Lord Lovat is my nearest legitimate male connection of the Fraser name.

My self-imposed task would have been far shorter and less difficult if I had not found myself obliged to notice, and, as far as possible, to correct the errors into which former writers upon the Fraser genealogy have fallen; and although I cannot hope myself to have avoided mistakes, and facts with which I am unacquainted may hereafter be brought to light, I have spared no pains to establish the correctness of every statement in this history, which I must now leave to the judgment of the reader.

In the course of my researches I became aware of an accidental oversight upon the part of Mr. Hill Burton, in his well-known History of Scotland.

In his list of the Barons of Scotland, who in 1320 sent the famous letter to Pope John XXII., he has omitted the name of Sir Alexander Fraser.

I thought it right to bring this omission to his notice, and upon doing so received the subjoined courteous reply, in which, while acknowledging the mistake, he promises that it shall be rectified at the earliest opportunity.

"CRAIGHOUSE, LOTHIANBURN,
"*Edinburgh,* 21*st October* 1871.

"MY LORD,—I have the honour of your Lordship's of the 11th, which only reached me yesterday. I showed it immediately to my father-in-law, Cosmo Innes, who said he had no doubt it was a correction of a mistake. I then looked at the original in the Register House, and there I found the name Alexander Fraser. I also saw how, in a careless transcription, it might be passed over. It comes between Menteith and Hay the constable, both with long titles: 'Johannes de Meneteth custos comitatus de Meneteth,' then comes, crushed in, 'Alex' Fras'.'

"In revising my book I shall not only see to the correction, but examine the several copies of the list, so that any who are interested may be warned against errors.

"Permit me to express my thanks to your Lordship for favouring me with this correction. I have occasionally received letters asking me to notice matters of family history which do not come within my scope. But certainly no house in Scotland that has the distinction of belonging to that group of patriots should wittingly let it be dropped out of remembrance.

"I have the honour to be, your Lordship's very obedient servant,

"J. H. BURTON.

"Lord Saltoun."

At pages 89, 90, 91, of vol. i., I have referred to the error of certain heralds of the seventeenth century, in blazoning the arms of "Lord Fraser of old," and of Fraser Lord Lovat, as *five "frays" placed saltireways*. It was not until after those remarks were printed that I met with a copy of Sir David Lindsay's work on Heraldry, of date 1542, which showed me that those heralds could claim his high authority for their statements.

But it also showed me that, whether originated by himself or before his time, Sir David Lindsay participated in the error; and it confirmed my view of the cause of the error having been the quarterings in the Yester arms; for the field of those quarterings on the shield of Hay Lord Yester, at page 56 of Sir David Lindsay's work, and that of the shield of "Fraseir Lord Frasere," at page 59 (the "Lord Fraser of old" of the heralds), are both sable; and as the field of the arms of Sir Simon Fraser, filius, whose daughter and co-heiress brought those quarterings into the Yester shield, was also sable (pp. 84, 95, vol. ii.), this affords additional evidence that the mistake originated through ignorance of the true ancient bearings of the Fraser family, as borne by that Sir Simon and his contemporaries of the name, viz., six rosettes or cinquefoils placed 3 . 2 . 1, and of their reduction from six to three placed 2 . 1, on the failure of the eldest male line during the fourteenth century (pp. 85, 86, vol. i.), and in the erroneous belief that the quarterings in the Yester shield represented those ancient bearings, as borne by the father of the heiress who brought them into the family of Hay.

It was my intention to have restricted this work within the limits of two volumes, but having in my possession a considerable number of letters, written by the late Lieut.-General Lord Saltoun during his military services in various parts of the world, it was suggested that selections from these might prove of interest, and hence a third volume has been added.

These letters range from the first entrance of Lord Saltoun upon active military service to within a few days of his decease; and they evince throughout the manly straightforwardness, the strong good-sense, the firm self-reliance, the obedience to the dictates of duty, the cheerful and contented temper, the sympathy with his fellow-man, and the warm affection to those more nearly connected with him that formed his character, while the last letter, written by a friend who was present at the closing scene of his life, shows how calmly and fearlessly this brave and good man rendered his spirit to God who gave it.

For the letters written to Lieut.-Colonel and Mrs. Charles Ellis, I am indebted to the kindness of the late Lady Parker, widow of Vice-Admiral Sir Charles C. Parker, Bart., and sister-in-law of Mrs. Charles Ellis; and to Mr. Francis Bayley, through whom I received them, I am also indebted for many valuable hints during my researches.

It may be of interest to point out the striking similarity between the early career of the late Lieut.-General Lord Saltoun and that of his distinguished ancestor, Sir Alexander Fraser the Chamberlain, though separated by an interval of five hundred years.

Either was born towards the close of a century; Sir Alexander about 1285, Lord Saltoun in 1785. Either lost his father at an early age. Either commenced an active military career at a similar time; Sir Alexander in 1306 when he joined Bruce, Lord Saltoun in 1806 in the expedition to Sicily. Either passed the next eight or nine years of his life in almost constant warfare. Either took part in the decisive victory that insured success to the cause for which he fought; Sir Alexander at Bannockburn in June 1314, Lord Saltoun at Waterloo in June 1815. Either married at a similar period; Sir Alexander about 1315-16, Lord Saltoun in 1815. Either, after a few years, was left a widower.

But there the parallel ends, for the former, while leaving issue, fell in battle at a comparatively early age; and the latter, while he had no child, nearly attained to the allotted threescore and ten years of man's existence.

Although I cannot flatter myself that the subject of which I have treated will be of much interest to the general public, I hope there are some to whom these volumes will afford pleasure, and serve as a record of the family to which they belong, or with which they are connected by ties of kindred or friendship.

I have to offer my best thanks to those friends who have

afforded me assistance during my labours, among whom are SIR ALEXANDER ANDERSON, MR. W. F. SKENE, MR. THOMAS DICKSON, and MR. HUGH FRASER. From the Authorities at the Record Office and the British Museum in London, and the General Register House and Advocates' Library in Edinburgh, I have also experienced much kindness, and I must mention with gratitude the help and encouragement I received from the late MR. COSMO INNES, and the late MR. GRANT LESLIE; and last, not least, my thanks are due to MR. WILLIAM FRASER, himself the author of many valuable Family Histories, who has given me not only the benefit of his great experience and vast research, but has also led my unaccustomed footsteps through the thorny paths of the press.

SALTOUN.

PHILORTH, *June* 1879.

PEDIGREE OF THE FRASERS OF PHILORTH, LORDS SALTOUN.

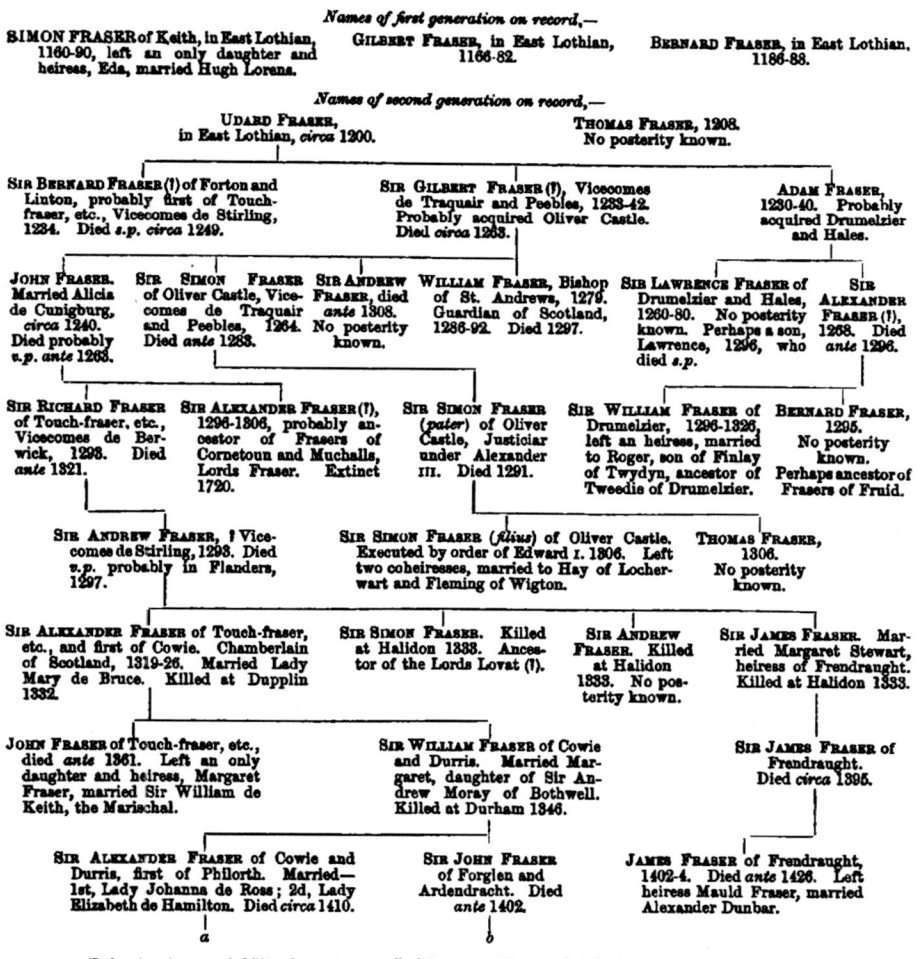

Names of first generation on record,—

SIMON FRASER of Keith, in East Lothian, 1160-90, left an only daughter and heiress, Eda, married Hugh Lorens.

GILBERT FRASER, in East Lothian, 1166-82.

BERNARD FRASER, in East Lothian, 1186-88.

Names of second generation on record,—

UDARD FRASER, in East Lothian, circa 1200.

THOMAS FRASER, 1208. No posterity known.

SIR BERNARD FRASER (?) of Forton and Linton, probably first of Touch-fraser, etc., Vicecomes de Stirling, 1234. Died s.p. circa 1249.

SIR GILBERT FRASER (?), Vicecomes de Traquair and Peebles, 1233-42. Probably acquired Oliver Castle. Died circa 1263.

ADAM FRASER, 1230-40. Probably acquired Drumelzier and Hales.

JOHN FRASER. Married Alicia de Cunigburg, circa 1240. Died probably v.p. ante 1263.

SIR SIMON FRASER of Oliver Castle, Vicecomes de Traquair and Peebles, 1264. Died ante 1283.

SIR ANDREW FRASER, died ante 1308. No posterity known.

WILLIAM FRASER, Bishop of St. Andrews, 1279. Guardian of Scotland, 1286-92. Died 1297.

SIR LAWRENCE FRASER of Drumelzier and Hales, 1260-80. No posterity known. Perhaps a son, Lawrence, 1296, who died s.p.

SIR ALEXANDER FRASER (?), 1268. Died ante 1296.

SIR RICHARD FRASER of Touch-fraser, etc., Vicecomes de Berwick, 1293. Died ante 1321.

SIR ALEXANDER FRASER (?), 1296-1306, probably ancestor of Frasers of Cornetoun and Muchalls, Lords Fraser. Extinct 1720.

SIR SIMON FRASER (pater) of Oliver Castle, Justiciar under Alexander III. Died 1291.

SIR WILLIAM FRASER of Drumelzier, 1296-1326, left an heiress, married to Roger, son of Finlay of Twydyn, ancestor of Tweedie of Drumelzier.

BERNARD FRASER, 1295. No posterity known. Perhaps ancestor of Frasers of Fruid.

SIR ANDREW FRASER, ? Vicecomes de Stirling, 1293. Died v.p. probably in Flanders, 1297.

SIR SIMON FRASER (filius) of Oliver Castle. Executed by order of Edward I. 1306. Left two coheiresses, married to Hay of Locherwart and Fleming of Wigton.

THOMAS FRASER, 1306. No posterity known.

SIR ALEXANDER FRASER of Touch-fraser, etc., and first of Cowie. Chamberlain of Scotland, 1319-26. Married Lady Mary de Bruce. Killed at Dupplin 1332.

SIR SIMON FRASER. Killed at Halidon 1333. Ancestor of the Lords Lovat (?).

SIR ANDREW FRASER. Killed at Halidon 1333. No posterity known.

SIR JAMES FRASER. Married Margaret Stewart, heiress of Frendraught. Killed at Halidon 1333.

JOHN FRASER of Touch-fraser, etc., died ante 1361. Left an only daughter and heiress, Margaret Fraser, married Sir William de Keith, the Marischal.

SIR WILLIAM FRASER of Cowie and Durris. Married Margaret, daughter of Sir Andrew Moray of Bothwell. Killed at Durham 1346.

SIR JAMES FRASER of Frendraught. Died circa 1395.

SIR ALEXANDER FRASER of Cowie and Durris, first of Philorth. Married— 1st, Lady Johanna de Ross; 2d, Lady Elizabeth de Hamilton. Died circa 1410.
a

SIR JOHN FRASER of Forglen and Ardendracht. Died ante 1402.
b

JAMES FRASER of Frendraught, 1402-4. Died ante 1426. Left heiress Mauld Fraser, married Alexander Dunbar.

(?) denotes strong probability of parentage ascribed, but no positive proof of the fact from documentary evidence.

PEDIGREE OF THE FRASERS OF PHILORTH, LORDS SALTOUN.

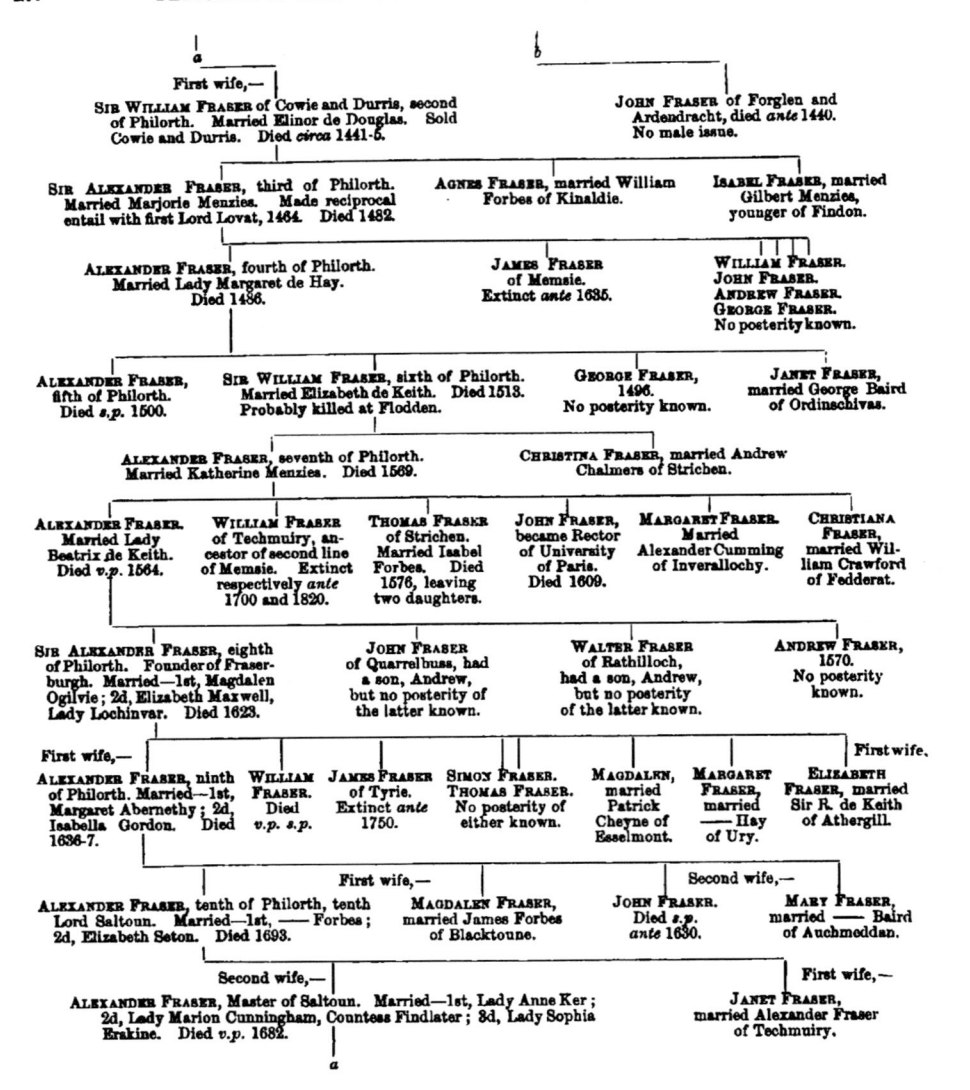

a

First wife,—
SIR WILLIAM FRASER of Cowie and Durris, second of Philorth. Married Elinor de Douglas. Sold Cowie and Durris. Died *circa* 1441-5.

b

JOHN FRASER of Forglen and Ardendracht, died *ante* 1440. No male issue.

SIR ALEXANDER FRASER, third of Philorth. Married Marjorie Menzies. Made reciprocal entail with first Lord Lovat, 1464. Died 1482.

AGNES FRASER, married William Forbes of Kinaldie.

ISABEL FRASER, married Gilbert Menzies, younger of Findon.

ALEXANDER FRASER, fourth of Philorth. Married Lady Margaret de Hay. Died 1486.

JAMES FRASER of Memsie. Extinct *ante* 1635.

WILLIAM FRASER.
JOHN FRASER.
ANDREW FRASER.
GEORGE FRASER.
No posterity known.

ALEXANDER FRASER, fifth of Philorth. Died *s.p.* 1500.

SIR WILLIAM FRASER, sixth of Philorth. Married Elizabeth de Keith. Died 1513. Probably killed at Flodden.

GEORGE FRASER, 1496. No posterity known.

JANET FRASER, married George Baird of Ordinschivas.

ALEXANDER FRASER, seventh of Philorth. Married Katherine Menzies. Died 1569.

CHRISTINA FRASER, married Andrew Chalmers of Strichen.

ALEXANDER FRASER. Married Lady Beatrix de Keith. Died *v.p.* 1564.

WILLIAM FRASER of Techmuiry, ancestor of second line of Memsie. Extinct respectively *ante* 1700 and 1820.

THOMAS FRASER of Strichen. Married Isabel Forbes. Died 1576, leaving two daughters.

JOHN FRASER, became Rector of University of Paris. Died 1609.

MARGARET FRASER. Married Alexander Cumming of Inverallochy.

CHRISTIANA FRASER, married William Crawford of Fedderat.

SIR ALEXANDER FRASER, eighth of Philorth. Founder of Fraserburgh. Married—1st, Magdalen Ogilvie; 2d, Elizabeth Maxwell, Lady Lochinvar. Died 1623.

JOHN FRASER of Quarrelbuss, had a son, Andrew, but no posterity of the latter known.

WALTER FRASER of Rathilloch, had a son, Andrew, but no posterity of the latter known.

ANDREW FRASER, 1570. No posterity known.

First wife,—
ALEXANDER FRASER, ninth of Philorth. Married—1st, Margaret Abernethy; 2d, Isabella Gordon. Died 1636-7.

WILLIAM FRASER. Died *v.p. s.p.*

JAMES FRASER of Tyrie. Extinct *ante* 1750.

SIMON FRASER.
THOMAS FRASER. No posterity of either known.

MAGDALEN married Patrick Cheyne of Esselmont.

MARGARET FRASER, married —— Hay of Ury.

First wife,
ELIZABETH FRASER, married Sir R. de Keith of Athergill.

First wife,—
ALEXANDER FRASER, tenth of Philorth, tenth Lord Saltoun. Married—1st, —— Forbes; 2d, Elizabeth Seton. Died 1693.

MAGDALEN FRASER, married James Forbes of Blacktoune.

Second wife,—
JOHN FRASER. Died *s.p. ante* 1630.

MARY FRASER, married —— Baird of Auchmeddan.

Second wife,—
ALEXANDER FRASER, Master of Saltoun. Married—1st, Lady Anne Ker; 2d, Lady Marion Cunningham, Countess Findlater; 3d, Lady Sophia Erskine. Died *v.p.* 1682.

First wife,—
JANET FRASER, married Alexander Fraser of Techmuiry.

a

PEDIGREE OF THE FRASERS OF PHILORTH, LORDS SALTOUN.

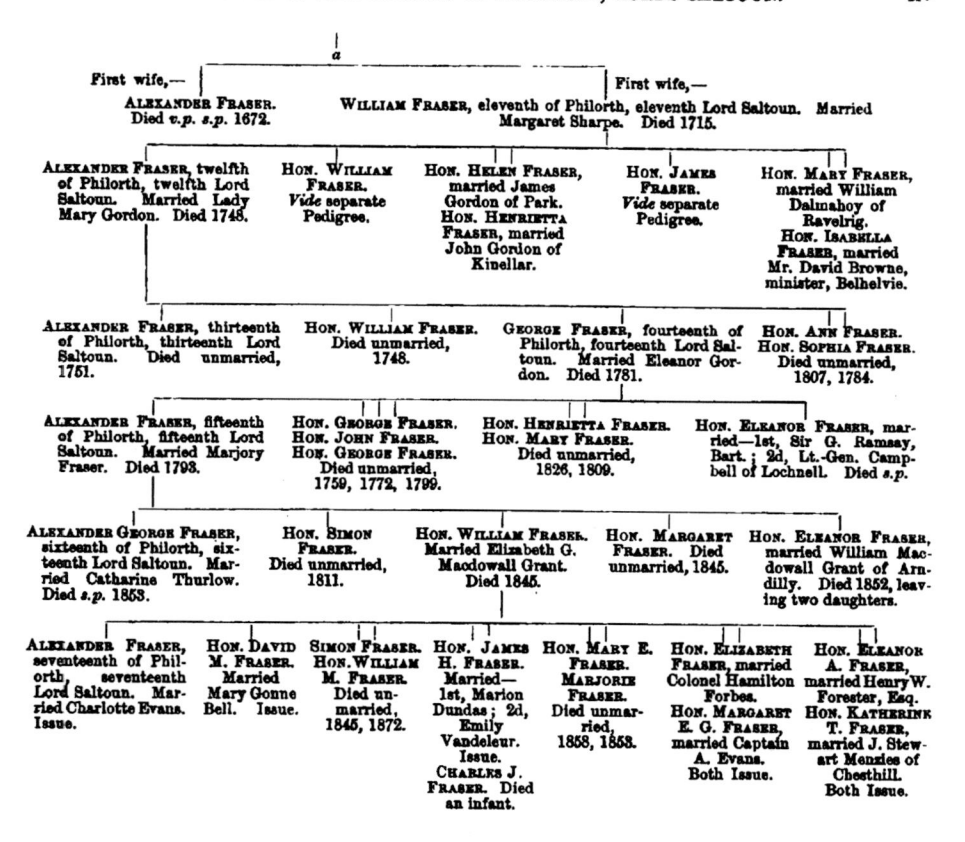

a

First wife,—
ALEXANDER FRASER. Died v.p. s.p. 1672.

WILLIAM FRASER, eleventh of Philorth, eleventh Lord Saltoun. Married First wife,—Margaret Sharpe. Died 1715.

ALEXANDER FRASER, twelfth of Philorth, twelfth Lord Saltoun. Married Lady Mary Gordon. Died 1748.

HON. WILLIAM FRASER. *Vide* separate Pedigree.

HON. HELEN FRASER, married James Gordon of Park.
HON. HENRIETTA FRASER, married John Gordon of Kinellar.

HON. JAMES FRASER. *Vide* separate Pedigree.

HON. MARY FRASER, married William Dalmahoy of Ravelrig.
HON. ISABELLA FRASER, married Mr. David Browne, minister, Belhelvie.

ALEXANDER FRASER, thirteenth of Philorth, thirteenth Lord Saltoun. Died unmarried, 1751.

HON. WILLIAM FRASER. Died unmarried, 1748.

GEORGE FRASER, fourteenth of Philorth, fourteenth Lord Saltoun. Married Eleanor Gordon. Died 1781.

HON. ANN FRASER.
HON. SOPHIA FRASER. Died unmarried, 1807, 1784.

ALEXANDER FRASER, fifteenth of Philorth, fifteenth Lord Saltoun. Married Marjory Fraser. Died 1793.

HON. GEORGE FRASER.
HON. JOHN FRASER.
HON. GEORGE FRASER. Died unmarried, 1759, 1772, 1799.

HON. HENRIETTA FRASER.
HON. MARY FRASER. Died unmarried, 1826, 1809.

HON. ELEANOR FRASER, married—1st, Sir G. Ramsay, Bart.; 2d, Lt.-Gen. Campbell of Lochnell. Died *s.p.*

ALEXANDER GEORGE FRASER, sixteenth of Philorth, sixteenth Lord Saltoun. Married Catharine Thurlow. Died *s.p.* 1853.

HON. SIMON FRASER. Died unmarried, 1811.

HON. WILLIAM FRASER. Married Elizabeth G. Macdowall Grant. Died 1845.

HON. MARGARET FRASER. Died unmarried, 1845.

HON. ELEANOR FRASER, married William Macdowall Grant of Arndilly. Died 1852, leaving two daughters.

ALEXANDER FRASER, seventeenth of Philorth, seventeenth Lord Saltoun. Married Charlotte Evans. Issue.

HON. DAVID M. FRASER. Married Mary Gonne Bell. Issue.

SIMON FRASER. HON. WILLIAM M. FRASER. Died unmarried, 1845, 1872.

HON. JAMES H. FRASER. Married—1st, Marion Dundas; 2d, Emily Vandeleur. Issue.
CHARLES J. FRASER. Died an infant.

HON. MARY E. FRASER. MARJORIE FRASER. Died unmarried, 1858, 1853.

HON. ELIZABETH FRASER, married Colonel Hamilton Forbes.
HON. MARGARET E. G. FRASER, married Captain A. Evans. Both Issue.

HON. ELEANOR A. FRASER, married Henry W. Forester, Esq.
HON. KATHERINE T. FRASER, married J. Stewart Menzies of Chesthill. Both Issue.

DESCENTS FROM HON. WILLIAM FRASER OF FRASERFIELD, SECOND SON, AND HON. JAMES FRASER OF LONMAY, THIRD SON OF WILLIAM, ELEVENTH LORD SALTOUN.

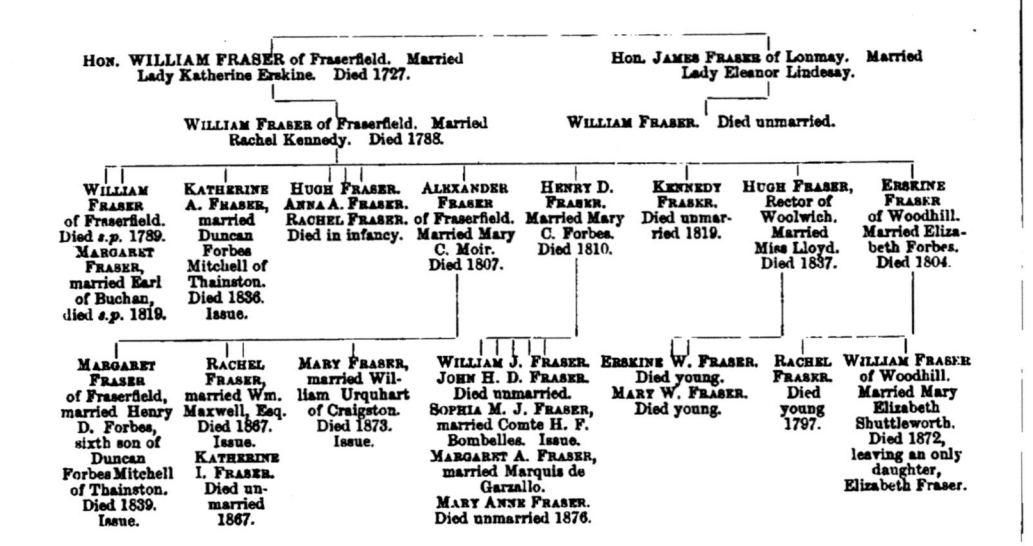

- **Hon. WILLIAM FRASER of Fraserfield.** Married Lady Katherine Erskine. Died 1727.
  - **WILLIAM FRASER of Fraserfield.** Married Rachel Kennedy. Died 1788.
    - **WILLIAM FRASER of Fraserfield.** Died s.p. 1789. **MARGARET FRASER**, married Earl of Buchan, died s.p. 1819.
      - **MARGARET FRASER of Fraserfield**, married Henry D. Forbes, sixth son of Duncan Forbes Mitchell of Thainston. Died 1839. Issue.
    - **KATHERINE A. FRASER**, married Duncan Forbes Mitchell of Thainston. Died 1836. Issue.
      - **RACHEL FRASER**, married Wm. Maxwell, Esq. Died 1867. Issue. **KATHERINE I. FRASER.** Died unmarried 1867.
    - **HUGH FRASER. ANNA A. FRASER. RACHEL FRASER.** Died in infancy.
      - **MARY FRASER**, married William Urquhart of Craigston. Died 1873. Issue.
    - **ALEXANDER FRASER of Fraserfield.** Married Mary C. Moir. Died 1807.
      - **WILLIAM J. FRASER, JOHN H. D. FRASER.** Died unmarried. **SOPHIA M. J. FRASER**, married Comte H. F. Bombelles. Issue. **MARGARET A. FRASER**, married Marquis de Garzallo. **MARY ANNE FRASER.** Died unmarried 1876.
    - **HENRY D. FRASER.** Married Mary C. Forbes. Died 1810.
      - **ERSKINE W. FRASER.** Died young. **MARY W. FRASER.** Died young.
    - **KENNEDY FRASER.** Died unmarried 1819.
    - **HUGH FRASER**, Rector of Woolwich. Married Miss Lloyd. Died 1837.
      - **RACHEL FRASER.** Died young 1797.
    - **ERSKINE FRASER of Woodhill.** Married Elizabeth Forbes. Died 1804.
      - **WILLIAM FRASER of Woodhill.** Married Mary Elizabeth Shuttleworth. Died 1872, leaving an only daughter, Elizabeth Fraser.
- **Hon. JAMES FRASER of Lonmay.** Married Lady Eleanor Lindesay.
  - **WILLIAM FRASER.** Died unmarried.

PEDIGREE OF THE FAMILY OF ABERNETHY, LORDS SALTOUN.

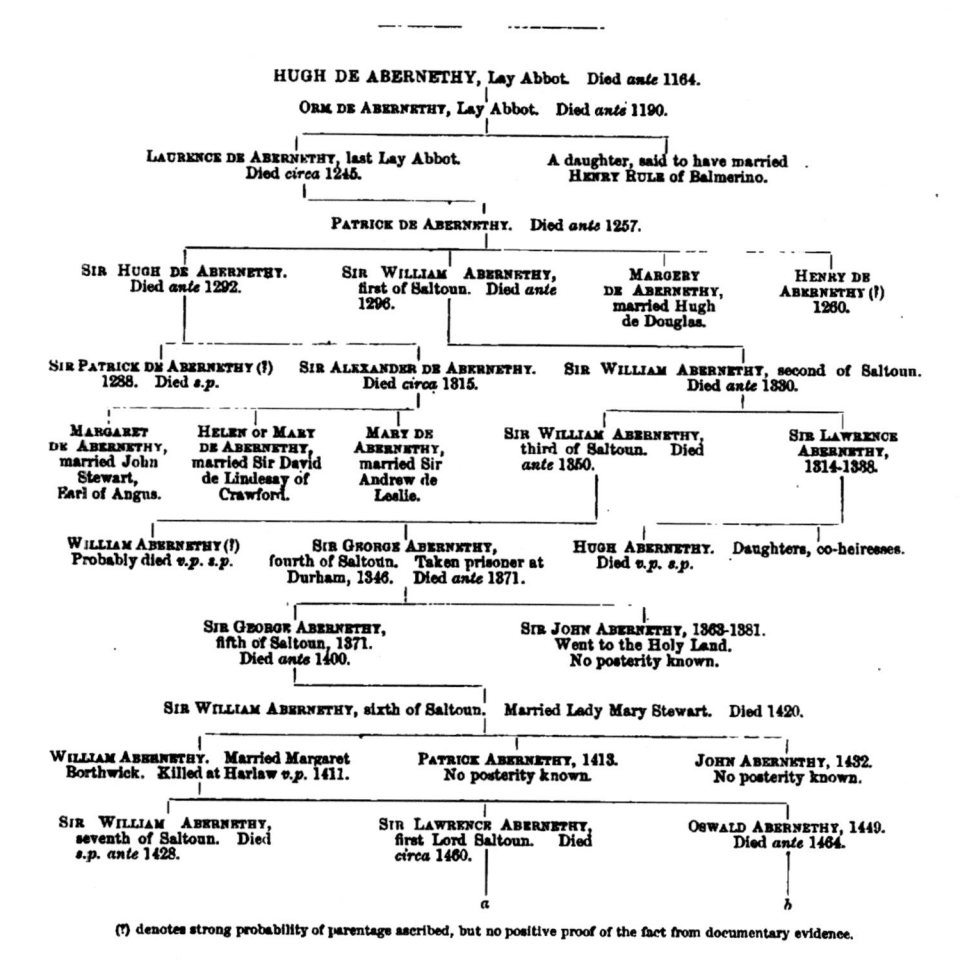

HUGH DE ABERNETHY, Lay Abbot. Died *ante* 1164.

ORM DE ABERNETHY, Lay Abbot. Died *ante* 1190.

- **LAURENCE DE ABERNETHY**, last Lay Abbot. Died *circa* 1245.
- A daughter, said to have married **HENRY RULE** of Balmerino.

PATRICK DE ABERNETHY. Died *ante* 1257.

- **SIR HUGH DE ABERNETHY.** Died *ante* 1292.
- **SIR WILLIAM ABERNETHY**, first of Saltoun. Died *ante* 1296.
- **MARGERY DE ABERNETHY**, married Hugh de Douglas.
- **HENRY DE ABERNETHY** (?) 1260.

- **SIR PATRICK DE ABERNETHY** (?) 1288. Died *s.p.*
- **SIR ALEXANDER DE ABERNETHY.** Died *circa* 1315.
- **SIR WILLIAM ABERNETHY**, second of Saltoun. Died *ante* 1330.

- **MARGARET DE ABERNETHY**, married John Stewart, Earl of Angus.
- **HELEN or MARY DE ABERNETHY**, married Sir David de Lindesay of Crawford.
- **MARY DE ABERNETHY**, married Sir Andrew de Leslie.
- **SIR WILLIAM ABERNETHY**, third of Saltoun. Died *ante* 1350.
- **SIR LAWRENCE ABERNETHY**, 1314-1388.

- **WILLIAM ABERNETHY** (?) Probably died *v.p. s.p.*
- **SIR GEORGE ABERNETHY**, fourth of Saltoun. Taken prisoner at Durham, 1346. Died *ante* 1371.
- **HUGH ABERNETHY.** Died *v.p. s.p.*
- Daughters, co-heiresses.

- **SIR GEORGE ABERNETHY**, fifth of Saltoun, 1371. Died *ante* 1400.
- **SIR JOHN ABERNETHY**, 1363-1381. Went to the Holy Land. No posterity known.

SIR WILLIAM ABERNETHY, sixth of Saltoun. Married Lady Mary Stewart. Died 1420.

- **WILLIAM ABERNETHY.** Married Margaret Borthwick. Killed at Harlaw *v.p.* 1411.
- **PATRICK ABERNETHY**, 1413. No posterity known.
- **JOHN ABERNETHY**, 1432. No posterity known.

- **SIR WILLIAM ABERNETHY**, seventh of Saltoun. Died *s.p. ante* 1428.
- **SIR LAWRENCE ABERNETHY**, first Lord Saltoun. Died *circa* 1460. — *a*
- **OSWALD ABERNETHY**, 1449. Died *ante* 1464. — *b*

(?) denotes strong probability of parentage ascribed, but no positive proof of the fact from documentary evidence.

PEDIGREE OF THE FAMILY OF ABERNETHY, LORDS SALTOUN.

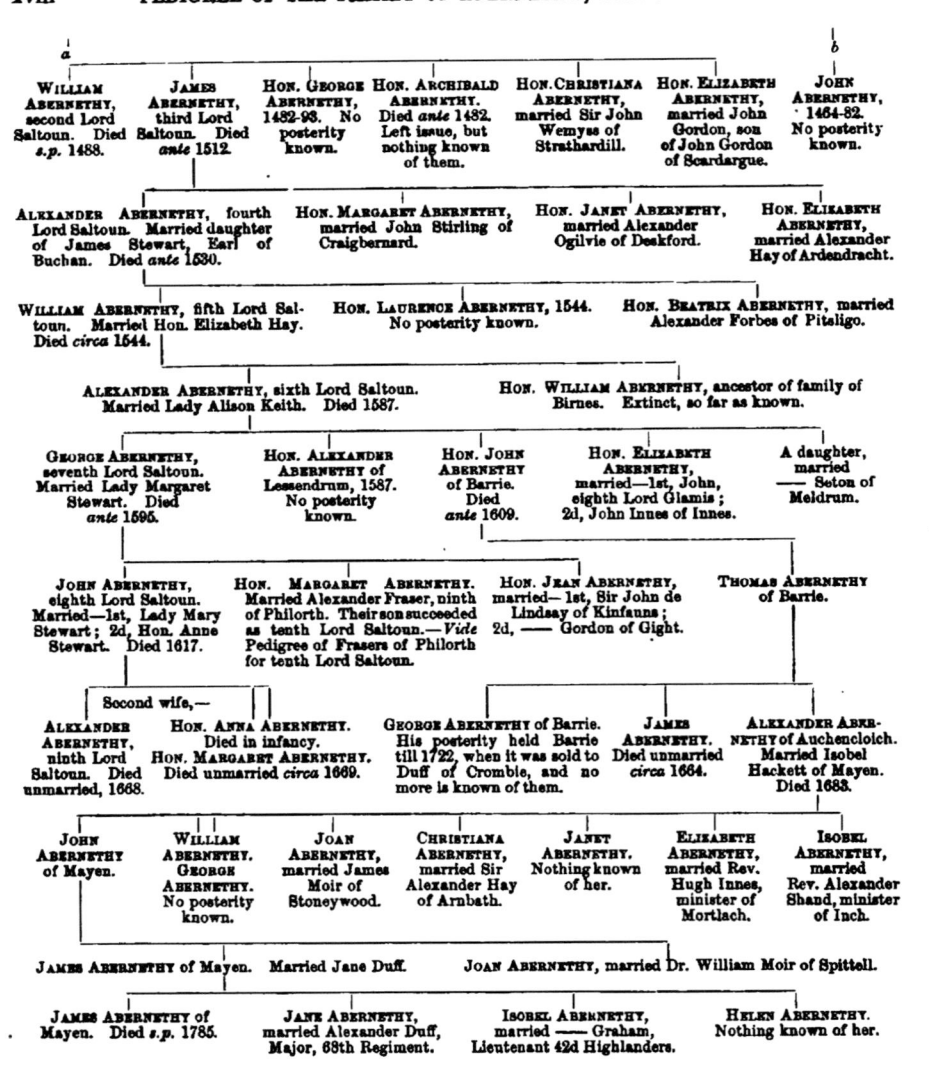

WILLIAM ABERNETHY, second Lord Saltoun. Died s.p. 1488.

JAMES ABERNETHY, third Lord Saltoun. Died ante 1512.

HON. GEORGE ABERNETHY, 1482-93. No posterity known.

HON. ARCHIBALD ABERNETHY. Died ante 1482. Left issue, but nothing known of them.

HON. CHRISTIANA ABERNETHY, married Sir John Wemyss of Strathardill.

HON. ELIZABETH ABERNETHY, married John Gordon, son of John Gordon of Scardargue.

JOHN ABERNETHY, 1464-82. No posterity known.

ALEXANDER ABERNETHY, fourth Lord Saltoun. Married daughter of James Stewart, Earl of Buchan. Died ante 1530.

HON. MARGARET ABERNETHY, married John Stirling of Craigbernard.

HON. JANET ABERNETHY, married Alexander Ogilvie of Deskford.

HON. ELIZABETH ABERNETHY, married Alexander Hay of Ardendracht.

WILLIAM ABERNETHY, fifth Lord Saltoun. Married Hon. Elizabeth Hay. Died circa 1544.

HON. LAURENCE ABERNETHY, 1544. No posterity known.

HON. BEATRIX ABERNETHY, married Alexander Forbes of Pitsligo.

ALEXANDER ABERNETHY, sixth Lord Saltoun. Married Lady Alison Keith. Died 1587.

HON. WILLIAM ABERNETHY, ancestor of family of Birnes. Extinct, so far as known.

GEORGE ABERNETHY, seventh Lord Saltoun. Married Lady Margaret Stewart. Died ante 1595.

HON. ALEXANDER ABERNETHY of Lessendrum, 1587. No posterity known.

HON. JOHN ABERNETHY of Barrie. Died ante 1609.

HON. ELIZABETH ABERNETHY, married—1st, John, eighth Lord Glamis; 2d, John Innes of Innes.

A daughter, married —— Seton of Meldrum.

JOHN ABERNETHY, eighth Lord Saltoun. Married—1st, Lady Mary Stewart; 2d, Hon. Anne Stewart. Died 1617.

HON. MARGARET ABERNETHY. Married Alexander Fraser, ninth of Philorth. Their son succeeded as tenth Lord Saltoun.—Vide Pedigree of Frasers of Philorth for tenth Lord Saltoun.

HON. JEAN ABERNETHY, married—1st, Sir John de Lindsay of Kinfauns; 2d, —— Gordon of Gight.

THOMAS ABERNETHY of Barrie.

Second wife,—

ALEXANDER ABERNETHY, ninth Lord Saltoun. Died unmarried, 1668.

HON. ANNA ABERNETHY. Died in infancy.

HON. MARGARET ABERNETHY. Died unmarried circa 1669.

GEORGE ABERNETHY of Barrie. His posterity held Barrie till 1722, when it was sold to Duff of Crombie, and no more is known of them.

JAMES ABERNETHY. Died unmarried circa 1664.

ALEXANDER ABERNETHY of Auchencloich. Married Isobel Hackett of Mayen. Died 1683.

JOHN ABERNETHY of Mayen.

WILLIAM ABERNETHY. GEORGE ABERNETHY. No posterity known.

JOAN ABERNETHY, married James Moir of Stoneywood.

CHRISTIANA ABERNETHY, married Sir Alexander Hay of Arnbath.

JANET ABERNETHY. Nothing known of her.

ELIZABETH ABERNETHY, married Rev. Hugh Innes, minister of Mortlach.

ISOBEL ABERNETHY, married Rev. Alexander Shand, minister of Inch.

JAMES ABERNETHY of Mayen. Married Jane Duff.

JOAN ABERNETHY, married Dr. William Moir of Spittell.

JAMES ABERNETHY of Mayen. Died s.p. 1785.

JANE ABERNETHY, married Alexander Duff, Major, 68th Regiment.

ISOBEL ABERNETHY, married —— Graham, Lieutenant 42d Highlanders.

HELEN ABERNETHY. Nothing known of her.

THE FRASERS OF PHILORTH.

INTRODUCTION.

WHEN the origin of the principal families of their native country first attracted the attention of Scottish authors, great difficulty existed in discovering the charters and historical documents by which alone the descent of each could be properly authenticated; and the most eminent genealogists were fain to take upon trust pedigrees already composed by bards and seanachies, in honour of the families to which they belonged or were attached, while no test of the truth of these statements was within the reach of those to whom they were presented.

Many of these pedigrees contained long lists of names, and recounted events that owed their existence solely to the fertile brains of the original composers; and a forced translation from the Gaelic, or a punning resemblance to a French word, satisfied the heralds and genealogists of succeeding ages, and induced them to lend the weight of their authority to family origins and histories, which had but very slender, if any, foundation in fact.

In this manner two accounts of the origin of the Fraser Family appear to have been produced; one deriving the lineage from Pierre Fraser, said to have come from France to Scotland in the age of Charlemagne, and giving a long roll of his posterity, Thanes of the Isle of Man; the other deducing it from Julius de Berri, a seigneur of the province of that name in France, who, on presenting a dish of strawberries to Charles the Simple, had his name changed from De Berri to De Fraise by that king.

INTRODUCTION.

It is unnecessary to enlarge upon the absurdity of these fabrications, unsupported as they are by any evidence. The first seems to be the older production, and is doubtless the work of some bard or seanachie, who selected the Isle of Man—probably little known to his circle in his day—as a spot where he might place his Thanes without fear of contradiction; and the second, an instance of the punning derivation of names, was probably invented when the increase of historical knowledge rendered the first untenable, and was supported by a further punning alteration of the rosettes, or cinquefoils —the family insignia—into "Frays," "Fraes," or "Fraises," meaning strawberry leaves, or flowers.

Both accounts may be discarded as fabulous, and the only particle of truth in either would appear to be the French or Norman origin assigned to the family.

The two appellations, "French" and "Norman," have the same signification. The "Normans," who composed the nucleus of the army of William the Conqueror, were called French by the Saxons and Anglo-Danes, whom they subdued; and with the French who accompanied them, or who, with Henry II. or other leaders subsequently settled in Britain, were at a later period termed Normans.

That the Frasers were not descended from any of the Celtic tribes of Scotland, nor from any of the Saxon or Danish immigrants,[1] but were of French or Norman extraction, is evident from their having been constantly designated by their surname at a period when patronymics only were used by Celts, Saxons, and Anglo-Danes or Scoto-Danes, and surnames were not universal even among the Normans; and it is worthy of observation that it was borne by them as a surname proper, and not as a territorial surname or personal appellation, the prefixes "de" or "le" being never used.[2]

The name appears in ancient records under the various forms of Fraser, Freser, Fresel, Frasel, Freshell, Frisel, Frysel, and Freysel,—sometimes with the letter "l" doubled, or a final "e" added.

---

[1] The term Saxon includes Angles, Jutes, etc., of the Saxon conquest during the sixth century, that of Dane all the various tribes of the Northmen of Scandinavia.

[2] Only one exception to this rule appears in the name "Hugh de Fraser" as a witness to a charter in 1367, which must have been an error on the part of the writer.

INTRODUCTION.

In the earliest Scottish documents the form "Fraser," as in use at the present time, is found, and from the year 1160, when the name first occurs (an original charter, still extant, granted between 1166 and 1182, authenticates that form having been then employed), the principal members of the family—in the charters they granted, the deeds they executed, upon those seals of which impressions have been preserved, and, at a later period, in their signatures—have almost invariably employed that form of the name; the exceptions being an early seal of Richard Fraser, and that of Margaret Fraser, on which the form Freser appears, and this, if not an error of the engraver, evinces that it was the same name; and the seal of Simon Fraser, Filius, on which Friser is found, which is certainly the engraver's mistake, as in the deed to which it is affixed his name is written Fraser, and in a later seal of Richard Fraser, also appended to the same deed, the name is spelt with an "a."

It may be of interest to notice here the time at which the name under the form of "Fraser" is first found in English records; and this appears to have been towards the end of the reign of Henry II., for the following is a translation from the Latin of certain historians referring to that period :—[1]

"The same year, 1188, Richard Count of Poitou" (afterwards Richard I.), "and Raymond, Count of St. Giles" (better known as Count of Thoulouse), "and Aymery Count of Angouleme, and Geoffry de Rancune, and Geoffry de "Lezinant" (Lusignan, brother of the King of Jerusalem), "and almost all "the principal men of Poitou, made war, all the others against the aforesaid "Richard, and he against them all, but he, the aforesaid Richard, overcame "them.

"And among those whom he captured in the country of the Count of St. "Giles, he took Peter Seillun, by whose advice the Count of St. Giles had "seized some merchants of the Count of Poitou's dominions" (whom he treated with great barbarity), "and had done much injury to him and his lands.

"Count Richard therefore placed this Peter in a strong place and very "strict captivity, and the Count of St. Giles, being unable in any way to "release him from it, searched throughout his own possessions for any "persons of the family of the King of England, or of that of Count Richard, "his son; and it happened, after a few days, that two knights of the house-

[1] Benedict of Peterboro', vol. ii. p. 35; Hoveden, vol. ii. p. 339.

" hold and family of the King of England, whose names were Robert Poer
" ('Power?'), and Radulph Fraser, passed through his country on their
" return from the shrine of St. James" (of Compostella), "to which they had
" made a pilgrimage, and journeyed by way of Thoulouse.

" The officials of the Count arrested them, and brought them bound before
" him, and he ordered them to be imprisoned.

" After a considerable time the Count proposed terms to them, saying,
" 'If the Count of Poitou will allow my servant, whom he holds in prison, to
" go free and unharmed, I will permit you both to go free and unharmed;'
" and upon this one of them, Radulph Fraser, was allowed to go to Count
" Richard of Poitou to treat for their own release and that of the servant of
" the Count of St. Giles.

" But Count Richard, hearing that they had been captured when returning
" from a pilgrimage to the shrine of St. James, replied that they should not
" be released by him, neither by request nor by ransom, because he should
" offend God and his blessed Apostle James if he gave a ransom for them,
" as the reverence due to a pilgrimage alone sufficed for their release."

The sequel is curious. "Therefore the King of France" (overlord of the Counts of Poitou and St. Giles) "commanded that they should be set free, not
" on account of love, or respect for the King of England, or his son Richard,
" but from respect and love for the blessed Apostle James. The Count of St.
" Giles therefore released them, not on account of the command of the King
" of France, but on account of the large ransom that he received from them."

In the first year of Richard I. of England, 1189-90, Radulph "Frasier" held lands in Oxfordshire, and in the same year payment of £25 was made to Radulph Fraser by order of the King for sustaining the castle of Kaermerdin in Gloucestershire, of which he may have been the keeper.[1]

He seems to have left daughters only, for in the time of Henry III. there is a notice of the *heredes* of Radulph Fraser, who held a knight's fee in Anestan, in the counties of Nottingham and Derby.[2]

About the end of the thirteenth century, when the interference of Edward I. in the affairs of Scotland brought English officials into that country, the forms of Fresel, Frasel, Freshell, Frisel, Frysel, and Freysel, first occur in

[1] Pipe Rolls, pp. 105, 163.   [2] Testa de Nevill, p. 17.

Scotland. They are often applied indiscriminately to the same individual in the Ragman Rolls, Rotuli Scotiæ, and other records of that period, and seem to have been used in consequence of the existence in England of a family bearing the name of Fresel, or Freysel, which was considered the same as that of Fraser.

In 1253-5, Jacobus Fresel was Escheator for Henry III. *citra*, or from an English point of view, south of Trent,[1] and in 1273 Richard Freysel was "Ballivus" of the Earl of Gloucester. Walter Freysel was also a landholder in that part of England in 1274, and William Freysel de Saxham, Ballivus of . . . . Blakeburn in the same year. John Freysel held property in Cambridgeshire in 1279, and Galfridus Fresel "tenet unum mansum in Burg Marlowe" in 1280.[2] Before 1341, another Jacobus Fresel held considerable possessions at Bledelaw (Bledlow), in the county of Buckingham.[3] Thomas Fresel was a landowner at Southton in 1345, and John Frisel was vicar of Houghton, in Norfolk, about 1332,[4] and a Margaret Fresel, the wife of Egidius Peche, on September 23d and November 16th, 1314, obtained safe-conducts to go to Scotland to negotiate for the ransom of William Peche.[5]

The other forms appear to be variations of Fresel, due to the defective orthography of that age, but were used exclusively by others to designate members of the Scottish family, who, as above noticed, always employed the forms Fraser or Freser when mentioning themselves.

At a later period, however, misled by the occurrence of these forms in early documents, genealogists, who had not the opportunity of examining still earlier records, fell into the error of adopting one of them, "Frisel," as the oldest form of the name to be found in Scotland.

The forms of Fraser, and perhaps Freser, in Scotland, and Fraser, Fresel, Freysel in England, are therefore the most ancient on record, and it has now to be seen whether these can be considered as variations of the same name, and in such an inquiry the pronunciation is of more assistance than the spelling, which in that age and for long afterwards was very arbitrary.

In Fraser the "a" has the sound of the French "é," and the "s" that of

---

[1] Excerpta e Rotulis finium, vol. ii. pp. 169-200.

[2] Hundred Rolls, vol. ii. second to eighth Edward I.

[3] His Will and Testament in Manuscript-room, British Museum.

[4] Calend. Inquis. post mortem, pp. 44, 141, 147.

[5] Rotuli Scotiæ, vol. i. pp. 131, 134.

"z;" it is pronounced exactly as "Frézèr" would be in the French tongue if the final "r" was sounded, and in favour of these and Fresel or Freysel having been variations of the same name, are the facts, first, that they all were surnames proper, used without the prefixes "de" or "le," and therefore neither territorial nor personal surnames; secondly, that about the end of the thirteenth century they were held to be identical by the clerks and writers of that age, and that no contradiction of that assumption has been found; and thirdly, that the pronunciation of the first syllable was exactly alike in all four.

It is certain that among the Anglo-Saxons and Anglo-Danes the slender sound of the letter "a," as in the words "grace," "place," was in use, and also that of the letter "e," as in "the," "he," "me," which are found in scarcely any other language than English; and it is very probable that if the name, pronounced Fréser or Frésel, were written by Anglo-Saxon or Anglo-Danish scribes, the accented "é" would be changed to "a;" and this suggestion is supported by the introduction of the letter "y" in one form "Freysel," evidently with the view of preserving the pronunciation of the name; while the final letters "r" and "l" are two liquids very susceptible of interchange.

The weight of evidence seems to incline to the four different forms of the name having been borne by persons of the same race, and it is not difficult to discover a source from which they may have sprung.

In Moreri's "Grande Dictionaire Historique," published at Paris in 1769, an account of the family of Frézeau or Frézel is given, from which an extract is here translated.[1]

"Frézeau, or Frézel, de la Frézelière, a family in Anjou, is one of the most ancient in the kingdom, and most illustrious in that province, where it has possessed from time immemorial the Seigneurie of Frézelière.

"As regards antiquity, few families can pride themselves on reascending so high. Even before custom had distinguished families by surnames, that is to say in the 11th century, the family of Frézel, or Frézeau, must have been very important, for in the Cartulary of the Abbey of Noyers, in Touraine, among the donations which were confirmed by King Robert about the year 1030, one is found in which mention is made of two Frézels, father

[1] Tom. iv. p. 455.

and son, who are both styled Chevaliers, a rank not then bestowed upon any except those equally distinguished by their nobility and their valour."

Moreri goes on to say that the civil wars and disturbances in France, extending to Anjou, caused the loss of the succeeding pedigree of the family until the year 1270, when a Chevalier Geoffry Frézel appears, from whom the descent proceeds in regular order, through successive Seigneurs de la Frézelière, to Lancelot Frézel, in 1405, who first adopted the form of Frézeau, under which the family continued as Seigneur, and latterly as Marquis, and Duke, de la Frézelière to the middle of the eighteenth century, when Moreri wrote.[1]

Aubert des Bois, in his "Dictionaire de la Noblesse," says that the Christian name of the Frézel who was a benefactor to the Abbey of Noyers, in Touraine, *circa* 1030, was René, and that he had issue two sons, René and Simon.

When it is found that the Frézels of Anjou and the English Fresels both used the name as a surname proper in that early age, it does not require much forcing to deduce the latter race from some junior members of the former, and, perhaps, a very possible contraction of Frézelière into Frésiere, or Frésere, may afford a clue to the cause of the final "l" being changed into "r" by the Frasers of England and Scotland.

It may be a matter of doubt whether the Frézels, or Frasers, were among those who accompanied William of Normandy to his conquest of England in 1066, or whether they entered Britain, at a later date, in the suite of Henry of Anjou, afterwards Henry II., when, in 1149, he visited his uncle, King David I. of Scotland, and was knighted by him at Carlisle.

The earliest appearance of the name, as yet discovered in Scottish charters or documents, occurs in 1160, some years after the last of the above two events, and, indeed, six years after the accession of King Henry II. to the throne of England; but, on the other hand, the member of the race then mentioned was a tenant-in-chief of the King of Scotland, while others of the name appear as vassals of the Earls of Dunbar in 1166; and it is certainly

---

[1] In the "Annals of the Frasers," published in 1805, which is a copy of a portion of a MS. in the Advocates' Library at Edinburgh, intended for publication 1749, the Duke de la Frézelière is mentioned as a connection, and the head of the French family in 1714; but the tradition of Pierre Fraser and the Thanes of the Isle of Man is also adopted, and the whole account is so overlaid with fiction as to be utterly valueless as an authority.

more probable that the Radulph Fraser of 1188-90, or his father, was a cadet of the race already settled in Scotland, who attached himself to the young Prince Henry on the occasion of his visit to King David, than that all of the name in Scotland should have emigrated from Anjou about that time, and leaving the fealty of their own sovereign, should have become the subjects of a neighbouring monarch.

There is not much dependence to be placed in the so-called Roll of Battle Abbey, for no proof exists that such a roll was ever compiled by the monks of that monastery. Joseph Hunter, the author of a paper in the "Sussex Archæological Collections," says: "There are ten lists professing to be lists of persons or families who are said to have come with the conqueror. All differ in many respects from each other; many names of families which are known not to have settled in England until long after the Conquest are inserted, many are omitted of whom there is the best evidence that they were in the expedition. It was not until the reign of Elizabeth that any claim was put forth on behalf of any of these lists to be the Roll of Battle Abbey, or to be in any way connected with the Abbey."

The number of lists is even greater than that given by Mr. Hunter. There are a dozen, or perhaps more; but the name as "Fraser" is not found in any of them.

In Holinshed's list it appears as Frisell.
„ Stowe's „ „ Frissell.
„ Scriven's „ „ Fresel.
„ Leland's „ „ Fresell.
„ Matthew of Westminster's Frysell.
„ Harl. MSS. 293, p. 37 „ Fresel.

But it is not in any of the other lists that have been inspected.

As, however, none of the name rose to any great power or influence in England, and the name had nearly if not quite died out in that country by the fifteenth century, the only reason for its preservation in some of the lists would seem to be that it had been found in some still more ancient record of the conqueror's companions.

A list has been recently prepared by M. Leopold Delisle, a justly celebrated antiquary, and in 1862 it was placed in the church of Dives, in Normandy.

The name of Richard Fresle occurs in it, and in Domesday Book it is recorded that "In burgo Snottingham Ricardus Fresle habet 1111 domos;" but although he bears the name as a surname proper, it is very doubtful whether it can be regarded as a variation of Fresel.

However this may be, neither the name of Fresel or Freysel, nor those of Freser or Fraser, appear in Domesday Book; but all Northumberland, Cumberland, Westmoreland, and Durham were omitted from that famous survey of England, and the connection which, at no great distance of time, existed between the descendants of Gospatrick, Earl of Northumberland, and the Frasers of Scotland, renders it not unlikely that the first settlement of the latter family was to the north of the river Humber.

Gospatrick the Saxon, or rather Anglo-Dane, contemporary with William the Conqueror, who created him Earl of Northumberland,[1] being shortly afterwards arbitrarily deprived of that earldom by the hand that conferred it, quitted England in disgust, and retiring into Lothian, where he had already considerable possessions, obtained an augmentation of these, with the title of Comes, or Earl, from Malcolm Canmore, which descended through his posterity, bearing the same name, to the year 1166, when Waldeve, the son of the last that was styled Gospatrick, became Earl upon the death of his father; and it will be found that one branch of the Frasers first appears as feudatory to this Earl Waldeve.

In tracing the common origin of families, the armorial bearings of each are of great importance up to an early date, but there is a still earlier age during which they afford scarcely any assistance.

The various insignia or arms, at first used to distinguish individuals, were not, necessarily, adopted by their descendants, and were also not unfrequently changed for others by the caprice of those who bore them; and it was not until the end of the eleventh century, and during the twelfth, that the hereditary descent of arms and the right of every member of a family to bear the insignia distinguishing the race gradually became established in the west of Europe; and as the separation of the Fresels, if they came into England with the Conqueror, from those of the name that remained on the Continent, took place in the middle of the eleventh century, it was prior to

[1] Caledonia, vol. ii. p. 238.

the age in which the armorial bearings of each might be of service in connecting one with the other, and as the Frasers were established as a Scottish family by, if not before, the middle of the twelfth century, their armorial bearings at that time are scarcely of more consequence.

The events of the latter portion of the Conqueror's reign, the numerous unsuccessful rebellions, especially in the Northumbrian district, not only of the conquered English, but also of many of his Norman followers, which were suppressed with great severity, and, above all, the discontent produced by the decisions of the King and the Great Council, held in 1086, upon the claims of many of the barons, caused a large emigration of Normans from England into Scotland, where they were well received by King Malcolm, who granted them lands, and was not sorry to see his kingdom strengthened by the influx of a considerable body of hardy, resolute, and well-trained warriors. The disturbances that occurred during the reigns of William Rufus and Henry I. largely augmented the number of Normans in Scotland, and the sons of Malcolm, Alexander I. and David I., followed their father's wise policy of cordially welcoming the gallant refugees.

From the foregoing observations it is apparent that no decision can, with certainty, be arrived at, as to whether the Fresels or Frasers entered Britain with the Conqueror, or at a later date; and, indeed, it is possible that various members of the race may have emigrated from Anjou at different times between 1066 and 1149.

It is also doubtful whether, at a more remote epoch, they were of Northman or Danish descent, or whether they derived their origin from a Frankish source. The etymology of the name affords no clue in any of the three forms, Frezel, Fresel, or Fraser. The estate of Frézelière, in Anjou, evidently took its name from the proprietors, and is an evidence of the surname having been very ancient; and this affords strong support to the idea of a Frankish origin, for the possession of so ancient a surname proper would argue descent from the older civilisation, founded on the ruin of Roman power, rather than from the more recent barbarism of the Northman and Danish tribes.

Having stated as concisely as possible the reasons for believing that the Frasers were of the same family as the Fresels of England, and that these were a branch of the Frézels de la Frézelière of Anjou, it only remains to add that almost every inquiry into the origin of families in that remote age must be more or less hypothetical, and that, in the preceding pages, the writer of this history does not pretend to do more than, rejecting fabulous pedigrees and punning derivations, to find a fairly probable origin for the Scoto-Norman family of Fraser, which the earliest authentic records prove to have been settled in East Lothian about the middle of the twelfth century, partly as tenants-in-chief of the Crown, and partly as feudatories of the great Earls of Dunbar, descendants of Gospatrick, Earl of Northumberland.

But although their establishment in the south of Scotland at that early age is thus authenticated, the lapse of time, and, still more, the unfortunate loss and destruction of records, due in no slight degree to the anarchy that prevailed in that country during its occupation by Edward I., render it difficult to frame any continuous history of the Frasers upon actual proof from charters or authentic documentary evidence, or even with approximate certainty to carry on the line from father to son, until about the beginning of the thirteenth century.

It is, at the same time, unsafe to rely upon the genealogists and authors who have hitherto written upon the subject, unless their statements are supported by unquestionable evidence, for some have put forward as facts assertions for which they have not adduced a shadow of proof, and these have been accepted by others without examination; thus all have, more or less, lent the weight of their authority to errors, which it will be the object of the writer of this history to avoid, and, if possible, to rectify.

Under these circumstances, it will be advisable to relate such information respecting those individuals of the race that flourished in Scotland before the middle of the thirteenth century as can be gleaned from the authentic, though meagre, data of the charters and other documents where their names occur, or from State papers in which they are mentioned; and by a careful consideration of the positions in which each is found, to connect one with another as far as possible, and then to carry on the history of that portion of the family to which this work is especially devoted from—to borrow the words of the talented author of "Caledonia"—a more perfect period of record.

PART I.

THE FRASERS IN EAST LOTHIAN.

SIMON FRASER OF KEITH.

IN 1160, during the reign of Malcolm the Maiden, Simon Fraser granted the Church of Keith, then written Keth, with a considerable tract of land in its vicinity, to the monks of Kelso.[1]

According to the learned author of "Caledonia,"[2] "The parish of Humbie comprehends the ancient districts of Keith-Hundeby and Keith-Marshal; the north-west half was called Keith-Hervey, and afterwards Keith-Marshal; the south-east half was named Keith-Simon, from Simon Fraser, which was afterwards changed to Keith-Hundeby."

In 1184 the name of Simon Fraser appears as a witness to a perambulation of the boundaries of the lands of Mordwheit or Morthwayt,[3] made by order of King William the Lion, who gave them to the Abbey of Newbottle; and his death must have taken place during the next few years, for, in 1190,[4] his daughter and heiress, Eda, with her husband, Hugh Lorens, confirmed his charter of the Church of Keith to the monks of Kelso, and the issue of this marriage was a daughter and heiress, also named Eda, who became the wife of Philip, the King's Marischal,[5] and the two districts of Keith were united in the possession of their son Hervey, the Marischal,[6] by whom, and by his son John de Keith, in his turn also Marischal,[7] the grant of Simon Fraser to the monks of Kelso was confirmed.

[1] Cart. Kelso, No. 85.
[2] Caledonia, vol. ii. p. 532.
[3] Cart. Newbottle, No. 20.
[4] Cart. Kelso, No. 86.
[5] Cart. Kelso, No. 87.
[6] Ibid. Nos. 87, 89.
[7] Ibid. No. 88.

CHARTER by EARL WALDEVE to the MONKS OF MELROSE, of Pasture on Lammermuir. [1166-1182.]

COMES WALDEUUS, omnibus fidelibus et amicis, Francis et Anglis, salutem. Sciant tam futuri quam presentes me dedisse et confirmasse hac mea carta, concessione heredis mei, Deo et Sancte Marie de Melros, et monachis ibidem Deo seruientibus, communem pasturam super Lambermoram mecum et cum hominibus meis, per has diuisas, scilicet, de Baldredestan per altam uiam usque ad Ealingcloh et inde deorsum sicut Healingcloh cadit in Bothkyl, et inde usque in diuisas de Inuerwic; pro salute anime mee et antecessorum meorum et successorum meorum, in perpetuam elemosinam, ita libere et quiete et honorifice ab omnibus secularibus seruiciis et consuetudinibus, sicut aliqua elemosina liberius et quietius et honorificentius datur uel tenetur: Si autem dimiserint pasturam de Inuerwic, caule eorum sequentur pecora sua cum logiis suis que pertinent ad ipsas caulas infra has prenominatas diuisas sine manuali opere, et meis propriis logiis de Beltun: Hanc donationem ego et heredes mei warantizabimus predictis monachis contra omnes homines inperpetuum: His testibus, Aelina Comitissa, Radulfo capellano, Johanne capellano, Waltero capellano, Hugone de Duns, Patricio fratre comitis, Edwardo auunculo comitis, Gilbert Fraser, Adam filio Alden, Alden senescaldo, Gamello de Pethcox, Adam de Foghou, Gilberto filio Walteri, Stephano Papedi, Warino Lemalla, Adam filio Eggari, Adam de Edintun.

[*Vide* Translation on page fourth of this sheet.]

Comes Waldeuus Omnib; fidelib; 7 amicis francis 7 a[
mals hac mea carta concessione heredis mei deo 7 s[
comuné pasturá sup lambermora meam 7 cú bon[
tam mã tilqs ad ellingelok 7 inde decisli hait hellu[
uic p salutte aïe met 7 ancessor meor 7 successor[
rifice ab oib; sctarib; seruias 7 consuetudinib; sicut
tenet. Si aú dimiserint pasturá de Inuerwic ea ule[
causas infra has pnotatas diuisas sine manuali op[
7 heredes mei warantizabim pdictis monachis con[
. . . capellō. Johe capt. Walto capt. Hugone de
frater. Adã filio aldris. Alden senescaldo. Gar[
Steph o papedi. Warino temalla. Adã filio e[

...anglis sal. Sciant tam sūti qm pñtes: me dedisse 7 confir-
...se marie de melros. 7 monachis ibidem deo serunetib;
...entib; meisp has diuisas saliez de baldredestan p al-
...lingelos cadit in bothkyl 7 inde usq; in diuisas de Inu-
...oz meoz in ppetua elemosina ita libere 7 quiete 7 hono-
...aliq; elemosina libers 7 quiets 7 honorificenti dat uel
...le coz legitio pecora sua cū logys siui q ptinent ad ipsas
...ope 7 meis ppriis logys de beltun. hanc donatione ego
...cont os hoiel inppetuū. his testib;. Aelina Coc. Radul.
...dunl. Patcio fre coc. Edwardo auuncto coc. Gilbt
...mello de pethcox. Adā de foghou. Gilberto filio Walti
...eggari. Adam de edintun.

TRANSLATION OF THE FOREGOING CHARTER.

EARL WALDEVE, to all his faithful men and friends, French and English, greeting. Know all men, present and to come, that I have given and, by this my charter, confirmed, with consent of my heir, to God and St. Mary of Melrose, and the monks there serving God, common pasture upon Lambermoor, with me and with my men, by these marches, to wit: From Baldred's Stane by the highway as far as Ealingcloh, and thence downwards as Healingcloh falls into Bothkyl, and thence as far as the marches of Inuerwic; for the safety of my soul and the souls of my predecessors and successors, in perpetual alms, as freely and quietly and honourably, free from all secular services and customs, as any alms is freely and quietly and honourably given or held. And if they shall quit the pasture of Inuerwic, their sheepcots shall follow the flocks, with their bothies that pertain to the said cots within the before-named marches, without manual labour, and along with my own bothies of Beltun. This gift I and my heirs shall warrant to the foresaid monks against all men for ever. Witnesses, Aelina the Countess, Radulf the chaplain, John the chaplain, Walter the chaplain, Hugh of Dunn, Patrick brother of the Earl, Edward uncle of the Earl, Gilbert Fraser, Adam son of Alden, Alden the steward, Gamell of Pethcox, Adam of Foghou, Gilbert son of Walter, Stephan Papedi, Warin Lemalla, Adam son of Edgar, Adam of Edintun.

Chalmers, in "Caledonia," says that the above grant was confirmed by King Malcolm, and quotes Cart. Kelso, No. 90, in support of this; but that confirmation relates only to a grant made by the King himself, and he did not confirm Simon Fraser's charter.

Both that charter and the confirmation by his daughter and her heirs were, however, confirmed by William the Lion and Alexander II,[1] without the intervention of any subject-superior, and it therefore appears that the lands were held in chief of the Crown.

Simon Fraser's line, probably the senior and most influential, from having been tenants-in-chief of the Crown at that date, therefore terminated in a daughter and heiress, through whom and her heirs the estates belonging to him passed into the family of De Keith.

GILBERT FRASER.

CONTEMPORARY with Simon Fraser of Keith in 1166, Gilbert Fraser appears as a witness to a confirmation by William the Lion, of a charter granted by Waldeve the Earl, son of Gospatrick, to the monks of Coldinghame,[2] and he was also a witness to another charter from the same Earl Waldeve to the monks of Melrose,[3] which, though without date, must have been granted before 1182, as the Earl died in that year.

A facsimile of this last charter is in the National Manuscripts of Scotland, and the name there appears "FRASER."

Whether Crauford be the originator of a mistake now to be noticed, or copied it from some earlier source, it appears in his "Lives of Officers of State,"[4] has thence been adopted by Chalmers in "Caledonia,"[5] and, upon his authority, transferred to the pages of other writers.

It consists in the confusion of this Gilbert Fraser with a certain "Kylvert, Culvut, or Kylward," for his name is found under these different forms, who was contemporary with him, and who, with his descendants, became

---

[1] Cart. Kelso, Nos. 91, 93.
[2] Cart. Coldinghame, No. cxiv.
[3] Cart. Melrose, No. 76.
[4] Lives of Officers of State, p. 270.
[5] Caledonia, vol. i. p. 555.

allied to the Frasers in the next generation; and it will be necessary here to give the reasons for differing from these authorities on this point, and regarding Gilbert Fraser and Kylvert as separate persons.

In spite of the similarity of sound, Kylvert does not seem to be a form of Gilbert.

Gilbert is a Norman or French name, a contraction from its old form "Gislebert,"[1] while Kylvert, and its variations Kylward and Culvut, are a Saxon name, and are so found in Simeon of Durham and other writers; but, independently of this, there is still stronger evidence in the fact that all the individuals of the Fraser family are found bearing that surname, the single temporary exception to this rule being an "Adam," who calls himself Adam, filius Udardi, in two of his charters, though in others he styles himself Adam Fraser, filius Udardi Fraser, but in no instance are Kylvert or any member of his family found to bear the surname of Fraser, or any surname whatever (with the exception of his daughter Maria, who took the territorial surname of "de Hales"), and this is the more remarkable, as their names occur repeatedly in the same charters with those of the Frasers.

The Saxon and Scoto-Danish families in Scotland continued the use of patronymics instead of surnames for a considerable time after their association with the Normans, of whom many bore surnames proper, or territorial, at the time of the conquest of England in 1066, while the remainder assumed them not long after that event; and of this the great Earls of Dunbar, descended from a Saxon or Anglo-Danish race, are a conspicuous example.[2]

This great family, from the time of its retirement into Scotland during the latter half of the eleventh century down to the middle of the thirteenth century, and even later, shows a succession of several Gospatricks, a Waldeve, and a further succession of Patricks, without a surname having been borne by any of the line; and the following are among some of the most curious instances of this:—

---

[1] Domesday Book, vol. iii. p. 532.

[2] This powerful family is found under the designations of Earls of Dunbar, Earls of March, and occasionally Earls of Lothian, but the first of these titles is applied to them in these pages.

1st, The notice of a visit made by Patrick,[1] the first of that name, Earl of Dunbar, to the shrine of St. Cuthbert, at Durham, which is thus recorded—

"Comes Patricius junior filius Waldevi Comitis
Patricius avunculus ejus et Cecilia uxor illius
Et Willelmus filius ejus."

2d, William, Earl Patrick's second son, married Christiana Corbet, heiress of Walter Corbet, and their two sons, Patrick and Nicolas, both assumed their mother's surname of Corbet, though Foghou, to which Patrick succeeded, Nicolas receiving their mother's estate of Makarston, had been given to their father by Earl Patrick.[2]

3d, Another William, the son of Earl Waldeve's brother Patrick, having married his cousin Ada, a widow, who had received the lands of Home from her father, Earl Patrick, on her first union with one of the De Courtenay family, took the name of Home as a territorial surname, which was afterwards used by his descendants as a surname proper.[3]

The fact that Kylvert and his children never bore the surname of Fraser, renders it impossible to consider them members of that family; and the absence of any surname whatever, with the exception noticed above, points to his having been of Scoto-Saxon or Scoto-Danish race.

He, or his son, appears to have held the lands of Hales, in East Lothian, as a feudatory of the Earls of Dunbar, and they also seem to have had large possessions in the district of Tweeddale.

His family will be seen to have consisted of two sons,[4] Oliver and Adam,[5] and two daughters, one married to a Fraser, the other styling herself Maria de Hales.

UDARD FRASER.

ALL that is known of Udard Fraser is gathered from the occurrence of his name in the charters of some of his descendants,[6] from which it appears that he lived during the latter half of the twelfth century, and that he

---

[1] "Liber Vitæ," p. 99.
[2] Caledonia, vol. ii. p. 367.
[3] *Ibid.* vol. ii. p. 241.
[4] Cart. Newbottle, Nos. 73, 92.
[5] Adam, filius Kylverti, a different person from Adam, filius Udardi, or Adam Fraser, was a witness to a charter by his sister, Maria de Hales, filia Kylverti.—Cart. Newbottle, No. 92.
[6] Cart. Newbottle, Nos. 74, 76, 77.

married a sister of Oliver, son of the Kylvert just mentioned, who is said to have been the founder of Oliver Castle, in Tweeddale,[1] and in all probability was so, and whom Adam Fraser, Udard Fraser's son, will be found to call *avunculus*, which, though sometimes used for uncle on either side, means maternal uncle, unless the context affords evidence to the contrary; *patruus* being the proper term to express that relationship on the father's side.[2]

THOMAS FRASER.

IN several charters granted by the first Patrick, Earl of Dunbar, who held the earldom from 1182 to 1232, and in others by Walter, son of Allan, "dapifer" to William the Lion, the name of Thomas Fraser is found as a witness.[3]

He also witnessed an agreement between the Earl and the monks of Melrose,[4] to which Bricius, Bishop of Moray, was an assenting party *in curia regis*, 1208; and his having been at that time of sufficient age and rank to be present at a Court, where the documents show that the King presided in person, renders it probable that he was contemporary with Udard Fraser, but no trace remains of his parentage or descendants.

During the first half of the thirteenth century the names of Bernard Fraser, Gilbert Fraser, and Adam Fraser are found, and the last of these is expressly designated as the son of Udard Fraser; but as the three appear to have been closely connected, in giving some account of each they may be taken in the order which their relative importance would seem to assign to them.

---

[1] Caledonia, vol. i. p. 555; vol. ii. p. 918.

[2] An instance of *avunculus* being used for paternal uncle appears in the passage from the Liber Vitæ of Durham, but the evident jingle between *Patricius* and *patruus* may have offended the ear of the monkish chronicler, and induced him to substitute the less correct, but more euphonious expression.

[3] Cart. Melrose, Nos. 48, 72, 74, 77, 101, 104.

[4] Acts of the Parliaments of Scotland, vol. i. pp. 69*, 70*.

It will be necessary, however, before relating the career of the first of these three, to notice that there appears to have existed a Bernard Fraser of earlier date.

In the register of the Priory of St. Andrews there is found an agreement made by G. (Gilbert I.), the Prior and the Convent of St. Andrews, with Bernard Fraser " et heredes de Drem," concerning a chapel at Drem, and some lands for the sustentation of the chaplain.[1] The date appears to be fixed between 1186 and 1188, by that having been the duration of the first Gilbert's tenure of the office of Prior, and by there having been no other whose name began with G. until the election of Gilbert II. in 1258. Bernard Fraser is not styled dominus de Drem, and the expression " et heredes de Drem," invariably repeated after his name in the document, seems to distinguish them from his own heirs, and they may have been female heirs-portioners, of whom he was either the feudal superior, or had received the ward or guardianship.

A second agreement is also found in the register of St. Andrews, word for word the same as the one above mentioned, except that the initial S. (for Simon, who was Prior from 1211 to 1225) is inserted instead of G.[2]

It appears certain that this last agreement is a copy of that made between 1186 and 1188, and that the initial letter of the Prior's name had been mis-read, for the witnesses are identical in both, and the names of at least two of them, Simon Fraser and Willelmus de Grame, belong to the former era.

In the agreement it is stated that Bernard Fraser " et heredes de Drem " shall hold the chapel as freely and quietly as any knight among their equals holds one, " adeo liberam et quietam sicut aliquis miles de paribus suis habet."

It would seem, therefore, that this earlier person of the name had attained to a certain importance before 1186; and he cannot be regarded as the same Bernard Fraser who is found in positions of minor importance during the earlier years of the thirteenth century, and only rose to influence and power under the Crown about 1230. There must, therefore, have been two persons of the name, both of whom will be found to have had some connection with the estate of Drem, although other circumstances hereafter related militate against their being considered father and son.

[1] Reg. Priorat. St. Andrews, p. 40.   [2] *Ibid.* p. 322.

Nothing, except his agreement with the Prior of St. Andrews, is to be found respecting the first; but the second became a person of considerable importance, and is also the earliest concerning whom information can be obtained, beyond the mere proof of existence from an isolated mention of a name.

SIR BERNARD FRASER.

His name, or that of the above-mentioned elder Bernard, is found as a witness to a charter by Patrick, Earl of Dunbar, and also to another by Walter, the son of Alan the "dapifer," during the reign of William the Lion;[1] but it must have been he who witnessed several other charters of later date, granted by Earl Patrick, and by his two sons (Patrick, who succeeded to the earldom about 1332, and William, who married Christiana Corbet), during their father's lifetime.[2]

Bernard Fraser appears as a witness to charters of lands in Milnehalech of North Hales, granted by Maria de Hales, daughter of Kylvert, and sister of Oliver, in her widowhood, to the monks of Newbottle;[3] and he also witnessed the confirmation of these charters by the Earl of Dunbar;[4] but, notwithstanding this, he afterwards laid claim to the very same possessions, and succeeded in evicting them from Maria de Hales by virtue of his hereditary right to them, which right she acknowledged in the court of the overlord, the Earl of Dunbar, at the same time confessing that she had no such right. He, however, only took this step for the purpose of regranting them to the monks of Newbottle in his own name.

His charter was witnessed by the king, Alexander II., the Chancellor, William de Bondington, who received that appointment in 1230-31, and Nesius de Londres, and was therefore not earlier than the above date.[5]

It is rather difficult, from the meagre records of these documents, to clearly understand this transaction, for as Bernard Fraser had hereditary right to those lands, which Maria de Hales acknowledged, it does not appear

---

[1] Cart. Melrose, Nos. 120, 73.
[2] Cart. Coldingbame, Nos. cxviii., cxxv., cxxvi., cxxxiii., cxxxiv.
[3] Cart. Newbottle, Nos. 91, 92.
[4] Ibid. No. 93.
[5] Cart. Newbottle, No. 94.

how she obtained the power of granting charters of them,[1] unless, indeed, it was an usurpation on her part, from her relationship to Kylvert and Oliver, which ultimately was overcome by Bernard Fraser's stronger hereditary right, probably derived from the same persons.

Bernard Fraser was dominus or lord, if not of the whole, at all events of a considerable portion of Forton and Linton, both situated in East Lothian; for he confirmed charters affecting lands therein, which had been granted by Nesius, the son of Nesius, and by the two sons of John de Londres, Nesius de Londres, and John de Murreff or Moravia. He terms Nesius de Londres "fratre meo," my brother (in law), but he does not extend the same appellation to John de Moravia as he would have done had he married a sister of both: Nesius de Londres may have married a sister of his.

It is necessary here to advert to, and, as far as possible, rectify some confusion respecting the name of Nesius, into which various authors appear to have been led by the mistake of confounding the earliest Gilbert Fraser with Kylvert, which has been already noticed.

They have employed the name of "Ness" as a family or generic name, and have vaguely stated that Maria de Hales, a daughter of Kylvert or Gilbert Fraser, married a "Ness," and that Bernard Fraser's mother was a daughter of "Ness," Lord of Forton, without in any way defining which individual of that name is referred to in each case.

Nothing can be found in support of either assertion in the charters, nor evidence of any other matrimonial connection between the Frasers and any one of the name of Ness, except that above mentioned existing between Bernard Fraser and Nesius de Londres; and it will be also seen that Nes, or Nesius, was a personal or Christian name, and not the surname of a family at that time.

A Nesius, son of William, attended the court of Malcolm IV., and that of William the Lion, before 1171.[2]

---

[1] In her charters Maria de Hales mentions the marches between the lands of North Hales and those belonging to her "nepotis," probably nephew, Randulphi. A Randulphus Nobilis was a witness to a charter by John de Moravia, Cart. Newbottle, No. 113, and designated as son of William Nobilis, granted lands in Peffer and East Forton to the monks, No. 118. The name of Maria's husband may have been "Noble."

[2] Acts of the Parliaments of Scotland, vol. i. pp. 53*, 64*.

THE FRASERS IN EAST LOTHIAN.

A Nesius, son of Nesius, witnessed, in company with the Countess Ada, natural daughter of King William, a charter granted by her husband, Patrick, Earl of Dunbar,[1] not later than 1200, as she, according to Fordun, died in that year.

Nesius, son of Nesius, granted two charters to the monks of Newbottle during the first few years of the thirteenth century.[2] One of these, granted in 1205, was confirmed by Nesius de Londres not later than 1214,[3] in which year John, Bishop of Dunkeld, one of the witnesses to the confirmation, died.[4]

John de Londres, contemporary with Nesius, son of Nesius, witnessed charters at the court of William the Lion before 1200.[5]

Nesius de Londres, in his charters to the monks of Newbottle, styled himself son of John de Londres, and called Nesius, son of Nesius, whose charters he confirmed, "avunculus," or maternal uncle,[6] from which it may be inferred that John de Londres had married a sister of Nesius, son of Nesius, and that Nesius de Londres succeeded to his uncle's property through her, his mother. His grant was "in feudo meo de Forton."

It is apparent from the above short sketch that "Ness" was not the surname of this family. The two earliest that bore it appear to have had no surnames, but to have been designated by patronymics, and the third bore it as a Christian name before his surname of de Londres, which he inherited from his father, and there is no trace of any connection between the family and Maria de Hales, or any of Kylvert's children.

Bernard Fraser, as superior, or as successor of Nesius de Londres, confirmed the charters of both Nesius, son of Nesius, and Nesius de Londres; and in the confirmation, to which Queen Ermengarde, who died in 1233,[7] was a witness, Nesius de Londres, who had witnessed his charter of Milnehalech not earlier than 1230-31, is said to be dead. "Sicut in cartis utriusque Nesii continetur et sicut eodem anno et die quo predictus Nesius de Londres frater meus vivus fuit et mortuus."[8]

---

[1] Cart. Newbottle, No. 75.
[2] Ibid. Nos. 109, 111.
[3] Ibid. No. 112.
[4] Chron. Melrose, p. 115.
[5] Acts of the Parliaments of Scotland, vol. i. p. 65*.
[6] Cart. Newbottle, Nos. 107, 112.
[7] Chron. Melrose, p. 143.
[8] Cart. Newbottle, No. 110.

John de Murriff, or Moravia, in the two charters granted by him, is called son of John de Londres, and brother of Nesius de Londres.[1] It is possible that these expressions may mean son-in-law and brother-in-law. He acquired lands from Nesius de Londres in West Forton and Linton, and in one of his charters affecting lands in Linton, he styled Bernard Fraser " domino meo ;"[2]—Patrick, Earl of Dunbar, in his confirmation of the other in West Forton as overlord, stating that Bernard Fraser had already confirmed it.[3]

These properties in Forton and Linton, probably in part paternal lands, and in part acquired by succession to Nesius de Londres, together with a portion of North Hales, which seems to have been derived hereditarily from another source, formed a considerable estate in the most fertile part of Scotland, of which Bernard Fraser was the owner and mid-superior, for he himself appears to have held it as a feudatory of the great Earls of Dunbar.[4]

In the charters and documents of that day the name of de Londres is also written de London, and de Lundin, and if Nesius de Londres or Lundin was related to the illegitimate children of William the Lion, Robert, and William, who bore that surname, the connection between him and Bernard Fraser may in some degree account for the latter having entered the service of the Crown about the year 1230. He may also have distinguished himself in the various wars and expeditions carried on by Alexander II., and by that means may have attracted the notice of the King.

However this may be, after that date he appears in very constant attendance at the royal court, and soon rose to eminence under his wise and gallant sovereign. He was a frequent witness to charters by him or others, in which his name is found in a very high position, and in general immediately following that of the Senescallus (Steward), or some other high official of the kingdom.[5]

He was appointed Vicecomes, or Sheriff, of Stirling, and in the recital of a charter granted by Alexander II. to the monks of Newbottle in 1234, he appears in that capacity as " noster Vicecomes de Striveline," associated with

---

[1] Cart. Newbottle, Nos. 113, 114.
[2] Ibid. No. 114.
[3] Ibid. No. 115.
[4] Ibid. No. 115.
[5] Cart. Moravia, No. 40. Cart. Newbottle, Nos. 22, 24. Cart. Holyrood, No. 58. Cart. Melrose, Nos. 73, 130, 203, 213, 215, 218, 219, 228, 248, 257, 278, 302.

Elyas, Abbot of Holyrood, in an arbitration and perambulation of marches, upon which the royal charter is based.[1] After this date his name is usually found as "Dominus Bernardus Fraser, Miles" (Knight).

It is probable, from his appointment as Vicecomes of Stirling, that he had acquired possessions in that district, and that the estate of Touch-fraser took its appellation from him; but the fact cannot be established by authentic evidence, in consequence of the paucity of early Stirlingshire records still extant. Not many years after his death, however, a family of the name, descended from Sir Gilbert Fraser, will be found holding that estate, with others in the district, which tradition affirms to be those that had belonged to him.

On the 17th of August 1233, at Stirling, Alexander II. confirmed an agreement between the prior and monks of the Isle of May, in the Firth of Forth, and Bernard Fraser, by which the latter feued to that priory, in perpetuity, the whole lands of Dremes-sheles (the schealings or upland grazings of Drem), to be held by the prior and his successors from him and his heirs.[2]

Although this document might seem, at first sight, to infer some succession on the part of the grantor to the elder person of the same name who, as already noticed, dealt with the estate of Drem, yet the terms of the two agreements are so different as not to afford much support to that conjecture. In this last there is no mention of the "heredes de Drem;" but Bernard Fraser deals with the lands as his own, and his heirs "heredibus suis" are only incidentally named as those of whom they are to be held after him. His hereditary right to other property, mentioned above, also appears at variance with his having succeeded to these lands in a similar manner. Perhaps he may have acquired his right to that part of the estate by marriage with one of the "heredes," if they were heirs-female; but whatever his connection with Drem, it seems to have terminated at or before his decease, for, so far as has been ascertained, that property is not among those held by any of the Fraser name in the next, nor any succeeding generation.

In 1237 Sir Bernard Fraser accompanied Alexander II. to the meeting with Henry III. at York, and was one of the "magnates" or barons of Scot-

[1] Cart. Newbottle, No. 165. [2] Cart. Isle of May (St. Andrews), No. 20. p. 16.

land that swore to the observance of the peace then concluded between his sovereign and the King of England.[1]

His name is found for the last time in 1247 as a witness to a royal charter in favour of the abbot and monks of Lindores,[2] and he seems to have died about the same time as the monarch whom he had so long served, viz., about 1249-50, for his name does not appear as that of a living man in any later document.

Mr. Anderson, "History of the Family of Fraser," p. 9, says that Sir Bernard Fraser lived until the year 1258, and in proof of this adduces a charter of the church of Foghou, from William, son of Patrick, Earl of Dunbar, to the monks of Kelso, which was witnessed by him, " though no date be mentioned," says Mr. Anderson, " evidently about the year 1258;" but the death of William, the grantor, in 1252 is upon record,[3] and therefore Mr. Anderson must have been mistaken as to the date.

He also, at the same page, states positively, " To Bernard Fraser succeeded his son, Sir Gilbert," and quotes " Caledonia," vol. i. p. 554; but that authority does not bear out his assertion. The word there used is not " son," but " relative," which is probable enough.

In the " Annals of the Frasers," published 1795, and some MS. histories, are statements that Sir Bernard Fraser married Mary Ogilvie, daughter of Gilchrist, Thane of Angus, and by her had four sons, Simon, Andrew, Gilbert, and William, and two daughters, Fenella, married to Sir Colin Campbell of Lochaw, and Helen, who died a nun at Coldinghame. Of these, so called, sons, three, Simon, Andrew, and William, will be found to have been the children of a Sir Gilbert Fraser; and for the marriage with Mary Ogilvie, and the existence of the two daughters, there is no authentic evidence.

Crawfurd, " Lives of Officers of State," p. 270, without giving any authority, also says that Simon Fraser was a son of Sir Bernard Fraser, and, p. 269, has the following passage :—" This Bernard was High Sheriff of the county of Stirling in the time of Alexander II., which we find continued in his descendants down to the grandchildren of the Lord Chamberlain, whose life I am writing."

[1] Rymer's Fœdera, vol. i. p. 376.   [2] Robertson's Index, p. 76, No. 92.   [3] Chron. Melrose, p. 179.

If this were correct, and the sheriffship had continued in the Fraser name without any break, it might lead to the inference that Sir Bernard Fraser left a son; but Crawfurd was mistaken, and it was not the case. During a great part of the reign of Alexander III. John de Lambyrton was Vicecomes of Stirling, after him Patrick de Grahame held the office down to 1292, and it is not until 1293 that a Fraser is again found in that position. It will be seen also that those of the name who afterwards possessed estates in Stirlingshire, with the sheriffship, and the one to whom the property in North Hales passed, were not Sir Bernard's actual descendants, but those of Sir Gilbert and Adam Fraser, and these considerations point strongly to the conclusion that Sir Bernard Fraser left no issue.

SIR GILBERT FRASER.

THE first notice that is found of the name of this Gilbert Fraser occurs in the charter of a meadow near Pouerhov, in East Lothian, granted by Nesius, son of Nesius, to the monks of Newbottle before 1214,[1] to which he was a witness along with Alexander de St. Martin Vicecomes, Hugh Giffard, and others. Though this is the only occasion upon which his name is found as a witness to any charter dealing with lands in East Lothian, it to a certain extent shows a connection with that district.

He appears to have had sufficient talent to raise himself to the position of an official of the Crown about the same time as Sir Bernard Fraser, for in 1233 Alexander II. addressed a precept to Gilbert Fraser, Vicecomes de Traquair, ordering him to try a cause then pending between William, Bishop of Glasgow, and a Mariota, daughter of Samuel, who resigned her claim to the lands of Stobhou, those in dispute, " in curiam Vicecomitis de Traquaire;"[2] and in the same year, as Vicecomes, he was a witness to a second resignation of those lands by Eugene, the son of Anabell, another daughter of Samuel.[3]

There are also extant two other precepts or mandates from Alexander II.

[1] Cart. Newbottle, No. 111. [2] Cart. Glasgow, No. 130. [3] Ibid. No. 131.

addressed to Gilbert Fraser, Vicecomes de Traquair; the date of the second is 1242, and the first was probably issued before that year.[1] It desires J. de Vallibus, Vicecomes of Edinburgh, G. Freser, Vicecomes of Traquair, N. de Heris, forestar, and W. de Penycook, to ascertain the boundaries of the pastures of Lethanhope, exclusive of the common pasture belonging to the town of Inverlethan, and to report their extent and value to the King; and the second orders him, in the exercise of his office, to imprison all excommunicated persons whom the bishop of Glasgow, his archdeacon, official, or dean should designate as having been for forty days under the censure of the church.[2]

His name is also found as Vicecomes of Traquair among the witnesses to a charter of Ingolfhiston, granted by Christiana, quondam filia Ade, filii Gilberti, to the chapel of St. Mary of Ingolfhiston, between the years 1233 and 1249.[3] The other witnesses are Sir David de Graham, Sir Alexander de Hunyot, William de Malvill, John Venator (Hunter), and some others.

An inquiry, by means of an assize or species of jury,[4] composed of dominus Nes Freser, dominus Henricus de Candela, Willelmus de Malevill, and nine others, was held in 1259 to ascertain the justice of a former verdict given at a trial, concerning the lands of Hopkelchoc, in the court of Gilbertus Fraser, miles, Vicecomes de Peebles.

The above records prove that Sir Gilbert Fraser held both sheriffships, Traquair and Peebles, and was the principal official of the Crown in that extensive district; and to attain to that position he must not only have been an able man, but in all probability must have acquired considerable estates there, to which supposition the possession of large property in the same district by his descendants, and the succession of one of his sons to the two sheriffships afford strong support.

It must have been during his tenure of office that the occurrence took place thus related by Fordun.[5] "On the 9th of May 1261, in the thirteenth year of King Alexander, a stately and venerable cross was found at Peebles, in the presence of good men, priests, clerics, and burgesses, but it is quite

---

[1] Caledonia, vol. ii. p. 920; A.D. 1241, Origines Parochiales, vol. i. p. 216; Cart. Newbottle, No. 121.

[2] Caledonia, vol. ii. p. 920; Origines Parochiales, vol. i. p. 220.

[3] Cart. Glasgow, No. 150.

[4] Acts of the Parliaments of Scotland, vol. i. p. 88, documents subjoined to preface.

[5] Fordun, Gesta Annalia liv. Translation by Mr. F. Skene.

unknown in what year and by what person it was hidden there. It is, however, believed that it was hidden by some of the faithful about the year of our Lord 296, while Maximian's persecution was raging in Britain. Not long after this a stone urn was discovered there, about three or four paces from the spot where that glorious cross had been found. It contained the ashes and bones of a man's body, torn limb from limb as it were. Whose relics these are no one knows as yet. Some, however, think they are the relics of him whose name was inscribed on the very stone wherein the holy cross was lying. Now there was carved on that stone, outside, 'Tomb of the Bishop Saint Nicholas.' Moreover, in the very spot where the cross was found, many a miracle was and is wrought by that cross; and the people poured, and still pour, thither in crowds, devoutly bringing their offerings and vows to God. Wherefore the King, by the advice of the Bishop of Glasgow, had a handsome church made there to the honour of God and the Holy Cross."

Sir Gilbert Fraser probably died about 1263, for his son is found as Vicecomes of Traquair in 1264. His wife's name was Christiana, but that of the family to which she belonged does not appear; she was certainly the mother of one of his four sons, and probably of the other three.

John, ancestor of the Frasers of Touch-fraser.

Simon, who succeeded to the sheriffships, mentioned as brother of Andrew and William.

Andrew, mentioned as son of Sir Gilbert Fraser.

William, mentioned as brother of Simon and Andrew.

ADAM FRASER.

OLIVER, the son of Kylvert, with the consent of Beatrix, his wife, granted to the monks of Newbottle a charter of some lands "in tellure de Hale."[1] The date of the gift is fixed in or before 1189, for Jocelyne, Bishop of Glasgow, and Ernauld, Abbot of Melrose, were witnesses to it, the latter of whom was translated to the Abbey of Rieville in that year.[2] Oliver, therefore, may have acquired the lands of Hales through his wife.

[1] Cart. Newbottle, No. 73.   [2] Chron. Melrose, p. 97.

Patrick, Earl of Dunbar, confirmed this charter by Oliver in or before 1200,[1] as the confirmation was witnessed by Ada, his Countess, who, according to Fordun, died in that year; Nesius, son of Nesius, being also a witness to it.

The record of a perambulation and arbitration is extant,[2] which was held to settle a contention between the monks of Newbottle and William de Vallibus concerning the marches of certain lands; and in the document " D. Oliverus Nesius William de Montfort and William de Grahame " appear as the arbitrators. If Oliver Nesius be the name of a single individual, there is no evidence to show who he was; but if, as is probable, the " D " stands for D^{ni} (Domini), which would embrace all the members of the Court, the names may be held to be those of this Oliver, and of the Nesius, son of Nesius, already noticed. There is no date affixed to the arbitration, but from the persons engaged in it, and the names of the witnesses to it, Richard Rydel, William de Grahame, Bernard Fraser, William Noble, etc., and from the matters with which it deals, it appears to have taken place during the first fifteen or twenty years of the thirteenth century.

Chalmers, in " Caledonia,"[3] ascribes the foundation of Oliver Castle, in Tweeddale, to this son of Kylvert, and it is probable that he is correct in doing so, for the first mention of that place, afterwards the seat of a branch of the Frasers, is found about the time when he flourished, in a description of the marches between Stobo, Hopprew, and Orde; two of the numerous witnesses being designated Adam and Cosvold, sons of Muryn " aput Castrum Oliveri."[4]

Adam, filius Udardi,[5] sometimes written Odoardi, confirmed the above charter granted by Oliver, using the same expression, " in tellure de Hale," and terming Oliver " avunculus meus;" and a passage in the confirmation, " per easdem divisas per quas illam tenuerunt " (the monks) " in vitâ predicti Oliveri," shows that it was granted after Oliver's death. Adam therefore succeeded his maternal uncle in the lands of Hales.

Under the same appellation he granted to the monks a second charter of

---

[1] Cart. Newbottle, No. 75.
[2] Ibid. No. 119.
[3] Caledonia, vol. i. p. 555; vol. ii. p. 918.
[4] Cart. Glasgow, p. 89, No. 104.
[5] Cart. Newbottle, No. 74.

certain lands, in augmentation of those already given to them, and these were also "in tellure de Hale."[1] This charter was witnessed "D^{no} Bernardo Fraser, Simone de Lindesay, Johanne de Cadela, et multis aliis."

But he also granted another charter of Suythrig, in Suythale—Southrig, in South Hale—to the monks,[2] and in it he termed himself Adam Fraser, and mentioned Constantia his wife.

The Earl of Dunbar, as overlord or superior of the lands of Hales,[3] in his confirmation of these charters, recites that the gifts are those of Oliver, the uncle of Adam Fraser, the son of Udard Fraser, " Oliveri, avunculi d^{ni} Ade Fraser, filii Odoardi Fraser," and the Earl's two sons, Patrick and William, with Bernard Fraser, Thomas de Gordoun, and others, were witnesses to the confirmation.

Adam, the son of Udard, was a witness to one of the charters[4] granted by Maria de Hales of those lands which Bernard Fraser evicted from her, and he is also found, in company with Bernard Fraser and John Giffard, a witness to a confirmation by William de Vallibus[5] of a charter granted by William Noble to the monks of Newbottle,[6] not earlier than 1214, as Hugh, Bishop of Dunkeld, who succeeded Bishop John in that year, was a witness to it ;[7] and with Bernard Fraser and others,[8] he witnessed an agreement between John de Morham and Richard, Abbot of Newbottle from 1214 to 1216.[9]

The temporary disuse of his surname by Adam Fraser is a curious fact, but the most reasonable explanation of it seems to be that he was brought up in the family of his maternal uncle, Oliver, a Scoto-Saxon or Scoto-Dane, where surnames were not in use, and where he would only be known as the son of Udard, though, after the death of his uncle, he resumed his surname on associating more freely with his own Norman relatives that bore it.

There is no record of the death of Adam Fraser, but he left at least one son,

Laurence, who will be found to have possessed the lands of Drumelzier, in Tweeddale, with those of Hales, in East Lothian, and also to have succeeded

[1] Cart. Newbottle, No. 76.
[2] Ibid. No. 77.
[3] Ibid. No. 79.
[4] Ibid. No. 91.
[5] Ibid. No. 117.
[6] Cart. Newbottle, No. 116.
[7] Chron. Melrose, p. 115.
[8] Cart. Newbottle, No. 90.
[9] Chron. Melrose, pp. 115, 124.

to that part of North Hales which had been the hereditary property of Sir Bernard Fraser, and who confirmed the charters affecting the lands of Hales, granted to the monks of Newbottle by Oliver, the son of Kylvert, by Adam Fraser, the son of Udard Fraser, and by Sir Bernard Fraser.

As the view which the writer of this history has taken respecting those individuals of the Fraser race that have been already noticed differs so materially from that hitherto countenanced by the highest authorities, it may be as well to review the circumstances upon which it is based, and to point out how they affect the argument as regards each person.

The three earliest names, those of Simon Fraser, the first Gilbert Fraser, and the first Bernard Fraser, appear contemporaneously from 1160 to 1190, and are followed by those of Udard Fraser and Thomas Fraser in the next generation.

Whether Gilbert Fraser and Bernard Fraser were Simon Fraser's brothers, or Udard Fraser and Thomas Fraser sons of Gilbert Fraser or Bernard Fraser, are points altogether lost in obscurity, upon which not a scintilla of evidence remains to enable an opinion to be formed, except the apparent connection of all five with the district of East Lothian. The positions in which their names are found, however, prove the existence of the race in Scotland by the middle of the twelfth century, and show that the members of it held a respectable rank among the barons and landowners of that part of the country.

With regard to the second Bernard Fraser, the second Gilbert Fraser, and Adam Fraser, there is a little more light afforded by the documents in which their names appear, and here it may be repeated that the entire absence of the use of any surname whatever (except in the case of Maria de Hales) by Kylvert and his family, is conclusive evidence that they were not Frasers, and affords good reason for believing that they were not Normans, and that a Scoto-Saxon or a Scoto-Danish descent may be ascribed to them.

Sir Bernard Fraser held considerable possessions and superiorities in East Lothian as a vassal of the Earls of Dunbar, which seem to have been, to some extent, the family estates inherited by him, yet he also asserted and maintained his hereditary right to Milnhalech, and other lands in North Hales; and as all Hales, both north and south, with exception of those lands, appears to have belonged to Oliver, the son of Kylvert, the only way in which he could acquire that hereditary right would seem to have been through some member of Oliver's family. Tradition also asserts, with great probability, that Sir Bernard Fraser possessed estates in Stirlingshire, of which district he was the vicecomes or sheriff in 1234.

Sir Gilbert Fraser is not found in possession of any property in East Lothian, but still seems to have had some connection with that district during his earlier days, as he witnessed a charter of lands there granted by Nesius, son of Nesius.

In 1233, however, he held the sheriffship of Traquair, and probably about the same time, or a little later, was appointed to that of Peebles, and this, with the fact of Oliver Castle having been the seat of some of his descendants, if the tradition assigning the erection of that castle to Oliver, son of Kylvert, be correct, would suggest that he obtained considerable estates in Tweeddale from that person.

The fact of some of Sir Gilbert Fraser's descendants being found in possession of property in Stirlingshire, and of the sheriffship of that district also, favours the idea of a close relationship between him and Sir Bernard Fraser.

Adam Fraser, who was undoubtedly a son of Udard Fraser, is found possessing the lands of Hales, in East Lothian, not as part of his paternal inheritance, of which there is no trace, but as succeeding his maternal uncle, Oliver, son of Kylvert, in them, which would suggest the failure of all male issue of that family; and his son Lawrence, in addition to Hales, possessed the lands of Drumelzier, in Tweeddale, which may have been obtained from the same source.

Laurence Fraser also succeeded to Milnhalech and the other lands in North Hales, which had belonged hereditarily to Sir Bernard Fraser, and this evinces a near connection between his father, Adam Fraser, and Sir Bernard.

The circumstances thus presented in one body seem to justify the deduction that Kylvert was a powerful personage of Scoto-Saxon or Scoto-Danish race, who held large possessions in Tweeddale, embracing perhaps nearly the whole of that district, and that either he or his son Oliver acquired the estate of Hales, in East Lothian; that Udard Fraser married one of his daughters, and with her obtained, as her marriage portion, Milnhalech and other lands in North Hales, and that Bernard, Gilbert, and Adam were sons of this marriage.

That Bernard Fraser, the eldest son, succeeded his father, in some parts of Forton, Linton, and his other possessions in Athelstaneford and Linton, obtained others from the de Londres family, and acquired his hereditary right to Milnhalech and other lands in North Hales through his mother, by which right he forced Maria de Hales to restore them to him.

That Oliver, the last of Kylvert's family, his brother Adam, the son of Kylvert, and his sister Maria de Hales, having no children, at his death divided the large property which he had inherited from his father, or had himself acquired, between his two younger nephews, bequeathing to Gilbert Fraser extensive estates, with Oliver Castle, in Tweeddale, and to Adam Fraser, Drumelzier, in that district, and Hales, in East Lothian, except those parts of the latter that belonged to Bernard Fraser.

From the Sheriffship of Stirling having passed for a time into other families, until restored to the Fraser name in the person of a descendant of Sir Gilbert, from the great probability that estates in Stirlingshire found in the possession of Sir Gilbert's grandson, Sir Richard Fraser, had belonged to Sir Bernard, and from the acquisition of Sir Bernard's property in North Hales by Adam Fraser's son, Sir Lawrence Fraser, it appears impossible to doubt that Sir Bernard Fraser left no issue, and that the bulk of his possessions descended to Sir Gilbert Fraser and Adam Fraser, or their heirs.

Such is the conclusion to which a careful examination of the charters and documents bearing upon the subject has led the compiler of this history. Upon such meagre evidence it is impossible to arrive at certainty, or to assert positively that events thus happened; but there is nothing upon record adverse to that conclusion, and the evident close connection between the three, together with the circumstances in which they and the descendants of two of them appear, can scarcely be accounted for in any other manner.

The separation of the Frasers into different branches during the next generation is very apparent, of which the three principal may be distinguished from each other, as that of Touch-fraser, near Stirling, descended from Sir Gilbert Fraser through his son John; that of Oliver Castle, in Tweeddale, also descended from him through his son Simon; and that of Drumelzier, in the same district, descended from Adam Fraser.

It is very difficult, if not impossible, to decide whether the Touch-fraser family or that of Oliver Castle, represented the main stem of the race. The succession of Sir Gilbert Fraser's son Simon to the sheriffships held by his father, and the fact of his son, also a Simon, having been the only layman of the name that attended the Parliament at Scone in 1283-84, and the still more numerous and important Parliament at Briggham in 1289-90, point to the Oliver Castle family having been the most powerful in their day; but, at the same time, the members of the Touch-fraser family are found in possession of extensive and widely-distributed estates, and holding appointments of very considerable trust and importance, and there can be no doubt that its representative was the head of the whole race during the reign of Robert I. The succession of Sir Gilbert's son Simon to the sheriffships may also be accounted for by his having obtained the estates with Oliver Castle, in Tweeddale, and by the son of his brother John, who afterwards possessed those in Stirlingshire, having been a young man at Sir Gilbert's death.

The Oliver Castle family, and that of Drumelzier, which seems never to have risen to the same status as the other two, both failed in heirs-female in the course of a few generations, without leaving any male cadets whose posterity can be traced; and the line of Touch-fraser was that from which the family whose history is related in this work, and most, if not all, of the name existing at the present day are descended. It has therefore been thought advisable to follow the succession of this latter in the text, and to give some account of the two former in the Appendix, where will also be found a memoir of the son of Sir Gilbert Fraser that rose to the greatest eminence, but who, as an ecclesiastic, could leave no legitimate posterity.

In the Appendix are also inserted some notices of other early members of the race, respecting whom nothing but their names, or isolated facts, are known, together with such accounts of the families descended at later periods from cadets of the line followed in the text, as may serve to show their origin.

PART II.

THE FRASERS OF TOUCH-FRASER, ETC., AND COWIE.

JOHN FRASER—ALICIA DE CUNIGBURG.

THE name of John Fraser appears here and there in the mythical histories of the race constructed by genealogists. According to some writers, a John Fraser acquired Oliver Castle and a magnificent estate, during the reign of Malcolm Canmore, by marriage with a lady called Eupham Sloan, heiress of Tweeddale, while by others a John Fraser is styled Sheriff of Tweeddale and Laird of Oliver Castle, in 1214, and two very circumstantial lines of descent are brought down from these individuals; but as they do not agree with each other, and as there is not a tittle of evidence to support either, it is scarcely necessary to say that no reliance can be placed upon these statements.

The first notice of any John Fraser, in trustworthy authorities, is that in the "Liber Vitæ" of Durham, where not only his name appears, but his parentage is also recorded—

"Gilbertus Fraser et Christiana uxor ejus
Et Johannes filius illorum"[1]

and although no dates are given in that catalogue of pilgrims to the shrine of St. Cuthbert, the other names found in that part of the roll, and the handwriting in which their visits are recorded, belong to the first half of the thirteenth century.

[1] Liber Vitæ, p. 99.

The next notice of John Fraser that is extant records his marriage with Alicia, the daughter of William de Cunigburg, Lord of Stapilgorton, in the county of Dumfries, and his having received as her portion the lands of "Rig," which his father-in-law held as a feudatory of Roger Avenel, Lord of Eskdale.[1]

This event seems to have occurred, therefore, before the year 1243, when Roger Avenel died;[2] and as a son of Sir Gilbert Fraser would be of an age to marry about that time, there appears no reason to doubt that Alicia de Cunigburg's bridegroom was the John Fraser whose name is found in the "Liber Vitæ" of Durham.

In the Ordnance Survey recently published, "Rigfoot" is placed about a mile to the north, and a little to the westward of Arkelton. Its situation in the old manor of Stapilgorton, now a part of the parish of Langholm, suggests that it was the property thus acquired by John Fraser; and the fact of his having received an estate near Arkelton is important, as serving to connect the next in the series with him.

No further information respecting this John Fraser can be found. It is probable that his life was not a long one, for there is no appearance of his name after his father's death, about 1263; and this affords ground for the presumption that he predeceased his father, which would account for his not being found in possession of the Stirlingshire estates, though, after the death of Sir Gilbert Fraser, they are seen to have been held by the same person that possessed a small estate near Arkelton, viz, Richard Fraser, which appears to warrant his being considered John Fraser's son, and it is not unlikely that John was also the father of another son, Alexander. See Appendix.

SIR RICHARD FRASER.

THE period during which Sir Richard Fraser lived exactly agrees with his having been the son of John Fraser, who received the lands of Rig, near Arkelton, as the marriage portion of his wife, Alicia de Cunigburg;

[1] Reg. Hon. de Morton, vol. ii. No. 9.   [2] Chron. Melrose, p. 155.

and his possession of a small estate close to that town,[1] together with his having been styled "cousin" by Sir Simon Fraser, filius,[2] who, as a great-grandson of Sir Gilbert, would have been first cousin once removed to any son of John Fraser, seems sufficient evidence to support the assumption that he was so.

Sir Richard Fraser's name is first found in 1276, when, with the rank of "Miles" (Knight), he was a witness to the resignation of the lands of Pencaitland, in East Lothian, granted by John de Pencaitland in favour of Herbert de Maxwell, to which the seals of Hugh de Berkeley, justiciar of Lothian, and Sir Simon Fraser (son of Sir Gilbert Fraser, and Sir Richard's uncle) are said to have been affixed, in addition to that of the grantor of the deed,[3] because the seal of the latter was not very ancient or well known.

He next appears in 1289, when, associated with his first cousin, Sir Simon Fraser, pater, Sir John de Lindesay, and several monks and clerks of the "rotuli regis," he was one of the "Attornati," or representatives, sent by his uncle, William Fraser, Bishop of St. Andrews, and his co-executors of the late King Alexander III., to attend on their behalf at a Court, held at Carham-on-Tweed, on the 3d of February in that year, by order of Edward I., desiring Thomas de Normanville and Guiscard de Charrun to try the justice of the claim of John de Massun, a merchant of Gascony, who alleged that the King of Scotland died indebted to him in considerable sums, an allegation disputed by the bishop and his co-executors.[4]

The name of Sir Richard Fraser does not appear among the Barons that attended the Parliament at Brigham in 1290; but in the competition for the Crown of Scotland that ensued on the death of the young Queen Margaret, he sided with Baliol, as did all of his name at that time.

He swore fealty to Edward I. on the 8th of July 1291,[5] and was appointed one of the auditors that were to hear the pleadings of the various competitors, and report thereon to that Monarch, to whom the decision upon their claims had been referred. In the list of these auditors, of whom there were forty

[1] Palgrave, p. 305.
[2] Original Document in Record Office, London.
[3] Original Resignation printed and lithographed in Book of Carlaverock, by William Fraser, vol. ii. p. 406.
[4] Historical Documents of Scotland, vol. i. p. 73.
[5] Ragman Rolls, p. 13.

for Baliol and those of his party, forty for Bruce and those who sided with him, and twenty-five added by Edward I., his name is found seven places below that of his cousin, Sir Simon Fraser, pater.[1]

In 1292 the auditors made their report, declaring that the competitors had terminated their pleadings, and that Edward I. might proceed to give judgment, and when that judgment had been given in favour of Baliol towards the end of the year, Sir Richard Fraser was a witness to the two homages paid by the newly-made King of Scotland to Edward, as his feudal superior, at Norham on the 20th November, and at Newcastle-on-Tyne on the 26th December, in one of which documents his name immediately precedes that of Sir Andrew Fraser, and in the other those of Sir Andrew and Sir Simon Fraser, filius.[2]

He seems at this time to have been in favour with the King of England, and on the 14th of November 1292 Edward I. granted him the ward or guardianship of the lands of the late Richard de Glen, in the county of Peebles,[3] with the "maritagium" or power over the marriage of the young heir, who was Richard, the son of Duncan de Glen, and probably nephew or grandson of the late proprietor, he engaging to pay one hundred merks for this privilege, by instalments of twenty-five each, for which Walter de Huntercombe and Allan Penyngtone became his securities.

In 1293 Sir Richard Fraser was appointed vicecomes of Berwick by John Baliol, and he held that office when one of the early causes of difference between the King of Scotland and Edward I. occurred, viz., the demand for the surrender of William Thorold, who had fled thither from English jurisdiction, to which demand he answered that he must consult his sovereign on the matter, as he had but recently been appointed to the sheriffship.[4]

Upon the commencement of hostilities the grant of the wardship of Richard de Glen's estates was revoked, as indorsed on one of the copies,

---

[1] Rymer's Fœdera, vol. ii. pp. 553, 555.
[2] In these homages, as printed in Rymer's Fœdera and Palgrave's Scottish Records, the name of "Johan de Strivelyn del Cars" is found between those of Richard Fraser and Andrew Fraser; but its insertion there is erroneous, for in the original documents in the Record Office, examined 12th May 1870, no name appears so placed, and the two names in the one homage, the three in the other, stand together in the order described in the text, without any intervening name.
[3] Rotuli Scotiæ, vol. i. p. 11.
[4] Historical Documents of Scotland, vol. i. p. 392.

"quia testatum est quod est nunc inimicus Regis;"[1] but Sir Richard Fraser made his submission early in 1296, and on the 3d September his lands were restored to him, the restoration to date from the Friday of the Paschal week, Good Friday, on which day, so runs the order, the castle of Berwick was surrendered.[2] This seems to show that he was taken prisoner on that occasion, and subsequently readmitted to the favour of Edward I.; indeed, Pierre de Langtoft says that William de Douglas and Richard Fraser were made prisoners when Berwick was taken.[3]

Sir Richard Fraser twice swore fealty to Edward I. for his lands in Stirlingshire and Dumfriesshire on the 28th of August 1296 at Berwick,[4] but he does not appear to have been one of the Barons carried captive into England, for on the 24th of May 1297, invitations to serve Edward in his war with the King of France were sent to him and others resident in Scotland,[5] and on the 28th of the same month he was accepted as surety for his cousin, Sir Simon Fraser, filius, who was released from captivity upon undertaking to serve under Edward I. in his war with France, and the obligation to that effect was sealed by the two cousins at Brembre, Bamborough Castle, in Northumberland.[6]

Sir Richard does not appear to have served personally in Edward's expedition to Flanders, for on the 26th of September in the same year he was one of the Scottish Barons summoned to assist Brian Fitzallan, Custos of the kingdom, against Wallace and his followers;[7] but after this no further mention of him is found until the year 1306, when he probably joined Bruce in his first effort for independence, as he certainly shared in the misfortunes of the defeated Scottish party, and various requests for his estates were made by the rapacious soldiers of England in that year.

John de Luc asked for the lands of Tulchfraser (Touch-fraser), in the county of Stirling, belonging to Richard Fraser.[8]

Alexander de Baliol made a request for the lands of Richard Fraser, and

---

[1] Historical Documents of Scotland, vol. i. p. 367.
[2] Rotuli Scotiæ, vol. i. p. 26.
[3] Metrical Chronicle of Pierre de Langtoft, vol. ii. p. 235.
[4] Ragman Rolls, p. 162.
[5] Historical Documents of Scotland, vol. ii. p. 169.
[6] Original Document in Record Office, London.
[7] Rotuli Scotiæ, vol. i. p. 50.
[8] Palgrave, p. 303.

John de Bristowe demanded "le petit terre qui feust a Richard Fraser a Arkelton, en la conté de Dumfries."[1]

It is remarkable how completely genealogists have overlooked the position in the family held by Sir Richard Fraser, some ignoring him altogether, others only mentioning him in a cursory manner as cousin to Sir Simon Fraser, filius, and one, Craufurd, suggesting that he belonged to the Makarston branch,[2] but none in any way according him the very high rank in the family that the account of his career, meagre as the record may be, shows him to have held, for he is not only found engaged in affairs of considerable public importance, viz., as a representative of the executors of Alexander III. in 1289, as an auditor on the part of Baliol at the competition for the crown in 1291, and as vicecomes of Berwick-on-Tweed, a very responsible post at that time, in 1293, but he appears with the rank of Knight as early as 1276; and it is evident from the terms of the mandate for the restoration of his estates by Edward I. in 1296, which, reciting the order addressed to the Sheriff of Stirling, adds that the same Richard had similar letters to the Sheriffs of Berwick, Roxburgh, Dumfries, Peebles, and Edinburgh, that he held possessions in nearly, if not quite, every district in Scotland into which the Frasers had then penetrated; and it may here be noticed that he is the only person of the name found in possession of lands in England as well as in Scotland, for he appears as proprietor of Eddirstone, in Northumberland,[3] although he probably held that estate as a sub-feudatory of the Scottish King.

In the orders issued by Edward I. for the restoration of their lands to Scotchmen, where these were held from a subject-superior, that fact is very generally mentioned in the order; and it may therefore be inferred, from the absence of any such notice in regard to Sir Richard Fraser's lands, that he was a tenant-in-chief of the Crown.

Some of his possessions he may have acquired by marriage, but there is no trace to be met with of the name or family of his wife, or even of her existence.

It has already been observed that it is open to doubt whether the representative of the Touch-fraser family, or that of the Oliver Castle family,

---

[1] Palgrave, pp. 304, 305.
[2] Remarks on the Ragman Rolls, p. 12.
[3] Historical Documents of Scotland, vol. ii. pp. 46, 49.

was the head of the whole race; but it is apparent from the above that Sir Richard, whose existence has been almost ignored by genealogists, occupied a very high position in the race, and was one of the most influential members of it, and that he obtained as his principal inheritance those estates in Stirlingshire which may, with good reason, be supposed to have belonged to Sir Bernard Fraser, and from him to have passed to Sir Gilbert Fraser.

The question of seniority between these two branches is, however, of little importance, for the Oliver Castle family failed in the male line in 1306. But two facts may here be stated that seem to lead to the inference that although the eminent abilities of the three Sir Simons raised them high in the service of the State, and gave precedence to the names of the two first over those of other laymen of the race contemporary with them, yet the Touch-fraser family was the elder line, and John, from whom it descended, the eldest son of Sir Gilbert Fraser. In the first place, John is the one of whom earliest mention is found; and secondly, when the Oliver Castle family failed in the male line in 1306, no alteration was made in the armorial bearings of the various remaining branches of the race, such as will be seen to have taken place at the failure of the eldest male line of the Touch-fraser family about the middle of the same century.

It is also worthy of notice that the field of the armorial bearings of the Oliver Castle branch was sable instead of azure.[1] Nisbet, in his Heraldry, says that a change in the tincture of the field is a mark of cadency; but it is now impossible to determine which was the original bearing.

There is no record of Sir Richard Fraser's death, but he survived the year 1306, fatal to so many of the best and bravest of the Scottish nobility, for a petition addressed by him to Edward I. in the spring of the succeeding year is extant.[2] It sets forth that he had enjoyed the guardianship of Richard de Glen, the son of Duncan de Glen, for only three years after it was granted to him, and that he was deprived of it at the time of the first war in Scotland, that others had held it since then, and that he had obtained no advantage or profit from it; and therefore prayed that an inquiry might be instituted, and that he should only be responsible for what he had received during the three years, and also—which seems the gist of the petition—that the debt of 100

---

[1] See Appendix, Sir Simon Fraser, filius. [2] Placita in Parl., vol. i. p. 211.

merks, due from him to Edward I. for the grant, should be reduced within proportionate limits, if, indeed, the King would demand any portion of it from him. To this petition the stern reply was made, that he had been "inimicus regis," a rebel, after the guardianship was granted to him, and was so at that present time; that his petition was refused; that the debt must be paid in full; and that an order should be issued to seize his goods, cattle, lands, and tenements for it, which order was accordingly sent to John de Landels, the English King's Chamberlain of Scotland, on the 1st of April 1307.

Sir Richard Fraser's possessions were all situated within those districts of the kingdom at that time completely under the domination of England, and, therefore, unless he became a fugitive, he had no choice but to submit to whatever oppression might fall to his lot, fortunate if his life were spared, until the reconquest of the country by Bruce enabled him to end his days in peace; and as his successor in Touch-fraser, Sir Alexander Fraser, did not receive his charter of that property until about 1321, he may have been alive nearly down to that date, though, if this were the case, he was incapacitated by some cause, probably age and infirmity, for he would have been nearly seventy years old, from joining King Robert in 1307, when that Alexander appears as leader of the Frasers.

Two impressions of Sir Richard Fraser's seals have been preserved, the earlier one before the dignity of knighthood had been conferred upon him. Both bear on a triangular shield six rosettes or cinquefoils, disposed 3.2.1, and the inscription round the first is S. Ricardi Freser; that around the second, which is attached to the obligation of his cousin, Sir Simon, filius, is S. Ricardi Fraser M., showing the surname in those two different forms.

Although there is no positive evidence of the fact, yet there is good reason to believe that he had a son, named Andrew.

Richard Fraser, *ante* 1276.   Sir Richard Fraser, 1297.

SIR ANDREW FRASER.

IMMEDIATELY following the name of Sir Richard Fraser, upon two important occasions, appears that of Sir Andrew Fraser. It is impossible to doubt that he was very closely connected with Sir Richard, for his son Alexander was Sir Richard's successor in the estate of Touch-fraser, but, unfortunately, no distinct record of the nature of that connection has been preserved.

The constant warfare, which, commencing in 1296, lasted for many years, and the numerous executions by order of Edward I. in 1306, cut off many of the younger scions of Scottish families almost contemporaneously with the decease of their relatives of the two preceding generations; and where two individuals of a family bore the same Christian name, this has been very apt to mislead genealogists into confounding them together, and considering them one and the same person. In this manner appears to have originated the mistake into which it is believed that Mr. Anderson has fallen,[1] of regarding this Sir Andrew Fraser as identical with a Sir Andrew Fraser, son of Sir Gilbert, and brother of John Fraser, Sir Simon Fraser, Sheriff of Traquair and Peebles, and William Fraser, Bishop of St. Andrews, and therefore uncle to Sir Richard Fraser, of which a little reflection will show the improbability, and, indeed, it might almost be said the impossibility.

It is not probable that the name of Sir Richard should precede that of his uncle Andrew whenever they occur together, but a still stronger argument is drawn from the positions in which this Sir Andrew Fraser is found. He was the father of a young family in 1296;—that his children were then young is shown by the dates at which his sons subsequently married, viz.,—Alexander, in 1316; Simon, not mentioned as a married man until 1329, though he probably was so a few years earlier; and James, in 1322. This by itself, though important, would not be conclusive, for an aged man might have had a young family; but this Sir Andrew will be found to have been ordered by Edward I. to reside south of the Trent in 1296, and to have been vigorous enough to accompany that monarch to Flanders during

[1] History of the Family of Fraser, page 33.

his war with the King of France in 1297, a service not required from Sir Richard Fraser, but also performed by Sir Simon Fraser, filius, one of the next generation to that to which Sir Richard belonged.

John Fraser probably died at a comparatively early age; but Sir Simon, the Sheriff of Traquair and Peebles, died between 1280 and 1283, and the Bishop of St. Andrews ended his life in 1297—both advanced in years; and it seems an improbability, amounting to impossibility, that their brother, Sir Andrew, should appear, in 1296 and 1297, in positions that would naturally be occupied only by a young man in the full vigour of life, or that Edward I. should have required his services as the price of his freedom, or, indeed, should have thought it worth while to send an aged worn-out man a prisoner into England, south of the Trent, when he did not consider it necessary to treat Sir Richard Fraser, one of the next generation, and a most important member of the race, in a similar manner.

The above considerations have caused the writer of this history to entertain the opinion that this Sir Andrew Fraser was not the son of Sir Gilbert who bore that name, but a far younger person, and the reasons for deeming him to have been Sir Richard Fraser's son must now be advanced.

These are, in the first place, the very near connection between them, evinced by the succession of Sir Andrew's eldest son to Sir Richard's principal estate of Touch-fraser and other lands in Stirlingshire.

In the second place, the sequence of Sir Andrew's name to that of Sir Richard, whenever the two occur together.

In addition to these facts it may be observed that it is evident that Sir Andrew Fraser was a person of considerable consequence, for he was an auditor on the part of Baliol in 1291-2, he was Sheriff of Stirling in 1293, and Edward I. sent him and his whole family to reside south of the Trent in 1296; and yet it does not appear that he was in possession of any great estate at that time, for he is only found as a tenant or vassal of the Bishop of St. Andrews, and of Elye de Kininmunth, and Adam de Valoines, in the county of Fife, and he received his wife's dower lands for his support and that of his family during his captivity, though from the lands of Dripp, in Stirlingshire, having been in possession of his son Alexander before Sir Richard's death, they had probably belonged to him.

The consequence which he enjoyed, though, perhaps, partly due to his personal character, may, therefore, have arisen in a great degree from his position in the family rather than from his actual territorial power at the time; and this may not only explain his being found in offices of responsibility, but may afford a reason for Edward I. having carried him and his family into England, as even more valuable hostages than Sir Richard himself.

The position of son to Sir Richard has therefore been accorded to this Sir Andrew Fraser in these pages upon the foregoing grounds, and whatever credit that conclusion may be held to deserve, at all events the succession to Touch-fraser shows that his eldest son Alexander was Sir Richard's nearest relation and heir at the date of the decease of the latter.

The first notice of Sir Andrew Fraser occurs at the competition for the Crown of Scotland, when, upon the 17th July 1291, he swore fealty to Edward I.,[1] and about the same time was appointed one of the auditors on the part of Baliol; and, with the other auditors, in 1292, he sealed the letters testimonial, announcing the conclusion of the pleadings for the several competitors.[2]

Towards the end of the same year, on the 20th November at Norham, and on the 26th of December at Newcastle-on-Tyne, he witnessed the homages of Baliol to Edward I.; and in the record of these his name immediately follows that of Sir Richard Fraser, and precedes that of Sir Simon Fraser, filius, in the homage also witnessed by the latter.[3]

He appears as vicecomes of Stirling in 1293,[4] and was the first of the name that held that office after the decease of Sir Bernard Fraser about the year 1249, but it will be seen to have become hereditary in his descendants down to the year 1407.

In 1293 Macduff, the brother of Colban, a former Earl of Fife, was sentenced in the Court of King John Baliol to the forfeiture of his estates of Rareys and Crey in that Earldom (of which transaction an account will be found in the Appendix); and Sir Andrew Fraser, probably by order of the King or the Bishop of St. Andrews, led an armed force against the house of

---

[1] Ragman Rolls, p. 15.
[2] Rymer's Foedera, vol. ii. p. 555.
[3] Original Documents in Record Office, London.
[4] Cart. Newbottle, No. 175.

Rareys, and plundered it and the adjacent lands of arms, jewels, cattle, and other property to the value of two hundred merks (a large sum in those days), according to a statement in one of the mandates addressed to Baliol on that occasion by Edward I., to whom Macduff had appealed.[1]

On the 21st of November 1295 King John Baliol granted a charter to William de Silkyfwrth of some lands in the tenement of Colbanston; the charter was dated at Stirling, and the witnesses to it were William, Earl of Ross, Andrew Fraser, David de Beton, and Gilbert de Haia, Knights.[2]

Sir Andrew Fraser supported Baliol in his ineffectual resistance against the power of the King of England in 1296, and after the overthrow of that feeble prince by Edward, submitted to the victor like the other barons of Scotland, and swore fealty to him twice, on the 28th of August at Berwick-on-Tweed, as Andreas Fraser del conté de Fyf, tenant l'evesque St. Andreu,[3] and as Andreas Fraser del conté de Fyf, and on the 3d of September some lands in that district, which he held as vassal of Elye de Kininmunth and of Adam de Valoines, were restored to him by the King's order.[4]

He was one of those carried captive into England in that year by order of Edward I., and on the 1st of October two mandates were issued by the King in favour of Andrew Fraser,[5] then residing "ultra," from Morpeth, in Northumberland, where the orders were dated, south of Trent, the first being for a pension of one hundred merks yearly, for the support of himself, his wife, and family, from his wife's dower lands in Catania, the district of Sutherland and Caithness, to be supplemented to that extent by John de Warrenne, Earl of Surrey and Governor of Scotland, to whom the orders are addressed, if the lands did not yield so much; and the second a grant of the lands themselves to the value of one hundred merks yearly, to be in like manner supplemented if they did not yield that amount.

Upon the ground of these mandates from Edward I., Mr. Anderson[6] has founded an erroneous theory of large possessions in that northern part of Scotland, held by Sir Andrew Fraser in right of his wife, and descending to Simon Fraser, whom he styles Sir Andrew's eldest son (relegating Alexander

---

[1] Rotuli Scotiæ, vol. i. p. 10.
[2] Cart. Coldinghame, lxxviii.
[3] Ragman Rolls, pp. 147, 157.
[4] Rotuli Scotiæ, vol. i. p. 27.
[5] Ibid. vol. i. p. 35.
[6] History of the Family of Fraser, pp. 35, 36.

to the position of second son), and from him passing to another Simon, and thence to one whom he calls the brother of this last Simon, Hugh, the progenitor of the Frasers of Lovat; but for these statements he adduces no better authority than the apocryphal "Annals of the Frasers," published in 1795; and the first of them, viz., that Simon was Sir Andrew's eldest son, will be found completely refuted in the succeeding account of Alexander Fraser, and also in the Appendix, in the account of that Simon Fraser; but although there is no record in these mandates, or elsewhere, of the name or family of the lady who was Sir Andrew's wife, and had dower lands in Catania, a fragment of information still extant, of which Mr. Anderson seems to have been ignorant, affords some clue by which her family can be traced with at all events greater probability than belongs to the theory advanced by him.

This fragment of information is in the shape of a charter from David II., dated October 18th, 1363,[1] which recites royal letters granted by Robert I. on the 6th of November 1312, declaring that nothing in the agreements ordered or arranged by the king between Lady Mary, widow of the late Sir Reginald le Chen, and Alexander Fraser, concerning the lands of Duffus, should prejudice the status of inheritance of Lady Mary in those lands, or in any way be construed into her disinheritance of them. And the charter from David II. confirms the above royal letters in favour of Lady Mary's heirs, giving them the same force and validity as they had during his father's reign.

It is evident that Alexander Fraser, who was Sir Andrew Fraser's son, had claims upon the property of the le Chen family in 1312 that were so far legal and just as to be recognised by King Robert, and made the subject of agreement by his order; and the necessity of the royal letters to protect the hereditary rights of Lady Mary, upon that agreement being made, implies that those claims were also of an hereditary nature.

Freskin de Moravia, dominus de Duffus, who flourished during the first half of the thirteenth century, married Johanna, Lady of Strathnaver, in Catania,[2] and, dying before 1269, left issue two coheiresses, Mary, married

---

[1] Spalding Club, Antiquities of Aberdeenshire, vol. iv. p. 611.
[2] Cart. Morav., preface, p. xxxiii.

to Sir Reginald le Chen, junior,[1] and Christian, the wife of William de Fedreth, between whom his estates were divided;[2] but as Sir Reginald is styled dominus de Duffus in 1269, while William de Fedreth appears as "portionarius" of that estate in 1286, it is probable that Mary was the elder sister, both being also heirs-portioners of other properties in various parts of the kingdom, including Strathnaver, in Catania; but Sir Reginald, by purchase from, or agreement with William de Fedreth and his wife, obtained their portion of Strathnaver in 1286.[3]

It was this Mary, Lady of Duffus, who in her widowhood made the agreement, by order of Robert I., with Alexander Fraser. She was the wife of Sir Reginald le Chen before 1269, and a daughter of theirs might have been of an age to become the wife of Sir Andrew Fraser between 1280 and 1290, and might have received dower lands in Catania; and if, during the disturbances of that stormy period, the part of Lady Mary's estates where those dower lands were situated had been lost, or alienated by her, Alexander Fraser might have just claims upon her other possessions, in lieu of the inheritance to which he had right through his mother, but which it was no longer in Lady Mary's power to grant him; and, so far as can be ascertained, there is no other reason to be found for any such pretensions on the part of Sir Andrew's son.

This view of the case may also suggest a cause for the confirmation of the royal letters by David II. in 1363, for the Sir Reginald le Chen, then Lord of Duffus, probably Lady Mary's grandson, was the last male of that line, and his possessions were divided among his daughters, who were married about that time, when it is possible some revival of the claims may have been tried by Alexander Fraser's heiress Margaret, and her husband, Sir William de Keith, the Marischal.

It has been necessary to anticipate the course of events, in order to show

---

[1] Crauford, Officers of State, p. 264, makes the mistake of saying that Sir Reginald le Chen, senior, married Mary, Lady of Duffus, and that Sir Reginald, junior, married Eustachia de Colville; but the charters referred to here prove his error: it was Sir Reginald the senior that married Eustachia de Colville. She was not the mother of Sir Reginald the junior, but the second or perhaps third wife of his father.

[2] Antiquities of Aberdeenshire, vol. iv. p. 600.

[3] Ibid. p. 602.

the probability that Sir Andrew Fraser's wife, who had dower lands in Catania, was a lady of the family of le Chen.

Sir Andrew continued his enforced residence to the south of the Trent until the middle of the succeeding year, 1297, when, upon the 23d of June, he entered into an obligation or engagement to attend Edward I. abroad, and serve under him in the war with the King of France,[1] and he was thereupon permitted to proceed to Scotland in order to make preparations for that expedition;[2] and he seems to have enjoyed the favour of the King of England, for on the 25th of the same month he received from him a grant of the estate of Ugtrethrestrother—Struthers—in Fife, taken from Macduff, who is stated in the document to be then in rebellion.[3]

There can be no doubt that Sir Andrew Fraser performed his engagement to serve Edward I. in his foreign war; the mistake into which Abercromby and other authors have fallen in supposing that the barons of Scotland abandoned the engagements that were the price of their freedom, or deserted the standard of England in face of the enemy, is shown in the Appendix, in the account of Sir Simon Fraser, filius; but Sir Andrew evidently left valuable hostages behind him in the persons of his wife and children, and an additional proof of his fidelity to his engagement is found in the fact of his son being in possession of Ugtrethrestrother in 1306, for those lands would certainly have been at once resumed by the English monarch if he had broken faith.

It is, however, rather remarkable that Edward I. should have bestowed a portion of Macduff's lands upon the very person whose conduct, in plundering Macduff's house of Rareys, he had so severely reprobated about three years before.

After 1297 Sir Andrew Fraser does not appear in any record as alive, and it is possible that he was killed or died while abroad in Flanders; he certainly was dead before the year 1306, when Thomas de Grey petitioned Edward I. for the lands of Alexander Fraser, "qui fut le filz de Andrew Fraser,"[4] and a second request by de Grey shows that these lands were those of Ugtrethrestrother; and although the expression above quoted would appear

---

[1] Original Document in Record Office, London.
[2] Historical Documents of Scotland, vol. ii. p. 185.
[3] Rotuli Scotiæ, vol. i. p. 42.
[4] Palgrave, pp. 303, 314.

more applicable to a deceased Alexander, yet its bearing the meaning here ascribed to it is proved by the facts that an Alexander, son of the late Sir Andrew Fraser, was living in 1312, and that the granddaughter and heiress of that Alexander possessed the estate of Ugtrethrestrother in 1392.

His decease before the year 1307, when Sir Richard was alive, proves that Sir Andrew never succeeded to the estate of Touch-fraser, and therefore he cannot have been the Sir Andrew Fraser of Touch mentioned by Cranford in his remarks on the Ragman Rolls attached to Nisbet's Heraldry,[1] and by other writers; but in the Appendix the possibility of this individual having been his son of the same name is shown, though if this latter held any property bearing the not uncommon prefix of Touch, it was not Touch-fraser, which was inherited by his elder brother, Alexander.

The seal of Sir Andrew Fraser has been preserved; it is attached to his obligation to serve Edward I. in his war with the King of France, which is

Sir Andrew Fraser, 1297.

one of similar documents still in existence at the Record Office in London. It bears on a triangular shield six rosettes or cinquefoils, disposed 3.2.1, and the inscription around the seal is S. Andree Fraser, Militis.

He left issue, four sons—
Alexander, the successor of Sir Richard Fraser.
Simon, see Appendix.
Andrew, see Appendix.
James, see Appendix.

[1] "Remarks on Ragman Rolls," p. 13.

SIR ALEXANDER FRASER, LADY MARY DE BRUCE,
CHAMBERLAIN OF SCOTLAND.   SISTER OF ROBERT I.

NEARLY every genealogist that has touched upon the subject has fallen into error respecting the parentage of this distinguished member of the race, and that error has been universally adopted by other authors. They have placed him in the Oliver Castle branch, and have called him the younger son of Sir Simon Fraser, pater, and younger brother of Sir Simon Fraser, filius, executed in 1306 by order of Edward I. The principal causes of this mistake on their part were the high positions in which the two Sir Simons are found, the brilliant career and tragical death of the younger, and the eminence to which Sir Alexander attained; together with their oversight of the separate line of Touch-fraser, and their having been unaware of the fact that, during the period assigned by them for Sir Alexander's career, there were three persons of the race in existence, bearing that Christian name, who will be noticed in the present work.

1st. Sir Alexander Fraser, a knight in 1268, who died in or before 1295.[1]

2d. Sir Alexander Fraser, who was baron and knight in 1296.[2]

3d. This Sir Alexander Fraser, who certainly was not a knight before 1309, and probably not until after 1312, who certainly was brother-in-law to Robert I., and to whom a Sir Simon Fraser,[3] killed at Halidon, was brother.

The earlier genealogists appear to have confounded the above three together, and one author, Abercromby, has added a mistake peculiarly his own, for he says, "In the reign of Robert I. there were two eminent gentlemen, the one designed Sir Alexander Fraser of Touch, the other Sir Alexander Fraser of Cowie."

Mr. Anderson, in his "History of the Family of Fraser,"[4] has avoided the above-mentioned error, and is correct in saying that his father was a Sir Andrew Fraser, though mistaken as to the identity of that Sir Andrew; but without giving any authority for his assertion, he goes on to state that Alexander was a second son, and that his brother Simon was the elder, and their

---

[1] See Appendix, Frasers of Drumelzier.   [3] See Appendix, Frasers of Lovat.
[2] See Appendix, Frasers of Cornetoun.   [4] History of the Family of Fraser, pp. 33-37.

father's heir, and also heir to extensive estates belonging to their mother in Catania (Caithness).

In the notice of that brother, Simon Fraser, it will be seen that his name appears, in company with that of Alexander Fraser, in a manner applicable only to the younger of the two; but, independently of that refutation of Mr. Anderson's mis-statement regarding their respective seniority, it has already been shown, in the immediately preceding account of their father, Sir Andrew Fraser, that the settlement in 1312 between Alexander Fraser and Lady Mary of Duffus in all probability had reference to his mother's lands in Caithness; and a very complete chain of evidence, of which the links are established on documentary authority in the course of the succeeding pages, and of which a short summary is given below, effectually proves that Alexander Fraser, the son of Sir Andrew Fraser, was heir to him and to Sir Richard Fraser, and therefore his eldest son, and that he was consequently not more nearly related than cousin to either Sir Simon, pater, or Sir Simon, filius; that there were not two gentlemen of the name, one of Touch, the other of Cowie, during the reign of Robert I., but that the same individual possessed both those estates, with many others, and that he was brother-in-law to the King.

This chain of evidence is composed of—

1*st.* The descent of the Sheriffship of Stirling from Sir Andrew Fraser, 1293, through Sir Alexander Fraser, 1328, to Margaret Fraser, granddaughter and heiress of the latter, 1407.

2*d.* The descent of the lands of Ugtrethrestrother from Sir Andrew Fraser, 1297, through Sir Alexander Fraser, 1306, to the same Margaret Fraser, 1392.

3*d.* The descent of the estates of Touch-fraser from Sir Richard Fraser, 1306, through Sir Alexander Fraser, 1321; and of Drippis, or Dripp, from Alexander Fraser, 1306, to the same Margaret Fraser, 1407.

4*th.* The assedation of the lands of Torry by Bernard, Abbot of Arbroath, to Alexander Fraser, the son of the late Sir Andrew Fraser, 1312.

5*th.* The mention of Mary, the King's sister, as wife of Sir Alexander Fraser, in the charter of a tenement in Auchincarnie, 1324; and that of Sir Alexander Fraser's son, John, the father of Margaret Fraser, as the King's nephew, in the charter of the forest of Cowie, 1327.

6*th*. The descent of the forest and thanage of Cowie, granted by Robert I. to Sir Alexander Fraser, 1327; the forest to the same Margaret Fraser, 1359; the thanage to his second son, William Fraser, 1341-46.

Although it somewhat anticipates the narrative of events, it may be here observed, as accounting in some degree for Abercromby's mistake, that owing to Margaret Fraser having carried the bulk of her grandfather's possessions, and among them Touch-fraser, into another family, future writers styled Sir Alexander Fraser "Thane of Cowie," as if that had been his principal and hereditary estate, and they, perhaps, were misled by its having been the only part of his vast property that continued in the Fraser name to the third generation after him; but it is not probable that he was ever so designated during his life, for Cowie did not come into his possession by inheritance, and was the last, and by no means the largest, grant that he received from the bounty of his friend and sovereign.

When Sir Andrew Fraser was carried prisoner into England by Edward I. in 1296, and obliged to reside south of the river Trent, he appears to have taken his wife and children with him;[1] and as that monarch, after his usurpation of the Crown of Scotland upon the compulsory abdication of John Baliol, required the young Scottish nobility to attend the English Court, it is possible that Alexander Fraser, like the young Robert Bruce, and others, passed a considerable portion of his earlier years in that then unrivalled school for warriors, and there contracted that friendship with his future king, some ten or twelve years his senior, to which Barbour will be seen to allude, and that this friendship was a prominent cause of the change in the political views of the Fraser race, which had previously adhered to the party of Baliol.

In Barbour's historical poem "The Bruce," a Sir Alexander Fraser is said to have been taken prisoner at the disastrous battle of Methven in 1306,[2] in which Sir Aymer de Valence, Earl of Pembroke, defeated the recently-crowned Robert I.; but it is very doubtful whether it was this Alexander Fraser, or

[1] Rotuli Scotiæ, vol. i. p. 35.　　　　[2] Spalding Club Edition, The Bruce, p. 40.

the Sir Alexander Fraser mentioned above who appears in 1296, that sustained the misfortune of being captured on that occasion. If it were this Alexander Fraser, Barbour is mistaken in styling him "Sir," for he was not then a Knight, and he must have found means to escape from captivity, for his name does not appear among those who, like Thomas Randolph, the future renowned Earl of Moray, were pardoned, and returned for a time to the service of the King of England; but if it were the Sir Alexander Fraser of 1296, it is probable that he was one of those who perished by the hand of the executioner, for his name does not again appear in any document, except the demand for his lands by John de Luc.

Alexander Fraser, the subject of this Memoir, had, however, also embraced the cause of Bruce, for his estates were seized and partitioned among some of the followers of Edward I.

Thomas de Grey asked for the lands of Alexander Fraser, the son of Andrew Fraser, and a second application by the same Thomas shows that these lands were those of Ugtrethrestrother.[1]

William de Montfitchet demanded the lands of Dripp, in Stirlingshire, belonging to Alexander Fraser.[2]

John de Weston asked for lands in the county of Edinburgh, the property of Alexander Fraser, and John de Lisle for some in Fife, remaining from those already granted to Walter Gilbert.[3]

In the winter of 1306 Bruce, after many wanderings and adventures in the mountains during the autumn, had temporarily abandoned Scotland, and sought an asylum in the little island of Rachrin, on the Irish coast, where he passed the winter; but on the return of spring he once more appeared in arms, and crossing to the island of Arran, and thence to Carrick, spent the summer and autumn of 1307 in gallant and desperate exploits in the southwest of Scotland, including his victory of Loudoun Hill over his former con-

[1] Palgrave, pp. 304, 313.
[2] Ibid. pp. 303, 305.
[3] Ibid. pp. 314, 317. Ugtrethrestrother and Dripp were certainly this Alexander Fraser's possessions, the former, and perhaps the latter, had belonged to his father, and both descended to his granddaughter; but it is uncertain whether the lands in the county of Edinburgh demanded by John de Weston, and those in Fife granted to Walter Gilbert, and asked for by John de Lisle, were his, or belonged to the elder person of the same name noticed above, who, in all probability, possessed the estate of Cornetoun, asked for by John de Luc.

queror, the Earl of Pembroke, which enabled him, after the death of Edward I. and the retreat of his feeble successor from the Border, to turn his attention to the northern portion of the country.

From some cause or another, Alexander Fraser appears to have been prevented from joining Bruce during the winter of 1306 and the spring and summer of 1307, which rather supports the suggestion of his having been made prisoner at Methven; but however this may be, in the autumn of the latter year he and his brother Simon are found preserving their fidelity to King Robert, and Barbour expressly says that, in resolving to march northward, he calculated in some degree on the aid he should obtain from them.

> "And he thocht wele that he would far
> Out our the Month with his menyhe,
> To luk quha that his frend wald be.
> Into Schir Alexander the Fraser
> He trastit, for tha frendis war,
> And in his brother Symon, tha twa,
> He had mistere wele of ma." [1]

In some editions of Barbour's poem the word "cosyngis" is printed instead of "frendis" in the passage just quoted, and, misled by this, Crawford and other writers have stated that consanguinity existed between Robert I. and this Alexander Fraser; but they were certainly mistaken, for although the children of each became cousins (probably the origin of the error), no blood-relationship of any sort can be traced between themselves, and in no one of the numerous charters and other documents of that reign, where his name appears, is Alexander Fraser ever once designated "consanguineus," or cousin, to the King, as, in accordance with the custom of the age, would assuredly have been the case in many, if not all, had such relationship existed between them. For this reason, the reading of the Cambridge copy of Barbour, as printed by the Spalding Club, has been adopted; but the talented editor of that edition, the late Mr. Cosmo Innes, has also been misled, for he says, at page 496, in his notes of various readings, "Frendis, so in Cantab, meaning perhaps 'relations,' as the word in Scotland still means;" but it is

[1] The Bruce, p. 187.

very evident, from its use in the passage quoted above, that Barbour did not employ the word "frend" in that sense.

It may also be noticed here that Barbour in his poem mentions the name of Alexander Fraser four times, all prior to the year 1309, and that on three of these occasions, in the extant editions of the poem, the title "Sir" is prefixed to the name,[1] although the Alexander Fraser of whom this is the account was not made a Knight until after 1312; but it is remarkable that, with the exception of the first of these lines,

"And Schir Alexander Fraser,"[2]

which, as already noticed, may have applied to the elder person of the name, they appear by the use of that appellation to be rendered too long for Barbour's eight-syllable metre, and that if the title "Sir" is left out, together with the definite article "the" before the surname, the lines return to the eight-syllable metre, which raises a presumption that the insertion of these words may have been the work of some transcriber, misled by the title having been given on the first occasion of the name being mentioned in the poem, and, therefore, applying it in the subsequent instances.

The lines are these—

"Into Schir Alexander the Fraser,"
"Schir Alexander the Fraser wicht,"[3]

which, under the above-mentioned eliminations, would read—

"Into Alexander Fraser,"
"Alexander Fraser the wicht."

In the remaining instance the title is not applied, though the line is still too long—

"Quhar Alexander Fraser him met;"[4]

and in this case the word "quhar" seems to have been an interpolation, hardly necessary to preserve the sense of the passage, which would read as well without it. The mention of his brother Simon shows that the last three instances apply to this Alexander Fraser, however it may be with the first.

[1] The Bruce, pp. 40, 187, 192, 221.
[2] *Ibid.* p. 40.
[3] The Bruce, pp. 187, 221.
[4] *Ibid.* p. 192.

To return from this digression to the narrative. The battle of Loudoun Hill was fought on the 10th of May, and King Robert's victory appears to have disposed of all the force that the Earl of Pembroke could bring into the open field; indeed, according to Barbour, that leader, after his defeat, rode to England, and resigned the "wardanry" of Scotland to Edward I., who was then at Carlisle.[1]

While, however, his great adversary was yet alive, and preparing to lead a large army over the western border, King Robert could not venture from that part of the country, but was obliged to hold his small force together, and watch the course of events.

He was soon relieved from his most dangerous opponent. Edward I.—"Scotorum Malleus," the hammer of the Scots—died at Burch-on-the-Sands, near Carlisle, on the 7th July 1307; and his son, Edward II., after an inroad as far as Cumnock during the month of August, before which Bruce retreated, returned to Carlisle in the beginning of September, and retired from the border into the heart of England.[2]

Upon the retreat of the English monarch, King Robert again overran all Galloway, accepting or compelling the submission of the inhabitants, preparatory to his projected movement towards the north, for which his victory at Loudon Hill in May had, to a certain extent, opened the way; and it may be also fairly surmised that the recent events in England had made all the great nobles of that country desirous of being present at the Court, and had prevented fresh forces being sent to reinforce those that were then defeated and dispersed.

It has been asserted by some writers that the expedition of Bruce to the north was undertaken in consequence of his defeat by a body of English troops under the command of the Earl of Richmond. There is no good authority for this statement, and yet Lord Hailes, in his Annals, seems to favour it, for he remarks: "The evidence of this fact rests on the authority of the Chronicle of Lanercost, quoted by Tyrell, vol. iii. p. 225. Abercrombie, vol. i. p. 583, seems to question the truth of it, and yet, unless it is supposed to be true, it will be difficult to account for the march of Bruce to the north."

When writing this passage, Lord Hailes does not appear to have remem-

[1] The Bruce, pp. 178, 186.   [2] Rymer's Fœdera, vol. iii. pp. 4-13.

bered that the danger of leaving large districts in his rear unfriendly to his cause, and the information which Bruce had doubtless received, although afterwards made more fully acquainted with details by the two Frasers, that influential barons in those districts were preparing for active hostilities against him, were quite sufficient reasons for his determination to reduce the north to submission upon the first opportunity; and that a defeat which put him to flight, far from accounting for his taking such a measure, would, on the contrary, have been the event most likely to render him utterly powerless to attempt a movement of that nature, for although the English garrisons were not strong enough to oppose his small but resolute and well-disciplined army on its march, they would have been able to inflict severe loss on a disheartened and flying body of troops.

There is no doubt that Edward II., on the 30th of September, sent orders to the Earl of Richmond to repel Bruce's invasion of Galloway;[1] but the story of the defeat of the latter cannot be accepted, and his march to the north was evidently caused by the skill and forethought that distinguished his military career.

King Robert must have commenced the expedition to the northern parts of the country about the end of September or beginning of October 1307. In the following passage Barbour says :—

> " And turn we to the nobill King
> That with the folk of his leding
> Toward the Month has tane the way
> Richt stoutly and into good array,
> Quhar Alexander Fraser him met.
> And als his brothir Symon hat (hecht)
> With all the folk tha with tham had :
> The King gud countenans tham mad
> That was richt blyth of thar cumyn.
> Tha tald the King all the covyn
> Of Johnne Cumyn the Erl of Bouchane,
> That till help him had with him tane
> Schir Johne Mobra and othir ma,
> Schir David the Brechyn alsua,

---
[1] Rymer's Fœdera, vol. iii. p. 14.

With all the folk of thar leding
'And yharnis mar than ony thing
Vengeans on yhou, schir King, to tak
For Schir Johne the Cumynis sak
That quhilom in Dumfries was slane.'"[1]

Alexander Fraser and his brother Simon, with such forces as they could assemble, therefore, met King Robert on his arrival at the Month, *i.e.* on the southern side of the great Grampian range of mountains. A short review of the position of affairs on both sides will show in how dangerous a situation the champion of Scottish independence was even then placed.

Although the victory of Loudoun Hill, and the other causes noticed above, had cleared the open country of English troops to some extent, yet they still held the garrisons of Bothwell, Rutherglen, Edinburgh, Linlithgow, Stirling, Perth, and almost every other fortress or castle. The Lothians, with Berwickshire, and the whole south-east of Scotland, were completely in their possession, while their steadfast ally, John of Lorn, and his father, Alexander of Argyll, held those districts, and were paramount in the Western Highlands.

The country around Inverness, where the Earl of Ross was powerful, Moray, and the district of Badenoch, under the sway of the Red Comyns, were in alliance with them, and hostile to Bruce; and in the north-east, comprising the counties of Forfar, Kincardine, Aberdeen, and Banff, were situated the territories of his most bitter enemy, the Earl of Buchan, who was not only prepared to resist any attack, but, in concert with Sir John de Mobray and Sir David de Brechin, had assembled forces, and was on the point of marching southward against him.

On the other side, Douglas, who, with very insufficient force, had been left in the south-west, was unable to do more than maintain a gallant resistance in the forest that then covered a great part of the southern hill-country; and the position of King Robert himself, with his army, was most critical, almost in presence of the superior force led by the confederate barons of the north-east, whose march to the south it was all-important to him to prevent, but whom he did not dare to attack in front while his rear was liable to be

---
[1] The Bruce, p. 192.

assailed by detachments from the English garrisons, which he was not strong enough to blockade.

In this state of affairs King Robert decided upon a course that strikingly illustrates his knowledge of the art of war, and his superiority in it to most of his contemporaries.[1]

He at once passed the Month, or Grampian chain, by the shortest route, and marched straight upon Inverury, in Aberdeenshire, thus completely turning the flank of the confederate barons.

The consequences of this manœuvre were most important; the communication of the confederates with Aberdeenshire was seriously perilled, the co-operation of the English garrisons in the districts of Perth and Stirling rendered impossible, the possessions of the principal leader, the Earl of Buchan, threatened in the absence of any to defend them, and but for the severe illness that prostrated King Robert on reaching Inverury, it is more than probable that he would quickly have made himself master of Aberdeen, and that the battle would have been fought to the south of that town, instead of to the north-westward of it, as afterwards happened.

The results, however, were very advantageous to the royal cause. The march of the confederate barons to the south, and their junction with the English troops, were frustrated, and the Earl of Buchan, with his allies, had to return to protect his own country, though, from the expression used by Barbour, "He sent efter his men in hy;" and as some days elapsed before he could lead his forces against the King, it would seem that they had been well on their way to their former destination.

On his arrival at Inverury, however, King Robert was attacked by a very serious illness, that incapacitated him from all exertion, mental or bodily; but in Edward de Bruce, his brother, one of the most renowned warriors of that day, his followers found a leader equal to the duties that devolved upon him in consequence of this misfortune.

Unwilling to risk a battle in the open country under such dispiriting

[1] In relating the events of this campaign, the account given by Barbour has been followed in preference to that found in Fordun's Gesta Annalia, and very generally adopted by subsequent historians; and the reasons for this preference will be found in the Appendix, as they do not affect the family history, and are necessarily of a length that would interfere with the thread of the narrative if they were inserted here.

circumstances, Sir Edward, after consultation with the other barons then following the King, decided on retreating from Inverury to a strong position in the course of the Slevach,[1] a brook descending from the Foudland Hills, bordered, as its name implies, by marshy ground, where there was a wood at that time, according to Barbour.[2]

Here he constructed some defences, and probably formed such sort of entrenched camp as the engineering skill of the age suggested, and the means at his disposal enabled him to make ; and soon after Martinmas—about the end of November—the Earl of Buchan, Sir John, and Sir Philip de Mobray, and Sir David de Brechin appeared in front of the position with a superior force, hoping to obtain an easy victory, as they had heard of the King's dangerous condition.

Sir Edward de Bruce, however, could not be tempted to relinquish the advantage of ground that he held, or to sally from his camp, but for three days maintained his impregnable position, merely repulsing with his archers the assaults of the bowmen and light-armed troops of the enemy.

His wise and patient behaviour upon this occasion is the more remarkable, as his characteristic quality was bravery carried to the extreme of rashness, and may be attributed to the temperate counsels of the other leaders, as well as to his own feeling of responsibility.

After three days, provisions becoming scarce, and the enemy continually receiving reinforcements, a further retreat was resolved upon, but it was conducted in no ordinary fashion.

Placing the invalid King in a litter, Sir Edward de Bruce marshalled his forces around him in battle array, and deliberately and boldly marched out of the camp in full view of the adverse host, which, daunted by this resolute demeanour, and the strict discipline maintained by the royal army, dared neither attack nor pursue, but allowed him to pass on his way unmolested, and themselves retired to the eastward.

Sir Edward continued his retreat to Strathbogie, where he remained undis-

---

[1] The Bruce, p. 193, et seq.

[2] Some authors have believed this place to be Slains, probably from the name having been written "Slenach" in Fordun's Gesta Annalia, but it is absurd to suppose a retreat into the very heart of the enemy's country. The burn of the Slevach lies in the direct route between Inverury and Strathbogie, to which district Edward de Bruce continued his retreat.

turbed until the King began to recover his health. This welcome change in his condition took place towards the end of December, when it was decided to advance again to Inverury, as Barbour relates, for the greater facility of obtaining provisions, but doubtless also in pursuance of the object for which the campaign had been undertaken; and it may here be noticed that this movement to Inverury, for the purpose, amongst others, of procuring supplies, together with no mention of reinforcements having joined the royal army during its stay in Strathbogie, are very strong evidence that Barbour was aware that it had no communication with the districts of Moray and Inverness, and that those parts of the country had not then been reconquered.

The King, with his forces, returned to Inverury shortly before Christmas; and upon hearing of his approach the Earl of Buchan, Sir John de Mobray, and Sir David de Brechin reassembled their troops at Old Meldrum two days before Christmas.

On the morning of Christmas Eve Sir David de Brechin advanced towards Inverury, and surprising some outlying portions of the royal army, put them to flight, and killed a few of their number.

Roused by this attack, King Robert ordered his troops to be put in battle array, and though far from restored to full strength, called for his horse and armour, replying to the remonstrances of his friends that the boast of the enemy had done more for his recovery than any medicine, and announcing his intention of himself taking the command.

Leading his army towards Old Meldrum, he attacked the confederate forces, and in spite of their numerical superiority, inflicted upon them such a defeat and total rout that they were entirely dispersed, and unable ever to rally or make head again.

The Earl of Buchan fled to England; but immediately after this decisive victory King Robert ravaged and devastated his whole earldom, so, to quote Barbour—

"That eftir that wele fifty yhear
Men menit the herschip of Bouchane;"[1]

[1] The Bruce, p. 203.

and by this vigorous proceeding he utterly broke down and destroyed the power of the great Comyn family, his irreconcilable enemies, whose influence had been so adverse to his cause.

The submission of all the more north-westerly parts of the kingdom followed the victory of Inverury and the devastation of Buchan, though it is probable that the King either marched in person through Morayshire to Inverness and the adjacent country, or detached a considerable force thither; and those districts being subdued, he returned southward through Kincardineshire towards the counties of Forfar and Perth, and the central parts of Scotland.

The policy of Bruce at this time, and for a year or two afterwards, appears to have been the reduction of all the open country to submission, without wasting time in the siege of any castle or fortified town too strong to be carried by a *coup de main*; and in this manner he swelled his ranks by the adhesion of those who secretly favoured his cause, but had hitherto been powerless to espouse it, and was doubtless also joined by many who found it convenient to change sides on the dispersion of their former feudal lords and protectors. Thus many castles and towns, especially those on the sea coast that were capable of relief by water, remained for a time in the hands of the English, and it was not until the years 1311-12 that Bruce seems to have turned his attention to their systematic reduction, though his possession of the open country must have enabled him to keep a pretty strict blockade upon them.

Having thus established his authority in the northern provinces of the kingdom, which do not appear to have again revolted from him, or to have been again overrun by the English during his reign, King Robert found his forces so increased that he was able to detach his brother, Sir Edward de Bruce, to Galloway, where Sir Ingrahame de Umphraville had restored the sway of England during their absence in the north, while he himself determined to destroy the power of his two other great adversaries, Alexander of Argyll and John of Lorn, as he had that of the Comyns.

James of Douglas, who, during the King's absence in the north, had gallantly held the great southern forest against enormous odds, and had surprised and captured Sir Thomas Randolph, the King's nephew, and Sir Alexander Stewart of Bonkill,[1]—Sir Adam de Gordon, who was of their party, making his escape,—about this time rejoined King Robert, bringing his prisoners with him.[2]

The story of Sir Thomas Randolph's insolent demeanour when brought into the presence of his royal uncle, of his subsequent repentance and reconciliation, and of his future faithful and gallant career as the renowned Earl of Moray, is well known.

About the beginning of August 1308, the King led his army towards Argyll, advancing on that district by the passes at the head of the Tay, through Glen Dochart and Tyndrum, amid scenery, the wild magnificence of which must have been painfully brought to his recollection, and to that of Douglas and others who had shared his wanderings among those mountains during the summer and autumn of 1306, and his terrible defeat there by John of Lorn, which was now about to be avenged.

He arrived on the confines of Argyll about the third week in August; but the news of his approach had preceded him, and John of Lorn resolved on resistance, and having good intelligence of the movements of the royal army, prepared an ambuscade in a narrow pass at the foot of Ben Cruachan, where that mountain abuts on Loch Awe, hoping to entangle the King in a position where he could be attacked, not only on land, but also from a powerful fleet of galleys on the lake, and where the Knights and men-at-arms could not advantageously act against his Highlanders.[3]

But King Robert, with the same warrior instinct that had prompted his flank march to Inverury in the last campaign, and which it is to be regretted so few of his descendants inherited, as they, almost all, did his courage, saw through the designs of his enemy, and on approaching the defile, detached a large force of archers under Douglas, who, as Barbour says, took with him

---

[1] The Bruce, p. 217.
[2] Cranford, Lives of Officers of State, p. 273, quoting Barbour as his authority, states that Alexander Fraser was one of those captured by Douglas on this occasion; but he is totally in error, not only as regards the fact, which is disproved by Alexander Fraser having met King Robert at the Month in the autumn of 1307, but also as regards the authority he quotes, for Barbour, pp. 217-18, says no such thing, and does not mention his name at all at that place.
[3] Fordun, Gesta Annalia, cxxvi.

> "Schir Alexander the Fraser wicht,
> And Wilyham Wisman ane gud knight,
> And with tham gud Schir Andro Gray,
> Thir with thar menyhe held thar way."[1]

This force had orders to ascend the mountain by a circuitous route, and to attain a position commanding any that could be occupied by enemies in the defile; and this having been effected, the King marched boldly with his main army into the pass.

The event approved his wise precaution. When fairly engaged in the defile, the hitherto concealed enemy assaulted his right flank, but repulsing them vigorously with light-armed troops, he converted his defence into an attack on their position, when Douglas and his companions, also charging them from the heights above, the result was the complete rout of the men of Argyll and Lorn after a furious battle and desperate resistance, numbers being slain or drowned, and the victors pushing the pursuit so eagerly as to prevent the breaking down of the bridge over the Awe, by which the King and his army were enabled to cross that river at their ease.

John of Lorn, who had watched the fight from a galley on Loch Awe, fled by water; but Alexander of Argyll retired to the castle of Dunstaffnage, where he was soon besieged by the King, when he submitted, yielded up the castle, and swore fealty. There was no further opposition at that time in Argyll and Lorn; but John of Lorn, who continued persistently in the English interest, appears soon afterwards to have re-occupied the castle of Loch Awe,[2] and it was his doing so that probably caused King Robert to make another expedition into that district in the following year, of which, however, little is known, except that he was again at Dunstaffnage Castle on the 20th of October 1309.[3]

These two campaigns, and especially that of the winter of 1307-8, in the north, have been more particularly noticed, as they afford evidence of King Robert's military talent; and as the earlier of the two was the first in which Alexander Fraser appears to have been able to accompany his royal master,

---

[1] The Bruce, p. 221.
[2] Rotuli Scotiæ, vol. i. p. 58.
[3] Robertson's Index, p. 80, No. 137.

after the unfortunate battle of Methven, and, also, as the fact of their meeting having taken place at the southern base of the Grampians shows that the seat of the Fraser power was then in that district, and tends to disprove their possession, at that time, of large estates near Inverness, as stated, without a scintilla of authority, by some genealogists, who, misled by Fordun's account of the campaign, have also said that the meeting between the King and the Frasers occurred in the neighbourhood of that town.

After the conquest of Argyll and Lorn, the King seems to have marched to the south, and to have joined his brother Edward, who had performed brilliant exploits in Galloway, and had once more reduced that part of the country to obedience; and after threatening the English border,[1] he appears to have again moved northward towards Fife in the beginning of 1309.

It was probably about this time, or it may have been before the expedition to Argyll, that Alexander Fraser made the attempt to draw Thomas de Grey, the English governor of Cupar Castle, into an ambush, which is thus related in the pages of an old writer:—

"Another tyme Alexander Fresile, a Scotte, frend to Robert Bruce, was sette within a little of Couper Castel, with an embuschment, and caused certen of his to pille a village thereby, so supposing to bring Thomas Gray into a trappe; the which, hearing the cry, went to horse to see what it was. The embuschment, seeing that, rode of force to the very castel gates. Thomas, seeing this, returned his horse, and cam fair and softly through the toun of Cuper, and then laying spurres to his horse, and rode through them, and got within the barres of the castel, wher he found his owne meny arrunning out to help hym."[2]

There is no further information to be found about this affair, or whether Alexander Fraser ever succeeded in getting Thomas de Grey into his power; but if the latter were the same person that had demanded, and probably obtained, his estate of Ugtrethrestrother from Edward I. in 1306, it may account for his desire, in the quaint language of the old chronicler, "to bring Thomas Gray into a trappe."

Towards the end of 1308, Philip, King of France, made some attempts to bring about a peace or truce between Edward II. and King Robert, and for

[1] Rotuli Scotiæ, vol. i. p. 57. [2] Leland's Collectanea, vol. ii. p. 545.

that purpose addressed a letter to the latter, and the nobles of his party, which appears to have been received in the beginning of 1309, according to present computation.

The King upon this assembled a Parliament at St. Andrews, in Fife,[1] and on the 16th of March, the barons that attended it, among whom appears the name of Alexander Fraser, affixed their seals to a reply to the French monarch, in which they declared Robert de Bruce to be the rightful King of Scotland, and thanking Philip for his expressions of good-will, and approving of his design to undertake another crusade, promised to aid him in it when the affairs of Scotland should have been restored to order.[2]

The destruction of the power of the Comyns and their allies, followed by the forfeiture of their estates, placed extensive tracts of land at the disposal of the Crown, out of which the King now proceeded to reward his faithful followers; and as Alexander Fraser had done good service in the campaign that proved the turning-point of his sovereign's fortunes, so he now shared his prosperity.

About the year 1309 he received royal grants of the following lands in the sheriffdoms of Forfar and Kincardine :—

> Panbryde.
> Garuocis (Garvocks).
> Strathean (Strachan), de Essuly (Essintuly ?), Ballebrochy, and Auchincross.
> Culpressache.[3]

He also obtained from the King the lands of Obyne (Aboyne), at first on a lease, or in feu-farm, for a term of years, which was subsequently changed to hereditary tenure of them.[4]

He maintained amicable relations with his neighbours, the monks of Arbroath, and in 1312 Bernard, the Abbot, with consent of the chapter, gave

---

[1] Acts of the Parliaments of Scotland, vol. i. p. 99.

[2] Original Letter in H. M. General Register House, Edinburgh. Unfortunately the part where the name of Alexander Fraser occurs has been destroyed, and his seal is also lost from it; but on the tag to which the seal was attached is written "S. Alex¹ fraser."

[3] Robertson's Index, p. 1, Nos. 7, 14, 15, 18.

[4] Reg. Episc. Aberdon., vol. i. pp. 157, 159.

him an assedation for life of the lands of Turry, or Torry, in the parish of Nigg, near Aberdeen, in lieu of a pension from the rents of Conveth, to which he was entitled by the gift of John, the late Abbot; and in the assedation, and also in his resignation of the pension, he is styled "Alexander Fraser, filius quondam Domini Andree Fraser, militis."[1]

About the year 1312 he had put forward those pretensions or claims upon the estates of Mary, Lady of Duffus, in Moray, and of Strathnaver, in Caithness, the widow of Sir Reginald le Chen, junior, which have been already noticed in the account of his father, Sir Andrew Fraser.

This dispute was settled by the King in person, who caused certain agreements to be made between the parties,—of these unfortunately no record remains,—and at Elgin, on the 6th November 1312, issued royal letters in favour of Lady Mary, declaring that nothing in the agreements ordered by him between her and Alexander Fraser, concerning the lands of Duffus, should prejudice her status of inheritance in those lands, nor in any way be construed into her disinheritance of them,[2] from which it may be reasonably inferred that Alexander Fraser's claims were founded upon some hereditary right alleged by him, and the only possible way in which any such right could have accrued to him seems to be from his mother (Sir Andrew Fraser's wife, who in 1296 had dower lands in Catania—Caithness) having been a member of Lady Mary's family.

Neither in the assedation from the Abbot of Arbroath, nor in the royal letters from Robert I., is Alexander Fraser styled "Miles" (Knight), and he therefore seems not to have attained that rank of chivalry in 1312; and this conclusion is supported by his name being found as that of a witness (certainly not before the end of 1308, and probably later) to the King's pardon of Gilbert de Carrick, for having surrendered the castle of Lochdoune to the English in 1306.[3] In the list of witnesses Edward de Bruce, James Senescallus or Stewart, Thomas Randolph, John de Menteith, and Nigel Campbell are called "militibus" (knights), while James de Douglas, Alexander Fraser, and Walter de Bykyrton are not so designated; and the

---

[1] Antiquities of Aberdeenshire, vol. i. p. 258.
[2] Ibid. vol. iv. p. 611.
[3] Robertson's Index, p. 135, No. 8.

proof that the pardon was not of an earlier date, consists in Sir Thomas Randolph having been one of the witnesses, for he was not retaken by Douglas until the summer of 1308, nor released from imprisonment and reconciled to his uncle until late in that year, after the expedition to Argyll at the earliest.

After the year 1308 Barbour does not again mention the name of Alexander Fraser, and there are no means of tracing any particular service upon which he was employed, nor any particular actions at which he was present, but it cannot be doubted that one who, as will be seen, rose to considerable eminence in the state, became closely connected by marriage with his sovereign, and constantly received tokens of his friendship and favour, must also have borne a worthy part in the glorious events of the next few years, including the three invasions of the northern counties of England in 1311-13, and the reduction of all the fortresses in Scotland, with the exception of Stirling, down to the great victory of Bannockburn in 1314, which crowned King Robert's heroic efforts, and for a time freed Scotland from the presence of the English invaders; and as after that period the designation "Miles" always accompanies his name, it is probable that Alexander Fraser was knighted, with Walter the Steward, James of Douglas, and other distinguished leaders, immediately before that decisive battle.[1]

His name is not mentioned among those who accompanied Sir Edward de Bruce on his invasion of Ireland in 1315, but he probably took part in the King's expedition to the Hebrides during that year, when, drawing his fleet across the isthmus of Tarbert, Robert I. reduced the western isles to obedience, and having succeeded in capturing his old and inveterate enemy, John of Lorn, sent him at first to Dunbarton, and thence to the castle of Loch Leven, where he died.

About the following year, 1316, Sir Alexander Fraser married Lady Mary de Bruce, the King's sister, and widow of Sir Neil or Nigel Campbell.

That lady having been made captive in 1306 by the Earl of Ross when accompanying the Queen in her flight from Kildromie to Tain, was by him delivered to Edward I., by whom she was sentenced to imprisonment in Roxburgh Castle, and ordered to have similar treatment to that commanded

[1] The Bruce, p. 288.

for Isabella, Countess of Buchan, in the castle of Berwick, which some authors have described as being put into a wooden cage, and hung over the walls of the fortress; but the order for the incarceration of the Countess, of which the following is a translation, will not warrant such an exaggeration:—[1]

It is ordered and commanded, by letters under the Privy Seal, to the Chamberlain of Scotland, or his Lieutenant at Berwick-on-Tweed, that in one of the towers within the castle there, in whatever place he shall find most convenient, he shall cause to be made a cage of strong latice of . . . , and barred, and well secured by a lock, in which he shall place the Countess of Buchan, and that he shall cause her to be so well and so securely guarded in the cage that she cannot get out of it in any way. And that he shall assign one woman, or two, of the said town of Berwick, English, who is not, or are not, under any suspicion, . . . understands, or understand, how to serve the said Countess with food and drink, and other things necessary to her in . . . residence; and that he cause her to be so well and strictly kept in that cage that she shall speak to none, neither man nor woman, of the Scottish nation, nor any other . . . to her, except only the woman, or women, assigned to serve her, and those who have the custody of her.

And that the cage shall be so made that the Countess shall there have the convenience of a private closet, but that it shall be so very securely arranged that she has no speech but in presence of the guard of the said Countess. And that he who shall have the custody of her be responsible for her, body for body, and that he have the allowance "des custagis."

In the same manner it is ordered that Marie, sister to Robert de Bruce, late Earl of Carrick, be sent to Roxburgh, to be kept . . . in the castle in a cage.[2]

---

[1] Matthew of Westminster and others.

[2] Rymer's Fœdera, vol. ii. p. 1014. This mandate, though it ordains a very strict and almost barbarous imprisonment, yet completely contradicts the assertions made by some authors as to the outrage upon all decency and humanity, which the suspension of these ladies in cages outside the walls of the castles would have been considered even in that rough age. The order expressly says that the "kage" is to be constructed in one of the turrets within the castle. The opposite story seems, according to Lord Hailes, to have originated with Matthew of Westminster, whom other writers, especially Abercromby, have copied.

Having endured this severe imprisonment for four years, Lady Mary de Bruce at length found a termination to her sufferings. On the 4th July 1310 she was exchanged for nine nobles or gentlemen, either English, or Scots in the English interest, who were then prisoners of war to King Robert. Their names were—

John de la Moubra.
Michael de Menilevre.   Robert de Lindelles.
Gerard de la Farde.   Nicholas de Cesp.
Peter de Courteys.   John de Boysy.
John de Baillo.   William de Coupeland.

And by this arrangement she was again restored to her country and friends.[1]

It is doubtful whether she had been married to her first husband, Sir Neil Campbell, before her captivity; but by his death, about 1315, she was left a widow, and in 1316, as above mentioned, her hand was bestowed upon Sir Alexander Fraser.

In 1318 Sir Alexander was one of the barons who in Parliament, on the Sunday after St. Andrew's Day, enacted the order of succession to the Crown, declaring that, in case of the heir succeeding while a minor, the Earl of Moray, or, failing him, the good Sir James of Douglas, should be Regent.[2]

This settlement had become necessary in consequence of the untimely fate of Sir Edward de Bruce, the king's brother, who had been recognised as his heir, but who fell on the field of battle at Carrickfergus, in Ireland, gallantly fighting against enormous odds, which he had encountered, according to his usual custom, without regard to disparity of numbers.

About 1319 the office of "Camerarius," or Lord Chamberlain of Scotland, which had been held by Sir William de Lindesay, becoming vacant, the king conferred it upon Sir Alexander Fraser, who, on the 3d August in that year, was ordered in that capacity to determine the marches between Ardlogie, belonging to the Abbey of Arbroath, and the King's Park at Fyvie, in

---

[1] Rotuli Scotiæ, vol. i. p. 86.
[2] Acts of the Parliaments of Scotland, vol. i. p. 105. Robertson's Index, Appendix, p. 10.

Aberdeenshire, which duty he performed through his lieutenants;[1] and on the 10th December in the same year he was a witness,[2] as Chamberlain, at Berwick, to a charter from the King to the burgesses of Aberdeen (of which body he was an honorary member),[3] of the burgh of Aberdeen and forest of the Stocket.

On 6th April 1320, the barons of Scotland, assembled at Arbroath, affixed their seals to the celebrated letter to Pope John XXII.,[4] which in simple but unmistakeable language expressed the sentiments which influenced those who signed it, and is especially remarkable as being almost, if not altogether, the first public expression in Scotland of true patriotism, or love of country, and independence, and also for the declaration, worthy of freemen, that they had determined to maintain King Robert's right to the Crown, because he had by so many and such great labours and achievements restored their independence; but that, if ever he should alter his conduct and attempt to subject them or their country to the King of England, or the English, they would expel him as a subverter of his own and their rights, and would choose another king who would defend them, "for, so long as one hundred remain alive, we will never in any way be subject to the dominion of the English . . . for we do not fight for glory, riches, or honours, but for freedom alone, which no good man will lose except with life."

Sir Alexander Fraser was one of the gallant men who in these energetic words expressed the feelings which they supported by their actions, and although he is not expressly designated as "Camerarius," or Chamberlain, in the document, of which a duplicate is preserved in the Register House at Edinburgh, his name is placed immediately before those of Sir Gilbert de la Haye, the Constable, and Sir Robert de Keth, the Marischal of Scotland. The impression of his seal, of which a woodcut is given in this work, is still attached to the parchment, and on the lower side of the tag connecting it is written "S' Alexi' Fras'."

About the year 1321 he received a charter of his hereditary estate of

---

[1] Antiquities of Aberdeenshire, vol. iii. p. 545.
[2] Ibid. vol. iii. p. 212.
[3] Spalding Club Miscellany, vol. v. p. 10.
[4] H. M. General Register House, Edinburgh. Acts of the Parliaments of Scotland, vol. i. p. 114.

Touch-fraser, in Stirlingshire,[1] and the date of this occurrence raises a presumption that his predecessor, Sir Richard Fraser, who certainly escaped the fatal autumn and winter of 1306, and was alive in April 1307, may have lived long enough to have his last years cheered by the sight of his country's restoration to independence.

At the same time, although Sir Alexander Fraser succeeded to the estate of Touch-fraser and others, in the centre of Scotland, neither he nor his heirs are found to have been in possession of the properties in the Sheriffdoms of Berwick, Edinburgh, Roxburgh, and Peebles, which, by the mandate of Edward I. for their restoration, appear to have belonged to Sir Richard Fraser in 1296.

It is possible that some of these were merely superiorities, and that they may have been bought up by the tenants of the lands; but Edward I. very largely distributed the possessions of those who joined King Robert's first rising, or shared in earlier attempts at independence, and many of these lands may have fallen to individuals who, afterwards changing sides, earned by their services during the long war the right to retain them, or were too powerful to be safely dispossessed of them, or in the then disorganised state of the kingdom, some may have been taken possession of by faithful and constant adherents to the cause of Bruce.

An instance of the first kind is found in the case of Sir Alexander Fraser himself, who held the estate of Ugtrethrestrother, in Fife, which in 1297 Edward I. had taken from Macduff, then in rebellion, and had given to his father, Sir Andrew Fraser; and one of the second in the charter from Robert I. to the good Sir James de Douglas, of the whole of the great forest which he had so bravely and successfully defended, and which extended over large portions of the counties of Lanark, Peebles, Selkirk, Roxburgh, and Dumfries.[2]

It may therefore be inferred that the large grants in the districts of Aberdeen, Kincardine, and Forfar, bestowed by the King upon Sir Alexander Fraser, were not only rewards for his eminent services, but were also given and accepted in compensation for such of his hereditary lands in the southern counties as it was not in the sovereign's power to restore without incurring

---

[1] Robertson's Index, p. 8, No. 86. [2] *Ibid.* p. 10, Nos. 15-26.

the opposition and enmity of those whom he must have dispossessed in doing so.

As required by the duties of his office of Chamberlain, Sir Alexander Fraser's attendance upon the King was very constant; his name is found as a witness to numerous royal charters, and he seems to have accompanied him in most of his expeditions or changes of residence. In 1323 a peace was concluded with Edward II., and he was one of the barons of Scotland that swore to the observance of it.[1]

Lady Mary de Bruce did not survive the year 1323 (although the date of her death is unknown), for at Kinross, on the 22d of September in that year, the King gave a charter of confirmation of six acres of land in the royal tenement of Auchincarnie, near the royal manor of Kincardine, together with a right of pasturage in the thanage of Kincardine, to his beloved and faithful Sir Alexander Fraser, to be held by him and his heirs legitimately procreated between him and the late Mary de Bruce, the King's sister.[2]

He had also obtained the barony of Cluny, in Aberdeenshire; but no charter or notice of a charter granting it to him is extant, except that of the 18th of June 1325, by which he received from the King the lands of Cardenye, with the fishings of the loch of Skene, in augmentation of his barony of Cluny.[3]

He also obtained the barony of Kinnarde, probably by purchase, as it was granted to him on the resignation of Thomas de Kinnarde; and he had a charter of "an annual furthe of Pendreche," in Stirlingshire, but to what amount is not said.[4]

Sir Alexander Fraser appears to have held the office of Chamberlain of Scotland for seven years, from 1319 to about 1326. Crauford, "Lives of Officers of State," pp. 275-6, says that he did not become Chamberlain until 1325, and retained that office until the close of the reign of Robert I. in 1329, and also that he succeeded Robert de Peebles in it. But Sir Alexander's tenure of the Chamberlainship, and the fact of Robert de Peebles having succeeded

---

[1] Rymer's Fœdera, vol. iii. p. 1025.
[2] Robertson's Index, p. 17, No. 51. Haddington Collections, in Advocates' Library, vol. ii. p. 53, last division.
[3] Antiquities of Aberdeenshire, vol. iii. pp. 116, 117. Robertson's Index, p. 16, No. 24.
[4] Ibid. p. 17. No. 45; p. 23, No. 7.

him, are very distinctly shown by his name appearing without that designation as a witness to a royal charter granted in favour of Henry le Chen, Bishop of Aberdeen, on the Tuesday following St. Andrew's Day 1318,[1] by the order addressed to him in that capacity on the 3d of August 1319, to determine the marches between Fyvie and Ardlogie:[2] by the last extant document in which he appears as Chamberlain, a precept or order from him to the alderman and bailies of Roxburgh to pay twenty shillings yearly to the canons of Dryburgh, being dated the 1st of November 1325 ;[3] and by his name appearing without that designation, as a witness to a royal charter granting the Church of Rathen to the chapter of Aberdeen, on the 20th of March 1327, and to another in favour of the hospitallers of Turriff, on the 6th of October 1328,[4] in which last year Robert de Peebles, then Chamberlain, collected arrears due in the time of Sir Alexander Fraser's tenure of the office.[5]

In 1327, further tokens of his sovereign's favour were bestowed upon him, and on the 6th of April the King granted a charter to his beloved and faithful Sir Alexander Fraser, and John, his son, the King's nephew, of the forest of Craigie, in the thanage of Collie—Cowie (called in other documents the forest of Cowie), in the Sheriffdom of Kincardine, in which the King was causing an enclosed park to be made, containing 1500 "particates" of land, to be held by them and their heirs, under burden of keeping up the said park for the King ;[6] and about the same time Robert I. conferred the thanage of Cowie and Craiginning Glasculloche upon Sir Alexander Fraser by another charter.[7]

The mistake of supposing the thanage of Cowie to have been Sir Alexander Fraser's principal estate has been already referred to, and this error has led some genealogists and historians of the family to assert, without any authority, that it was in the possession of Frasers from a much earlier period. Not only is there no evidence of any kind to support that assertion, but all that exists tends to prove the contrary. The forests of

---

[1] Reg. Episc. Aberdon., vol. i. p. 45. Acts of the Parliaments of Scotland, vol. i. p. 118.

[2] Antiquities of Aberdeenshire, vol. iii. p. 545.

[3] Cart. Dryburgh, No. 306.

[4] Reg. Episc. Aberdon., vol. i. p. 48.

Antiquities of Aberdeenshire, vol. ii. p. 339.

[5] Chamberlain Rolls, vol. i. p. 26.

[6] Haddington Collections, Advocates' Library, vol. ii. p. 63, last division. Robertson's Index, p. 17, No. 55.

[7] Robertson's Index, p. 17, No. 61.

Cowie, Durris, and Aberdeen were in the hands of the powerful Comyn family, as keepers of them, in the end of the thirteenth century, for Edward I. ordered a mandate to be addressed to John Comyn, Earl of Buchan, in that capacity in 1292,[1] and the charters of 1327 are certainly the first in which any person of the name of Fraser is found connected with Cowie.

The various grants of land that have been enumerated in the preceding pages show that Sir Alexander Fraser had acquired very extensive estates, and these, together with his alliance by marriage to the royal family, must have rendered him one of the most powerful and influential barons in the north of Scotland; and the lines in which Barbour describes the cause of the steadfast friendship that existed between King Robert and James de Douglas are equally applicable to him—

> "For he servit aye lelely,
> And the other full wilfully,
> That was both worthy, wicht, and wise,
> Rewardit him wele his service."[2]

Sir Alexander Fraser was Vicecomes or Sheriff of the Mearns or Kincardine. He is so designated in a charter granted by Robert Janitor (Porter) of Kincardine,[3] to which he and his brother Simon were witnesses. He was also Vicecomes of Stirling,[4] which office, as already noticed, descended to his granddaughter, and had been enjoyed by his father, Sir Andrew Fraser, in whom, therefore, it first became hereditary in the family, although at a former period, 1234, held by Sir Bernard Fraser.

Upon the death of the great restorer of the independence of Scotland, the good King Robert Bruce, which event occurred on the 7th June 1329, the quiet and prosperity which during the latter years of his reign had gladdened and enriched his country, ere long gave place to scenes of a far different nature.

Although the young King David II. was but eight years of age when he succeeded to the throne of his glorious father, two eminent guardians had been appointed to protect his youth and inexperience; and had it pleased

---

[1] Rotuli Scotiæ, vol. i. p. 10.
[2] The Bruce, p. 40.
[3] Arbuthnot Charter-chest.
[4] Chamberlain Rolls, vol. i. p. 13.

Providence to prolong their lives, the fate of Scotland in that age might have been very different.

But, alas! the good Sir James of Douglas fell on the field of battle in Spain, whilst conveying his late sovereign's heart to the holy sepulchre, in obedience to his last request; and Sir Thomas Randolph, the great Earl of Moray, after a brief but wise regency, was cut off by illness, some say by poison, in the month of July 1332.

About this time Edward de Baliol, the son of the former King John de Baliol, with many of those nobles who had forfeited their lands in Scotland, supported by the power of Edward III. of England, encouraged also by the nonage of King David, the death of one guardian, and the approaching decease of the other, determined to make an energetic attempt for the recovery of the throne which his father had lost through his failure to preserve its independence, and which he himself only proposed to hold as a vassal to the English Crown.

Landing in Fife, he dispersed some troops hastily collected to oppose him, and marching onward to the river Erne, found himself, near Dupplin, in presence of a large force commanded by Donald, Earl of Mar, who, after the Earl of Moray's death, had been appointed Regent, and to whose incapacity the fate of Scotland and her young King was then intrusted.

No order was maintained in the Scottish army; feasting and drunkenness prevailed throughout the camp, and being informed of this negligence and misrule, Baliol decided on making a night attack, passed the river by a ford, and advanced to the assault.

Some few only of the leaders of the Scottish army preserved discipline, and kept watch as became the old soldiers of Robert Bruce.

These were Thomas Randolph, Earl of Moray, the son of the late Regent, Robert de Bruce, Earl of Carrick, an illegitimate son of the late King, Murdoch, Earl of Menteith, and Sir Alexander Fraser,[1] who, with such of their men as they could assemble, not much exceeding three hundred, made a desperate resistance; but, unsupported and, indeed, overwhelmed by the disorganised and panic-stricken remainder of the army, after having slain many of the assailants, they fell overpowered by numbers, and on this field,

[1] Buchanan, lib. ix. cap. vi.

fatal to Scotland as to himself, Sir Alexander Fraser gloriously ended a life devoted to the service of his King and country.[1]

By his wife, Lady Mary de Bruce, he left two sons—

John.

William.

Sir Alexander Fraser, 1320.[2]

[1] Fordun, Gesta Annalia, No. cxlvi. Wyntoun, cap. xxvi. The print of Wynton's Metrical Chronicle, in mentioning the leaders of the Scottish army at the battle of Dupplin, has the following couplet:—

"The Erle Menteith, Murthak alsua,
Alexander the Fraser yhoung with tha."

This epithet "yhoung" could not be applied to the Sir Alexander, who had been Chamberlain; but on referring to the four MS. copies of the Chronicle in the British Museum, the following are the readings of the second line:—

Nero, DXL, late fifteenth century: "Alexander Freser zangᵉ wᵗ ya."
Royal, 17, D. 20, ,, : "Alysandʳ ye frysar yhoung wᵗ ya"
Lansdowne, 197, early sixteenth century: "Alexr. fraseᵉ wes ane of yai."
Harley, 6909, seventeenth century: "Alexander the fresall younger with tha."

But the Chronicle was composed in eight-syllable metre, and it is most probable that the earliest of the epithets, "zangᵉ," was an interpolation of some transcriber, as the definite article before the surname in two of the copies assuredly was, and that the couplet, as originally written by Wyntoun, stood thus:—

"The Erle Menteith, Murthak alsua,
Alexander Fraser with tha."

Neither Fordun nor his continuator Bowyer, nor any other chronicler, apply the epithet.

[2] In Laing's Scottish Seals, vol. i. No. 349, the shield on this seal is said to be charged with *three* cinquefoils, but this is a mistake, the number is six, 3.2.1, as depicted in the facsimile of the letter of 1320 to the Pope, Acts of the Parliaments of Scotland, vol. i., and verified by inspection of the original in H. M. General Register House, Edinburgh.

JOHN FRASER,

ELDEST SON AND HEIR OF SIR ALEXANDER FRASER, CHAMBERLAIN.

THE invasion of Scotland by Edward Baliol in 1332, and its extraordinary success, had revolutionised the kingdom, and though he was vigorously opposed, and driven to great straits, during the remainder of that year, the power of England soon engaged in the contest, and in 1333 the victory of Halidon put an end to all further general resistance, and once more for a time brought the mass of the population under the English yoke.

Thereafter, for a period of eight or nine years, the independent spirits who would not brook the domination of a king forced upon them, nor the tyranny of England, fought as best they could for life and liberty.

Retreating into impregnable strengths, or moving in flying columns across the more accessible districts, attacking a fortress here or defending a strong position there, often victorious, and at times defeated, as the fortune of war might chance, retiring before the powerful invasions of Edward III. in 1334 and 1335, but renewing their efforts on his return to his own country, under the leadership of Sir Andrew Moray of Bothwell, Sir William de Douglas, Robert the Steward of Scotland, afterwards Robert II., and other brave chieftains, they maintained the desperate contest with gradually increasing success down to the year 1341, when their gallant and patriotic efforts, aided by the outbreak of war between England and France in 1337, had so far restored their independence that the young King, David II., was enabled to return from the latter country, to which he had been sent as a secure asylum.

Sir Alexander Fraser's sons were not of sufficient age to take a prominent position during the earliest years of this second struggle for freedom.

Born, certainly not before the end of the year 1316, or beginning of 1317, John Fraser, his eldest son, was not above sixteen years old at his father's death; and though he may have been present at the battles of Dupplin and Halidon Hill, could not have held any important command at either.

He is mentioned in the charter of the forest of Craigie, in the thanage of Cowie, to his father and himself, where he is called nephew by Robert I.; and his name also appears in the title of a missing charter of the thanage of Aberbothnet (Arbuthnot), bestowed upon him by that King.[1]

A story is related by Kennedy in his Annals of Aberdeen, and perhaps by others, of the citizens of that good burgh, under the command of a John Fraser, having attacked and taken the castle of Aberdeen, razing it to the ground, and putting the garrison to the sword; and of their having also defeated, with great slaughter, a body of English troops marching to its relief. The date of these events is placed by Kennedy in May 1308, after the battle of Inverury, won by Robert I.; and he also states that, in penance for certain cruelties committed at the time, the citizens were enjoined to repair every Sunday to a chapel at the castle, there to pray for the souls of their victims, and that after the Reformation the people continued to proceed to the terrace of the castle hill every Sunday as soon as the forenoon sermon was over, without knowing the original cause of the custom.

The late Dr. Robertson effectually disproved the correctness of the above date,[2] by showing that Edward II. ordered the castle to be revictualled on the 10th of July 1308, which is pretty good evidence that it had not been razed to the ground in May of that year, and by other arguments; and upon the ground of its non-appearance in the pages of Barbour, and other contemporary historians, he characterised the whole story from beginning to end as a clumsy and ill-devised falsehood, to which he might have added that there is no hint to be found anywhere of the existence of a John Fraser in 1308 in any way connected with Aberdeen.

There are, however, certain circumstances that seem to point to the story not being altogether such a myth as Dr. Robertson considered it, and to the possibility of such an occurrence having taken place in the course of the second struggle for independence, during the minority of David II.

The attack and capture of the castle is said to have taken place after a defeat of the Comyns by the partisans of Bruce. Henry de Beaumont, who represented the Comyn family, and had recovered the possessions from which Robert I. had expelled the Earl of Buchan in 1307, was driven from them by Sir Andrew Moray, and forced to surrender his castle of Dundarg,

[1] Haddington Collections, Robertson's Index, pp. 17, 18, Nos. 55, 60.
[2] Book of Bonaccord, p. 33.

in Buchan, and to retire into England in 1334; and during the next two years Sir Andrew overran and wasted all Kincardine and Forfar, compelling such friends of Baliol as could escape to fly for their lives.[1]

The origin assigned for the prayers performed by the citizens in the chapel of the castle on each Sunday is probable enough, and their continued resort to the same spot at similar times, after the cause of their assembling in that manner was forgotten among them, shows that it was a custom of very long standing.

About 1334, also, there was a John Fraser in existence, who, from his position, as nephew to the late King, son and heir of Sir Alexander Fraser, and a rightful owner of large estates in the neighbourhood, of which he had been deprived by Edward Baliol's party, and from the connection of his family with the burgh of Aberdeen (his father, and, at least, one of his uncles, Simon, had been honorary burgesses),[2] was a most likely person to raise the citizens in support of the royal family, from which they had received so many favours, and to lead them to the victory that they are credited with by Kennedy.

A passage occurs in the Chamberlain Rolls, where the heirs of Robert de Keith and of Alexander Fraser of "Ewnysedale" are said to have usurped the office of Vicecomes or Sheriff of Aberdeen for several years prior to 1345-6.[3]

The date of the entry is 1348, and at that time Sir Edward de Keith was Marischal; but down to 1346 he had been heir to his grandnephew, Sir Robert de Keith, the Marischal, who was killed at the battle of Durham.

As Sir Edward's son, William, married John Fraser's only daughter, Margaret, there can be little doubt that their respective fathers were the persons to whom the passage refers, and perhaps John Fraser's successful leadership of the citizens of Aberdeen may have enabled him and his friend, Sir Edward de Keith, to seize upon that office for a time.

It is not easy to decide upon the interpretation of the word "Ewnysedale" in the passage, for no estate of that name appears to have been in the posses-

---

[1] Fordun, Gesta Annalia, cl., clvi.
[2] Spalding Club Miscellany, vol. v. p. 10.
[3] Chamberlain Rolls, vol. i. p. 287.

sion of Sir Alexander Fraser, the Chamberlain, nor of any other member of the family, or is found in any other record.

Perhaps it may have been a variation of Strathean or Strathechin (as Clydesdale is of Strath Clyde), where one of Sir Alexander Fraser's residences may have been situated, for in 1351 the above-mentioned William de Keith, with consent of his wife, Margaret Fraser, granted a charter which was dated, "Apud mansum capitale nostrum de Strathekin."[1] From his daughter having been styled heir to her grandfather instead of to him, John Fraser seems to have died before he could make up any title to his hereditary possessions, though whether he fell in one of the many conflicts of that stormy age or died a natural death, there is no record to prove.

He left no male issue, and there is no information to be obtained of the name or family of his wife.

He was succeeded by an only daughter and heiress, Margaret.

MARGARET FRASER, SIR WILLIAM DE KEITH,
DAUGHTER OF JOHN FRASER, GRANDDAUGHTER AND HEIRESS OF SIR ALEXANDER FRASER. THE MARISCHAL.

THE fact of Margaret Fraser having made good her title as heir to her grandfather, Sir Alexander Fraser, of whose estates she inherited nearly the whole, evinces her to have been the only daughter of his eldest son, John.

Her father could only have reached his twentieth year about 1336-7, and in all probability she was not born much before then, though, from her eldest son having been, in his turn, a father before 1375, her birth cannot be placed much later.

At an early age she was deprived of her father's protection by his death, but she found security against the dangers to which so rich an heiress would be exposed in those troubled times, by her betrothal to William, eldest son of Sir Edward de Keith, the Marischal.

Sir William de Keith, who had become Marischal on the death of his father before 1351, in that year called Margaret Fraser his wife, in a charter

[1] Antiquities of Aberdeenshire, vol. ii. p. 72.

of the lands of Wester Mathers, near Arbuthnot, which he declared himself to possess in her right.[1]

She made up her title as heir to her grandfather, and successfully asserted her right to his large estates, for, in a charter granted by herself and her husband, jointly, in 1361, she is styled " neptis et heres bone memorie quondam Domini Alexandri Fraser, Militis ;"[2] and one of these estates was the forest of Cowie, which is found in the Marischal's possession in 1359.[3]

Margaret Fraser and her husband enjoyed long and prosperous lives; they survived until near the end of the first decade of the fifteenth century, and had several children. Their eldest son, John, died in the latter part of the year 1375, having married a daughter of King Robert II., by whom he had a son, Robert,[4] who also predeceased his grand-parents, leaving an only daughter, Jean, married to the first Earl of Huntly.

About 1380, or perhaps a little earlier, Robert Stewart, Earl of Fife, afterwards the famous Regent Duke of Albany, third son of King Robert II., having been left a widower by the death of his first wife, Margaret, daughter of Allan, Earl of Menteith, espoused Murielle, daughter of Sir William de Keith and Margaret Fraser, by whom he had issue three sons, John, afterwards the renowned Earl of Buchan, Andrew, and Robert Stewart.

It was doubtless in consequence of this alliance that, on the 2d of May 1407, Margaret Fraser, conjointly with her husband, the Marischal, granted a charter of the barony of Obeyn (Aboyne), in Aberdeenshire,[5] to John Stewart, Lord of Buchan, and his heirs-male; whom failing, to Andrew Stewart[6] and Robert Stewart, and their heirs-male successively; and failing these, to Robert de Keith, their own second son, and his heirs-male; and also upon the same day granted another charter of the lands of Touch-fraser and

---

[1] Spalding Club Miscellany, vol. v. p. 248.
[2] Antiquities of Aberdeenshire, vol. ii. p. 73.
[3] Chamberlain Rolls, vol. i. p. 339.
[4] Antiquities of Aberdeenshire, vol. ii. p. 74.
[5] Robertson's Index, p. 163, No. 20. Antiquities of Aberdeenshire, vol. ii. p. 35.

[6] Crawfurd, Officers of State, p. 306, says that Andrew was a son of the Regent Albany by his first marriage, but it is not probable that an elder half-brother would have been interposed between two sons of the Regent by his second marriage in the destination of these charters.

Drippis, in Stirlingshire, with the office of vicecomes of that county, to the same individuals in similar succession.[1]

Another daughter of the Marischal and Margaret Fraser, Elizabeth, married Sir Adam de Gordon, Lord of Strathbogie, and seems to have received from her parents some portion of her mother's estates, for her daughter, Elizabeth de Gordon, who married Sir Alexander de Seton, appears in 1436 to have taken steps to assert her hereditary right to a part of these by obtaining a transumpt of the charter of Cardenye, etc., granted to Sir Alexander Fraser in augmentation of his barony of Cluny by Robert I. in 1325.[2] Elizabeth de Gordon's son, Alexander, the first Earl of Huntly, married his cousin Jean, as above noticed.

The office of Marischal, and most of the estates jointly held by Sir William de Keith and Margaret Fraser, however, descended to their second son Robert,[3] and hence arose the contention between the families of Seton-Gordon, Earls of Huntly, and Keith Marischal, respecting the lands that had belonged to Margaret Fraser as heiress of her grandfather, which continued with great acrimony until its settlement, about 1442-4, by their partition between the two families.

By the charter that Alexander, the first Earl of Huntly, received from James II. in 1450 the lordship of Strathbogie, the lands of Cluny, Tulche, Obyn, Glentanner, and Glenmuick were erected into a free barony, to be called Huntly, and together with the barony of Panbride and the lordship of Gordon, were granted as the earldom of Huntly to him and his heirs by his third wife, Elizabeth de Crichton;[4] and of these, Cluny, Obyn (Aboyne), and Panbride had certainly been the property of Sir Alexander Fraser, and consequently of Margaret Fraser, and in all probability Tulche,[5] Glentanner, and Glenmuick also; and the Earl seems to have acquired his right to them partly through his mother, and partly from his first wife, Jean de Keith, though he had no issue by her.

There is, however, a little obscurity in the descent of some portions of

---

[1] Robertson's Index, p. 163, No. 19.
[2] Antiquities of Aberdeenshire, vol. iii. p. 316.
[3] Ibid. vol. ii. p. 74; vol. iii. p. 230.
[4] Antiquities of Aberdeenshire, vol. iv. p. 340.
[5] This Tulche is Touch, in Strathdee, a part of the old barony of Cluny, not Touch-fraser, or Tulchfraser, in Stirlingshire.

Margaret Fraser's estates that may require some explanation. It has been seen above that the lands of Aboyne, in Aberdeenshire, with those of Touch-fraser and Drippis, in Stirlingshire, were given by the Marischal and his wife to their grandson, John Stewart, Earl of Buchan, in 1407. The Earl of Buchan left an only daughter and heiress, Jean or Margaret, who before 1436 married George de Seton of Seton, afterwards first Lord Seton, a second cousin of the first Earl of Huntly, and they had male issue.

But as Aboyne formed a part of the earldom of Huntly according to the charter of 1450, and the ancestor of the family of Seton of Touch-fraser was Alexander de Seton, eldest son of the first Earl of Huntly by his second wife, Egidia de la Hay (the earldom being limited to his heirs by his third wife, Elizabeth de Crichton), it is evident that these lands must have passed from the possession of the Earl of Buchan and the substitutes in the charter of 1407 into the hands of the Earl of Huntly, and it is not easy to trace how this occurred.

Genealogists have solved the question by saying that they were part of the inheritance of his second wife, Egidia, the daughter and heiress of Sir John de la Hay of Touch and Tullibody; but, besides that this will not account for Aboyne, whatever lands she may have brought to her husband, it is impossible that Touch-fraser could be among them, unless there had been some transference of it from the Earl of Buchan to the de la Hay family, of which there is no trace.

In a pedigree of the name of Hay, in order apparently to account for Egidia's possession of that estate, a Sir Andrew Fraser of Touch and Tullibody is introduced among her ancestors; but whatever truth there may be in this, it is certain that the Touch there referred to was not Touch-fraser, which was in Margaret Fraser's hands down to the year 1407.

Touch, or Tulch, also written Tullich, and contracted into Tuly or Tilli, derived, according to the trustworthy authority of Mr. W. Skene, either from the genitive form of Tulach, a little hill, or of Tealach, a family,[1] is a very common prefix or affix to Scottish names of places; and if there ever was a Sir Andrew Fraser of Touch, he was probably one of the individuals of that name of whom some account will be found in the Appendix.

[1] Historians of Scotland, Fordun, vol. ii. Appendix, p. 443.

It appears then pretty evident that these estates, Aboyne, Touch-fraser, and Drippis, were not brought into her husband's family by Egidia de la Hay, and it is probable that Sir Robert de Keith, the second son of Sir William de Keith, the Marischal, and Margaret Fraser, who succeeded his father as Marischal, acquired these possessions in terms of the charters of 1407, upon the death, without male issue, of John Stewart, Earl of Buchan, and his brothers Andrew and Robert, to whom they had been successively granted; and that the first Earl of Huntly put forward his pretensions to them, as he did to the other parts of Margaret Fraser's property, and that they fell to his share upon the partition of her estates, which put an end to the contention between the families of Seton-Gordon and Keith-Marischal, about 1442-4. The Earl seems to have incorporated Aboyne in the earldom on account of its position within the barony of Huntly, but he granted the distant estates of Touch-fraser and Drippis to his eldest son, Alexander de Seton, as they were situated at no great distance from that of Tullibody, which the latter inherited from his mother, Egidia de la Hay.

It is probable that the sheriffship ceased to be an hereditary office; but from a Sir Alexander de Seton of Touch-fraser having received that appointment for life in 1488, the possession of that estate may have given him some claim to it.

A third daughter of the Marischal and Margaret Fraser, Christiana, is said to have been married to Sir James de Lindesay of Crawford; for Wyntoun relates how she was besieged in the castle of Fyvie by her nephew, Sir Robert de Keith, in 1395, until relieved by her husband, who, gathering together four hundred men, defeated her assailant near Bourtry, killing fifty of his followers;[1] but the poet seems to have mistaken the name of the one or the other.

The thanage of Arbuthnot was conferred upon John Fraser by King Robert I., and it is probable that his daughter, Margaret, succeeded him in it; but a family bearing that territorial surname had been Thanes of Arbuthnot for seven or eight generations previously. It is not unlikely that their repre-

---

[1] Wyntoun, Lib. IX. c. xvi. The contents of the excambion of Dunnottar, quoted further on, prove that Sir William de Lindesay of the Byres was the husband of Christian, daughter of the Marischal and Margaret Fraser, in 1392.

sentative was an adherent of the Comyns, and at the destruction of that party in 1307-8, had forfeited the thanage, which the King bestowed upon his own nephew. A descendant, however, Philip de Arbuthnot, seems to have made his peace with King David II., and possibly asserted a right to the thanage.

If this were so, the dispute was arranged by his marriage to Janet, a daughter of the Marischal and Margaret Fraser; but he is said to have had no male issue by her, the Lords Arbuthnot being descended from his second marriage to Margaret, daughter of Sir James de Douglas of Dalkeith.[1]

The seal of Margaret Fraser is still extant, appended to a charter of excambion, entered into by her and her husband in 1392, with their son-in-law, Sir William de Lindsay of the Byres, and Christian de Keith, his wife. Sir William was the ancestor of the Lords Lindsay of the Byres and the Earls of Lindsay, who were so famous in the history of Scotland. By that contract of excambion Margaret Fraser and her husband exchanged the lands of Ugtrethrestrother (Struthers), Petyndreiche, and Wester Markinche for the castle and estate of Dunnottar.[2]

The seal of Margaret Fraser contains three separate shields, touching at the base points; that in the centre is upright, and bears the six rosettes or cinquefoils, disposed 3.2.1, for Fraser; another, couché on the proper right, bears the arms of Keith Marischal, a chief paly of six; and the third, couché on the proper left, has a fess chequé between 3 fleurs-de-lis, 2 and 1.

The Fraser shield on this seal is the latest instance of six rosettes or cinquefoils disposed 3.2.1 representing that name, and in that generation the number was reduced to three, placed 2.1, as exemplified in the seal of Hugh Fraser of Lovat, 1377-90.[3]

There must have been a reason for this reduction, for in that age everything relating to armorial bearings was arranged with scrupulous care, and no one could make any important change in them without proper authority from the Crown, through the heralds or kings-at-arms.

Among the marks of cadency in ancient use, Nisbet gives diminishing the number of the figures, and, perhaps, there could not be a more expressive typical illustration of the failure of an eldest line in an heir-female, than

---

[1] Douglas Peerage, by Wood, vol. i. p. 78.
[3] See Appendix.
[2] Original Excambion in Charter-chest of the Earl of Glasgow at Crawford Priory.

that afforded by cutting off the figures in the chief of the shield, leaving those in the fess and base to be borne by the still existing junior branches.

The shield of Sir James Fraser of Frendraught, in the year 1371, bore six rosettes or cinquefoils, 3 in chief, and 2.1 below a fess chequé,[1] but he was of the same generation as Margaret Fraser's father, and in the next generation, that to which she belonged, James Fraser of Frendraught bore only three upon his shield in 1402; and Janet de Dunbar, Countess of Moray, in 1454 quartered a fess chequé between three rosettes or cinquefoils, as the arms of Fraser of Frendraught, in the shield on her seal.

There is of course no possibility of verifying the statement, made by some early genealogists, that the Fraser insignia were originally azure, semée with cinquefoils argent, but, in that case, their disposition on a triangular shield would cause each line to be one less in number than that immediately above it, and the reduction of the number, accompanying the failure of the eldest line in Margaret Fraser, may suggest that, when a former eldest line failed in Simon Fraser's daughter Eda, about 1160-80, they may have been disposed 4.3.2.1; and if the row on the chief of the shield were then cut off, they would become 3.2.1, as borne by all of the race down to the next failure of the eldest line in a female, when they were reduced to three, disposed 2.1, and the fact of this not having taken place at the time of the failure of the Oliver Castle branch, by the death of Sir Simon Fraser, filius, in 1306, leaving daughters only,[2] is an argument against that having been the senior line of the race.

With regard to the third shield on the seal of Margaret Fraser, upon one point there can be no doubt; the arms are not those of another husband; for Margaret Fraser was assuredly the wife of Sir William de Keith, the Marischal, from 1351 to 1407 at the least.

Although the keen heraldic eye of Nisbet failed to read the charges on the third shield of the seal of Margaret Fraser, and he left it as an entire blank in the engraving of the seal which is given in one of his works on heraldry, close inspection of the shield shows that it bears a fess chequé and three fleurs-de-lis, two in chief and one in base. The seal must be considered as Margaret Fraser's own, as that of her husband, the Marischal, had

[1] See Appendix. [2] Ibid.

been also appended to the document. Although the seal of Sir William de Keith has been broken off, the tag to which it was originally attached still remains. The reading which gives the most satisfactory explanation of the three shields used by Margaret Fraser, is that they were those of herself, her husband, and her mother. The name or family of her mother is not known through any documentary evidence, but the arms on the third shield, if so considered, denote her to have been the offspring of an alliance between a Stewart and a member of a family bearing fleurs-de-lis, and taken in conjunction with her daughter's christian name of Margaret, and other circumstances to be narrated, suggest a possible descent for her.

In the Appendix will be found a short memoir of the Frasers of Frendraught, in which it is shown that James Fraser, youngest brother of Sir Alexander Fraser, Margaret's grandfather, married the daughter and heiress of Sir John Stewart of Frendraught, who had supplanted the ancient family of Frendraught in that estate about the beginning of the fourteenth century, and whose wife may have been the heiress of that family. The Frasers of Frendraught carried the Stewart fess chequé between their own rosettes or cinquefoils, six or three in number, and they also bore a wolf's head as a crest, and the old Frendraught arms were three wolves' heads.

Some former connection by marriage must have existed between the Frasers and the Stewarts, though its nature is not traceable, as a dispensation had to be obtained in 1322 from Pope John XXII., for the marriage of James Fraser and Margaret Stewart of Frendraught, who were related within the prohibited degrees. Such close relationship often led to further alliances between families; and it is not unlikely that Margaret Fraser's father may have married a younger daughter of Sir John Stewart of Frendraught, who, however, could scarcely have been full sister to Margaret Stewart, but may have been her half-sister by a second marriage of their father with a lady whose arms were fleurs-de-lis, and Margaret Fraser may have been named after her aunt, Margaret Stewart.

The seal of Margaret Fraser, of which an engraving is given on page 89, bears an inscription which, although much defaced, can still be read " S. Margarete Freser." It is attached to the above-mentioned charter of excambion of the lands of Ugtrethrestrother (Struthers), Wester Markinche, and other lands in the county of Fife, for the lands and the celebrated Castle of Dunnottar, the picturesque ruins of which are still an object of great interest on the rocky coast of the Mearns, in the parish bearing the name of the castle. The great family of Keith continued in possession of Dunnottar from its acquisition under that excambion in 1392, till their forfeiture in the year 1716. Dunnottar was subsequently acquired by purchase by a cadet of the Keiths, and it remained with him and his descendants till within the last few years, when the castle and lands were sold by Sir Patrick Keith Murray of Ochtertyre, Bart. As the excambion by which the Keiths acquired Dunnottar is of some historical interest, an abstract of it is here given.

William of Keith, Marischal of Scotland, and Margaret [Fraser] his spouse, with joint consent and assent, after full consideration of their common weal and that of their heirs, grant and confirm to Sir William of Lyndesay, Knight, and their well-beloved daughter, Christian [Keith], his spouse, and the longer liver of them, and to the lawful heirs of their bodies; whom failing, to the heirs and assignees of Sir William Lyndesay, the lands of Ochtirothirstruthir, of Wester Markynch, of Petyndreich, with eight pounds annualrent out of the lands of Dunotyr with the castle thereof, in excambion for the lands of Dunotyr and the castle, with all their right pertinents, as in their charters made thereupon: And in case it should happen that William of Keith, or Margaret his spouse, or any of their heirs, successors, or assignees should gainstand the premises in whole or in part, or come in the contrary thereof by word or deed, they bind themselves in the sum of one thousand pounds sterling money of Scotland, to be paid to Sir William Lyndesay and Christian his spouse, and the heirs of their bodies; whom failing, to their heirs and assignees whomsoever, without any gainsaying or exception, in name of skaith and expenses; and further, in the sum of one thousand pounds sterling, in name of penalty, to be proportionally paid to the fabric of the kirks of St. Andrews, Aberdeen, and Glasgow, before they be heard before any judge, spiritual or secular, in plea or complaint anent the premises: With a clause of warrandice in the usual terms: Renouncing for themselves and their heirs all remedy of law, canon and civil, in the contrary of the premises: And for greater faith, Margaret [Fraser], touching the holy evangels, gave her bodily oath not to come at any time in contrary of the premises. They also bind and oblige themselves to surrender of new, at any future time, all charters and evidents of these lands; to grant infeftment therein and fulfil all other things needful for security: For the observance of all which they bind themselves by oath, their heirs and executors, and all their goods, moveable and immoveable, their lands and tenements, to be distrained, taken, poinded, and led away, at the will of Sir William Lyndesay and Christian his spouse, without license of any judge, to be possessed or sold till satisfaction be made. In witness of all which they caused their seals to be appended at Fetheresso, the eighth day of the month of March 1392.

The observations upon the subject of these seals would not be complete without adverting to what Mr. Anderson says respecting the proper armorial bearings of the Frasers of Lovat.

In a note to pages 47 and 48 of his work,[1] he refers to and quotes from the MS. Index of Matriculations of Arms "in the Lyon Records, written partly by Robert Porteous, Snaddoun Herald, and Joseph Stacey, Ross Herald," before 1663-4, giving the following extracts; and he further alludes to the arms of Lord Lovat, as described in the MS., having been illuminated by John Sawers, herald painter, before 1654, and places a copy of that drawing as the frontispiece of his work.

"FRAISER LORD LOVAT,

"Beirs 2. coats first fraiser: azure 5. frays alias strawberrey leves a lacing^r argent: Secondly; argent three antiant crowns. Gules: supported be 2 buks sceant eatch in ane hollin bush proper. Crist: a buks head errashe: or: armed wyt 6 tynes azure. Motto—I am readi."

[1] History of the Family of Fraser.

"37, Fraser Lord Fraser *of old* az : 5 fraes strawberrey leves salterwayes, 2.1.2. argent. 38, Fraser of Lovat, *the same*. 39, Fraser of Mucehall, quarterlie, 1 Fraser, 2 argent, a lyon sable. 40, Fraser of Phillorth, quarterly, 1 azure, 3 fraes, argent gules, a lyon rampant argent."[1]

Mr. Anderson follows these extracts with an argument, which need not be repeated here, if it be shown that the premises on which it is based, the above statements of the heralds of 1663, are fallacious.

Who these heralds imagined to have been the person they called "Lord Fraser *of old*" will be found below; but the earliest seals of the race extant, those of William Fraser, Bishop of St. Andrews, 1279 to 1297, Sir Richard Fraser, before 1276 and in 1297, Sir Andrew Fraser, 1297, Sir Simon Fraser, filius, 1297, Sir Alexander Fraser, 1320, Sir James Fraser, 1371, and Margaret Fraser, 1392, all show the rosettes or cinquefoils, six in number, disposed in the shield 3.2.1, and upon the seal of a William Fraser, 1296, they are still six in number, although not on a shield, and the three-pointed label on which they are placed forces their disposition to be two on each point.[2]

It is evident that the heralds of 1663 knew nothing of these seals, and from the mis-spelling of the name, "Fraiser," and the mention of "frays," and "fraes," if they themselves were not the inventors of the punning derivation of the name, it had been at all events suggested by that time and accepted by them, and it is not difficult to discover the source from whence they took the five "fraes" placed "salterwayes."

One of the daughters and co-heiresses of Sir Simon Fraser, filius, executed by order of Edward I. in 1306, married Sir Gilbert de Hay of Locherwart, and their descendants, the Lords of Yester (now Marquis of Tweeddale), quartered the rosettes or cinquefoils of Fraser in consequence of that alliance. They appear to have done this by placing five of them saltireways, at all events, in the upper quarter, though the shape of the shield in the earlier Yester seals prevented their being so placed in the lower quarter, and four are found there, or three, though not disposed 2.1, as may be seen in Mr. Laing's first vol. of Scottish Seals, where plates of those of John, second Lord Hay of Yester, 1513, and John, fourth Lord Hay of Yester, 1556, show that arrange-

[1] These extracts are strictly copied from Mr. Anderson's work.
[2] See Appendix.

ment; but in 1564, William, fifth Lord Hay of Yester, adopted a form of shield broader at the base upon his seal, and then the five rosettes or cinquefoils, placed saltireways, are found in both the first and fourth quarters.[1]

The Hays of Tallo, in the barony of Oliver Castle, a junior branch of the Tweeddale family, adopted four, disposed 2.2.,[2] and in the second and third quarters of the shield, on a seal of John, Earl of Wigton and Lord Fleming, in 1644—the descendant of the Sir Patrick Fleming that married the other daughter and co-heiress of Sir Simon Fraser, filius—six rosettes or cinquefoils are found, but they are disposed 2.2.2.[3] All of these various dispositions by the posterity of Sir Simon Fraser, filius, effectually difference their bearings from the Fraser coat of arms, either before or after the reduction from six, 3.2.1, to three, 2.1.

It can scarcely be doubted that the heralds of the seventeenth century, in their ignorance of the ancient bearings of the family, imagined that the disposition found in the arms of the Lords of Yester was that used by Sir Simon Fraser, filius, whom they chose to style "Lord Fraser of old;" and that this error, coupled with the absurd punning derivation of the name, led them into the utterly fallacious heraldry recorded in the above extracts, which Mr. Anderson did not possess sufficient acquaintance with the subject to detect, but which has been long rejected by the Lords Lovat, who bear the three rosettes or cinquefoils, placed 2.1, of their ancestor Hugh Fraser.

---

[1] Laing's Scottish Seals, vol. i. Plate 28, Nos. 2, 5, 8; pp. 224, 225, Nos. 1225, 1228, 1230.

[2] Laing's Scottish Seals, vol. i. p. 223, No. 1223.

[3] Ibid. vol. ii. p. 63, No. 367.

PART III.

THE FRASERS OF COWIE, DURRIS, AND PHILORTH.

IN the preceding pages the eldest male line of the family of Touch-fraser and Cowie has been followed to its extinction by the marriage of Margaret Fraser, granddaughter and heiress of Sir Alexander Fraser, the Chamberlain (as he may be styled, to distinguish him from others of the same name), to Sir William de Keith, the Marischal; and the greater part of her grandfather's extensive estates are seen to have passed with her into that powerful family, to be eventually partitioned between the Earls Marischal, the Earls of Huntly, and the Setons of Touch-fraser. Upon this failure in an heir-female the representation of the male line of the Chamberlain reverted to the descendants of his second son,

SIR WILLIAM FRASER OF COWIE AND DURRIS, who married MARGARET MORAY, DAUGHTER OF SIR ANDREW MORAY OF BOTHWELL.

As, however, one author has disputed the generally admitted fact that this William Fraser was a son of Sir Alexander Fraser, the Chamberlain, and has endeavoured to suggest a different parentage for him, it may be as well to dispose of his objections and suggestions before proceeding further.

This author is Mr. Anderson, and in his "Historical Account of the Family of Fraser,"[1] he has brought forward a specious argument in support of his view, which, to a person unacquainted with the documents referred

[1] History of the Family of Fraser, page 38, note.

to; who took his statements upon trust, might have a plausible appearance. The whole passage is therefore quoted here for the purpose of inquiring how far it is borne out by fact:

"Sir Alexander Fraser, knight, the Chamberlain, having been only married to the widow of Sir Neil Campbell about 1316, and his line having terminated in a female descendant, who inherited all his estates, and carried them into other families, it is surprising that our peerage-writers should have confounded him with an Alexander Fraser of Cowie and Durris, the undoubted male ancestor of the ancient and respectable family of Philorth. To expose the fallacy of this opinion requires but a very few remarks. It has always been admitted by every one, and cannot be disputed, that this very ancient line of the Frasers is descended from William, son of an Alexander Fraser (evidently the latter Alexander), who flourished principally during the early part of the 14th century, and succeeded to his father as proprietor of the estates of Cowie and Durris. This is further apparent from the title of a missing charter of David II. in Robertson's Index, containing a grant to William of the lands of Durris, but more especially of Collie, 'whilk thanedom of Collie' (it is added) 'was Alexander Fraser his father's'" (*sic*).

"Here it cannot escape observation, that Alexander of Collie is not, even after his death, termed *knight*, a title which, as has been proved, Sir Alexander the Chamberlain held from 1308, and continued to enjoy ever afterwards. But independently of this striking fact, there is the evident failure of the male line of the Chamberlain before 1355, and the impracticability of instructing that he ever possessed the estate of Collie or Cowie. Besides it may be added that there is explicit proof by Ragman's Roll" (*sic*), "that on the 7th July 1296 'William Fraser, the son of the late Alexander Fraser,' swore fealty to Edward I. among the barons of the neighbourhood, at Fernel, Forfarshire, contiguous to the quarter of Scotland where the family estates were situated. Alexander Fraser, therefore, ancestor of the house of Philorth, for such the latter Alexander must be presumed to be, was dead long before the period when the Chamberlain commenced his career, and obviously was a different person from him."

With the exception of some complimentary allusions to the family of Philorth, which need not be repeated here, the above is Mr. Anderson's argument, but some parts of it appear to have no real bearing upon the question at issue, for instance whether the Chamberlain was a Knight as early as 1308, or did not attain to that dignity until after 1312; the fact that a William Fraser, son of an Alexander Fraser, happened to be at

Fernel, in Forfarshire, when he swore fealty to Edward I. in 1296 (without anything appearing in the document to connect him with that district, and not "among the barons of the neighbourhood," as Mr. Anderson says), and the failure of the Chamberlain's eldest male line in a female, of which there can be no doubt, but which does not disprove the existence of a second male line; and when these are eliminated the argument appears to be based on the three following statements, which it is trusted are here fairly extracted from the above quoted passage :—

1*st*, That the Alexander Fraser who had a son named William, and was dead before the 7th July 1296, was the proprietor of the estates of Cowie and Durris, and that his son William succeeded him in those estates.

2*d*, That the omission of the title of Knight, even after death, in Robertson's Index, shows that Alexander Fraser of Cowie was not the same person as Sir Alexander Fraser the Chamberlain.

3*d*, That it is impracticable to instruct that Sir Alexander Fraser the Chamberlain ever possessed the estate of Cowie.

If, in contradiction of these statements, it can be shown by good evidence—

1*st*, That it is impossible that the Alexander Fraser, dead before 1296, could have possessed Cowie and Durris, or his son William have succeeded him in those estates;

2*d*, That the omission of the title of Knight in Robertson's Index, even after death, is of no importance.

3*d*, That it is not impracticable to instruct that Sir Alexander Fraser the Chamberlain did possess the estate of Cowie, the refutation of Mr. Anderson's argument would appear to be complete, and to this the following observations are directed—

1*st*, Mr. Anderson's assertion that the Alexander Fraser, dead before 1296, possessed Cowie and Durris, rests entirely upon his *ipse dixit*; he adduces no authority for it; and it may here be mentioned that no document of any sort has been found in existence or upon record, giving even the slightest hint that any person of the name of Fraser held lands in that district or neighbourhood before 1309.

The forfeiture of Durris by John Comyn, Earl of Buchan, is upon record in Robertson's Index,[1] and this certainly did not take place before the accession of Robert I. to the throne in 1306, and probably not before the destruction of the power of the Comyn family in 1308.

The keepership of the forest of Cowie, and that of the forest of Durris, were held by the Comyns, as is proved by the mandate of Edward I., mentioning the Earl of Buchan in that capacity in 1292;[2] and it is not probable that they lost the former before the latter, nor either until their overthrow in 1308.

But the forest and thanage of Cowie were granted to an Alexander Fraser by Robert I. in 1327.[3]

It is impossible that the Alexander Fraser, dead before 1296, could have been proprietor of Durris, which was not forfeited by the Earl of Buchan until 1308, and it is also impossible that he could have been the person of that name who obtained the charters of Cowie from Robert I. in 1327, and it is evident from this that he did not possess those estates, and that his son William could not have succeeded him in them.

2d, With regard to the omission of the title of Knight, even after death, which might have been of weight had it applied to a name in the body of a charter, it may be pointed out that in Robertson's Index, a list of the titles of ancient charters, many no longer extant, where the omission occurs, the designation of Knight, attached to any name, is very exceptional; and that by Mr. Anderson's reasoning most of the individuals mentioned in that Index, who were knights, would be deprived of that rank, and among them the Chamberlain himself, for in the titles of his charters of Auchincarnie and of the forest of Craigie in the thanage of Cowie, elsewhere called the forest of Cowie, he is not styled Knight, although that designation is bestowed upon him in the charters themselves, of which copies are still extant.[4]

This shows that the omission upon which Mr. Anderson lays so much stress is utterly unimportant; but a rather curious evidence of his not having gone very deeply into the subject is found in the fact, entirely overlooked by him, that the Alexander Fraser, dead before 1296, was also a knight; he is

---

[1] Robertson's Index, p. 68, No. 8.

[2] Rotuli Scotiæ, vol. i. p. 10.

[3] Robertson's Index, pp. 17, 18, Nos. 55-61. Haddington Collection MSS., Advocates' Library, Edinburgh, vol. ii. p. 63, last division.

[4] Robertson's Index, p. 17, Nos. 51-55. Haddington Collection MSS., Advocates' Library, vol. ii. p. 63, last division.

so designated in his son Bernard's agreement with John de Lambyrton, on the Sunday after St. Matthew's day, 1295, at which date he was dead,[1] and he is also found as a witness with that rank before 1268;[2] so that, if the argument on the omission of the title of Knight in Robertson's Index were worth anything, it would apply as forcibly to this Alexander as to the Chamberlain.

3*d*, It is difficult to understand how Mr. Anderson could venture to assert the "impracticability of instructing that" the Chamberlain "ever possessed the estate of Cowie," for it is evident that he had consulted Robertson's Index, and the Haddington Collection, both of which authorities he quotes at page 37 of his work, in proof of charters granted to Sir Alexander Fraser the Chamberlain, especially that of Auchincarnie, and yet he says nothing of the charter of the forest of Craigie, in the thanage of Cowie, granted to the same Sir Alexander Fraser, as is proved by the tenor of the document, which is also in the Haddington Collection; nor does he notice the titles, in Robertson's Index, of that charter, and of another of the thanage of Cowie, to Alexander Fraser, although they are both in the same roll of the Index with that of Auchincarnie, which he does mention, and the three are numbered respectively 51, 55, and 61, and the suppression of evidence, so adverse to his argument, with which he must certainly have been acquainted, throws grave suspicion upon his good faith as an historian, and with the refutation of the two other statements on which his argument is based, effectually disposes of it.

To return, however, to the question of the Chamberlain's having possessed Cowie.

In the account of his life it has been already noticed that, towards the close of the thirteenth century, there were three members of the race in existence bearing the name of "Alexander."

Of the above three persons, two were considerably older than the third, and it is shown in the foregoing remarks that one, the Sir Alexander Fraser, father of the William Fraser who swore fealty to Edward I. in 1296, died in or before 1295, and could not have possessed Cowie in 1327. It has been also shown that a second Sir Alexander Fraser was a Baron and Knight,

---

[1] Cart. Glasgow, No. 251. [2] Reg. Hon. de Morton, vol. ii. No. 7.

"Miles," in 1296, that in all probability he was made prisoner at the battle of Methven, and was the person whose lands of Cornetoun were demanded by John de Luc in 1306; that he probably perished in that year, at all events, that there is no further mention of him to be found during the reign of Robert I.; but he, by his having been a Knight in 1296, is distinctly marked as a different individual from the third Alexander Fraser, who is shown, in the account of his career, to have been the son of Sir Andrew Fraser, and not to have attained to the rank of Knight until after 1312, and whose identity with the brother-in-law of Robert I., Chamberlain of Scotland from 1319 to 1325, is completely established by his granddaughter having succeeded to possessions held by him in both capacities, viz., Ugtrethrestrother, as heir of Sir Andrew, and the forest of Cowie granted to him by the king.

The contents of the charter prove that it was the brother-in-law of Robert I., Sir Alexander Fraser, that obtained the grant of the forest of Craigie in the thanage of Cowie, for his son John is called the King's nephew in the charter, which is dated April 6th, 1327,[1] and it is impossible to doubt that it was the same Sir Alexander Fraser who also received the charter of the thanage of Cowie and Craigining Glasculloche about the same time;[2] and it is evident that the William Fraser who received from David II. a charter of the thanage of Cowie, which had belonged to Alexander Fraser, his father, must have been the son of the individual to whom it was given in 1327.

In Robertson's Index the title of the charter from David II. to William Fraser runs thus,—"To William Fraser, and Margaret Murray, his spouse, of the thanedom of Durris and thanedom of Collie, whilk thanedom of Collie was Alexander Fraser's, his father, with the lands of Eskyltuh in Kincardine."[3]

The particular notice of the thanage of Collie (Cowie), having been Alexander Fraser's property, which may have been taken from some expression in the charter itself, would lead to the inference that the thanage of

---

[1] Haddington Collection MSS., Advocates' Library, Edinburgh, vol. ii. p. 63, last division.

[2] In the reign of Robert II., Robert de Keith, second son of Sir William de Keith, the Marischal, and Margaret Fraser, got a charter (evidently upon the resignation of his parents in his favour) of lands thus described,—"the forrest of Colly, the forrest called the Forrest of the Month, the lands of Ferachy, Glastolach (Glasculloche?), Cragy, Clochnahule, whilk of old was of the thanedom of Colly, and vicecom. Kincardin."—Robertson's Index, p. 117, No. 72.

[3] Robertson's Index, p. 60, No. 14.

Durris had not belonged to him, and this agrees with what is known of the Chamberlain's possessions, for Durris is not found among them, and the wording of the passage is also suited to William Fraser's position as a second son, for he is not termed heir to his father.

After this somewhat long but necessary digression to prove the parentage of William Fraser, the account of what is known concerning him may be proceeded with.

His father having married Lady Mary de Bruce about the year 1316, and there having been an elder son of the union, the birth of William Fraser cannot be placed at an earlier date than 1318, and he would have attained to an age for commencing an active military career about 1334; but his acquaintance with the hardships and perils of a soldier's life was probably hastened by the misfortunes that had overtaken his country and his family, and as, in those days, boys often accompanied their parents or relatives to the field of battle when very young, he may even have witnessed the rout at Dupplin, and the disastrous conflict at Halidon Hill, during the two preceding years, though debarred by youth from being more than a spectator of those fatal encounters.

He seems, however, to have joined the brave Sir Andrew Moray, Sir William de Douglas, and the other leaders that maintained the long struggle against English domination, probably served under the command of the first of these during his campaigns from 1334 to 1337, and, after that leader's death in 1338, appears to have joined Sir William de Douglas, with whom he is found associated in the surprise and capture of Edinburgh Castle, on the 17th of April 1341.[1]

Sir William Bullock, of whom the chronicler says, "ceteros suo tempore ingenio præcellebat," effected an arrangement between Walter Currie, the

---

[1] Fordun, Gesta Annalia, cap. clx.; Scotichronicon, lib. xiii. cap. xlvii.; Wyntoun, lib. viii. cap. xxxviii.

Froissart calls the Fraser that participated in the capture of Edinburgh Castle "Simon," and Buchanan has followed him in this. Boethius, who is copied by Major, makes the name "Walter," but the fact of two persons called "Guilelmus" (sic), and two named "Gualterus," being mentioned in the same sentence, suggests how this error originated.

The authority of Froissart or Boethius is not of the same weight as that of Fordun in his Gesta Annalia, Bowyer in the Scotichronicon, and Wyntoun in his Metrical Chronicle, who all join in calling him William.

master of a vessel then lying at Dundee, and the Scottish leaders, Sir William de Douglas, William Fraser, and Joachim de Kynbuk, for their passage, with two hundred chosen men, to the Island of Inchkeith in the Firth of Forth, and his assistance in their subsequent operations.

Upon arriving there Walter Currie, who seems to have been a resolute and intelligent man, accompanied by one servant, visited the Governor of Edinburgh Castle towards evening, pretending to be an English merchant that had a cargo of excellent wine, ale, and other provisions for sale. He confirmed his story by producing two flasks, one of wine, the other of ale, carried by his servant, and, persuading the Governor to taste their contents, promised early next morning to bring him a barrel of each, with two cases of biscuit prepared with spices, on condition of receiving permission to dispose of the remainder of his merchandise.

The Governor willingly agreed to this proposal, and gave orders that when Currie should arrive next morning with the present, the gates were to be opened for him.

Sir William de Douglas placed his forces in ambush near the Castle gates that night, and very early in the morning Walter Currie, with twelve selected companions, disguised in sailors' clothing over their armour, and each having a stout staff in his hand, approached the castle openly, leading two horses laden with cases and barrels filled with water, and entering it by the great gate, thrown open for them according to the Governor's orders, they immediately slew the porter and his two assistants, placed a strong stake, provided for the purpose by Currie, under the portcullis, to prevent it being lowered, and throwing the boxes and barrels into the entrance of a tower close at hand, called the "Turnipyk," blew a loud blast on a horn, the signal to Douglas, who, on hearing it, broke from his ambush, and hastened to their assistance.

The English, alarmed at the noise, also hurried from all parts of the Castle to the gate, where a furious fight ensued, but Currie and his comrades gallantly held their ground until Douglas and his men arriving, the garrison were all put to the sword or forced over the ramparts, and the Castle was won.

Upon the death of the brave and wise Sir Andrew Moray in 1338, Robert

Stewart (afterwards Robert II.), grandson of Robert I., succeeded him as Guardian of the Kingdom, and his efforts, with those of his loyal comrades, had proved so far successful in 1341, that a great part of the country was again freed from English rule, and the young King, David II., with his Queen, was enabled to return from France, and landed at Inverbervie, in Kincardineshire, on the 2d of June in that year.[1]

The King is said to have held his Court at Perth soon after his arrival in his own country, and there to have bestowed lands and other rewards upon those who had signalised themselves in his service, or whose parents had lost their lives at Dupplin, Halidon Hill, or in other conflicts, during the nine years of incessant warfare that had elapsed since Edward de Baliol's successful invasion in 1332.[2]

William Fraser, whose merit under either of these categories was so conspicuous, obtained a grant of the thanages of Durris and Cowie, with the lands of Eskyltuh, Essintuly, in Kincardine, but unfortunately the charter, by which these possessions were conferred upon him and his wife, is one of those no longer extant, or at all events still undiscovered, and the title of it in Robertson's Index is all that remains on record.[3]

He also received by a royal order in 1342 an assignation or gift of £13, 6s. 8d., a considerable sum at that time, from the rents of the lands of Anauch,[4] which may have been situated on the banks of the Annack water, that passes by Stewarton, in Cunningham, and falls into the Irvine river.

Margaret Murray or Moray, who is mentioned as William Fraser's wife in the title of the charter of Durris and Cowie, appears to have been a daughter of the illustrious Sir Andrew Moray. In order, however, to avoid needless repetition, the reader is referred to the account given of her son, Sir Alexander Fraser, where the facts that seem to warrant this parentage being assigned to her will be found.

She is mentioned in Robertson's Index in close proximity to John Moray, Sir Andrew's eldest son, as receiving various grants and pensions for the term of her life,[5] and in the Chamberlain Rolls appears a notice of the

---

[1] Fordun, Gesta Annalia, cap. clx.
[2] Boethius.
[3] Robertson's Index, p. 60, No. 14.
[4] Chamberlain Rolls, vol. i. p. 280.
[5] Robertson's Index, p. 37, Nos. 10, 13, 14, 16.

remission in her favour, of a contribution due to the Crown from her property, at the same time that a payment of money to John Moray is recorded.[1]

She survived her husband William Fraser many years, for in 1360 an entry in the Chamberlain Rolls shows her in receipt of a pension from the lands of the thanage of Cowie.[2]

In 1392 Robert de Caldwell, dominus de Todrig, caused a copy to be made of a former charter from Margaret de Moravia, granting him her lands of Aynachil, . . . de Unthank "in dominio de Robertone in baronia de Conynghame, infra Vic. de Are;"[3] and as in the loose orthography of those days Aynachil and Anauch might easily mean the same place, it is at least probable that William Fraser received his gift of money from the lands of Anauch in right of his wife.

It may have been from the hand of his Sovereign, when the two thanages were bestowed upon him, that William Fraser received the honour of knighthood, to which rank the record of his death and the mention of his name in a charter to one of his sons show that he attained.

In all probability he served in the earlier expeditions of David II. into the northern counties of England, but his career, though active and useful, and giving promise of eminence, was not destined to rival that of his father in length, for in 1346 the king resolved once more to invade that country, influenced by the request of the King of France, and under the impression that many of the best warriors of England being engaged with Edward III. in the siege of Calais, the kingdom was left comparatively defenceless, and Sir William Fraser, as in duty bound, joined his standard.

As Wyntoun relates, the King assembled his forces at Perth, but, in consequence of the murder of Ronald, Lord of the Isles, by the Earl of Ross, and the quarrels engendered by the commission of that crime, great numbers deserted from him.[4]

However, undeterred by the diminution of his army, David marched to the border, and after taking the peel or small castle of Liddel, advanced into England in spite of the wise advice of Sir William de Douglas, who counselled retreat, and penetrated as far as Durham.

---

[1] Chamberlain Rolls, vol. i. p. 280.
[2] Ibid. p. 380.
[3] Reg. Hon. de Morton, vol. ii. p. 186, No. 197.
[4] Wyntoun, lib. viii. cap. xl.

In the meantime the Archbishop of York, with Lord Percy and other nobles, had assembled the power of the country north of the river Trent, and had so well concealed their measures that the Scottish army had no notice of their approach until they surprised and defeated Douglas when on a foraging excursion; he, however, escaped and brought the intelligence to the King, who immediately set his troops in battle array, divided into three "escheles" or large divisions, of which he himself commanded one, the Earl of Moray and Sir William de Douglas another, and Robert Stewart of Scotland the third, which was considerably the largest.

It is a proof of how little the experience of one generation benefits the next, that the advice and offer of the gallant Sir John de Grahame to charge the English archers with cavalry, a plan that Robert I. had so successfully adopted at Bannockburn, was altogether rejected, and this mistake, combined with a faulty choice of ground, resulted in the complete defeat of the royal army after a long and desperate battle, in which David II. was taken prisoner with many of his nobles and followers; and Sir William Fraser, with the Earl of Moray, Sir David de Hay the Constable, Sir Robert de Keith the Marischal of Scotland, Sir David de Lindesay, and many more, were slain.[1]

Crauford thinks it probable that Sir William Fraser was not killed at the battle of Durham, but taken prisoner, and bases his opinion upon the fact of a William Fraser afterwards getting a safe-conduct to pass through England on his way beyond sea,[2] but investigation shows that this is not a good foundation for his conjecture. A person of the name did get a safe-conduct in 1365, and again in 1374,[3] but in the latter of these he is styled Armiger, or Squire, and could not be the same as William Fraser, Miles, mentioned in the Scotichronicon, or the deceased William Fraser, Miles, whose name is found in a charter to his son John Fraser, from Robert II., in 1373.

Crauford also says that Margaret Moray was his second wife, and that he had been previously married to a lady of the house of Douglas, and, as authority for this, notices a charter of a fourscore merk land in Aberdour, given as a marriage portion with that lady, which he had seen in the inventory of the writs of the Saltoun family, but he is totally in error in this state-

---

[1] Scotichronicon, lib. xiv. cap. iii.   [2] Lives of Officers of State, p. 277.
[3] Rotuli Scotiæ, vol. i. pp. 893, 966.

ment, and must have misapprehended the document, which is still extant.[1] The fourscore merk land in Aberdour was granted not to Sir William Fraser, but to his son Sir Alexander, and was not mentioned as any lady's marriage portion, and there is not the slightest evidence of any such connection with the house of Douglas until the marriage, about the beginning of the next century, of Sir William's grandson, also a William, with a lady of that name, from which Crauford's mistake probably arose.

Sir William Fraser left two sons—

Alexander, who succeeded him in Cowie and Durris.

John, who is mentioned in a charter of the lands of Wester Essintuly, in the thanage of Durris, granted to him by Robert II. in 1373, as filio quondam Willelmi Fraser, "Militis,"[2] and was the first of the family of Forglen and Ardendracht.[3]

SIR ALEXANDER FRASER OF COWIE AND DURRIS, AND FIRST OF PHILORTH. LADY JOHANNA DE ROSS, DAUGHTER OF WILLIAM EARL OF ROSS.

THIS Alexander Fraser is the last in the series of whose parentage it is necessary to adduce circumstantial evidence, for the line of his descendants is sufficiently established by successive inquests, retours, and other registers; and the following circumstances evince him to have been the son and heir of Sir William Fraser, of which any one by itself would suggest the probability, but the four, taken together, afford conclusive evidence.

1. That he was a cousin or blood-relation of David II. and Robert II.
2. That he succeeded to the thanages of Cowie and Durris about the time when, as a son of Sir William Fraser, he would have attained the age of twenty-one.
3. That he had a younger brother, John Fraser, in 1376 and 1385, that a John Fraser was designated as a son of the late Sir William Fraser in 1373, and that this John appears in connection with the barony of Durris on two of these occasions.

[1] Philorth Charter-room.
[3] See Appendix.
[2] Roll ii. of Great Seal Record, No. 17. Antiquities of Aberdeenshire, vol. iii. p. 355.

4. That he was a cousin or blood-relation of the fourth Earl of Douglas, and James Douglas, Lord of Abercorn, but not of their father the third Earl, and that this relationship could only have arisen through their mother, Johanna or Jean Moray of Bothwell, and Margaret Moray, Sir William Fraser's wife, having been related to each other.

By the death of their father at the battle of Durham, in 1346, Alexander Fraser and his brother John were deprived of his protection at a very early age, and during their long minority they were probably wards of the Crown, and were doubtless also befriended by the Marischal, the Morays, the Douglases, and their other powerful relatives and connections.

A statement by Crauford, that Alexander Fraser pursued his studies at the University of Oxford,[1] is of very doubtful authenticity; such was not the course of education deemed most suitable for a youth of good family in that age, unless he were intended for the Church, and more of his hours would be passed in the tilt-yard or the hunting-field than in the chamber of study; indeed, there were but few that could read or write. An Alexander Fraser did obtain safe-conducts to proceed to England in 1361 and 1363, but he was the person of whom some notice will be found in the Appendix. However, although the safe-conduct of 1366, to which Crauford alludes, was granted to a number of clerks or clergymen going to study at Oxford, the Alexander Fresille, whose name appears with theirs, was not designated as a cleric, and as he had a retinue of eight persons, while the prepositus of St. Andrews was accompanied by only six,[2] he was a person of some consequence, and Crauford may be right.

The earliest documentary evidence extant respecting this Alexander Fraser, shows that he succeeded to Durris and Cowie, the two thanages that had been conferred upon Sir William Fraser by David II., and some remarks upon the thanages of Scotland, and the tenure by which they were held, may be permitted here, as their nature and origin have been the subject of discussion by various antiquaries.

None, however, have so ably handled it as Mr. William Skene, in the Appendix to a recently published translation of Fordun's History, where he

[1] Lives of Officers of State, p. 278.   [2] Rotuli Scotiæ, vol. i. p. 905.

has clearly shown that, in the earliest time of which there is any knowledge, the "Tuath" or district in the possession of each Celtic tribe was held in the following manner:—"The Indfine, or commonalty of the Fine or Tribe, possessed the tribe land. The arable land was distributed at stated intervals among the Ceile or free members of the tribe, each having their share, and a redistribution taking place as fresh claimants for a share appeared; the pasture land was pastured in common, according to the number of cattle possessed by each, and the waste land separated each Tuath from another."

"The Orba, or inheritance land, was possessed by the Flaith or nobles of the Fine as individual property," which descended in their families under peculiar laws.

He then relates how "in Scotland proper, that is in the north-eastern lowlands, extending from the Forth to the Moray Firth," by the gradual change from Celtic to Saxon customs and institutions, and by the increasing power of the Crown, "the land possessed by the tribe communities came to be viewed as *terra regis*, or Crown land, and the King became the *dominus* or superior. The tribe land occupied by the commonalty was considered royal demesne, and the inheritance land became the *Thanagium* holding of the King," while he shows in another place that the chief of each tribe, "the Toisech, became the Thane."

He also points out that "the waste land, where it existed, became the royal forest," and that the forest was sometimes separated from the thanage, and each severally dealt with by the sovereign: and, further on, he notices the gradual supersession of the ancient Celtic burdens on the land by those of feudal tenure, and, after the reign of Alexander III., when most of the thanages are found in the hands of the Crown, the change of them into holdings for military service, brought about by the constant conflict with England, and the succession of kings of the Norman race, which was generally followed by their conversion into baronies.[1]

For much other interesting information on the subject the reader is referred to the work whence the above extracts have been taken, in the

[1] Historians of Scotland, Fordun; translated by F. J. H. Skene, Appendix by W. F. Skene, p. 444 to p. 456.

concluding sentences of which it is satisfactory to see that Mr. Skene hopes to recur to the subject at a future time; but it may be here remarked that from the thanage having been the Orba or inheritance land of the nobles of the tribe, the residence of the chief must have been situated there, and it may reasonably be inferred that, after the change which brought the whole tribal possession into the hands of the Crown, such residence, when it was suitable for the purpose, would be converted into a royal castle or fortress, and placed in the custody of the person upon whom the thanage or orba was conferred, while the royal demesne, which had been the tribe land, was also granted to tenants holding direct from the Crown, and not as feudatories of the thanage; and of this last-mentioned tenure an example is found in the charter of Wester Essintuly to John Fraser, the second son of Sir William Fraser, which recites that he was to pay the feu-duty, if demanded, at the Castle of Mount Durris (in the same manner as John de Dalgarnock, his predecessor in the lands, had been bound to do) to the King, not to Sir Alexander Fraser, although the latter was lord of the barony of Durris at the time.

The latter part of this gradual alteration of tenure, as explained by Mr. Skene, is well exemplified in the case of the thanages of Cowie and Durris, for in that of Cowie Robert I. appears dealing separately with the thanage and the forest, inasmuch as he gave a separate charter of each, though both were granted to the same person, Sir Alexander Fraser the Chamberlain, and in the next reign this separation is more distinctly marked, for Sir William de Keith the Marischal obtained the forest in right of his wife, the Chamberlain's granddaughter and heiress, while the thanage was conferred by David II. upon William Fraser, the Chamberlain's second son.

The charter of the forest of Cowie from Robert I. to the Chamberlain and his son, John Fraser, in 1327, conveyed an hereditary right, for it was granted to them and their heirs-general; but it is doubtful whether the Chamberlain held the thanage by a precisely similar destination, and it is very possible that a grant, which may have included the custody of a royal castle, would have been limited to heirs-male. From the charter being no longer extant, however, this point cannot be decided, but must be left to conjecture.

The temporary supersession of all the grants, from Robert I., in the north-east of Scotland, that followed Edward de Baliol's success in 1332, has thrown obscurity over many of the territorial arrangements of that part of the kingdom during the few succeeding years; for the representatives of the Comyns and other exiled families resumed possession of their forfeited estates until again expelled, but it would appear that, when David II. returned to Scotland in 1341, the thanage of Cowie was held to have reverted to the Crown, or at least to have been in ward from the decease of the Chamberlain at the battle of Dupplin (a royal gift or assignation from its revenues was made to John de St. Clair in 1341-2),[1] and that it was granted anew to Sir William Fraser, his second son, and nearest surviving male relative, while the forest passed to his granddaughter and heiress, and her husband, by the destination to heirs-general contained in the charter affecting it.

Upon the early death of Sir William Fraser at the battle of Durham in 1346, the thanage of Cowie and that of Durris, which he had also received, seem again to have been in the hands of the Crown, in ward, as the hereditary estates of his eldest son and heir, Alexander, during his minority; there are found royal gifts or pensions from the revenues of that of Cowie to his mother Margaret de Moravia or Moray, and also to the Countess of Angus, in 1360 and 1362,[2] but these cease about the time when he would have attained to the age of twenty-one; and he appears to have succeeded to both thanages a little before 1367, when, in a Parliament held at Scone in September, it was enacted that all lands of the royal demesne, with the reversions due from them, all rents, cane customs, forest offices, etc., should revert to David II. as fully and thoroughly as his father Robert I. had possessed them at the time of his death; and in a list made in the following January of certain sums collected, or to be collected, for the Crown in consequence of that Act of Parliament, xlix. libř. and xiij. libř. vi. s. viij. d. are said to have been recently in the hands of Alexander Fraser, on account of the thanages of Cowie and Durris respectively.[3]

On the 4th of September 1369, David II. granted "dilecto consanguineo nostro Alexandro Fraser" the whole royal lands of the thanage of Durris, erecting them into a free barony, to be held by him and his heirs from the

---

[1] Chamberlain Rolls, vol. i. p. 281.
[2] *Ibid.* pp. 377, 380, 396.
[3] Acts of the Parliaments of Scotland, vol. i. pp. 168, 170.

Crown for three attendances each year at the Head Court of the sheriffdom of Kincardine, and the service of an archer in the royal army.[1] Although the record of the transition of the thanage of Cowie into a barony in his favour is no longer extant, it probably occurred at this time, for he appears as lord of the barony of Cowie in 1376.

He must have received the honour of knighthood about the same time that he obtained the charters of his baronies, for though not styled "Miles" in that of Durris, he bore the rank in the succeeding year but one at the coronation of Robert II.; and he was also appointed Vicecomes or Sheriff of Aberdeen, in which capacity his name first appears in the Chamberlain Rolls of 1369,[2] when Philip de Dunbreck made a payment as his lieutenant in that office.

The term "consanguineus" (cousin), applied to him in the charter of Durris, was not at that time the mere title of courtesy used by the Sovereign to persons of a certain rank, that it became in a considerably later age, but actually meant what it expressed, blood-relationship, though in a more remote degree than uncle or nephew, of which there is abundant evidence in many royal charters, where the terms expressing various degrees of relationship, avus, pater, mater, filius, filia, patruus, avunculus, nepos, neptis, consanguineus, are found attached to the names of some persons, while those of others, often of the highest rank, who were not related by blood to the King, had no such designation, and although occasionally, but rarely, these terms were not attached to the names of those entitled to them, they were never misapplied to those of others. "Consanguineus" (cousin) correctly defines the relationship between David II. and Sir Alexander Fraser, arising from Lady Mary de Bruce having been the aunt of the former and grandmother of the latter; and it has been shown in the account of Sir Alexander Fraser

---

[1] Copy of Charter, Appendix. The date of this charter is the 4th of September in the fortieth year of the King's reign, which would properly be 1368, but at page 39 of the preface to the first vol. of the Acts of Parliament of Scotland, the late Mr. Cosmo Innes has shown that David II. after his return from his English captivity, in all his charters and public instruments counted the years of his reign one short of the truth, making from 7th June 1357, to the same date 1358, the twenty-eighth year, whereas it really was the twenty-ninth, and consequently the fortieth year of his reign as named in the charter, was in reality the forty-first, or from 7th June 1369 to 7th June 1370.

[2] Chamberlain Rolls, vol. i. p. 506.

the Chamberlain that no blood-relationship could have existed between Robert I. and him.

Sir Alexander was Sheriff of Aberdeen for nearly all the remainder of his life, certainly until the year 1399.

On one or two occasions in 1382 John Fraser's name is found as Vicecomes of Aberdeen;[1] it is possible that during some temporary absence of Sir Alexander, his brother John might have held that appointment, but he himself appears as Vicecomes both before and after that date, and it may be a clerical error, for a John de Forbes acted as his lieutenant in 1374.[2]

As Vicecomes of Aberdeen Sir Alexander Fraser was a witness to a gift by William de Meldrum to the church of St. Nicholas at Aberdeen, and although in the Antiquities of the shires of Aberdeen and Banff, published by the Spalding Club, the date of this charter is stated to be 1342,[3] there is evidence in the document itself that this must be an error, for Alexander, Bishop of Aberdeen, and Sir William de Keith, the Marischal, were also witnesses to it, and no Bishop of Aberdeen bore that name from the death of the first Alexander Kinninmond, on the 14th of August 1340, to the succession of the second Alexander Kinninmond in 1355,[4] while Sir William de Keith did not become Marischal until the death of his father, Sir Edward de Keith, who himself was not Marischal until after the battle of Durham in 1346, where his grandnephew, Sir Robert de Keith, whom he succeeded, was killed; the correct date, therefore, must be later than 1355, and there is good reason for believing it to be 1372, for Sir Alexander Fraser is designated "Miles," or Knight, a rank that he will be seen to have held in 1371, at the coronation of Robert II., but probably had not obtained in 1369, as he is not so styled in the charter of the barony of Durris, which he received in that year.

David II., King of Scotland, died in February 1371, according to present computation of time, and was succeeded by Robert Stewart, who, though his nephew, was several years his senior, and had been guardian of the kingdom during his captivity in England, from 1346 to 1357.

On the 26th of March 1371 Sir Alexander Fraser was one of the barons

[1] Reg. Episc. Aberd., vol. i. p. 142.
[2] Chamberlain Rolls, vol. ii. p. 73.
[3] Antiquities of Aberdeen, vol. iii. p. 45.
[4] Reg. Episc. Aberd., vol. ii. p. 248.

that attended the coronation of Robert II., and on the following day did homage to the King, and affirmed in Parliament the order of succession to the Crown; and two years later, on the 4th of April 1373, he attended another Parliament, where a second and more precise settlement of the succession was enacted; and on both of these occasions his name immediately follows that of Sir James Fraser of Frendraught, his father's first cousin, who was therefore of the generation preceding him, and probably his senior in knighthood.[1]

In 1375 Sir Alexander Fraser married Johanna, second daughter of William, Earl of Ross, whose elder daughter and heiress married Sir Walter de Leslie, a younger son of Sir Andrew de Leslie, and his wife Mary, daughter and co-heiress of Sir Alexander de Abernethy.

The earldom of Ross was an ancient dignity. King Malcolm the Maiden addressed a precept in favour of the Abbey of Dunfermline to Malcolm, Earl of Ross, in 1162; and Ferquhard, Earl of Ross, appears between 1222 and 1231,[2] and is said to have founded the Abbey of Fern. He was succeeded by his son, William, who, in 1258, confirmed his father's charter to the monks of Fern,[3] and was probably the Earl present at the Parliament held in 1283-4, to regulate the succession to the throne. His son, William, sat as Earl of Ross in the Parliament at Brigham, in 1290, and was one of the auditors appointed on the part of Baliol at the competition for the Crown.[4] In 1306 he took part against Robert I., and the Queen having fallen into his hands after she fled from Kildromie Castle, he surrendered her to the English authorities;[5] but on the reconquest of the north of Scotland by Bruce in 1308, he submitted, and continued a faithful liegeman, having been a witness to the treaty between the King and Haco, King of Norway, in 1312.[6] He left two sons and a daughter.

Hugh, his successor in the earldom.

John, who married Margaret, daughter of the Earl of Buchan, and with her received a grant from the Crown of half the lands of that earldom,[7] which had been forfeited in 1308, but they had no issue.

[1] Acts of the Parliaments of Scotland, vol. i. pp. 181, 185.
[2] Douglas Peerage, quoting Cart. Dunferm., 186. *Ibid.* quoting Cart. Morav., 314.
[3] *Ibid.* quoting Cart. Morav., 312.
[4] *Ibid.* quoting Rymer's Fœdera.
[5] Barbour's Bruce, p. 76.
[6] Acts of the Parliaments of Scotland, vol. i. p. 103.
[7] Robertson's Index, p. 2, No. 44.

Isabella, who was the wife of Sir Edward de Bruce, the King's brother.

The eldest son, Hugh, Earl of Ross, seems to have become possessed of the half of the earldom of Buchan on the decease of his brother John, for in 1330 he renounced the advowson of the Church of Philorth, in that district, in favour of the Crown.[1] He commanded one of the divisions of the Scottish army at Halidon Hill, and fell in that battle after a long and desperate struggle.[2] He had no issue by his first wife, Jean, daughter of Walter Steward of Scotland; but by his second, Lady Matilda de Bruce, sister of Robert I., he had two, perhaps three, sons and two daughters.[3]

William, who succeeded him in the earldom.

Hugh, generally known as Hugh of Rarichies, to whom his father, or brother, appears to have given a considerable portion of the half of the earldom of Buchan.

Euphemia, who married, first, John Randolph, Earl of Moray, killed at the battle of Durham in 1346; and, secondly, Robert Stewart, afterwards Robert II., at whose accession she became Queen of Scotland.

Janet, who married, first, Sir John de Monymusk; and, secondly, Sir Alexander Moray of Abercairny.

William, Earl of Ross, joined the army assembled at Perth in 1346 by David II. for the invasion of England, but having slain Ranald, Lord of the Isles, at Elihok (Elcho), in that neighbourhood, he deserted with all his men, and retired to his own district of Ross, and his proceedings caused many others to abandon their sovereign's standard, and materially reduced his forces.[4]

He is said to have married a daughter of Malise, Earl of Strathearn, and by her had a son, William, who was nominated one of the hostages for the payment of the ransom of David II. in 1357, but was too ill at the time to proceed to England,[5] and seems to have died soon afterwards; and two daughters, Euphemia and Johanna.

Euphemia, the elder of the two, before 1365, and apparently against the will of her father, married, as already mentioned, Sir Walter de Leslie, who

---

[1] Robertson's Index, p. 29, No. 22. Acts of the Parliaments of Scotland, vol. i. p. 153.
[2] Wyntoun, lib. viii. c. xxvii.
[3] Ibid. lib. viii. c. vii.
[4] Wyntoun, lib. viii. c. xl.
[5] Rymer's Fœdera, vol. v. p. 792; vol. vi. pp. 35-47.

was in high favour with David II.; and the king, who evidently remembered the Earl's crime and its consequences, not only countenanced their union, but took measures to prevent him from punishing his daughter's disobedience, and for that purpose compelled him to resign his whole earldom and possessions for reinfeftment.

Upon his resignation at Perth on the 23d of October 1370, the King granted a charter of the whole earldom of Ross, the lordship of Skye, and all the other lordships, lands, and pertinents within the kingdom that had belonged to the Earl before his resignation, with the exception of those within the sheriffdoms of Aberdeen, Dumfries, and Wigtown, first, to the Earl himself and the heirs-male of his body; whom failing, secondly, to Sir Walter de Leslie and Euphemia, his wife, or the survivor of them, and to the heirs of the body of Euphemia, with the proviso that if heirs-male should fail, then the eldest daughter, whether of Euphemia or her heirs, should take the whole earldom, lordships, lands, etc., granted by the charter, without division or partition in any way; and should the issue of Euphemia fail, then, thirdly, to Johanna, younger daughter of the Earl, and her heirs, with a similar proviso as to the succession of the eldest daughter, failing heirs-male.[1]

A "querimonia," or petition, is extant from the Earl of Ross to Robert II., complaining that his lands and those of his brother, Hugh de Ross, in Buchan, had been taken from them by David II. without their having been cited, tried, and convicted of any offence, and that these lands had been bestowed by that king upon Sir Walter de Leslie. The querimonia, after detailing these and other grievances, affording a glimpse at the rough proceedings of the age, goes on to declare that the Earl only ratified this gift of his own, and his brother's, lands to Sir Walter under compulsion, and in fear of the anger of King David if he had refused to do so. He also complains that Sir Walter had married his daughter Euphemia against his will, and says that up to the death of the late king he had not made any concession of lands or goods to her, nor any agreement with her, except such as he was compelled to enter into by David II.[2]

[1] Acts of the Parliaments of Scotland, vol. i. p. *177. Antiquities of Aberdeen, vol. ii. p. 386.

[2] Philorth Charter-room. Antiquities of Aberdeen, vol. ii. p. 387.

However, the "querimonia" appears to have had no effect,—perhaps it was considered a bad precedent to question the rights of the Crown,—and Sir Walter de Leslie, with his wife, Euphemia, after her father's death within the next two years, enjoyed the dignities and estates conferred by the charter in full right and peaceful possession, Sir Walter as Dominus de Ross, and his wife as Countess.

The lands in the sheriffdoms of Aberdeen, Dumfries, and Wigtown, taken by David II. from the Earl and his brother Hugh, were evidently the half of the earldom of Buchan that had been granted by Robert I. to their uncle John on his marriage with Margaret de Comyn; and on John's death without issue they seem to have come into the possession of their father, Hugh, Earl of Ross, and so to have passed to them.

The king would seem to have claimed these lands as properly reverting to the Crown, in consequence of the failure of John's issue, instead of to the Earl of Ross; and having enforced his claim, he granted them to Sir Walter de Leslie, who out of them, as will immediately appear, satisfied the claims of Johanna, as coheiress of the estates of the earldom of Ross, without infringing the restrictions in the royal charter of 1370, which forbade partition between heirs-female.

On the 4th June 1375 Sir Alexander Fraser and his wife, Johanna, received a charter from Sir Walter de Leslie, Dominus de Ross,[1] of all the lands of Philorth, which are thus enumerated: "terras de Kirktoun, Cairnbuilg, Inuerolochy, Ardglassey, Kinglasse cum molendino, Kinbog, Ardmakren, duos Brakours, Auchintuin, Auchmacludy, Braklawmoir, terras de maiore Drumquhendill et minore Drumquhendill, Auchinchogill, Plady, Loncardy, et Delgady, cum le Querell, terras de maiore Fintrie, Balchern, et Blaktoune," all within the sheriffdom of Aberdeen; the lands of Ferdonald, in Ross, with a pension of £80 sterling, in the sheriffdom of Inverness; and the lands of the barony of Kregiltoun, with "quadraginta libras tenendriarum," in Galloway (Sir Walter reserving to himself, and his wife Euphemia, the castle of Kregiltoun, "cum residuo tenendriarum"), to be held by them, or the survivor, and their heirs, in chief of the Crown, as fully and freely as Sir Walter and Euphemia held their own lands, and in

[1] Transumpt, Philorth Charter-room. Antiquities of Aberdeen, vol. iv. p. 87.

compensation and satisfaction of Johanna's claims as heir-portioner upon the lands of the earldom of Ross.[1]

This charter and another of similar import were confirmed by Robert III. on 28th October 1405, thirty years after they had been granted.[2]

These lands, constituting the ancient lordship of Philorth, seem to have comprised very considerable portions of the present parishes of Fraserburgh, Rathen, Pitsligo, Aberdour, Tyrie, and Strichen, lying around the Hill of Mormond, the highest land in Buchan, which attains an elevation of 800 feet above the sea, from which it is distant from three to four miles on its northern and eastern sides. The surrounding country is undulating, and even in that early age must have contained many tracts of considerable fertility, which recent reclamation and improvement have extended to the whole area, with trivial exceptions. The north branch of the river Ugie flows in a south-easterly direction at no great distance to the south of Mormond, and forms a junction with the southern branch a few miles further on, the united waters falling into the sea near the town of Peterhead. A small stream, called the water of Philorth, rises in the uplands to the west of Mormond, and, taking an easterly course, runs along the northern base of that hill, and passing Rathen enters the sea near the south end of the bay of Fraserburgh, formerly called the bay of Philorth. About three furlongs from the sea, upon a little knoll close to the south bank of the stream, stands the old Manor Place of Philorth, now called the castle of Cairnbulg, an extensive and picturesque ruin; there are signs of a moat having once surrounded the knoll, and as the land is flat for a considerable distance on every side except the south, and was at that time very marshy, the castle must have been a strong fortress, for the rising ground on the south is not near enough to have enabled the rude engines used in war before the introduction of cannon to command it. The country generally is bare of wood, except in the vicinity

---

[1] A slight inaccuracy in "The Bruces and the Comyns," by Mrs. Cumming Bruce, may here be corrected. At page 427 the authoress terms the Lords Saltoun, i.e. the Frasers of Philorth, "descendants" of the second son of Hugh, Earl of Ross. The word "successors" in place of "descendants" would rectify the error in an otherwise correct passage, as they did succeed Hugh de Ross in some of his lands, though descended from his elder brother William, through Johanna de Ross.

[2] Transumpt, Philorth Charter-room. Antiquities of Aberdeen, vol. ii. p. 351.

CAIRNBULG CASTLE,

THE OLD MANOR HOUSE OF PHILORTH.

of the mansions of Crimonmogate, belonging to Miss Bannerman, Cairness, to J. W. Gordon, Esquire, and Cortes, to W. F. Cordiner, Esquire, towards the east; while upon and beyond the southern boundary of the district the estates of Strichen, Pitfour, Aden, and Brucklay are tolerably clothed. About a mile to the north-west of the old castle the present house of Philorth stands in the midst of extensive plantations, and about two miles further westward, and the same distance to the north of Mormond Hill, a low wooded range of rising ground runs for about a mile and a half east and west, with a breadth of a little over a quarter of a mile, called the Sinclair Hills, having derived its name from a family anciently settled in the district. Hugh de Ross, Lord of Philorth (from whom, with his elder brother, the Earl of Ross, David II. evicted the half of the lands of the earldom of Buchan, and bestowed them on Sir Walter de Leslie, as above related), granted the lands of Easter Tyrie to Alexander de St. Clair, the son of Thomas de St. Clair; and though the king had dispossessed the granter, Hugh de Ross, in October 1370, he confirmed the charter to the sub-tenant in November of the same year.[1] Although this branch of the St. Clairs left its name to a feature of the country, it does not appear to have remained long in that district, and having possessions in other parts of Scotland, probably soon abandoned those it held in Buchan.

About two miles northward of the Sinclair Hills, near the north-eastern corner of the coast, stood, at that date, the village of Faithlie (the site upon which, in after ages, the town of Fraserburgh was built), which, with a small tract of land around it, including the high bluff of Kinaird's Head (probably of old "Ceann ard," the high head), the promontorium Taixalium of Ptolemy, seems to have been then distinct from the lordship of Philorth. Sir Walter de Leslie and his wife, Euphemia, Countess of Ross, granted Faithlie and Tyrie to Andrew Mercer in 1381, and they remained in the possession of his descendants until sold by Sir Henry Mercer of Aldie to Sir William Fraser of Philorth in 1504.[2]

There were also various small estates within the area above referred to, such as Pitblae, Aucheries, New Forest, etc., held by sub-tenants from the

[1] Robertson's Index, p. 58, No. 10; p. 91, No. 273.
[2] Philorth Charter-room.

Earls Marischal and other superior lords; but by far the greater part was included in the estate or lordship of Philorth, which Sir Alexander Fraser acquired by his marriage with Lady Johanna de Ross, to which must be added outlying properties of considerable extent in Aberdeenshire and Banffshire, some of which he almost immediately bestowed upon his brother, John Fraser.

In 1376 Sir Alexander Fraser, Lord of Cowie, granted to his brother, John Fraser, the lands of Auchinshogill, Plady, Loncardy, Delgady, and others in that neighbourhood, in the valley of the Deveron.[1]

This John Fraser, described as son of the late Sir William Fraser, in 1373 had obtained from Robert II. a charter of the lands of Wester Essintuly, resigned by Sir John de Dalgarnok, for which he was to do suit and service at the royal castle of the thanage of Durris; and about 1387-8, having come into possession of the lands of Forglen by a grant from the Abbot of Arbroath, he was styled dominus of that place.[2]

The estates bestowed upon his brother by Sir Alexander were part of those he had received from Sir Walter de Leslie, and it seems for some years to have been doubtful how far it was in his power to alienate estates acquired by his marriage, for in 1385 Sir Alexander gave to his brother John a letter of obligation, to the effect that he should have the whole lands of the barony of Durris in compensation, if by any legal process he should be ejected from possession of Auchinshogill, and the other properties in Buchan that he had granted to him. No such eviction, however, occurred, and John Fraser retained those estates, which, by the terms of the charter of 1376, were to be held by him and his heirs as feudatories of Sir Alexander and his heirs, for the delivery of a pair of gilt spurs at the manor place of Philorth, on each feast of Pentecost; and this charter was confirmed in 1397, during his father's lifetime, by William Fraser, who is styled son and heir of Sir Alexander Fraser, Lord of Cowie.[3]

---

[1] Antiquities of Aberdeen, vol. i. p. 470.
[2] *Ibid.* p. 511.
[3] In the Antiquities of Aberdeenshire, published by the Spalding Club, vol. ii. p. 352, the name of the granter of this obligation is printed "John," in mistake for "Alexander." In the original document, Philorth Charter-room, the name is contracted, and much defaced; this may have caused the error, which is evident from the name of the recipient being "John," and from the charter of 1376, printed in vol. i. p. 470 of the Antiquities.

THE FRASERS OF COWIE, DURRIS, AND PHILORTH.

A dispute having arisen between Adam, Bishop of Aberdeen, and John, Lord of Forbes, it was settled by arbitration in 1387, and Sir Alexander Fraser, Vicecomes of Aberdeen, John Fraser of Forglen, and Thomas Fraser of Cornetoun, with some others, were the arbiters appointed on the part of the bishop.[1]

In the same year, on the 19th of October, Robert II. confirmed a charter from Sir Alexander Fraser, whom the king terms "consanguineus noster," to Alexander Bannerman, burgess of Aberdeen, of the lands of Alesick, now Elsick, in the barony of Cowie.[2]

In 1388 Sir Alexander Fraser accompanied the heroic James, second Earl of Douglas, on his expedition into Northumberland. Froissart, in his Chronicle, says that the main Scottish army, under Sir Archibald Douglas, Lord of Galloway, the Earl of Fife, and Sir Stephen Freseyle,[3] marched towards Carlisle, while a smaller division, commanded by James Earl of Douglas, with the Earls of Moray and March, and other leaders, entered Northumberland, crossed the Tyne at Brancepeth, and ravaged the country as far as Durham. It then retired, and laid siege to Newcastle-on-Tyne, which was defended by Sir Henry Percy and his brother, Ralph, where, in one of the encounters at the barriers, Douglas captured Percy's pennon, and, on raising the siege, vowed to carry it into Scotland, and to place it on his Castle of Dalkeith.

To recover his pennon and avenge the insult, Sir Henry Percy, having collected a considerable force, pursued the Scottish army, and overtaking their leisurely march at Otterbourne, where they had halted to reduce the castle of that name, fought the desperate battle in which "Douglas, though victor, was slain, and the Percy led captive away," having surrendered to Montgomerie of Eaglesham, ancestor of the Earls of Eglinton.

Froissart, who received his information from two French knights present at the engagement, describes it as the most fiercely fought and severest encounter of his time, and says that he can only liken one other to it, that of Cocherel.

[1] Reg. Episc. Aberdon., vol. i. p. 176.
[2] Antiquities of Aberdeen, vol. iv. p. 642.
[3] He may have been a Fraser of Fruid, or perhaps one of a family that bore the territorial name de Freslay or de Freslaw, and were domini de Arringrosk and Fourgy. Reg. de Cambuskenneth, pp. 6-23.

118   THE FRASERS OF COWIE, DURRIS, AND PHILORTH.

He gives the numbers of the English as 9000, and those of the Scottish forces as but 3000, an enormous disproportion of three to one, but points out that the latter had the advantage of rest, position, and the wise precaution taken by the Earl of Douglas to organise his plan of battle, in case of a night attack, which foresight was one cause of Percy's defeat, who, as anticipated by his adversary, did make his attack in the night, and his front being engaged in the assault of the Scottish camp, where it encountered desperate resistance, was himself assailed on the flank by a large force, led on by Douglas in person.

The effect of this attack in flank was tremendous, and altogether disorganised the English array, and though, upon a rally being made by part of their army, Douglas was overpowered by numbers and mortally wounded, far in advance of the bulk of his forces, who could not reach the spot to which his prodigious strength and heroic valour had carried him in time to save his life; yet, as the English were unaware that it was he whom they had slain, the exertions of the Earl of Moray and the other commanders, who by his dying orders concealed his fate, raised his banner and continued his war-cry of Douglas! Douglas! as if he were still leading them on, completed the defeat of the English, which speedily became an utter rout.[1]

Sir Henry Percy and his brother, Sir Ralph, with many other gentlemen, were made prisoners, and their dispersed army chased for miles from the field of battle, 1040 having been slain in the flight, and 1840 falling in the pursuit, while the Scottish loss was only 100 killed and 200 taken prisoners.

The name of Sir Alexander Fraser is recorded by Froissart among those of whom he says, "Il n'y avoit nul qui n'entendist bien, et vaillement, a faire a besogne" in this desperate encounter;[2] and he had the good fortune to escape the fate that befell his gallant leader and some of his brave comrades.

After a rest of three days, and holding at bay the Bishop of Durham (who

[1] The account of the death of Douglas at Otterbourne, by Froissart, is one of the most interesting and graphically told events in the pages of that eloquent chronicler of gallant and knightly feats of arms.

[2] Buchon's ed. of Froissart, vol. ii. p. 730.

with 20,000 men appeared the day after the battle, but retired without daring to attack), the army, under the Earl of Moray's command, continued its retreat into Scotland with its prisoners (among whom were more than forty knights), and the booty it had gained during the expedition, but at the same time carrying the dead body of its late beloved leader in mournful procession.

Sir Archibald Douglas, surnamed the Grim, Lord of Galloway and Bothwell (who became third Earl of Douglas), granted a charter, confirmed by Robert II. in 1378, of 80 merks worth of the lands and mills of Aberdour, in the sheriffdom of Aberdeen, to Sir Alexander Fraser, whom he terms "confederato nostro" (our ally or comrade),[1] to be held of the Earl and his heirs; whom failing, of his Countess Johanna and her heirs, Lords of the lordship of Aberdour, which seems to infer that this lordship was part of the estate which the Countess brought to her husband.

On the 31st October 1408, James of Douglas, Lord of Abercorn and Aberdour, younger son of the third Earl, granted a charter of Little Drumquhendil to Patrick Reed Ramsay,[2] upon the resignation of Sir Alexander Fraser, whom he calls "Domini Alexandri Fraser, Militis, consanguinei nostri" (our cousin), which was confirmed by Archibald, fourth Earl of Douglas, and although Sir Alexander is not named as a cousin of his own by the Earl, he must have borne that relationship to him also, for both brothers styled his son William "consanguineus" in other documents.[3]

The third Earl of Douglas had become Lord of Bothwell by his marriage with Johanna or Jean, daughter and heiress of Sir Thomas Moray, who was second son of the famous Sir Andrew Moray of Bothwell, and had succeeded

---

[1] Philorth Charter-room. Antiquities of Aberdeen, vol. iv. p. 113. This is the charter of the 80 merk land in Aberdour seen by Crawfurd.

[2] Slains Charter-room. Antiquities of Aberdeenshire, vol. i. p. 448.

[3] Philorth Charter-room. Antiquities of Aberdeenshire, vol. ii. p. 375. The lands of Little Drumquhendil had been given to Sir Alexander Fraser in 1375, by Sir Walter de Leslie, as part of the lordship of Philorth, to be held in chief of the Crown; but here, a few years later, the Lord of Aberdour and his brother, the fourth Earl of Douglas, appear as overlords of them. It is probable, as was not uncommon, that one portion of the estate was included in the lordship of Philorth; and another portion in that of Aberdour, which last may have been part of the 80 merks worth of land given by the third Earl to Sir Alexander Fraser before 1378.

his elder brother John, who died without issue; and the terms of these charters evince that, although there was no blood relationship between the third Earl and Sir Alexander Fraser, whom he calls " confederato nostro," such relationship did exist between the latter and the two sons of the former, the fourth Earl and James de Douglas, who were the children of his wife, Johanna Moray of Bothwell; and as this blood relationship could only have originated through her, it affords good ground for the conclusion that Margaret Moray the wife of Sir William Fraser, was Sir Alexander's mother, that she was of the Bothwell family, and a daughter of Sir Andrew Moray, which is strengthened by the appearance of her name in such close proximity with that of John Moray, as already noticed, and also by the probability referred to above that Aberdour was part of Johanna Moray's own estate, upon which Sir Alexander may have had some claim through his mother.

Lady Johanna de Ross, Sir Alexander Fraser's first wife, died before 1400, for in that year a lady of the name of Hamilton appears as his wife, who is said to have been of the family of Cadzou, ancestors of the ducal house of Hamilton.

In 1400 he granted, with the consent of his wife, Lady Elizabeth de Hamilton, who seems to have been infeft in the estate to secure her jointure, certain lands in the barony of Durris to his illegitimate son, Alexander Fraser, to be held under himself and Elizabeth de Hamilton, or the survivor, and under the heirs of this second marriage; and failing such heirs, he granted him the whole barony of Durris, to be held under himself and his heirs, with a proviso that if the grantee should die without legitimate issue, the barony should revert to himself or his heirs.[1]

As there was no issue of the second marriage, this Alexander Fraser obtained the whole lands of the barony in accordance with the terms of the charter, and was the immediate ancestor of the family of Durris.[2]

A charter is on record, granted in 1406 by Alexander Fraser, Lord of Philorth and Clogstoune, to his cousin, Joneta Makgillumquha, giving her the lands of Closerath and Drumdowle, in the barony of Clogstoune and

[1] Antiquities of Aberdeen, vol. iii. p. 362.
[2] See Appendix, The Frasers of Durris.

sheriffdom of Wigtown; but who this lady was, or how her cousinship with him arose, cannot be ascertained.[1]

The seal of Sir Alexander Fraser has not been discovered, but it may be noticed that from his acquisition of Philorth and other estates by his marriage with the heiress, Johanna de Ross, their descendants quartered the arms of the Earls of Ross with the Fraser rosettes or cinquefoils.

These arms were gules, three lions rampant argent, as appear on the seals of Euphemia, Countess of Ross, and her uncle, Hugh de Ross, Lord of Philorth.

It is also probable that he adopted the crest that has since been used by the family, an ostrich holding a horse-shoe in its beak, which may have been taken from the supporters of the arms of the great family of Comyn, Earls of Buchan, of whose property Philorth had formerly been a part.

After an active life, Sir Alexander Fraser died in or shortly before 1411, as in October of that year William, his only son by his first marriage, appears as Dominus de Philorth, and in possession of the family estates.

By his second wife, who survived him, he had no issue.

Euphemia, Countess of Ross, 1381.   Hugh de Ross, Lord of Philorth, 1365.

SIR WILLIAM FRASER,
OF COWIE AND DURRIS, AND SECOND OF PHILORTH.

ELINOR DE DOUGLAS,   MARJORIE?
PROBABLY NATURAL DAUGHTER OF SECOND
EARL OF DOUGLAS.

In the year 1397, William Fraser confirmed his father's charter of Auchinshogill, Plady, Loncardy, Delgattie, etc., to his uncle, John Fraser.[2] He is

[1] Antiquities of Aberdeen, vol. iv. p. 642.
[2] Charter-room, Slains. Antiquities of Aberdeenshire, vol. i. p. 470; vol. ii. p. 352.

styled "filius et heres domini Alexandri Fraser, militis, domini baronie de Cowy, ac dominus de Filorth," and, therefore, he was probably born about 1376, and infeft in Philorth on his mother's decease.

About 1404 he married a lady of the Douglas family, for, on the 8th of December in that year, Isabel de Douglas, Countess of Mar and the Garioch, gave a charter of the lands of Tibarty and Utlaw, in the barony of "Strauthaveth," in the sheriffdom of Banff, " dilecto nostro affini Gulielmo Fraser, et Elinore de Duglas, sponse sue . . . in libero maritagio."[1]

The parentage of Elinor de Douglas is uncertain. Crawfurd says that she was a daughter of Archibald the Grim, third Earl of Douglas. The same view is taken in the Peerage by Douglas, who erroneously calls her husband "Alexander Fraser." This account of her parentage seems scarcely correct, for if she had been a daughter of the third Earl, his two sons, the fourth Earl and James de Douglas, Lord of Abercorn, would have been brothers-in-law to her husband, William Fraser, and would have designated him accordingly, instead of by the term "consanguineus," or cousin, which they will be seen to have used to him.

Taking into consideration the probable date of her birth, about 1385, and that she was dowered by Isabella, Countess of Mar, it may be conjectured that she was an illegitimate daughter of that lady's brother, the gallant James, second Earl of Douglas and Earl of Mar, who fell at Otterburn in 1388.

William Fraser obtained the lands of Over and Nether Pittullie, Pitsligach, Culburty, and others, all within the barony of Aberdour, in 1408, on the resignation of his father, who reserved his own superiority and the terce of Lady Elizabeth Hamilton, his second wife. In pursuance of the resignation, the superior, James de Douglas, Lord of Abercorn and Aberdour, granted a charter of these subjects "carissimo consanguineo nostro Willelmo Fraser," which was confirmed in the same year by Archibald, fourth Earl of Douglas, who used similar terms in the designation of the grantee.[2]

[1] Antiquities of Aberdeenshire, vol. iii. p. 576. The grandfather of the Countess, Donald, Earl of Mar, and William Fraser's grandmother, Margaret Moray, were half brother and sister, children of Lady Christian de Bruce by her first husband, Gratney, Earl of Mar, and her third, Sir Andrew Moray of Bothwell.

[2] Philorth Charter-room.

THE FRASERS OF COWIE, DURRIS, AND PHILORTH.

On the 10th of July 1410, the fourth Earl of Douglas gave a bond for one hundred merks, "dilecto consanguineo nostro Vilhelmo Fraser de Philorth, militi,"[1] which shows that William Fraser had received the honour of knighthood before that date. His succession to the estates must have occurred before the end of the next year, for, on the 31st October 1411, as dominus de Philorth, he issued to his bailie, John de Inchmartyn, canon of Aberdeen, a precept of sasine in favour of Alexander, dominus de Forbes, of the lands of Mykle Fintra, the half of Tulymald, Blactoun, with the Smithill, Miltoun of Kynnedwart, Belcors, and an annualrent of ten shillings from the town of Edane, all in the barony of Kynedwart. It is probable that the Lord of Forbes had purchased these properties from him.[2]

During Sir William Fraser's life the power and influence of the family of Philorth suffered serious diminution, in consequence of his having been obliged to part with very considerable portions of the estates which he inherited from his parents.

There is no positive information as to the cause of these misfortunes and pecuniary difficulties, but they may have arisen from his having been implicated in some of the political disturbances of that unquiet age. One of the most serious of these commotions was connected with the earldom of Ross, and in this he may have been involved by his near relationship to Alexander de Leslie, Earl of Ross, and his sister, Margaret de Leslie, the wife of Donald, Lord of the Isles, who were his first cousins.

Alexander de Leslie, Earl of Ross, married Isabel, daughter of Robert, Duke of Albany, afterwards Regent, by whom he had an only daughter, who bore the name of Euphemia after her paternal grandmother, and on her father's death in 1402, succeeded to the earldom of Ross.

It was probably the old contention, so often met with, that among heirs-female, a daughter is nearer heir than a son's daughter, which induced Donald, Lord of the Isles, to assert the claim of his wife, Margaret de Leslie, to the earldom of Ross; but the claim was repelled by the Regent, and the result was the rebellion of the Lord of the Isles, his devastation of the northern districts nearly as far as Aberdeen, and the battle of Harlaw, in the summer of 1411, after which he was compelled to retreat.

[1] Antiquities of Aberdeenshire, vol. iv. p. 85.　　　[2] Ibid. vol. iii. p. 534.

Whether Sir William Fraser was implicated in this rebellion it is impossible to say, but let the facts be noticed, that, in October 1411, he sold certain lands to the Lord of Forbes; that two years later he was obliged to make a further sacrifice of his estates, and on the 10th October 1413 sold the baronies of Collie (Cowie) and Durris (saving the right of his stepmother, Lady Elizabeth de Hamilton, who was infeft in them) to William de Hay, Lord of Errol and Constable of Scotland, "for a sowme of sylure beforehand in my mykyle mistre to me payit;" and it will not seem improbable that, upon the repulse of the Lord of the Isles at Harlaw in 1411, and his forced submission in the following year, Sir William may have been heavily fined for acts of commission or of omission during the preceding disturbances.

The connection of Cowie with the Fraser name ceased altogether, and there is no later trace of it, with the exception of a service in 1461 of the son and successor of Sir William, as heir to his grandfather, which will be mentioned in its place; but Durris eventually passed to the Alexander Fraser to whom it had been granted if there was no issue of his father, Sir Alexander's, second marriage, and his descendants continued in possession of that estate for many years.[1]

Sir William Fraser also sold the lands of Ardlaw, with the mill of Bodychell, to John, natural son of Sir John, Lord of Gordon, in 1418, and the sale was confirmed by Sir James de Douglas, Lord of Abercorn and Aberdour, in 1423.[2]

In 1423 he had to encounter a most serious danger, and not only lost further parts of his property, but was forced to resist an attack upon his position as a tenant-in-chief of the Crown.

The second Euphemia, Countess of Ross, took the veil, and became Abbess of Elcho, a course doubtless highly approved by the crafty Regent who before 1415 had obtained from her a resignation of the earldom, for a regrant to herself and the heirs of her body; whom failing, to John Stewart, Earl of Buchan, the Regent's eldest son by his marriage with Muriel de Keith, and the heirs-male of his body; whom failing, to the Earl's brother, Robert Stewart, and the heirs-male of his body; whom failing, to revert to the Crown; and on the 15th June in that year he granted a charter

[1] See Appendix, Frasers of Durris. [2] Antiquities of Aberdeenshire, vol. ii. p. 378.

of the earldom to her and the other heirs in that succession.[1] The design of the Regent may partly have been to reduce the power of one of the great feudatories of the Crown; but in these proceedings it is evident that while he maintained to a certain extent the charter of 1370 from King David II. to William, Earl of Ross, by which alone could Euphemia pretend to any right in the subjects that she resigned, he sought to set aside the further destinations contained in that charter, and to reverse them in favour of his own sons.

Some success may have attended his designs; but if so, it was only temporary, for Margaret de Leslie was Countess of Ross before her death in 1429, and was succeeded in the earldom by her son, Alexander, Lord of the Isles, who, in 1449, was succeeded by his son, John, Lord of the Isles.

Sir William Fraser had two daughters; Agnes, probably the elder, married William de Forbes of Kinaldie, whose elder brother, Sir Alexander, dominus de Forbes, was one of the most steadfast allies and intimate friends of John Stewart, Earl of Buchan. Isabel, the other daughter, married Gilbert Menzies.

In pursuance of the plans originated by the Regent, the Earl of Buchan, by virtue of the charter of 15th June 1415, and upon the retirement of Euphemia without heirs of her body, ignored altogether the charters of 1375 from Sir Walter de Leslie and his wife, the first Euphemia, Countess of Ross, to Sir Alexander Fraser and his spouse Johanna, the sister of the Countess. He granted charters, of date 24th September[2] and 6th November[3] 1423, in the latter of which he claimed, as superior of the barony of Kinedwart, and upon the recital of a resignation of the subjects by Sir William Fraser, to re-grant the lands of the lordship of Philorth to William Fraser and Marjorie his wife, or the longer liver of them, and to the heirs-male of the body of William Fraser; whom failing, to William de Forbes of Kinaldie, and Agnes his wife, daughter of William Fraser, or the longer liver of them, and the heirs of the body of William de Forbes; whom failing, to Sir Alexander de Forbes, Lord of Forbes, and the

[1] Original Charter in the Rothes Charter-chest.
[2] Antiquities of Aberdeenshire, vol. iv. p. 86.
[3] Forglen Charter-chest.

heirs of his body: thus setting aside the heirs of the body of Agnes Fraser, and also Sir William Fraser's other daughter, Isabel, and her heirs, and providing for the succession of the Forbes family, in the event of the decease, without issue, of Sir William Fraser's only son Alexander.

The resignation by Sir William Fraser, embodied in this charter, cannot have been an act of his free will. It is possible that it may have been inserted without his knowledge, or, more probably, it may have been extorted by force, and, therefore, not regarded as binding by him. There is not sufficient evidence extant to determine which was the case, but Sir William Fraser, either upon becoming aware of the Earl's proceedings, or upon regaining freedom of action, on the 4th March 1425, procured a transumpt or judicial copy, under the Great Seal, of the confirmation by King Robert III. in 1405 of the charters given in 1375 by Sir Walter de Leslie and his wife, the Countess, to Sir Alexander Fraser and his spouse, Johanna de Ross,[1] evidently for the purpose of resisting the usurpation of superiority on the part of the Earl, by proving that those charters, which granted the lordship of Philorth, and the other lands conveyed by them, to be held in chief of the Crown, were genuine documents, and had received the royal confirmation.

He appears to have succeeded in establishing this, and to have maintained his right to hold Philorth direct from the Crown, without the intervention of a subject-superior, for although, on the 30th May 1432, the Earl of Buchan's charter was confirmed by King James I.,[2] and, in 1437, Sir William's son, Alexander Fraser, procured a transumpt of the charter of 1375 by Sir Walter de Leslie and his wife, the Countess[3] (the confirmation having been probably obtained by the Forbes family privately, to be used should opportunity occur, and the transumpt having been, in all likelihood, due to some revival of their claim), no further serious action seems to have been taken in the matter, and the pretended superiority of the Earl of Buchan was never admitted, or legally enforced.

But Sir William Fraser was obliged to give a considerable part of his remaining estates as a marriage portion to his daughter Agnes; and on the 24th August 1424, he granted to her and William de Forbes of Kinaldie, and

[1] Philorth Charter-room.   [2] Forglen Charter-chest.   [3] Philorth Charter-room.

the heirs of their bodies; whom failing, to Sir Alexander, dominus de Forbes, and the heirs of his body; the lands of Glaslach, Culcoak, Tulynamolt, Nether, Over, and Middlemas Bulgny, Achlun, Petslegach (Pitsligo), etc.; and this charter, with its confirmation by James de Douglas, Lord of Balvenie, the superior of Aberdour, was confirmed by King James I. in 1426.[1]

A former charter of these lands had been granted by Sir James de Douglas, on the 24th July 1423, to William de Forbes and his wife, Agnes, upon the resignation of her father; and the further destination of them to the Lord of Forbes in 1424, may have arisen from some attempt at a compromise.

There can be no doubt that the possessions in the districts of Ross, Inverness, and Galloway, acquired by Sir Alexander Fraser on his marriage with Lady Johanna de Ross, were also lost by their son, Sir William, for they no longer appear among the family estates; but the records of their transference to other hands have not been discovered. There is, however, some reason to believe that those in the district of Inverness fell to William de Forbes and Agnes Fraser, the progenitors of the Pitsligo family, and, about a century later, passed by sale from that family into the hands of Lord Fraser of Lovat.

The unhappy loss of so many estates was doubtless the cause of the representative of the Philorth family not having been raised to the dignity of a peerage, when barons by patent began to be created in Scotland, as he would, in all likelihood, have been selected for that honour, if the possessions and influence of Sir Alexander Fraser, first of Philorth, had been preserved intact.

In 1430, Alexander, Earl of Mar and the Garioch, confirmed a charter of the lands of Tibberty and Utlaw from Sir William Fraser to his son and heir, Alexander Fraser, and Marjorie Menzies, the wife of the latter; and in the same year Sir James de Douglas, Lord of Balvenie, issued a precept of sasine in Culburty, Memsie, Over and Nether Pittullie, and Rathen, in favour of Alexander Fraser, on the resignation of his father,[2] and these properties were evidently the provision for the heir-apparent at the time of his marriage. The date of this precept is printed 1420 in the Antiquities of Aberdeenshire, published by the Spalding Club, vol. ii. p. 378; but the original document, though a good deal damaged, seems to have had a third numeral x, and that

[1] Antiquities of Aberdeenshire, vol. ii. p. 380.   [2] Philorth Charter-room.

date coincides with the marriage of the heir, who in 1420 would have been too young to require a separate establishment.

It would appear, from the destination in the charter of the Earl of Buchan, that Sir William Fraser was a second time married; but the lady's surname is not mentioned, and no notice has been found of the family to which she belonged.

It is probable that Sir William Fraser died before 1441.[1]

He left one son and two daughters:—

Alexander, who succeeded him.

Agnes, married William de Forbes of Kinaldie.

Isabel, married Gilbert Menzies (probably younger of Findon).

SIR ALEXANDER FRASER,　　MARJORIE MENZIES,
THIRD OF PHILORTH.　　DAUGHTER OF MENZIES OF FINDON.

THE birth of this Alexander Fraser may be placed in the first decade of the fifteenth century, for his father, Sir William, was married about 1404, and he himself appears as the husband of Marjorie Menzies in 1430.

Shortly after his succession, Alexander Fraser was engaged in a lawsuit with the Hays of Ardendracht and the Thorntons of that Ilk, to enforce his superiority over the lands of Auchinshogill, Plady, Delgattie, etc., which had passed into their possession upon the failure of the male line of his granduncle, Sir John Fraser. In this dispute he was successful.

In the year 1450, William, eighth Earl of Douglas, and many other distinguished Scots, attended the Jubilee at Rome, and Alexander Fraser is said by Crawfurd to have been among those who made that journey.[2]

After his return to his own country, he resigned all his possessions into the hands of James II. for re-infeftment. At Spynie, in Morayshire, on the 9th February 1456, the King granted him a charter, erecting the lands of Philorth, and those belonging to him in Aberdour, with Tibberty and Utlaw in Banffshire, into a free barony of Philorth, to be held in chief of the Crown by him and his heirs;[3] and this the king was enabled to do from

---

[1] Lives of Officers of State, p. 280.　　[2] Ibid. p. 281, quoting Holinshed, p. 391.
[3] Philorth Charter-room.

having succeeded to the earldom of Mar, in which the superiority over Tibberty and Utlaw was vested, while the barony of Aberdour was also in the royal hands by the forfeiture of the ninth Earl of Douglas and his family during the preceding year; and this instance of his sovereign's favour is an evidence that Alexander Fraser had adhered to the king's party in the struggle that decided whether a Stewart or a Douglas was to reign in Scotland.

The name of Alexander Fraser of Philorth is found among those of the twenty-one influential nobles and gentlemen that composed the assize of error, or inquest, held at Aberdeen on the 5th November 1457, in the course of the law-suit between the Crown and Thomas Lord Erskine, respecting the half of the earldom of Mar, which the latter claimed as having been the property of his father, Robert Lord of Erskine. His claim, however, was rejected by the verdict of the inquest, which found that the half of the earldom had never rightfully belonged to his father, but had been possessed by King James I., on whose decease it descended to James II.[1]

Crawfurd says that Alexander Fraser received the honour of knighthood from James II.,[2] and it was about this time that he attained to that rank, for on the 14th of April 1461, under the designation "Miles," he was served heir to his grandfather, Sir Alexander Fraser of Cowie, by an inquest held at Kincardine;[3] but this service seems to have been merely accessory to the establishment of the title of Nicholas, second Earl of Errol, to that estate, which had been given by the first Earl of Errol in 1447 to his uncle, William de Hay of Ury, second son of the Sir William de Hay who had bought it from Sir William Fraser in 1413, but was to revert to the earldom, if Hay of Ury died without issue, which event occurred about three months before the inquest was held.

A transaction that occurred in the year 1464 deserves some notice. Reciprocal entails were made by Sir Alexander Fraser, dominus de Philorth, and his cousin, Hugh dominus Fraser de Lovat; for, on the 13th July in that year, the former executed a charter of tailzie or deed of entail, by which, after destining his whole lands to his own six sons, and the heirs-male of each

---

[1] Miscellany of Spalding Club, vol. v. p. 272.
[2] Lives of Officers of State, p. 281.
[3] Philorth Charter-room.

in succession, and, failing them, to any other heirs-male of his own body that might be; upon the failure of all these, he disponed them "dilecto consanguineo meo Hugoni domino Fraser de Lowet, et heredibus suis masculis de corpore suo legitime procreatis, aut procreandis quibuscunque;" and upon their failure, "heredibus legitimis cognominis nostri vocati Fraser, nobis propinquioribus, et masculis, quibuscunque."[1] Hugh, Lord Fraser of Lovat, also made a similar entail, for although the deed itself is no longer in the Charter-room at Philorth, a copy of it, made in 1698, has been preserved, which shows that he destined, if he should happen to die without an heir-male, the whole of his estates of Lovat and Kinnell, etc., saving the tierce of his wife Violette Lyonne, "dilecto consanguineo meo Alexandro Fraser de Philorth, militi, . . . et heredibus suis masculis de corpore suo legitime procreatis, aut procreandis;" whom failing, "heredibus meis masculis et propinquioribus cognominis mei quibuscunque;"[2] and on the 24th of August 1464, he issued a precept of sasine to the same effect in favour of Sir Alexander Fraser and his heirs-male.[3]

Although this interchange of entails was inoperative, in consequence of the succession in each family having been carried on by direct heirs, yet it is interesting as a recognition of the relationship of the parties, and as reflecting a little light upon former generations; for the granters of the respective entails must be held to have been the nearest of kin to each other, by legitimate male descent, living at the time; and from the destination in both entails being eventually to heirs-male of the name of Fraser, without particularising any other cousin, the conclusion must be drawn that no other as closely related to either legitimately was then in existence.

The male line of Sir John Fraser of Forglen and Ardendracht seems to have failed about 1440, for his son and heir had died without male issue before that year, and there is no trace of any descendants of his other sons, Andrew and William; and therefore, in 1464, the third lord of Philorth and his sons were the only remaining legitimate descendants of Sir William Fraser, the Chamberlain's son.

---

[1] Philorth Charter-room.
[3] Ibid. Antiquities of Aberdeenshire, vol. v. p. 90.

[2] Copy made A.D. 1698, by Robert Fraser, from the original, then in possession of William Fraser, eleventh Lord Saltoun.

In the Appendix it will be seen that Hugh Fraser, first of Lovat, was a younger son, as is plainly evinced by the charged border of the shield upon his seal;[1] and that in all probability the Alexander Fraser, who first appears in 1337, and again in 1361, as brother-in-law to Sir Thomas Moray, was his father, and was a younger brother of a Simon who died without issue, and that they both were sons of Sir Simon Fraser the Chamberlain's brother; but if this were so, from the descendant of this Hugh having been the only person nearly enough related to the third Lord of Philorth to be termed cousin in the entail of 1464, it follows that the male line of any elder son of that Alexander must have become extinct before that date. In the Appendix there will be found some account of a Duncan Fraser of Tulifour in 1362-67, whose son Alexander was cousin to John Fraser of Forglen or Ardendracht, in 1414, and therefore also cousin to the Lord of Philorth, and whose male line appears to have failed about the same time as that of the family of Forglen and Ardendracht, or perhaps earlier, as there is no further notice of them to be found after the year 1414.

The above circumstances afford strong reasons for supposing that it was the failure of the male line of Sir John Fraser of Forglen and Ardendracht, on the one hand, and of that of Duncan Fraser of Tulifour, on the other, that brought the Lord of Philorth and the Lord of Lovat into the position of nearest of kin to each other in 1464; and they also support, in no slight degree, the descent of the latter family from Sir Simon Fraser the Chamberlain's brother; for it must be remembered that the male line of the Frasers of Frendraught descended from James, another brother of the Chamberlain, had also failed early in that century, and that there is no record of any male issue of the Chamberlain's brother Andrew. And it would therefore appear that in 1464 the Frasers of Philorth, and the Frasers of Lovat, were the only existing legitimate male descendants of the Sir Andrew Fraser who flourished in 1291-1297, and was the father of the Chamberlain, and his three brothers, Simon, Andrew, and James.

The absence of any mention by name of the Frasers of Cornetoun in the

---

[1] Though in very ancient heraldry it may be doubtful whether the border was a mark of cadency, it had become so at that period, for Boutell mentions a decision of King Richard II. in 1390, "that the Bordure is a mark of cadency properly so called."—Boutell's Heraldry, pp. 216-7.

entail of 1464, is also remarkable, for they were then an important family. It shows that they were not so nearly related to the Lord of Philorth as to be particularised as cousins, and this affords support to the belief that they were older cadets of the race, and were descended from the Sir Alexander Fraser who held that estate in 1306.[1]

Sir Alexander Fraser bought the lands of Scatterty and Byth, in the barony of Kinedwart, from Thomas de Grayme in 1470, and the charter of sale was confirmed by the superior, John Lord of the Isles, and Baron of Kinedwart, who also, in 1471, gave him a second charter, upon the resignation of Thomas de Grayme; and in both of these documents the Lord of the Isles terms him "dilecto consanguineo nostro."[2] This cousinship arose from Euphemia, Countess of Ross, great-grandmother of the Lord of the Isles, and Sir Alexander Fraser's grandmother, Lady Johanna de Ross, having been sisters.

An attempt was made by Sir Alexander Dunbar of Westfield to set aside this transaction, upon the ground of his pre-emption of these lands from Thomas de Grayme; and the Lord of the Isles being in rebellion at the time, he obtained a charter of them from James III. But Thomas de Grayme having made a declaration, and sworn that he had sold them to Sir Alexander Fraser three years and a half before he had any dealings respecting them with Sir Alexander Dunbar, the latter failed to make good his claim, and they remained in possession of the family of Philorth.[3]

On the 25th of June 1470, Sir Alexander Fraser of Philorth, and William Meldrum of Fyvie, became bound, as securities, before Alexander Irvine of Drum, Sheriff-depute of Aberdeen, that the Provost, Bailies, Council, and community of Aberdeen, and the tenants of their freedom, should be unharmed by Thomas Fraser of Stonywood, and Andrew Fraser, his son and heir, and their people.[4]

John Lord of the Isles was also Earl of Ross. That dignity descended from Euphemia, Countess of Ross, and Sir Walter de Leslie, Lord of Ross, to their son Alexander de Leslie, upon whose decease, without male issue, it passed to his daughter Euphemia, but was also claimed by Margaret de Leslie, his sister, the wife of Donald Lord of the Isles, and the battle of

---

[1] See Appendix.
[2] Philorth Charter-room. Antiquities of Aberdeenshire, vol. ii. p. 360; vol. iii. p. 526.
[3] Antiquities of Aberdeenshire, vol. iii. p. 528.
[4] Council Register of Aberdeen, vol. i. p. 56.

Harlaw, in 1411, was the consequence of her husband's attempt to enforce that claim, which, however, seems at last to have been admitted, probably after the death of her niece Euphemia, who had taken the veil. Margaret, Countess of Ross, was succeeded in 1429 by her son Alexander, Lord of the Isles and Earl of Ross, who, dying about 1449, left a son, the John Lord of the Isles and Earl of Ross above referred to.

The Lords of the Isles seem to have existed in a state of chronic rebellion against the Crown of Scotland (of which, indeed, they were scarcely vassals before the reign of Robert I.), yielding obedience only when its power was sufficient to compel submission, revolting and leaguing with its enemies whenever there was a prospect of doing so with success; and though repeatedly defeated and humbled in 1412, 1427, and 1429, they had hitherto escaped forfeiture; but in 1462, John Lord of the Isles entered into a deeply treasonable convention with Edward IV., contemplating nothing less than the transference of his allegiance from the Crown of Scotland to that of England, and the conquest and partition of the former kingdom, when he was to have the portion north of the river Forth.

This treason was concealed until about 1474, when, upon peace being made between the two countries, a clause in the treaty, requiring each sovereign to abandon all alliances made against the other, caused it to be discovered, and measures were soon taken by the King of Scotland against the offender.

The Lord of the Isles was summoned for high treason in 1475, and on the 1st December of that year was forfeited for that crime in a Parliament where he did not appear.

An expedition was sent into the district of Ross against him, but he soon made submission, and in July 1476 he was pardoned, and his possessions were restored to him, with the exception of the earldom of Ross, the lordship of Kintyre, and the vicecomitatus of Inverness and Nairn, which, says the king, "we reserve in memory of his offence and transgressions."

The earldom of Ross was inalienably annexed to the Crown of Scotland by Act of Parliament, on the 10th July 1476, with power, however, for the sovereign to bestow it upon a younger son.

John Lord of the Isles, though for a time restored to favour, could not subdue his hereditary propensity to rebellion, but in 1481 again entered into treasonable correspondence with Edward IV., and was forfeited of his remaining possessions, and died a fugitive about 1498.

The annexation of the earldom of Ross to the Crown was an arbitrary proceeding on the part of King James III. and his Parliament, for, by the terms of the charter from David II. in 1370, failing the heirs of Lady Euphemia, the elder daughter of William Earl of Ross, the earldom was destined to Lady Johanna, the younger daughter of the Earl, and her heirs.

If, therefore, Earl John in 1476, on account of his treason and consequent forfeiture, was considered dead in civil law as regarded the earldom of Ross, and it was no longer to remain in his family, it would have been more in accordance with justice if it had been allowed to descend to the heir of Lady Johanna, Sir Alexander Fraser of Philorth, whose right to it was not derived in any way from the Lords of the Isles, or from Euphemia, the elder daughter, but directly from the Earl, to whom that charter had been granted, through Johanna, his younger daughter, and who was not tainted by the treason that deprived the elder line of the dignity.

The Lord of Philorth was not, however, powerful enough to urge his claim to the earldom with any hope of success, and it might have been dangerous to recall the remembrance of his near connection with so indefatigable a rebel and conspirator as John, Lord of the Isles. Perhaps, also, some parts of his own father's political conduct were more safely buried in oblivion, and this may well account for his not having made any remonstrance on the subject.

As already noticed, the actual possession of the lands of Auchinshogill, Plady, Delgattie, etc., had passed from the Fraser name; but in 1477, Sir Alexander Fraser issued a precept to his bailie, William Crauford of Feddrett, desiring him to give sasine of those estates to William de Hay of Ardendracht, son and heir of Sir Alexander de Hay of Dronlaw, which shows that the superiority over them was still vested in the Philorth family.[1]

No distinct account exists as to the event about to be related; but from contingent evidence it appears that during the latter years of his life, while on a journey to or from Aberdeen, Sir Alexander Fraser and his cortége were waylaid and attacked at the Bridge of Balgounie, which crosses the river Don a short distance north of that city, by Alexander Irvine of Drum and his

[1] Antiquities of Aberdeenshire, vol. ii. p. 352.

associates. Two persons, an Alexander Fraser and a George Tailzour, who seem to have been dependants, and perhaps kinsmen, of the Lord of Philorth, were killed; and for this outrage, Alexander Irvine had to make compensation.

This Lord of Drum was pre-eminently turbulent in that not very peaceful age, and the royal pardon, afterwards received by him for the attack upon Sir Alexander Fraser and his friends, was granted, also, "pro crudeli dismembratione, et mutilatione, in suo loco de Drum, Domini Edwardi Makdowell, capellani;"[1] so that the Lord of Philorth and his friends might congratulate themselves on not having met with a similar fate to that of the unfortunate priest, or suffered further injury, their safety being doubtless due rather to their own stout resistance than to any forbearance on the part of their assailants.

In 1479, the Lord of Philorth and his son and heir-apparent, Alexander Fraser, were witnesses, at Aberdeen, to a precept of sasine granted by Lanslotus Futhas to James Innes of Innes, of the lands of Rothibrisbane;[2] and in the same year he seems to have been successful in a lawsuit, for on the 16th October, "The Lords Auditoris decretis and deliveris that William Cumyn of Cultir sall content and pay to Alexander Fraser of Fillorth, Knight, and James Fraser of Mamissy, the sowme of 1 c. pundis of the rest of a mare sowme, ocht to them by his obligationne schewin and producit before the Lordis."[3]

Sir Alexander Fraser died in April 1482; but his wife, Marjorie Menzies, survived him,[4] and on the 17th of April in that year she revoked all writs granted by him affecting the lands of Tibberty and Utlaw, in which she had been jointly infeft.

He had six sons by her:—

Alexander, who succeeded him.

James, ancestor of the Frasers of Memsie.[5]

William.
John.
Andrew.
George.
} These four sons are named in the entail of 1464, but nothing further respecting them is known. John was probably the John Fraser of Ardglassie.

[1] Antiquities of Aberdeenshire, vol. iii. p. 298.
[2] Ibid. vol. ii. p. 328.
[3] Ibid. vol. i. p. 299. Acta Dom. Audit. p. 90.
[4] Antiquities of Aberdeenshire, vol. iv. p. 90.
[5] See Appendix.

ALEXANDER FRASER,	LADY MARGARET DE HAY,
FOURTH OF PHILORTH.	DAUGHTER OF WILLIAM, FIRST EARL OF ERROLL.

ALEXANDER FRASER was served heir to his father, Sir Alexander, by an inquest held at Aberdeen on the 8th of May 1482.[1]

He married Lady Margaret de Hay, the daughter of William, first Earl of Erroll, probably about 1470, for the lands of Scatterty and Byth, which his father had bought in the previous year, were settled upon him and his wife,[2] and in 1474 he also received the lands of Memsie from his father;[3] but this last estate seems to have been resigned by him in favour of his brother James before 1479.

Little or nothing is on record respecting the career of this Lord of Philorth. He appears to have had no inclination or no opportunity to take any share in public matters during the lifetime of his more energetic father, and his own tenure of the family property was but a very short one.

Crawfurd, indeed, says that "he was of those barons who were preparing, as our historians tell us, to come to the assistance of King James III., when he fought the battle of Stirling, without waiting for his northern friends, anno 1488;" but he gives no authority for this; and circumstances that will appear in the account of his eldest son and successor, render it certain that he died in or before the year 1486.

By his wife, Lady Margaret de Hay, who survived him,[4] he left three sons—

Alexander, who succeeded him.

William, who succeeded his brother.

George, of whose descendants, if there were any, no record remains.

And perhaps a daughter—

Janet, married in 1512 to George Baird of Ordinschivas.

---

[1] Antiquities of Aberdeenshire, vol. iv. p. 90.

[2] Ibid. vol. iii. p. 530.

[3] Antiquities of Aberdeenshire, vol. iv. p. 125.

[4] Ibid. vol. ii. pp. 402-3.

ALEXANDER FRASER, FIFTH OF PHILORTH.

AT an inquest held in Aberdeen on the 4th October 1491, this Alexander Fraser was adjudged to be of weak mind, and incapable of managing his affairs; and the verdict went on to declare that he had been in this state for the previous five years, but that his brother William was careful of his own matters, and fully able to manage those of another person, and was then seventeen years old.[1]

Sir Walter Ogilvie of Boyne was appointed by the Crown curator or guardian of the Laird of Philorth and his estates, and exercised that office until 1496, when, at Sir Walter's request, William Fraser, then twenty-two years of age, his brother, George Fraser, and John Fraser of Ardglassie, were associated with him in the guardianship,[2] which appears from that time to have been principally administered by William Fraser.

There is no information to be obtained as to the origin of this affliction under which the fifth Laird of Philorth suffered, whether it were congenital or the result of an accident or illness cannot be decided; but the above proceedings were probably taken by his relations to prevent the family possessions falling into the hands of others, who had shown some disposition to take advantage of his incompetency.

William, third Earl of Erroll, and Sir Gilbert de Keith of Inverugie, purchased the marriage and ward of Alexander Fraser of Philorth from the Crown about 1486 (this evinces that his father was then dead, and that he was a minor), and the Earl of Erroll sold his share of it to the Thane of Cawdor.[3]

The Thane appears to have had the care of the young laird's person, and to have endeavoured to turn this to account, for an indenture is extant between William, Thane of Cawdor, and Alexander Fraser of Philorth, made about 1486-87, by which, after recital of the above-mentioned purchase of the marriage and ward, and the transfer of one-half of it, Alexander Fraser agrees to marry Margery Calder, the Thane's daughter; but it is stated that

---

[1] Philorth Charter-room. Antiquities of Aberdeenshire, vol. iv. p. 91.
[2] *Ibid.* p. 92.
[3] Book of Thanes of Cawdor, pp. 69, 70.

because they were god-brother and god-sister to one another, a Papal dispensation was necessary. He consents to severe penalties if he should fail to perform his engagement, viz., a fine of 300 merks to the king; 300 merks to the Bishop of Aberdeen, to be employed in building and repairing the cathedral; and 400 merks to Margery Calder for her virginity, and loss, skaith, etc.; in all, 1000 merks; and he also binds himself to reside with the Thane until the dispensation should arrive, and he should marry the lady. The indenture concludes thus :—" And becaus the saide Alexander Frasser has na seyle present of his awne, he has procurit with instance the seyl of ane honorabil lorde, Hew Frasser of the Lowet," and it is signed " Alexander Fraser de Fillorth manu propria."

Mr. Laing, in the second volume of his "Ancient Scottish Seals," No. 389, has fallen into the strange error of calling this Laird of Philorth a son of the Lord Lovat, whose seal is appended to the indenture. He has been misled by this fact, and has made the statement without due caution and inquiry.

The late Mr. Cosmo Innes, in "The Book of the Thanes of Cawdor," edited by him, says that the marriage took place, and that there was issue from it.[1] Not being acquainted with the pedigree of the Philorth family, he had fair ground for believing this; but the following facts will show him to have been mistaken, for though it is possible that the marriage may have been solemnised, the Laird of Philorth never had the power to make the settlements upon Margery Calder, for which he bound himself in the indenture; and from there being no mention of her, nor of him as a married man, in the proceedings of the inquest of 1491, or the appointment of his guardians in 1496, it is more probable that it never occurred. It is most certain that no issue of it was in existence at his decease.

In 1488-89, the Laird of Philorth gave a bond of manrent to William, Earl of Erroll, by which he bound himself to be the Earl's man,—as it was then termed,—and to serve him truly for three years, in return for his support.[2] To this bond, as to the former indenture, he had to affix the seal of an acquaintance, who, in this case, was William Cheyne, because he had none of his own; but he signed it in the same manner, " Alexander Fraser manu

---

[1] Family tree attached to Book of the Thanes of Cawdor.

[2] Miscellany of Spalding Club, vol. ii. p. 257.

propria;" and the desire of obtaining the Earl's assistance against those of his relatives that impugned his competency to manage his affairs was probably the cause of his entering into the engagement, but it was of no avail, and the verdict of 1491, and subsequent proceedings, put an end to his power of hurting himself or his family by any follies he might have committed since his succession.

He lived in retirement, but properly taken care of, and maintained according to his rank, as is expressly ordered in the appointment of his guardians, until the year 1500, when he died, and was succeeded by his brother William.

SIR WILLIAM FRASER, SIXTH OF PHILORTH.

ELIZABETH DE KEITH, DAUGHTER OF SIR GILBERT DE KEITH OF INVERUGIE.

By the verdict of the above-mentioned inquest held at Aberdeen on the 4th October 1491, William Fraser was said to be seventeen years of age at that time, which would place his birth in 1474, or the end of the preceding year; and from 1496, after he had been associated with some of his relatives and Sir Walter Ogilvie in the guardianship of his imbecile elder brother, he appears to have acted as the representative of the family.

In 1497, on the 23d of January, as "William Fraser of Fyllorth," he was one of the witnesses to a bond of manrent, given at Inverness, by Robert Stewart of Clawak to Alexander Lord Gordoun.[1]

His grandfather purchased the estates of Scatterty and Byth in 1469, and held them under the Lord of the Isles, superior of the barony of Kinedward. He had settled them upon his eldest son and Lady Margaret Hay at the time of their marriage, without obtaining the consent or confirmation of the feudal superior; and they passed to the eldest son of that marriage, the fifth Laird of Philorth.

James Stewart, Earl of Buchan, uterine brother of James III., in 1490 received a grant of the barony of Kinedward, after the final forfeiture of John,

[1] Spalding Club Miscellany, vol. iv. p. 191.

Lord of the Isles, and arraigned this omission in the Court of the barony, which adjudged the lands to have lapsed into his hands in consequence of it; but upon the payment of a sum of money (probably the fines due for the entries, with a penalty), he regranted them to William Fraser in the year 1495.[1]

Although too young to have been personally engaged in the skirmish at the Bridge of Balgounie, it fell to him, in company with John Fraser, James Fraser of Memsie, who seem to have been his uncles, James Fraser the bailie, William Fraser of the Kirktoun, and others of his kinsmen, to acknowledge the receipt of 100 merks from Alexander Irvine of Drum, "for the assithement . . . ande parte off . . . recompensation callit kynbutt, for the offences and violence committit ande done be the said Alexander Iruyn and his complices, one umquhile Schire Alexander Frasar of Philortht, knicht, and Alexander Frasar, his sone ande air, fader to me the said William, till us and utheris, our kyne and frendis, at the Brig of Polgony, of the quhilkis ane hundretht merkis in pairt of payment of the said offence we hald us weil content, etc.;"[2] and although there is no notice of any other payment, from the tenor of the receipt it would seem that the Laird of Drum had to make further atonement for his outrage, possibly in the way of masses for the souls of those killed by him or his associates.

William Fraser was served heir to his brother Alexander in the barony of Philorth, by the verdict of an inquest held at Aberdeen on the 10th of December 1501,[3] which also declared Alexander to have then been dead about a year and a half; and he married Elizabeth de Keith, daughter of Sir Gilbert de Keith of Inverugie,[4] in or before 1494, as their son will be seen to have attained majority in 1516.

In 1502, and the following years, various transactions took place between Sir William Fraser, who had received knighthood before that date, and Sir Gilbert, son and heir of Sir William de Hay of Ardendracht, respecting the lands of Auchinshogill, Plady, Delgattie, etc., the estates given in 1376 by Sir Alexander Fraser, first of Philorth, to his brother, Sir John Fraser, which,

---

[1] Antiquities of Aberdeenshire, vol. iii. p. 529.
[2] Ibid. p. 304.
[3] Antiquities of Aberdeenshire, vol. iv. p. 94.
[4] Ibid. vol. ii. p. 404.

by the failure of his male line, had passed to the Hays, and had been held by them as feudatories of the Philorth family; and though the record of these transactions is very meagre, the object of them was probably the purchase of the superiority by Sir Gilbert de Hay.

On the 31st of March 1502, Sir William Fraser resigned these lands into the hands of James IV., who thereupon granted them, on the 10th of May 1503, to Sir Gilbert de Hay, to be held by him and his heirs in chief of the Crown.[1]

The price, however, had not then been wholly paid, and Sir Gilbert conveyed some, if not all, of the lands back to Sir William Fraser, under a letter of reversion, by which the latter bound himself to restore them, upon payment of 500 merks, before Michaelmas 1504, and that sum having been paid before the 31st of May in that year, he returned to Sir Gilbert the estates, in which all interest of the Philorth family seems to have ceased from that time.[2]

Sir Walter de Leslie and Euphemia, Countess of Ross, had granted the lands of Faithlie (afterwards the site of the town of Fraserburgh) and Tyrie to Andrew Mercer in 1381, and his descendant, Sir Henry Mercer of Aldie, sold them to Sir William Fraser in 1504, to be held for an annual payment of 25 merks.[3]

Before 1505, James IV. appears to have claimed the barony of Kynedward, as heir and successor of John, Earl of Buchan, killed at Verneuil in 1424, who had obtained a charter of it on the resignation of Euphemia the Nun, Countess of Ross, which, however, seems to have been inoperative, for the barony remained in possession of the Lords of the Isles (also Earls of Ross) until the forfeiture of John, Lord of the Isles, about 1490, when it was granted by James III. to his uterine brother, James Stewart, created Earl of Buchan about 1469, from whom Sir William Fraser received the regrant of Scatterty and Byth in 1495. He died before 1500, and although he left male issue, James IV. seems, on his death, to have asserted his claim to the barony; but being unwilling, so runs the charter, that anything should arise therefrom to the prejudice of Sir William Fraser in the possession of Scatterty,

---

[1] Antiquities of Aberdeenshire, vol. ii. p. 354.
[2] Ibid. p. 356.   [3] Ibid. vol. iv. p. 124.

the King, in 1505, upon Sir William's resignation, regranted the lands to him, to be held in chief of the Crown,[1] which property, with the fishings attached to it, he soon afterwards sold to Sir John, the son of John Ogilvie of Mylnetoun, and the charter of sale was confirmed by the King in 1506.[2] On the 11th of October 1505, Sir William Fraser had received a remission for resetting, supplying, and intercommuning with sundry of the King's rebels; but there is no record of the occasion upon which he had committed the acts for which he was pardoned.[3] Walter Ogilvie, nephew and heir of the late Sir Walter Ogilvie of Boyne, with consent of his tutor, Sir William Ogilvie of Strathearn, in 1512 resigned the lands of Fetyhede, in the barony of Philorth, into the hands of the superior lord, Sir William Fraser, for disposal according to his pleasure.[4]

This sixth Laird of Philorth seems to have been an active man of business. He served on numerous inquests, and was a witness to many documents of the period.[5] He died in the autumn of 1513. Crawfurd says at Paris, on the 5th September; but as no other notice of his having gone abroad is to be found, and as his son and successor did make a journey to France, which Crawfurd does not mention, that author seems to have been misled upon this point, and it is more probable that Sir William Fraser was one of the many slain at the battle of Flodden, on the 9th of September in that year, whose names are not recorded.

By his wife, Elizabeth de Keith, he left one son—
Alexander, his successor.
And in all probability a daughter—
Christina, married to Andrew Chalmers of Strichen.

ALEXANDER FRASER,   KATHERINE MENZIES,
SEVENTH OF PHILORTH.   DAUGHTER OF GILBERT MENZIES OF PITFODELS, PROVOST OF ABERDEEN.

Two years and a half after the death of his father, Sir William, Alexander Fraser received sasine of the barony of Philorth by precept from the King's

---

[1] Antiquities of Aberdeenshire, vol. ii. p. 361.
[2] Ibid. vol. iii. p. 530.
[3] Pitcairn's Criminal Trials, vol. i. p. 104.
[4] Antiquities of Aberdeenshire, vol. iv. p. 95.
[5] Ibid. in many documents.

chapel, addressed to William, Earl of Erroll, then Sheriff of Aberdeenshire, and dated April 23, 1516, which shows that he had lately attained to full age, as the Earl was to take security from him for the payment of four hundred and fifty pounds for the mails of the lands during the time they had been in the hands of the Crown, and one hundred and eighty pounds for ward and relief of the same.[1]

Sir Lawrence Mercer of Aldie issued a precept to his bailies, John Fraser in Ardglassie, and others, in 1518, to infeft Alexander Fraser, son and heir of the late Sir William Fraser of Philorth, in the lands of Faithlie and Tyrie.[2]

In the Antiquities of Aberdeenshire and Banffshire, the date of this precept is erroneously stated as 1418; but this mistake of a century is evident from there having been neither a Lawrence Mercer of Aldie, nor an Alexander Fraser of Philorth in existence at that date, for Sir Andrew Mercer, who first received Faithlie and Tyrie from Sir Walter de Leslie and the Countess Euphemia, was succeeded by Sir Michael, who, dying about 1440, left a son, Sir Andrew, who was succeeded about 1473 by his son, Sir Lawrence, whose son, Sir Henry, sold the lands to Sir William Fraser in 1504, and left a son, a second Sir Lawrence Mercer, the grantor of the precept of sasine,[3] while the lands of Philorth were held by a Sir William Fraser from 1411 to 1441 at the shortest.

Crawfurd, upon the authority of a MS. account of the family no longer extant, but written, according to him, by Thomas Fraser, a great-grandson of this Laird of Philorth, says that Katherine Barclay of Gairntully was his wife, and the mother of his children;[4] and the author of Douglas' Peerage has followed Crawfurd as to this, but adds that Katherine Menzies was his second wife, though he had no issue by her.[5] Thomas Fraser ought to have known the name of his great-grandmother; but still, as Katherine Barclay's name never appears in any document connected with Alexander Fraser, seventh of Philorth, while Katherine Menzies will be seen to have been the first on the list of executors in his will of date 1532, and to have been his

---

[1] Antiquities of Aberdeenshire, vol. iv. p. 95.
[2] Ibid. p. 122.
[3] Pedigree of the Family of Mercer of Aldie.
[4] Lives of Officers of State, p. 282.
[5] Douglas Peerage, vol. ii. p. 474.

144   THE FRASERS OF COWIE, DURRIS, AND PHILORTH.

wife in 1556, there is reason to believe that in this statement Thomas was in error, and that Katherine Menzies was the only wife of this Alexander Fraser.

She was a daughter of Gilbert Menzies of Pitfodels, Provost of Aberdeen, and the marriage probably took place about 1516, or soon after that year, as several children are mentioned in 1532.

A royal license, or leave of absence from the king's host, or army, then serving at Wark, Solway, and other places on the border, was granted to Alexander Fraser of Philorth, and some of his kinsmen and near neighbours, in 1527.[1]

Upon Sunday, the 25th of June 1530, Alexander Fraser of Philorth, with several other persons, found caution or security that they would "thole a great assize for their unjust acquittal of John Dempster of Auchterless, and his accomplices, delated for art and part of the cruel slaughter of Patrick Stewart and certain persons, and for the mutilation of William Downy;" and upon the 5th of August George Gordon of Geicht became surety in 1000 merks that Alexander Fraser should underlie the law at the next justice aire of Aberdeen; but there is no further notice of the affair to be found.[2]

A dispute arose between the burgh of Aberdeen and Alexander Forbes of Brux during the summer of 1530, the latter having maltreated some of the citizens.

The Laird of Philorth took the side of his father-in-law, the Provost, in this quarrel; and at its termination, in December of that year, he was included among those for whose security against violence from any of his family Lord Forbes became bound before the Lords of Council at Perth.

"I, John, Lord Forbes, be the tenour heirof, becummis souerte and lawborgh for myself, John, Maister of Forbes, my sone, and the remanent of my sonnis, that Gilbert Menzies, Provost of Abirdeine, Alexander Fraser of Philorth, Thomas Menzies, Androw Menzies, and all other the said Gilbertis sonnis, Wm Lyon, and the bailzies, counsall, and communite of the burgh of Abirdeine sallbe harmless and skaithless of me, and my saidis sonnis, and

---

[1] Philorth Charter-room. The other names in the license are John Fraser of Forest, John Miln in Ardmacron, and Robert Miln, his son.
[2] Pitcairn's Criminal Trials, vol. i. p. 148.

our seruandis, and all that we may latt in tyme cumming, bot fraude or gyle bot as law will, under the pane of fuve thousand pundis, to be paide be me to the kingis grace, and his successouris, in case I, my saidis sonnis, or our seruandis, or any that we ma latt happen to brek the said lawborowiss in tyme to cum," etc. etc.[1]

It may have been in the course of this feud, or in some affray consequent upon it, that the Laird of Philorth killed David Scott; but no information is to be found on the subject of this affair, except the record of his having appeared on the 8th July before the itinerant court of justice then sitting at Aberdeen, and proffered a payment of ten pounds to the nearest relations and friends in satisfaction of that homicide, besides providing masses and other divine suffrages for the repose of the slain man's soul during a whole year, and engaging to undertake such pilgrimage or other penance as the Lords of the Council might impose upon him.[2]

He was ordered to perform a pilgrimage to the shrine of St. John of Amess,—Amiens,—in France; and as one of the preparations for an absence that was likely to be of some duration, he made his Will and Testament, which affords some idea of the personalty of a landed gentleman in those days.

"TESTAMENTUM ALEXANDRI FRASER DE PHILORTH.

Inuentarium omnium bonorum honorabilis viri, Alexandri Fraser de Philorth, factum apud Aberdein . . . tempore sue itinerationis apud Galliam.

Imprimis fatetur se habere in Pittouly viii^{xx} oves matrices, et ii veruices.

Item, in agnis, v^{xx}xiiij.

Item, in Tarwathie, etatis unius, duorum, et trium annorum, xx^{xx}xviij oves.

Item, in agnis in Tarwathie, viii^{xx}ix.

Item, in Cairnbulg, xii^{xx} oves matrices, ij veruices.

Item, in Pettowly, xxviij boves.

Item, viij vaccas, cum vitulis.

Item, vi buculos, iiij illorum quinque annorum, ij quatuor annorum.

[1] Council Register of Aberdeen, vol. i. pp. 131-9.

[2] Antiquities of Aberdeenshire, vol. iv. p. 96.

Item, viij buculos unius anni.
Item, in Tarwathie, decem boves.
Item, in buculis, et iuuencis, xlij, et illorum sunt ix unius anni, et duorum annorum.
Item, in Cairnbulg, xxviij boves.
Item, in vaccis xxiiij, et ix vitulas.
Item, in buculis, et iuuencis vltra etatem duorum annorum xxix.
Item, de equis viij.
Item, de equis qui quotidie laborant vi.
Item, in victualibus xxx cheldras.

Item, in debitis que debentur aliis.

Item, Domino de Stenewod xvi libras. Item, Johanni Keith de Balmuir xii libras. Item, Vilhelmo Adamsone in Edinburght xii libras. Item, Johanni Brebuner xl marcas, et xxv petras. Item, . . . xx libras. Item, Vilhelmo Jhonstoune in Doveransyd x marcas, secundum debitum computum et rationem.

Debita que sibi debentur.

Item, per dominum Comitem de Merchell octinginta mercas pro feodo heredis mei. Procautionarij deuenerunt Dominus de Arbuthnat, Gilbertus Mengzies de (Pitfodellis), et Thomas Mengzies, heres dictus apparens dicti Gilberti.

Item, per Valterum Melwein in Craig viij^{xx} marcas pro victualibus. Item, per Gilbertum Menzies vij^{xx} marcas in . . . Item, per dictum Gilbertum iiij^{xx} angelos quod refero Thome et Magistro Jacobo Menzies. Item, per . . . Lindsay iiij marcas in . . . Item, per Dominum de Lauristowne, pro tertia parte de Aurnehall et tertia parte annui redditus de . . . pro tribus annis. Item, per Joannem Stratoune pro tertia parte de Butre, pro spatio quinque annorum. Item, per Jacobum Ogiluy pro tertia parte de Butre, pro spatio trium annorum. Item, . . . Thome Menzies et me refero . . . dicto Thome. Item, in granis crescentibus in Cairnbuilg, Pettowlies et Tarwathie, per estimationem et . . . xlvi^{xx} bollas auenarum. Item, in hordio ix^{xx}, et ix bollas per estimationem.

Et ego vero dictus Alexander condo meum testamentum in hunc modum. Item, do et lego animam meam Omnipotenti Deo, et ejus dulcissime genetrici Marie, et corpus meum sepeliendum vbi Deus voluerit.

Item, do et lego bona michi pertinentia, prolibus meis equaliter diuidenda, excepta Margareta quia assignaui maritagium Alexandri Cumming sibi. Item, constituo Katerinam Menzies, Alexandrum Fraser, filium meum primogenitum, Magistrum Joannem Fraser, Magistrum Adam Duffus, Georgium Gordoun de Schiues, et Magistrum Alexandrum Gallwie rectorem de Kinkell meos exequitores superioris testamenti.

Subscryvit with my awin hand,

ALEX^r. FRASER OF PHILORTH."[1]

This description of the state of his affairs shows them in a tolerably flourishing condition, the assets being considerably greater than the debts; but the inventory is confined to his personalty without doors, and no mention is made of household furniture and effects, of which there was probably another schedule that has been lost.

He also took the precaution of obtaining the following royal letter of protection for his estates while he was abroad:—

"James, be the grace of God, King of Scottis, to all and sindry our wardanis, lieutenentis, justices, sheriffis, stewartis, justice clerkis, crovnaris, and thare deputis, and all vthiris our officiaris, jugeis, and ministeris of our law, spirituale and temporale, liegis, and subditis quham it efferis, quhais knaulege thir our lettres sal cum, greting. Forsamekile as our louit, Alexander Fraser of Phillorth, is now with our licence, quhilkis we gif and grantis to him to pass in France and vthiris partis beyond sey, to do his pilgramage at Sanct Johnne of Amess, and vthiris his lefull erandis. Tharfor we haue takin, and be thir our lettres takis the said Alexander, and all and sindry his lands, heretages, rentis, kirkis, frutis, malis, fermes, teyndis, takkis, stedingis, graynges, store places, cornis, catall, possessionis, and gudis, movabill and vnmovabill, spirituale and temporale, quhatsumever, quharever

[1] Philorth Charter-room. Antiquities of Aberdeenshire, vol. iv. p. 98.

thai be, within our realme, or outwith, vnder our speceale protectioun. . . . Gevin vnder our priue sele, at Edinburgh, the first day of Februare, the yeire of God j^{m}v^{c}xxxi yeris, and of our regne the xix yeire."[1]

It is doubtful how long the Laird of Philorth was absent from his own country, but he seems to have spent several years abroad, for the above royal letter of protection is said to have been published at the town crosses of Aberdeen and Banff in September 1535; and yet he appears to have returned before that time, as on the 15th June 1534 a Papal dispensation was obtained for the marriage of his son and heir, Alexander, to Beatrice, daughter of Robert de Keith, Master of Marischal.[2]

The Peerages by Crawfurd and Douglas state that this lady was a daughter of the third Earl Marischal; but the dispensation proves that his eldest son was her father, and if the statement in Douglas' Peerage that he was killed at Flodden Field in 1513 be correct, she must have been several years older than her husband, who could hardly have been born before 1516-17. The marriage seems to have been solemnised soon after, as the young couple had a charter of the lands of Tibberty granted to them on the 6th May 1535.[3]

The Laird of Philorth had obtained the maritagium of Alexander Cumming of Inverallochy, which he assigned as a portion to his daughter Margaret; and accordingly, before 1539, the young lady had become the wife of the young gentleman whose hand was in her own gift, and they had a son, William Cumming, who succeeded his father in Inverallochy before 1568.[4]

After his return from his wanderings abroad, the Laird of Philorth, in July 1537, was a member of the Court that tried John seventh Lord Glamis for high treason, in not having revealed the plots of his mother, Lady Glamis, against the life of James V. Lord Glamis was convicted and sentenced to death, but being under age, he was respited until he should attain majority. Meanwhile the informer against him confessed that his accusation was false, and Lord Glamis was released, but did not get back

---

[1] Antiquities of Aberdeenshire, vol. iv. p. 99.
[2] Philorth Charter-room.
[3] Reg. Mag. Sig., Lib. xxv. No. 192.
[4] Antiquities of Aberdeenshire, vol. iv. p. 683-4.

his estates until he brought an action for their recovery.[1] In 1542 Alexander Fraser received from James V. a charter of the whole fishings, " et piscium escula, vulgo lie fische bait," opposite his lands of Cairnbulg, Faithlie, Pitcarlie, and Coburty,[2] and in the next year he was engaged in some litigation with the Sheriff of Banff, which is only worth notice on account of a royal Act obtained by him, under the signature of the Earl of Arran, Protector and Governor of the realm for the infant Queen, to withdraw the tenants of his land of Utlaw, etc., in that county, from the jurisdiction of the Sheriff, so long as the lawsuit should continue.[3]

He seems to have been a man of considerable energy and intelligence, and to have devoted himself to the improvement of his estate and the acquisition of further possessions, having a keen eye for the natural advantages offered by the configuration of the sea coast, and in pursuance of these objects he is found from time to time obtaining royal grants and confirmations.

In 1546, on account of his having constructed a convenient harbour at Faithlie, and for other good services, he received a royal charter, erecting that place into a free burgh of barony, with the usual privileges to the burgesses, and authority to hold markets, and to practise various trades, etc.,[4] which concession seems to have given much umbrage to the authorities and people of the town of Aberdeen; for in the Council Register of that city there is an entry to the effect that in 1564 "the haill town being warnit, etc. etc., grantit and consentit to pursew to the final end the action and cause movit and persewit be thame against Alexander Fraser of Philorth anent the privilege usurpit be him of ane fre burght in the toune of Faithly, contrar the libertie and priveleges of this burght, presently dependan before the Lords of Council."[5]

This opposition, however, proved as unavailing to arrest the establishment of the burgh of Faithlie as were efforts of a similar nature to prevent the rise of its successor, Fraserburgh, at a later period.

The acquisition of lands in the neighbourhood made by the seventh Laird of Philorth was very considerable. In 1549 he purchased the Muircroft

---

[1] Pitcairn's Criminal Trials, vol. i. p. 199.
[2] Philorth Charter-room.
[3] Philorth Charter-room.
[4] Philorth Charter-room. Antiquities of Aberdeenshire, vol. iv. p. 645.
[5] Council Register of Aberdeen, vol. i. p. 356.

of Kirkton Tyrie, together with the superiorities of Ardlaw and Bodychell, which last estates had been sold by his ancestor, Sir William Fraser, in 1418, and had by annexation formed a part of the barony of Borthwick, and they were erected into a barony of New Muircroft by a royal charter in his favour.[1] About 1552-3 he exchanged part of his lands of Coburty with John Forbes of Pitsligo, for those of Pittalochy,[2] and bought the estate of Meikle Crichie from George Crawford of Fedderat;[3] and in 1560 he purchased Tulykeraw, Blair Mormond, and Park of Crimond from William Hay of Ury and Crimond,[4] and received from Gilbert Menzies sasine of 24 merks of annualrent out of the lands of Cowlie.[5]

Upon the 12th October 1556, in consequence probably of some family arrangements, he obtained, under the Great Seal of Queen Mary, a charter of the lands of Kinglasser and Mill of Philorth, in favour of himself and his wife, Katherine Menzies, which is only of importance as evidence of that lady having been his wife down to that date.[6]

The Laird of Philorth was one of an inquest that served a certain Robert Gordon heir to his "gudschir" John Gordon. It would seem that this service was proved to be contrary to fact, and the Lords of Council found the members of the inquest guilty of wilful error, and, according to the law in such cases, decreed the escheat of their moveable goods to the Crown; but he was relieved from this penalty by the gift of the escheat to him under the sign-manual of the Queen Regent, on the 13th January 1555.[7]

His daughter, Christiana, having married William Crawford of Fedderat, nephew and heir of the George Crawford from whom he had bought Meikle Crichie, he settled that property upon the young couple in 1561.

In 1564 he had to mourn the death of his eldest son, Alexander, whose marriage to Lady Beatrix de Keith has been already recorded, and who had by her four sons—

Alexander, who succeeded his grandfather.

Walter, who obtained the lands of Rathhilloch.[8]

---

[1] Antiquities of Aberdeenshire, vol. iv. p. 646.
[2] Ibid. p. 648.
[3] Ibid. p. 577.
[4] Ibid. p. 635.
[5] Antiquities of Aberdeenshire, vol. iii. p. 72.
[6] Ibid. vol. iv. p. 645.
[7] Ibid. p. 100.
[8] See Appendix.

John, who got those of Quarrelbuss.[1]

Andrew, a witness to the sasine of his brother Alexander in 1570, but of whom nothing more is known.[2]

The Laird of Philorth was by this time well advanced in life, but he seems to have preserved his energy and activity in prosecuting his plans for the increase of his property to his latest years, for in April 1568 he bought the sunny halves of Kindrocht and Denend, in the parish of Rathen, from his grandson, William Cumyn of Inverallochy; and the charter of sale was confirmed by James VI. in the succeeding year, a few days after the death of the purchaser.[3]

Alexander Fraser, the seventh possessor of Philorth, died on the 12th April 1569, being above seventy years of age, and having led an active and useful life, constantly engaged in improving and adding to his family estates. Tradition ascribes to him the building of the lower and more modern portion of the castle or manor-place of Philorth, which at a later date received the name of Cairnbulg Castle; but the great square tower or keep is of far more ancient date, and may have been built by the Comyns, Earls of Buchan, before their forfeiture in 1308, or even by some still older family, for there is no record of its erection: unfortunately the whole edifice is now only a picturesque ruin.

He had four sons and two daughters—

Alexander, who died in his father's lifetime, leaving four sons, already mentioned.

William, ancestor of the Frasers of Techmuiry.[4]

Thomas. See Frasers of Strichen.[5]

John.[6]

Margaret, married, 1st, Alexander Cumyn of Inverallochy; 2d, Alexander Annand of Ochterellon, and died in 1602.[7]

Christiana, married William Crawford of Fedderat.

---

[1] See Appendix.
[2] Philorth Charter-room. Antiquities of Aberdeenshire, vol. iv. p. 104.
[3] Philorth Charter-room. Antiquities of Aberdeenshire, vol. iv. p. 683.
[4] See Appendix.
[5] Ibid.
[6] Ibid.
[7] Monument in Ellon Church.

SIR ALEXANDER FRASER, EIGHTH OF PHILORTH,
FOUNDER OF FRASERBURGH.

MAGDALEN OGILVIE,
DAUGHTER OF SIR WALTER OGILVIE OF DUNLUGUS.

ELIZABETH MAXWELL,
DAUGHTER OF LORD JOHN HERRIES.

IN consequence of his grandfather's energetic and careful management of the family property, the eighth Laird of Philorth succeeded to a very considerable estate.

The date of his birth may be placed about the year 1537. He received a liberal education, and is said to have pursued his studies at Edinburgh.

About the year 1559 he married Magdalen, the daughter of Sir Walter Ogilvie of Dunlugus, when his grandfather settled the lands of Pittalochy upon them; and he succeeded to Pittulie in 1564, on the death of his father, who had enjoyed that estate under his marriage-settlement as heir-apparent.[1]

Under the designation of Alexander Fraser of Pettowleis,—Pittulie,—he witnessed William Cumyn's charter of sale of the sunny halves of Kindrocht and Denend in 1568;[2] and in the following year, under the same designation, he was served heir to his grandfather, and he received sasine of the barony of Philorth, and the other family estates, by royal precept, dated March 23, 1570.[3]

He had probably been fully conversant with his grandfather's efforts for the development of the town and harbour of Faithlie; but at all events, immediately after his succession, he began to carry out those designs with even greater vigour and perseverance.

On the 6th March 1570 he laid the foundation stone of a castle on Kinnaird Head, said to be the Promontorium Taixalium of Ptolemy, which was afterwards called the Castle of Fraserburgh; and in the next year he built a new church a short distance from it.

He then commenced the important operation of founding a new town

---

[1] Reg. Mag. Sig., Lib. xxxii. No. 504. Spalding Miscellany, vol. v. p. 358.
[2] Antiquities of Aberdeenshire, vol. iv. p. 683.
[3] *Ibid.* p. 101.

upon the site of the recently created burgh of Faithlie, and his designs in this undertaking were of a very enlarged and enlightened nature for that age and that part of Scotland, and he seems to have contemplated the foundation of a great city that should one day become the emporium of an extensive commerce, and also a seat of learning and science.

Although his aspirations were of a far grander nature than attendant circumstances might warrant, or the means at his disposal could enable him to carry into effect, yet, mistaken or not, his was a noble ambition, and the effort to promote the prosperity of that part of the country by the civilising influences of education and commerce showed an intelligence and public spirit certainly in advance of the age in which he lived, and deserving of all praise.

The bold and rocky promontory of Kinnaird Head is situated at the north-eastern angle of Aberdeenshire, the coast trending directly westward on one side, and towards the south-east on the other, it forms the northern boundary of a bay (anciently called the bay of Philorth) facing the north-east, and terminated at its other extremity by a reef of rocks projecting in that direction from Cairnbulg point. The coast is rocky for about half a mile southward from Kinnaird Head, after which sand-hills or " dunes" continue round the bay for about a mile and a half, until within a short distance of the Cairnbulg reef.

The position of the town of Faithlie was in the north-western corner of the bay, close under Kinnaird Head, which sheltered it on the north, and in some degree on the north-east.

To quote Crawfurd, the Laird of Philorth "continued to beautifie and inlarge the town with public buildings and fine streets," some of which were 40 feet broad, an unusual width in those days; and on the 9th of March 1576 he laid the first stone of a new harbour, "in nomine Patris, Filii, et Spiritus Sancti."[1]

Upon his resignation of all his possessions into the royal hands for reinfeftment, Alexander Fraser received a charter of them from James VI. on the 9th of April 1588, in which a grant of novodamus was inserted erecting Faithlie into a free port and burgh of barony, and granting to him and his heirs the advowson and patronage of the churches of Philorth, Tyrie, and Crimond.[2]

[1] Lives of Officers of State, p. 283.
[2] Philorth Charter-room. Antiquities of Aberdeenshire, vol. iv. p. 649, et seq.

Still vigorously pressing on his enterprise, on the 1st of July 1592 he obtained from the king another charter of all the lands and privileges granted in 1588, to which were added the estate of Inverallochy, recently acquired by him; and a grant of novodamus creating Faithlie a burgh of regality, with a free port, and ordaining that the same shall in all time coming be called the burgh and port de Fraser, and also authorising him to build a college or colleges, and to found an university in the said burgh, that should enjoy as ample rights, privileges, and immunities as those of any other university in the kingdom, with power to him and his heirs to appoint and remove the masters, teachers, and officials of the university, and to enact and cause to be obeyed such rules and regulations as might be necessary for its government.

This authority for the foundation of an university was confirmed by Act of Parliament on the 16th of December 1597, and the whole teinds and emoluments of the churches of Philorth, Tyrie, Crimond, and Rathen were granted for its support, under burden of providing for divine service in them; and on the 4th of April 1601, by a third charter, James VI. ratified and confirmed to Sir Alexander Fraser and his heirs all the grants mentioned in the two former of 1588 and 1592, with all the extensive powers and privileges conferred by them.

In virtue of the authority thus bestowed upon him, Sir Alexander Fraser entered into a contract with the feuars of Fraserburgh in the year 1613, appointing a Baron Bailie and Town Council, with other officials; and this contract, as modified from time to time by agreement between his descendants, the heritable Provosts, and the feuars of Fraserburgh, controls the government of the burgh at the present day.

The opposition attempted by the town of Aberdeen to the establishment of the burgh of Faithlie in 1564 appears to have been greatly stimulated by the founding of Fraserburgh.

On the 10th of March 1573, the Provost, Bailies, and Council of Aberdeen sent a petition to the Regent by the hands of their commissioner, Mr. Patrick Menzies, complaining of the lading of a Flemish ship within the port of Faithlie, "in hurt and prejudice of the privilege of this burght, comoditie, and jurisdictionne of the samen;"[1] and in the year 1605 the same authorities

[1] Council Register of Aberdeen, vol. ii. p. 10.

(1) KEEP OF FRASERBURGH CASTLE. (MADE THE LIGHT HOUSE.)
(2) THE WINE TOWER. (PART OF THE OLD FORT.)
(3) ANCIENT PIGEON HOUSE. (NOW REMOVED.)

FROM A DRAWING BY Mrs JAMES CARDNO AD 1850

of Aberdeen raised an action before the Court of Session for the purpose of obtaining a declarator that the privileges of trade, etc., granted to that town by former monarchs, included the whole sheriffdom or county of Aberdeen, and that therefore the creation of Fraserburgh as a burgh of regality and free port was illegal.[1] Their object appears to have been to obstruct the ratification of the royal charters by Act of Parliament, on the ground of the action being still undecided, and for that purpose they sent one of their burgesses, Mr. James Mowat, to Edinburgh, and seem to have spent considerable sums of money in following up the lawsuit, so that in the year 1606 they had succeeded in procuring letters of horning against Sir Alexander and his tenants of Fraserburgh, charging them to " desist and ceas from vsing any merchandice, packing, or peilling within the said towne, or hauldin of oppin buiths thairin, vsing or vsurping the libertie of frie burgesses of gild in tyme coming."

Sir Alexander Fraser resisted this somewhat selfish and tyrannical conduct, and managed to obtain letters of suspension against those of horning; and the lawsuit appears to have dragged on until the year 1616, when, in spite of resolutions passed at a rather stormy meeting, convened by Thomas Menzies, then Provost of Aberdeen, that it was "verie necessar and expedient that the saide actioune sall be prosequite and followit out cairfullie and diligentlie," it seems to have been abandoned, and Fraserburgh was left in the peaceful enjoyment of its privileges.[2]

Such is the record of the birth of Fraserburgh, and although the magnificent aspirations of its founder have not been realised,—although the projected university was but nominally established, and the college that was built soon became diverted from its original purpose,—although the feudal castle on the commanding but exposed elevation of Kinnaird Head was abandoned by his descendants for a more sheltered residence, and now performs the useful part of a lighthouse to guide vessels around that dangerous coast, yet much of the practically beneficial fruit of Sir Alexander Fraser's labour and expenditure remains to the present day; and the harbour, much improved and enlarged, and capable of infinitely greater development as a harbour of refuge, affords shelter to the ships engaged in the commerce of a thriving seaport, containing above 5000 inhabitants; and in the season of the herring-fishery,

---

[1] Council Register of Aberdeen, vol. ii. pp. 279, 284.   [2] *Ibid.* p. 336.

from June to September, is filled with a numerous fleet of boats from all parts of the coast, during which time the population of the town is about trebled.

Crawfurd has placed on record a Latin epigram by Mr. David Rattray, then minister of Philorth, who thus, according to the fashion of the age, celebrated the institution of the burgh:—

> "Hoc tibi Fraseria populis Rex curia nomen,
> Hoc dedit a proavis nobile nomen eques;
> Vive diu felix, vero pietatis amore:
> Vive memor tanti nominis usque tui."[1]

Which may be rendered into English in the following words:—

> The King, O Fraserburgh! has given to thee
> A name, through ages known to knightly fame.
> Long flourish thou! upheld by piety;
> And aye be mindful of thine honoured name.

The origin of Fraserburgh seemed of sufficient importance to warrant it being presented in a continuous narrative, and the more private history of the founder of that good burgh may now be resumed.

The eighth Laird of Philorth appears to have adopted the tenets of the Reformation, and to have adhered to the party supporting them during the troubled reign of Mary Queen of Scots.

The Earl of Morton, after his appointment to the Regency in 1572, among other wise measures for quieting the kingdom, committed some of the most notorious Border freebooters to the custody of those in the north of Scotland in whom he could confide, to be kept in a sort of honourable captivity at a distance from the scene of their former misdeeds; but having received additional security for their future good behaviour, he issued orders for their release in 1575, of which the following letter to the Laird of Philorth is one, and a similar letter, word for word (except the name of the prisoner), and of the same date, was addressed to the Laird of Arbuthnot, and probably to other gentlemen, which shows that the measure was a general one:—

"RYCHT TRAIST FREIND,—Efter our hairtlie commendationis. We haue laitlie ressauit new plegeis of the brokin men inhabiting the Bordouris,

---

[1] Lives of Officers of State, p. 283.

quhilkis we haue directit to be kepit in vther places; and thairefore it is our will, and we desire zow that ze let to libertie and fredome Johnne Baty, callit Johnne of the Corss, now being in zour cumpany and custody, that he may depairt hame to his duelling place or freindis at his pleasour, quhairvnto thir presentis sall serue zow for sufficient warrand. Sua we commit zow to God. At Halyruidhous, the xx day of December 1575.

"Your assuirit freind,

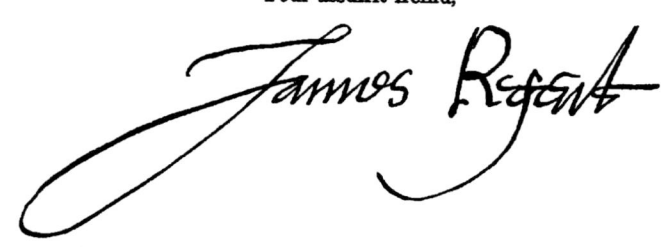

James Regent

"To our traist freind the Laird of Phillorth."[1]

In 1583, Sir Alexander bought the third part of Saithlie, near Tyrie, from Robert Innes of Kinkell; and he completed his grandfather's purchase of Kindrocht and Denend by buying the remaining or shady halves of those lands from George Gordon in the following year.[2]

Simon Fraser, Lord Lovat, who succeeded his father about 1576-7, when a mere child, passed a somewhat wild and unruly minority, that gave little promise of the good sense and estimable qualities which distinguished his future career. In 1586 he ran away from King's College, in Aberdeen, where his education was conducted, and went to Ireland, where, after a few months, his uncle and guardian, Thomas Fraser of Knockie and Strichen, heard that he was enjoying the hospitality of the Earl of Antrim. Strichen, apprehensive that he might do something to injure the interests of his family, prevailed upon him to execute, on the 15th of September 1587, an inhibition against his doing, directly or indirectly, anything that should hurt or lessen his estate or prejudice his heirs, without the consent and advice of certain curators

[1] Philorth Charter-room.
[2] Antiquities of Aberdeenshire, vol. iv. pp. 649, 683.

appointed, or any three of them, among whom Alexander Fraser of Philorth was one.[1]

The poverty of the exchequer of James VI. before his accession to the throne of England is matter of history; and the following letter, which is one of those addressed by him to his more wealthy subjects, not long before his marriage with Anne of Denmark, shows to what shifts the poor King was reduced to provide funds, even for a purpose of such public interest.

"TRAIST FREIND,—We greit zow weill. Mynding with all celeritie to direct ambassadouris for prosecutioun of the mater of our mareage, and wanting present moyen of our awin to furneis thame according to the honour and necessitie of that erand, we are forceit to have recourse to the favourable guid will of some specialis of our nobilitie, baronis, and vthers our loving subiectis best affectit to our weill and furtherance of our honourabill adois, of the quhilk nowmer [acc]ompting zow as ane we haif send this beirair to lay out vnto zow baith our intentioun and necessitie foirsaid, and to require zow in our name, as we do maist effectuuslie, that at this tyme, and in this purpois, tending sa heachlie to our weill, and to the weill of our haill realme sa mony wayes, ze will conforme to that advancement, and sowme quhairwith we haif commanded him to burden zow to the said vse contenit in his roll subscriuit with our hand, to be richt thankfullie refoundit to zow of the first and reddiest of our taxatioun of j° thousand lib., appointed be the commissioneris nominat to that effect be our lait act of Parliament, ze kepand this present, togidder [with] the resaverris tikket for zour warrand. Thus trusting to zour obedience, we commit zow to God, frome Halyruidhous, the vij day of Apryle 1588.

James R.

"To our Traist Freind, The Laird of Phillorth."[2]

[1] Anderson, History of the Family of Fraser, pp. 95, 96.
[2] Philorth Charter-room.

George, sixth Earl of Huntly, who had received a commission to pursue the rebel Earl of Bothwell on the 8th February 1591-2, took advantage of the power thus conferred upon him to attack and burn the house of Donibristle, and to murder (not without the suspected connivance of James VI.) the "bonny" Earl of Moray, whose beauty and gallant bearing had been praised by the queen, with somewhat imprudent earnestness, in her husband's hearing.

The Earl of Huntly afterwards surrendered himself, and was imprisoned for a time, but was at length dismissed without trial. Entering, however, into treasonable correspondence with Spain, he was again required to surrender, and, refusing to do so, was forfeited;[1] and upon the 9th of March 1592-3 a commission was issued to George, fifth Earl Marischal, constituting him his Majesty's commissioner in the counties of Kincardine, Aberdeen, and Banff, "to pas, searche, seek, and tak" George, Earl of Huntly, William, Earl of Angus, Francis, Earl of Errol, and their accomplices, for the treasonable fire-raising and burning of the place of Dynnibirsell, and murder of umq^{ll} James, Earl of Moray. One of the persons named as "counsallouris to the said Erll, be quhais advise, or any thrie of thame conjunctly, he and his deputis sall proceed," was Alexander Fraser of Philorth.

Alexander Fraser is said to have been one of those that attended at the baptism of Prince Henry on the 30th of August 1594, and to have received the honour of knighthood from the king's hand on that occasion;[2] and in 1596 Sir Alexander Fraser of Fraserburgh, as he was styled, and John Leslie of Balquhain, were unanimously elected commissioners to Parliament for the county of Aberdeen.[3]

His eldest son and heir-apparent, Alexander, married Margaret, daughter of George de Abernethy, seventh Lord Saltoun, in 1595, and Sir Alexander settled the estate of Pittulie upon the young couple.

He received a more familiar and rather curious letter from the king in the year 1596.

"RICHT TRAIST FREIND,—We greit zou hartlie wele. Heiring that ze haue ane gyirfalcoun, quhilk is esteamit the best halk in all that

---

[1] Pitcairn's Criminal Trials, vol. i. p. 284.
[2] Crawfurd, Lives of Officers of State, p. 283.
[3] Aberdeen Sheriff-Court Records.

countrie, and meatest for ws, that hes sa gude lyking of that pastyme; we haue thairfoir taikin occasioun effectuuslie to requeist and desyre zou, seing halkis ar bot gifting geir, and na vthiruise to be accompted betuixt ws and zou, being sa wele and lang acquented, that of courtessye ze will bestow on ws that zour halk, and send hir heir to ws with this berar, our seruand, quhom we haue anis earand directed to bring and carye hir tentilie. Quhairin as ze sall report our hartlie and speciall thankis, sa sall ze find ws reddy to requite zour courtessye and gudwill with na lesse plesour in any the lyke sutes, as occasioun sall present. Thus resting persuaidit of zour plesouring ws heiranent, we commit zou in Godis protectioun. From Perth, the Fift of Marche 1596.[1]

James

" To our richt traist freind, The Larde of Phillorth."

No doubt the king got the " halk " which he so " effectuuslie requeisted;" but it is amusing to see how plainly, and yet courteously, he intimated his wish that it should be made a present to him.

A third letter from James VI. to Sir Alexander Fraser is extant.

" RICHT TRAIST FREIND,—We greit zou hertlie wele. Being taiking ordour heir with the complaintis of our pure people, amang the rest it is heavilie meanit ws be this pure berare, callit Alexander Bruce, that zour seruand William Cheyne is awand to him the sowme of four scoir merkis xxxiij s iiij d. money of our realme, for a pece of land quhilk he had in wodsett, quhilk be his letteris obligatouris schawin to ws he wes obleist to pay at Witsunday 1598 zeiris, and notwithstanding postponis and deferris to do the samen, to the pure manis vtter wrak and vndoing. We haue thairfoir thocht gude to will and desire zou to caus the said William, zour seruand, satisfie this pure cumpliner of the said sowme, justlie addettit be him, sa that we be nocht fasched with forder complaint in that matir, as ze

[1] Philorth Charter-room.

tender our obedience and plesour. Sua we commit zou to God. From Perth, the last of Junij 1602.[1]

James R.

"To our richt traist freind, The Laird of Phillorth."

Although there is no record of the death of Magdalen Ogilvie, Sir Alexander's first wife, she did not survive the year 1606. He married, secondly, in the month of June 1606, or soon thereafter,[2] Dame Elizabeth Maxwell, Lady Lochinvar, eldest daughter of Sir John Maxwell, Lord Herries, the firm friend of Queen Mary. Lady Lochinvar was so styled as the wife of Sir John Gordon of Lochinvar, whom she married in 1563. He died on 23d August 1604. The mother of Lady Lochinvar was Agnes Herries, Lady Herries, who, in her will, dated at Terregles, on 13th March 1593, left to the Lady Lochinvar, her daughter, her new "black louse weluout gowne."[3] Lady Lochinvar obtained right to lands in the stewartry of Kirkcudbright by charter from her brother, William Maxwell, Lord Herries, in 1588; and she obtained a judicial transumpt of the sasine in her favour on 3d September 1614. In the judicial proceedings she is styled Dame Elizabeth Maxwell, Lady Lochinvar, and Sir Alexander Fraser of Fraserburgh, Knight, her spouse.[4] Lady Lochinvar and Philorth predeceased her second husband, Sir Alexander, for in his will he termed her "my umquhill spous."[5]

Sir Alexander Fraser had hitherto lived in happiness and prosperity; but his declining years were clouded by pecuniary embarrassment, from the pressure of the heavy debts which he had incurred in the prosecution of his enthralling project of founding the town of Fraserburgh; and the record of the remainder of his life consists of little more than an enumeration of the many and severe sacrifices that he and his eldest son were forced to make for

---

[1] Philorth Charter-room.
[2] Bond by Sir Alexander Fraser of Fraserburgh, Knight, in reference to his marriage, 31st May 1606, at Kenmure.
[3] Minutes of Evidence in Herries Peerage, p. 62.
[4] *Ibid.* p. 343.
[5] Philorth Charter-room.

the discharge of those obligations, which reduced the family possessions to a very considerable extent.

It is neither agreeable nor easy to follow these transactions in all their minutiæ; but a short and general statement of the circumstances is necessary.

During the first few years of the seventeenth century his creditors began to press Sir Alexander Fraser, and to institute proceedings at law for the recovery of their claims.

In 1608 he resigned to his son and heir, Alexander, a considerable portion of his property, the latter either paying his debts, or, more probably, becoming security for the payment of them; but this measure was not effectual, and he had shortly afterwards to apply for assistance to other kinsmen and friends.[1]

By various deeds, of date from the years 1608 to 1616, Simon Fraser Lord Lovat, the same to whom he had been one of the guardians appointed in 1587, George Ogilvie of Carnousie, his son Sir George Ogilvie, and William Forbes of Tolquhoun, were constituted trustees of his whole estates, with the exception of those settled upon his eldest son, for the purpose of selling, with his consent, such parts of the property as might be necessary for the payment of his liabilities, and of infefting his eldest grandson in all that could be saved of the family possessions.[2]

In pursuance of this arrangement, he and his trustees, in 1615 and 1616, sold the lands of Inverallochy to Simon Fraser, Lord Lovat; those of Kindrocht, Denend, and the third part of Saithlie, with Easter Tyrie, to Thomas Fraser of Strichen; and the lands of Cairnbulg and Invernorth, with a piece of land where stood the old manor-place of Philorth, at which he had ceased to reside after building Fraserburgh Castle, to Alexander Fraser of Durris and his son Robert, to whom he had granted them in pledge three years previously; but this last sale was made under certain restrictions, and upon the following conditions:—

First, that Alexander Fraser of Durris and his son Robert should not part with the lands of Cairnbulg and Invernorth during the lifetime of Sir Alexander Fraser, or of Alexander Fraser of Durris, under a penalty of

[1] Philorth Charter-room.   [2] *Ibid.*

£10,000, payable to Sir Alexander or his assignee; and secondly, that if Robert Fraser should wish to sell these lands after the decease of his father and of Sir Alexander, he should be bound to offer them to the heirs of Sir Alexander Fraser, or to any person he might nominate, bearing the name and arms of the family of Philorth, for the sum of fifty-seven thousand merks; and upon the refusal of that person to purchase, that he should be bound to offer them to the Lord Lovat, after him to Fraser of Strichen, and then to Fraser of Muchall, at such price as could be agreed upon, or as such land was worth at the time; and if they all refused to buy, that he should then have power to sell to whomsoever he chose.[1]

The Laird of Durris did not perform his part of this bargain, for, being deeply in debt to Fraser of Muchall, he sold him, during the lifetime of Sir Alexander Fraser, those lands which (in spite of an attempt on the part of Sir Alexander's grandson to set aside the sale and recover possession of them) then ceased to belong to the family, and in the lapse of time became the property of persons unconnected with the Fraser name, while the old manor-place of Philorth received the appellation of Cairnbulg Castle from the adjacent estate of that name, with which it was sold.

On her marriage, in 1606, to Sir Alexander Fraser, Dame Elizabeth Maxwell, Lady Philorth, appears to have been infefted in liferent in the lands of Cairnbulg. In order to protect her liferent right to these lands in the event of her surviving Sir Alexander Fraser, she made a protestation on 5th June 1613 in presence of Robert Fraser, sometime apparent of Durris, now of Cairnbulg, that no disposition of these lands should be prejudicial to her liferent right.[2]

The liabilities of Sir Alexander Fraser having been to a certain extent, if not altogether, met by these and other sacrifices of property, in 1620 he resigned the whole lands and barony of Philorth into the hands of the Royal Commissioners for new infeftment to be granted to Alexander, the eldest son of his heir-apparent, Alexander Fraser, by Margaret Abernethy, whom he terms his oy, or grandson; who, as will be seen, succeeded to this portion of the estates during his father's life, by consent of the latter to such arrangement; but Sir Alexander appears to have

[1] Philorth Charter-room.   [2] Original Protestation at Kenmure.

enjoyed the usufruct during his few remaining years, which he seems to have passed at his castle of Kinnaird Head, or at a house that he had in Edinburgh.[1]

He retained his mental faculties to the latest year of his long life, and this is evident from his having made his will upon the 12th July 1623, within a few days of his death, when he must have been eighty-five or eighty-six years of age.

By this deed he disponed his personal property in favour of Alexander Fraser, called his nephew, meaning thereby his grandson, which the word nephew or nephoy generally imports in ancient writings. This reading of the description nephew is confirmed by the testament itself, which mentions "Alex^r Fraser, my nephew," and "Andro Fraser, son to umquhill Walter Fraser, my brother."

The document commences thus—

"The Testament, letter Vill, and Legacie of Sr Alex^r Fraser of Fraserburghe, kny^t, maid be himselff 12 of Julij 1623 zeiris, Befor thir vitnesses, Alex^r Fraser, my nephew, Andro Fraser, sone to umquhill Walter Fraser, my broth[er], Alex^r Fraser, and Alex^r Harper, my servitouris.

Written be Mr William Forbes, Minister."

After lists of his debts and assets, the latter consisting principally of rents for 1621 and 1622, and arrears of feu-duties, which are signed by Sir Alexander Fraser, there follows:—

"My Legacie.

"Imprimis, I leiu to my nephew, Alex^r Fraser, my haill goldsmyth wark, whilkis was takin away be my umquhill spous, Dame Elizabeth Maxwell, and hir sone, James Gordoune. Item, I lieu to my said nephew all right and title that I had or micht hawe to the tearce and coniunct-fee of my umquhill spous, Elizabeth Maxwell. Item, I leiu to the said Alex^r, my nephew, my kist in Edinburghe, and my clothis and vther thingis conteaned therein. Item, I leiu to him my Courtingis, Nepperie, Cuschingis, and vther plenisching of my hous, which my said umquhill spous, Elizabeth Maxwell, had in keiping. Item, I leiu to the said Alex^r Fraser, my nephew, my buikis and plenisching

[1] Philorth Charter-room.

of my hous, as Weschell, Neppirie, Bedis, burdis, bedding, my clothis, and all vther thingis belonging to me within this hous of Kinnerds heid; my siluer wark also quhatsumewer. Item, I leiu to him all plenisching belonging to me in the Bredsie or any place quhatsumewer. Item, I leiu to him my hors, nolt, and scheip quhatsumewer, and I ordein the said Alex[r], my nephew, to intromet with the geir abou written, and my houssis, whow sone soewer it sall pleis the Lord to call me out of this present Lyff; and I, aboue all thingis, I exhort him to set his hart to feir God, and to doe his dewtie to all men, and to dowe wrong to no man, and to follow the adwyse of thes who ar appoynted to hawe a speciall cair of him and his effairis. I commend my saull into the handis of my heawenlie father, and I ordeane my bodie to be buried at the south syd of the kirk of Fraserburghe, and ane Ile to be buildit there, and ane litle woult to be buildit upon my corps, that my bodie may rest till the glorious appeirance of my blissed Sauiour the Lord Jesus Cryst, at which tyme I hope for a glorious resurrectioun with the rest of Godis santis: My will is that the Ile be woultit and ane chalmer to be buildit aboue the woult, to be ane cessioun hous or chalmer to the minister. The Ile to be thritte foot of heicht and als mekle of length, and ane steiple to be buildit on the Ile, and ane bell to be put thairin, and passag to be maid on the eist syd, that the minister may go in thereat to the pulpit.[1]

Sic subscribitur,

S[R] A. FRASER.

"M[r] W[m] Forbes, minister at Fraserburghe, writter of thir presentis.

"ANDRO FRASER, vitness heirof.

"ALEX[R] FRASER, vitness.

"GEORGE PROT, vitness."

Sir Alexander Fraser lived but a few days longer, as, according to the retour of his eldest son, Alexander, as his heir, he died in July 1623, though Crawfurd antedates that event to the 12th April, and he was buried in accordance with his last directions, at the south side of the church; but it is impossible to ascertain whether the vault and aisle were built as he had ordered, for the old church was pulled down, and another erected on the same spot in the year 1782.

[1] Philorth Charter-room.

He does not appear to have had any issue from his second marriage, but by his first wife, Magdalen Ogilvie, he had five sons and three daughters—

Alexander.

William, died unmarried.

James, a party to the contract of 1613 with the feuars of Fraserburgh. See Frasers of Tyrie, in appendix.

Simon, also a party to the contract of 1613.

Thomas, said by Crawfurd to have written an account of the family, but it is doubtful whether it is still extant, and nothing more is known of him.

Magdalen, married Patrick Cheyne of Esselmont.

Margaret, married Hay of Ury.

Elizabeth, married Sir R. Keith of Athergill.

In the portrait[1] of this Sir Alexander Fraser, his armorial bearings are depicted, and the shield displays, quarterly, three rosettes or cinquefoils for Fraser, and a lion rampant for Ross. From the annexation of the Earldom of Ross to the Crown in 1476, and the consequent disuse and disappearance of the arms belonging to that dignity, it would seem that *one* lion rampant, argent, had come to be regarded as the cognisance of the name of Ross by the heralds of the succeeding century, instead of *three*, which the seals of Euphemia, Countess of Ross, and of Hugh Ross of Rarichies, evince to have been the ancient insignia, and which were also borne by the Lords of the Isles, Earls of Ross, down to their forfeiture in 1476.[2]

The achievement of Sir Alexander Fraser also shows the motto, "The glory of the honourable is to fear God," which was disused by his successors until its restoration in the present generation.

---

[1] The name of the painter of this portrait has not been preserved; it is by a masterhand, somewhat in the style of Vandyck, but it was painted about the year 1593, before the birth of that eminent artist. It is the earliest in a series of portraits of successive proprietors of Philorth, lithographs of which, and of portraits of some other members and connections of the family, are inserted in this work.

[2] Laing's Scottish Seals, vol. i. Nos. 451-4, and Plate XII. figs. 4, 6.

George Jamesone. pinx.

ALEXANDER FRASER, NINTH OF PHILORTH.

MARGARET ABERNETHY,
DAUGHTER OF GEORGE, SEVENTH LORD SALTOUN.

ISABEL,
DAUGHTER OF SIR ROBERT GORDON OF LOCHINVAR.

His mother, Magdalen Ogilvie, having been very young at the time of her marriage, about 1559, it is probable that her first son, Alexander Fraser, was not born much before 1570.

He was contracted in marriage to Margaret Abernethy, daughter of George, seventh Lord Saltoun, by a deed dated on the 19th December 1595 and 1st January 1595-6. His father, Sir Alexander, settled Pittulie and some other lands upon him and his wife; but the cohabitation of the young couple appears to have been deferred for some years on account of the youth of the bride, for his eldest son, Alexander, was not born until the year 1604.[1]

In consequence of the arrangement already mentioned, he had obtained the lands of Aberdour, Scatterty, Tibertie, and Utlaw from his father before 1608, which, with Pittulie, made a considerable estate. This he seems to have pledged to his uncle, John Fraser of Quarrelbuss and Crechie, and his son Andrew, about that time, but to have redeemed the whole of it in the next year, 1609, with the exception of the lands of Aberdour, which, however, were at a later date reconveyed to his second son John by Andrew Fraser of Quarrelbuss, and on John's decease without issue, seem to have passed to his elder half-brother, Alexander.[2]

The young Laird does not appear to have taken any part in the further arrangements for the relief of his father Sir Alexander from his liabilities, except that he consented to waive his own rights in favour of his eldest son, Alexander, as regarded that portion of the estates not already in his possession; and although, on the 17th December 1624, he was served heir to his father in the lands and barony of Philorth and the other properties,[3] his succession to those that were then in the hands of the Crown, and of Simon Lord Lovat, and other trustees, for his eldest son's benefit, must have been

---
[1] Philorth Charter-room. [2] Ibid. [3] Appendix of Charters.

but nominal; and in succeeding years he and his eldest son, under the respective designations of Alexander Fraser of Philorth and Alexander Fraser, younger of Philorth, are found, either separately or together, engaged in various transactions down to 1636-37, about which time he died, for in a lawsuit between his son and Lord Fraser in 1637, his funeral is said to have recently taken place.[1]

The life of his first wife, Margaret Abernethy, was a very short one. Her parents were married by 1574, but she was not of age at her own wedding in 1595. She died before the year 1608, survived by her husband, who married, secondly, Isabel Gordon, youngest daughter of Sir Robert Gordon of Lochinvar, and Lady Isabel Ruthven, daughter of William, first Earl of Gowrie. Isabel Gordon, Lady Philorth, was the granddaughter of Elizabeth Maxwell, Lady Philorth, the stepmother of her husband: she was also sister of John, first Viscount Kenmure.[2]

By Margaret Abernethy, Alexander Fraser had one son and one daughter—

Alexander, afterwards tenth Lord Saltoun.

Magdalen, married James Forbes of Blackton.[3]

By Isabel Gordon he had also one son and one daughter—

John, died without issue before 1630.

Mary, married   Baird of Auchmedden.

[1] Philorth Charter-room.
[2] *Ibid.*
[3] Douay Register, 10th September 1643.

ALEXANDER FRASER,
TENTH LORD SALTOUN.
BORN 1604. DIED 1693.

PART IV.

THE FRASERS OF PHILORTH, LORDS SALTOUN.

ALEXANDER FRASER,
TENTH OF PHILORTH, AND TENTH LORD SALTOUN.

A DAUGHTER OF WILLIAM FORBES OF TOLQUHOUN.	ELIZABETH, DAUGHTER OF ALEXANDER SETON OF MELDRUM.

THE only son of the marriage between the ninth Laird of Philorth and Margaret, daughter of George de Abernethy, seventh Lord Saltoun, was Alexander Fraser. He was born in the year 1604, and, at an early age, had the misfortune to lose his mother, who died before 1608.

He received as good an education as the age afforded, and his name is recorded as having matriculated at King's College, Aberdeen, in 1619.[1]

If the almost hopeless state of disorder into which the pressure of pecuniary difficulties had thrown his grandfather's affairs had been allowed to continue, no very bright prospect of succession would have been opened to him, but, as already noticed, Simon Lord Lovat[2] and his co-trustees had been appointed in 1615 for the purpose, among others, of restoring to him all that could be saved out of the family property; and this trust was strengthened, in 1620, by his grandfather's resignation of the lands and

---

[1] Fasti Aberdon.

[2] Mr. Anderson, History of the Family of Fraser, p. 97, notices that Simon Lord Lovat had a charter of the Manor of Philorth, but, most disingenuously, omits to state that he held it in trust, with other co-trustees, for the young heir, and leaves it to be inferred that it was one of his own possessions.

barony of Philorth into the hands of the Royal Commissioners in his favour, and that of the substitutes named in the deed.

His grandfather dying in 1624, the succession to that portion of the estates, thus settled upon him, devolved on Alexander Fraser, to the exclusion of his father, who had, doubtless, given his consent to the arrangement; but his infeftment in these subjects was deferred for several years, and it was not until the 6th of March 1628 that Simon Lord Lovat and his co-trustees resigned their trust, which they had honestly and worthily executed, and all rights thereto belonging, into the hands of the Royal Commissioners, who thereupon gave the estates over to Alexander Fraser, which are described as those of Philorth, Cairnbulg, Invernorth, Benzietoun, Faithly, Burgh called Fraserburgh, Kinnaird's Head, Broadsea, Pitblea, patronage of the kirks of Philorth, Tyrie, and Rathen, etc. etc.,[1] and this was followed by a charter and precept of sasine in his favour, under the great seal of Charles I., which again was ratified by the King in 1633.[2]

About this time the young laird of Philorth married a daughter of William Forbes of Tolquhoun, who had been one of his trustees; but he was early left a widower by the death of this lady, by whom he had only a daughter.[3]

His second wife was Elizabeth, daughter of Alexander Seton of Meldrum, by whom he had an only son Alexander.[4]

In 1630 he sold Aberdour to Alexander Forbes of Pitsligo. This estate had been obtained in 1624 by his half-brother, John Fraser, from their cousin, Andrew Fraser of Quarrelbuss,[5] to whom their father had sold it in 1608; and John dying without issue, it seems to have passed to his elder half-brother.

From the time of Alexander Fraser's succession under his grandfather's destination, he is found engaged in various transactions, under the designation of "younger of Philorth," sometimes alone, at others in concert with his father, who is styled "of Philorth," or "elder of Philorth,"[6] until about 1636-7, when the latter died, and he succeeded to Pittullie, Pittendrum, etc., and became sole proprietor of all that remained of the once far more extensive family estates.

[1] Philorth Charter-room.
[2] Ibid.
[3] Lives of Officers of State, p. 284.
[4] Ibid.
[5] Antiquities of Aberdeenshire, vol. iv. p. 121.
[6] Philorth Charter-room. Dal. Decreets, vol. xxv.

In 1639 he appears, as Lord of the Regality of Fraserburgh, to have exercised the feudal right of repledging criminals to the Court of his Regality.

William Fraser, a merchant in Fraserburgh, his brother Alexander Fraser, and Andrew Fraser in Benzietoun, with some others, having been indicted at Edinburgh, on the 26th July 1639, for the murder of Edward Skellay, in the house of John Lyell, at Fraserburgh, on the 23d April in that year, Mr. William Forbes, advocate, appeared for Alexander Fraser of Philorth and Fraserburgh, lord of the regality thereof, and claimed the right of repledging the said prisoners, and any other of the inhabitants accused of any crime within the lordship, to the judgment and jurisdiction of his regality, producing the charter granted by James VI. in 1601, and its ratification by Charles I. in a Parliament held at Edinburgh in 1633, in support of the claim, which seems to have been allowed by the Court.[1]

In regard to the above-mentioned right of repledging criminals, Erskine thus explains it in his Institutes of the Law of Scotland:—"The civil jurisdiction of a lord of regality was in all respects equal to that of a Sheriff; but his criminal was truly royal, for he might have judged in the four pleas of the Crown, whereas the Sheriff was competent to none of them but murder. It was even as ample as that of the justiciary as to every crime except treason. Mack. Crim. Tr., p. 11, t. u. 85. And in this one respect it prevailed over it, that where a criminal was amenable to a regality the lord might have repledged or reclaimed him to his own Court, not only from the Sheriff, but from the justices themselves. He who had this right, or his procurator, appeared before the Court from whom he was to repledge, and demanded, judicially, that the person accused, because he resided within his special jurisdiction, might be sent to his Court to be tried there; and it behoved him to give security to the Court repledged from that he would minister justice to him within a year, which security was called 'culrach,' from the Gaelic 'cul,' which signifies 'back,' and 'rach,' 'cautioner.'

"If the repledger neglected to try the defender in that time he forfeited his right of holding courts for a year; the first judge might again proceed in the cause; and if the defender did not appear, the cautioner was to answer for him."[2]

[1] Philorth Charter-room. [2] Macallan's Edition, B. I. tit. iv. p. 76.

This privilege of the lords of regality was abolished by the Heritable Jurisdictions Act of 1747.

It is beyond the scope of this family history to enter further into the relation of public affairs than is necessary to explain the share taken in them by the individuals whose lives are recorded in these pages, and the references to the stirring events which occurred during Alexander Fraser's long life will be confined to those in which he took a part; but it would appear that the statement made by Crawfurd, that he "was a great Royalist, and suffered much for his adherence to King Charles I. during the Troubles," has no foundation in fact.[1]

Whether Alexander Fraser was an enthusiastic Presbyterian, or whether he had any strong objection to Episcopal government of the Church, is very doubtful; but he seems, like many others, to have acquiesced in the existing state of affairs, and yielded obedience and support to the then dominant party, and he subscribed the Solemn League and Covenant when it was brought to Aberdeen by Montrose in 1638. He was also a member of the General Assembly at Glasgow in 1639, when the resistance to the establishment of Episcopacy by the royal authority commenced, and in the same year he served in the army commanded by Montrose; and, with the tutor of Pitsligo, led a contingent of about 200 men during the expedition against the castles of Kellie and Gight.[2]

In April 1640 he was named a member of the committee or council of war appointed to assist the Earl Marischal, who commanded the forces of the Covenanters in the neighbourhood of Aberdeen;[3] and in June of the same year an event took place which had a rather curious termination. Gordon, Laird of Gight, a strong anti-Covenanter, having obtained forty-eight hours' safe conduct from the Earl Marischal, came into Aberdeen to treat about making his submission to the ruling powers, when from some cause or other, very possibly from the hereditary feud consequent upon the murder of Thomas Fraser of Strichen by a former Laird of Gight in 1576, a quarrel occurred between him and the Laird of Philorth, followed by a challenge to fight, although they must have been closely connected, for Philorth's aunt, Jean de Abernethy, had taken a Laird of Gight for her second husband in 1617.

---

[1] Lives of Officers of State, p. 284.
[2] History of Troubles, vol. i. pp. 193, 196.   [3] *Ibid.* p. 267.

The Earl Marischal hearing of this, in order to prevent the duel, made the Laird of Gight a prisoner before the expiry of his safe conduct, who, alarmed at this proceeding, and not knowing the Earl's real reason for it, effected his escape and fled to Germany.[1]

The Laird of Philorth and the Laird of Drum were chosen commissioners for the county of Aberdeen in 1643 to attend the Convention of Estates, held at Edinburgh, at which the Solemn League and Covenant of that year was agreed upon;[2] and in the same year they were appointed conveners of the county, for the purpose of levying taxes to maintain the Scottish armies.[3]

During 1644, the Laird of Philorth was associated with the Lord Fraser and the Forbes family, in support of the Marquis of Argyll against the Royalists, under the Earl of Huntly and the Marquis of Montrose;[4] and in the same year he was engaged in the following transactions with the Presbytery of Strathbogie, on behalf of James Urquhart of Old Craig, who appears to have been his ward.[5]

William Crichton, a brother of Viscount Frendraught, having been killed by Walter Urquhart of Crombie and some other persons, Mr. Douglas, minister of Forgie, appeared before the Presbytery of Strathbogie on the 4th January 1643, and in the name of the Viscount desired that process of excommunication might proceed against the slayer and his accomplices, who were consequently during that year cited to attend for trial, and on December 20th the various ministers reported that they had cited them to appear upon that day.

None of the accused appeared; but a letter from Alexander Fraser of Philorth was read, in which he said that he would have attended the meeting of the Presbytery if he had not been detained at Aberdeen by business of the Committee or Council of which he was a member, and in the name of James Urquhart of Old Craig, one of the accused, to whom he was guardian, requested information as to the time of the next meeting, in order that he might attend it.

[1] History of Troubles, vol. i. p. 287.
[2] Ibid. vol. ii. p. 254.
[3] Ibid. p. 266.
[4] History of Troubles, vol. ii. p. 338.
[5] Spalding Club, Presbytery Book of Strathbogie, pp. 35-54.

On the 10th of January 1644 he attended the meeting of the Presbytery held on that day, accompanied by Hugh Fraser of Easter Tyrie, and after stating that his ward, James Urquhart of Old Craig, was not in the kingdom, and was ignorant of the process instituted against him, requested the Presbytery to give him time to inform the said James of the circumstances, and to bring him home to answer for himself, which he would undertake to do if the Presbytery would suspend the process meanwhile.

The Presbytery replied that they could not suspend the process without authority from the Commissioners of the General Assembly, but consented to write a letter to them on the matter, which Philorth was to carry to them, and to return their answer to the Presbytery.

On the 28th February, at the meeting of the Presbytery, a letter was received from Philorth, excusing his not having returned them the answer of the Commissioners of General Assembly in time for their meeting, as that body was not to meet until the 25th of that month, but promising to send it as soon as possible, meanwhile requesting that the suspension of process against James Urquhart might be continued, and protesting that, if they proceeded in the matter, whatsoever they did should be referred to the Provincial Assembly.

The Presbytery, however, resolved to proceed, although on the 27th March they received a letter from James Urquhart and Patrick Meldrum, offering to make satisfaction for whatever transgressions they might have committed; and at their meeting on the 24th April, in reply to the demand of the Moderator, the members of the Presbytery reported that they had all given three public admonitions, and that some had offered up two public prayers in the matter of James Urquhart of Old Craig, Patrick Meldrum, sometime of Iden, and Adam Gordon, accomplices in the slaughter of William Crichton. Whereupon Mr. William Stewart, notar-public in Fraserburgh, appeared in the names of James Urquhart of Old Craig and the Right Honourable Alexander Fraser of Philorth, and offered, in their names, that James Urquhart should appear, within a competent time, to undergo his trial, and also protested against the Presbytery proceeding to excommunication in his absence, and that, if they did so, the matter should be referred to the General Assembly.

The Presbytery, in reply, decided that they had not power to delay the process, but promised that sentence should not be pronounced until " the . . . of May next, that Philorth might acquaint the . . . of the Generall (Assembly?) heirwith, that according to their . . . the Presbytery might proceed."

How the affair ended does not appear, but it is evident, from the record of this and of other transactions, that the Laird of Philorth not only obeyed, but gave active support to the party then in power, which was that of the Covenanters, and that he had considerable influence with the leaders of it.

On the 15th of July 1647, an Act of the Committee of Estates was passed, by which, "taking into their consideratioune the losses sustained be the Laird of Philorth and his tenentis, be the rebellis, and otherwayes," to the amount of "four score thousand merks, and finding it most just that some cours were tane for his reparatioune in some measure, and for a supplee to his subsistance," they modify to him the sum of sixteen thousand merks for a present supply, which was to include a sum of five thousand merks already granted to his tenants, and was to be levied out of the fines imposed upon Inverallochie, John Chessors, elder and younger, Alexander Hay of Bilbo, Patrick Strachan of Kinaldie, and young Glenkindie. This was followed by another decree from the same body, dated 29th February 1648, in which, after referring to the former Act, and the modification of sixteen thousand merks " as the fyft pairt of the losses sustained be him in this caus, conform to the report of the Commissioune given for tryall of the samen," and "considering that the said Alexander Frasser hes been a great sufferer for his affection to this publick work," they "doe find themselffes the more oblieged thereby to taik course for his satisfactioune in some measure;" and (as probably the fines mentioned in the first Act did not come very readily to hand) they ordered payment to be made to him out of the "loan, and first sevintene mounth maintenance of the shyres of Aberdeen, Murray, Banff, Inverness, Caithness, and Orkney."[1]

The Duke of Hamilton and the more moderate Presbyterian party had succeeded in wresting the government of Scotland from the hands of the Marquis of Argyll and his faction;[2] and in 1648, when the Scottish nation

[1] Philorth Charter-room.
[2] Clarendon's History of the Rebellion, vol. vi. pp. 8-14.

attempted to effect the deliverance of Charles I. from his captivity, the Laird of Philorth received a commission of Colonel from the Committee of Estates, in succession to the Master of Forbes in the following terms:—

"MUCHE HONORED,—The Maister of Forbes haveing quit his employment as ane Colonell in the present levey, and wee being confident of your affection to the publict service, have nominat yow to be Colonel, in place of the Maister of Forbes, and to have that division of the shyre of Aberdein allowed to him. These are therefore to desire yow, vpon receipt heirof, to goe about the leveying of that Regiment quhilk formerlie fell to the Maister of Forbes. Quherin expecting your care, we rest,

"Your affectionat Freinds,

A. HEPBURNE.   JAMES DUNDAS.   S. JA. FOULIS.

ARCH^D. SYDSERFE.   ROBERT INNES.

"Edinburgh, 23rd May 1648.
    Addressed thus:
        "For our worthie Freind, Alexander Fraser of Phillorth.
"To be communicat to the Committee of Aberden."[1]

[1] Philorth Charter-room.

As colonel of this regiment, it is not unlikely that the Laird of Philorth served in the army that invaded England under the Duke of Hamilton, and may have shared in the defeat of Preston, where that nobleman was routed and taken prisoner; but if so, he was fortunate enough to avoid captivity.

After the death of the royal martyr, Charles II. had been proclaimed King of Scotland in 1649, but he did not arrive in that country until June 1650 where he was subjected to many indignities, Argyll and the more fanatic of the Covenanters having again returned to power after the failure of the Duke of Hamilton's expedition and the subsequent invasion of the south of Scotland by Cromwell, though even they were compelled to acknowledge the young king as their sovereign, from the general indignation against his father's murderers. On the 15th July he was again solemnly proclaimed king at Edinburgh.

A few days afterwards, Cromwell once more crossed the Tweed, and advancing as far as Edinburgh retired from thence to Dunbar, where on the 3d September he gained the important victory of that name over the Scottish forces, and returning to Edinburgh invested the castle, which surrendered on the 12th December.

As it is recorded by Lord Clarendon, in his History of the Rebellion, that the Marquis of Argyll and his party allowed few or no soldiers or officers who had been in the expedition of the Duke of Hamilton, or who were thought to wish well to the king, to serve in the army at Dunbar, it is very improbable that Alexander Fraser of Philorth was in that engagement.[1]

The king, who had not been permitted to command the army, retired to Perth on Cromwell's advance to Edinburgh; and Argyll's power being considerably reduced by the defeat of Dunbar, his Majesty found himself more independent, and proceeded to raise a fresh army to the north of the Forth.

The Laird of Philorth was one of those who most ardently devoted themselves to his cause, and contributed sums of money towards it; besides which he is said, by family and local tradition, to have raised a regiment at his own expense, with which he joined the royal standard after the king's coronation at Scone on the 1st January 1651.

In the annals written by Sir James Balfour, Lyon King-of-Arms to

[1] Clarendon's History, vol. vi. ed. 1826, p. 453.

Charles First, the following passage is found in the record of the Parliament at Perth, under date March 31, 1651:—" Ordred by the King and Parliament, that the Laird of Philorthe stay wntill he be cleired anent his letting the pryese withe cheisse escape; and that one of each estait be addit to his examinators."[1]

This meagre notice is all that remains respecting the matter, but a few pages before occurs another passage, of date March 27, in the same year:— " A letter from the Magistrats of Aberdeen to the King and Parliament, shewing that one Capitane Binge of Jarsey, with a commissione from the Ducke of Zorke, as Admirall of England and Irland, had brought into Aberdeene ane Englishe shipe, as a prysse."[2]

This may have been the "pryese withe cheisse," that the Laird of Philorth was accused of allowing to escape, but he either cleared himself from the charge, or it fell to the ground, for he appears to have lost nothing of the royal favour.

The following letter, from King Charles the Second, also shows that his sovereign had recourse to him in his straits for pecuniary aid:—

" LAIRD OF PHILLORTH,—I am so confident of your good affection to me, and the aduancement of my affaires, that I doubt not but you wilbe willing to furnish me, for my present occasions, with the summe of two hundred pounds sterling, which I pray you to deliuer either to my selfe, or to the bearer hereof, my seruant, who shall bring you to me; and I shall not only take it as a testimonie of your affection, but shall also repay the same to you, and acknowledge it as an acceptable seruice done to me.

" Perth, the 28th day of March 1651."   Your *Louing frind*
  Charles R

Addressed: " For the Laird of Phillorth."[3]

[1] Balfour's Annals, vol. iv. p. 280.
[2] *Ibid.* p. 276.
[3] Philorth Charter-room. The words in the woodcut are holograph of the king.

The loan thus requested appears to have been made by instalments, and at a discount of ten per cent., as the following receipt will show:—

"*April* 8*th*, 1651.—Receaved, the day and yeer above written, of the Laird of Philorth, for His Majestie's use, to his Privy Purse, the sume of Fower score and tenne pound sterlin mouney, I say receaved by me, the day and yiere above written, the full sum of 90 Lib."

Signed "RIC. HARDING.

Which 90 Lib. sterlin is now, vpon the raising of mouney, become 100 Lib."[1]

After the capture of Edinburgh, Cromwell passed the winter in that city, and the king, having assembled his army, numbering about 18,000 men, held the line of the river Forth. Cromwell, having advanced from Edinburgh, after a while outmanœuvred the royal army, and succeeded in turning its left flank, and establishing himself in Fife about the end of July, thereby threatening its communications.

Upon this the king, finding the way clear, determined to move southward into England, and getting a few days' start of his great adversary, advanced by forced marches to Carlisle, which he reached on the 6th August, and thence through Lancashire and Shropshire to the city of Worcester, where he arrived on the 22d of the same month.

The king had expected to receive considerable reinforcements in England, but his expectations were not realised, and, save the contingent raised by the gallant Earl of Derby, who not long after suffered on the block for his devoted loyalty, and a few other kindred spirits, he obtained no accession of force, nor did any general rising in his favour take place.

As soon as he heard of the march of the royal army, Cromwell, though delayed for a few days by the necessity of making arrangements to secure his conquests, left General Monck to command in Scotland, and followed with all speed.

His army being strongly recruited by militia levies as he passed through England, he appeared with 30,000 men in the beginning of September before Worcester, where the king with his army, now reduced to 14,000, still remained, having partially fortified the town and broken down a bridge across the Severn some distance below the place.[2]

[1] Philorth Charter-room.   [2] Carlyle's Oliver Cromwell, vol. ii. p. 138.

On the 3d September, the anniversary of the battle of Dunbar in the previous year, Cromwell advanced to the attack from the south-east. Fleetwood, with Lambert's division, managed to cross the Severn by the bridge, which had not been thoroughly destroyed, and having also succeeded in passing the small river Teme, which runs into the Severn, drove the Scots on the western bank towards the town.

Cromwell having also passed the Severn with strong reinforcements to aid Fleetwood, the king and his advisers thought the opportunity a good one to attack the forces left upon the eastern bank, and made a furious sally upon them; but Cromwell, hastening back, resumed the command, repulsed the assailants, and both armies entered the city fighting desperately.

Various conflicting accounts have been given of the behaviour of the Scots in this action; Clarendon, who, however, seldom has a good word for that nation, accusing them of gross cowardice. But one may be allowed to rely on the testimony of Cromwell himself, who, in letters to the Speaker, Lenthall, bears witness to the severity of the battle; and when it is remembered that their adversaries were more than double their number, it may be concluded that the Scottish army fought well.

The following are extracts from these letters:—

"Indeed, this hath been a very glorious mercy, and as stiff a contest for four or five hours as ever I have seen."

"The battle was fought with various success for some hours, but still hopeful on our part, and in the end became an absolute victory."

"Indeed, it was a stiff business."[1]

At length, after a desperate resistance, fighting hand to hand through the streets, the Scottish army, overpowered and outnumbered, was utterly broken and put to flight, many being slain and a great number made prisoners.

Family tradition has handed down a report of the fate of the Laird of Philorth on that day. He is said to have been left for dead on that bloody field, and only to have been saved by his faithful servant, who, on finding his master's body, perceived that life still lingered therein, and was fortunate enough to be able to convey him to a place of concealment, where he recovered of his wounds.

[1] Carlyle's Oliver Cromwell, vol. ii. p. 143.

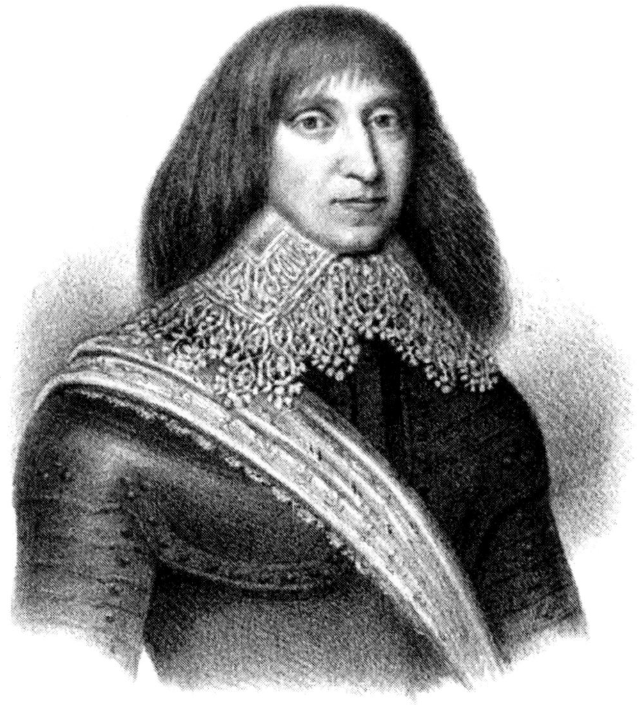

The same report says that they were the only two of the regiment who returned to Scotland, the remainder having been slain, or taken prisoners and sent as slaves to the colonies; and whatever exaggeration there may be in this, the tradition was doubtless founded on the fact that the corps suffered very severely.

After a while the Laird of Philorth succeeded in making his way back to Scotland, and on the 11th January 1652, at Newbottle, he signed the contract of marriage between his son and heir, Alexander, and Lady Ann Kerr, daughter of William, Earl of Lothian.

Before entering upon the dangerous career which he foresaw when he joined the party of his sovereign, he had drawn up his "latter will and testament;" and although, from his life having been prolonged many years, it never took effect, yet it is an interesting document, affording evidence of his having been a thoughtful and religious man, and also of a kindly and affectionate disposition.[1]

After some bequests to his half-sister, Mary, and other relations, he leaves his whole property to his son, and especially mentions his claim and right to the lands of Cairnbulg.

The sale of the old manor-place of Philorth, and of the lands attached to it, by Alexander Fraser of Durris, in contravention of the conditions under which he had purchased them from Sir Alexander Fraser of Philorth and Fraserburgh in 1616, has been already noticed, and the Laird of Philorth now attempted to set aside that transaction and recover the property.

About 1652 he commenced an action against Andrew Lord Fraser (the successor of the Laird of Muchalls, who had been the purchaser), for the reduction of the sale of the lands and castle, and for their revendition to him in the terms of the contract under which they were conveyed to the Laird of Durris, upon the ground that such sale had been in direct contravention of the stipulations in that contract, that these subjects should not be sold during the lives of his grandfather, Sir Alexander Fraser, and Alexander Fraser of Durris, and that, after their decease, they should be offered to his grandfather's heir at a fixed price.[2]

This lawsuit dragged on until 1665, when it was decided in favour of the

[1] Philorth Charter-room.   [2] Philorth Charter-room. Dal. Decreeta, vol. xv.

Lord Fraser, and, as was too often the case in those days, the authority of the law confirmed the possession of property wrongfully acquired.

In another litigation with the same adversary, the Laird of Philorth was more successful. Between 1631 and 1637, it had become necessary to rebuild the kirkyard dike of the parish church of Rathen, which work was apportioned amongst the heritors of the parish, and the stile or entrance to the kirkyard fell to the share of Lord Lovat and Andrew Fraser of Muchalls,[1] recently created Lord Fraser, the latter of whom not only encroached some feet upon the Philorth property, but also placed his arms over the kirk stile, which, doubtless, was considered by far the greater offence, as the Laird of Philorth was patron of the church of Rathen.

Philorth at first endeavoured to redress this grievance with the strong hand, and caused boards bearing his arms to be placed over the sculptured arms of Lord Fraser, who thereupon raised an action against him in the Court of Session.

The Lords of Council and Session found that wrong had been done to the Lord Fraser by the Laird of Philorth, but upon the latter declaring that "the setting up of the saides armes wes done be him vpon respect and for honour of his father's funerallis, and not out of any splene or contempt of the said Lord Fraser, nor of the honour, title, and dignitie conferred be his Majestie vpon him," they forbore censuring him, and merely ordered him to take the boards down before the 15th March 1637, and not to remove the arms of the Lord Fraser except in a legal way, upon decreet from the Judge Ordinary. The Laird of Philorth thereupon obeyed, and afterwards brought an action against the Lord Fraser, both as regarded the kirk stile and dike and the arms, which was decided in his favour in 1667.

But upon the petition of William the Earl Marischall, Simon Fraser of Inverallochie, and other heritors of the parish, who represented "Lyke as their Lordships knew that the armes of the Lord Fraser wes upon the said kirkstyle, and it was sufficientlie known what prejudice and animositie wes alreadie between the Lairds of Philorth and the Lord Fraser, and if this opportunitie wer puttin in Philorth's hand, be vertu of this decreit, to throw

---

[1] These had become heritors in the parish of Rathen in consequence of their respective acquisition of Inverallochy, and of Cairnbulg and Invernorth.

down and break in pieces the Lord Fraser's armes, which is a badge of honour conferred on his familie be the King's Majestie, thair Lordships by putting an end to this pley would occasion a farr greatter and worse between the saids pairties nor ever zet had bein." Therefore they "craved their Lordships would fall on some convenient way for accommodating the samyn, and recommend to indifferent and judicious men, who wer not ingaideged in either pairtie, to take cours in ordour to the saids armes befor the decreit wer put in execution as to the dyke and style." Whereupon their Lordships "recommendit, and heirby recommends to my Lord Fyvie, and, in his absence, anie two of the justices of peace, to be present at the removal of the foresaid armes off the kirk style above specified, and to cause the samyn to be done without defacing the armes."[1]

In consequence of the adverse decision in 1665 respecting the castle and lands of Cairnbulg, and his failing to recover the old manor-place of Philorth, Alexander Fraser determined to erect a new residence, and in 1666 built the present house of Philorth, about two miles to the south of Fraserburgh. The age of fortified castles had gone by, and that of Fraserburgh was in too exposed a situation for a pleasant residence, at all events during the winter.

In 1668 his cousin, Alexander de Abernethy, ninth Lord Saltoun, died without issue, and the decease of his only sister, unmarried, having soon followed, this Laird of Philorth inherited the dignity of Lord Saltoun, and he became the tenth Lord. He expede a service as heir of line, through his mother, Margaret de Abernethy, of his maternal grandfather, George, the seventh Lord.[2] As Lord Saltoun, the tenth Lord took the oaths and his seat in the Scottish Parliament on the 9th of August 1670. Lord Mordingtoun made a general protest, probably on the ground of precedency, but without effect. Only thirteen days thereafter, on 22d August 1670, the king and the Parliament passed an Act ratifying the dignity to Lord Saltoun, and that Act embodied in it a previous ratification, which was made by the king on the 11th of July preceding. The Act of Parliament is in the following terms:—

"At Edinburgh, the tuentie tuo day of August, on thousand sex hundreth and three score ten yeers.—Our Soveraign Lord, with advyce and consent of

[1] Philorth Charter-room. Dal. Decreets, vol. xxiii.

[2] Retour expede on 14th April 1670. Extract at Philorth. See Appendix.

the Estates of Parliament now presentlie convened, Ratifies and Approves, and for His Mātie and his successors, perpetualie confirmes to Alexander, now Lord Saltoun, and the aires of his bodie alreadie procreat and to be procreat, the Letters Patent vnder writtin made and granted be His Mātie, whereof the tenor followes. Sic suprascribitur, Charles R. Whereas wee have seen Alexander Frazer of Philorth, his generall service as air of Lyne to the deceast (George) Abernethie, Lord Saltoun, retoured to our Chancellarie; And wee being willing that the said Alexander and the aires of his bodie alreadie procreat and to be procreat, as nixt in blood and Linealie descended of the said familie, and conforme to ther right thereto, may injoy the title and dignitie of the Lord Abernethie of Saltoun, in all tyme comeing, Thairfor wee have not only ratified and approven the foresaid service and retour, Bot also ratifie and approve of the said Alexander his vseing and takeing vpon him as Air of Lyne and next in blood and Lineallie descended of the said familie, the Title, Dignitie, place, and rank therof, And will and declare that the said Alexander and the Aires Lineallie descending of him may vse and injoy the forsaid Title and Dignitie in all tyme comeing, as any other Lord Abernethie of Saltoun did in any tyme bygon vse and injoy the same, and all the honours and priviledges therto appertaining. Wherof wee will and comand all our Officers and others our Subjects to tak notice. Given at Our Court at Whytehall, the Elevint day of July 1670, And of our reigne the tuentie tuo yeer. By his Majesties comand sic sub^r Lauderdaill. In all and sundrie heids, articles, priviledges, Immunities, Honors, and Dignities therof above mentioned, and after the forme and tenor therof in all points."[1]

Beyond the acquisition of an ancient and honourable dignity, his succession to the title, and heirship to his maternal grandfather brought Lord Saltoun little advantage; on the contrary, it involved him in a sea of trouble and litigation, which lasted his whole life, and did not end until the time of his grandson, with disastrous results to the family.

In the history of the Abernethies of Abernethy and Saltoun, Part v., it will be seen that the eighth and ninth Lords Saltoun had become deeply embarrassed in their circumstances, and had parted with all, or nearly all their estates.

[1] Original Extract Act, signed by Sir Archibald Primerose, Clerk Register, in Philorth Charter-room.

Charles R

Whereas we have seene Alexanders
service, as air of lyne to the decd
Reponed to our Chancelary, of
Alexander Frazer, and the heires
be procreat, as next in ... and
family, and conforme to ...
dignitie of the ...
Therefore we have ...

his using and taking upon him an
lineally descended of the said family
thereof ... and declare ...
lineally descended of him may ...
dignitie in all tyme coming as any ...
did in any ... passage and ...
priviledges hereto apertaining ...
our officers and others our subts
at Whitehall the ... day of ... 16 ...

Alexander Fraser of Philorth his generall
the umquhile Lord George Abernethie Lord Salton
... And wee being willing that the sayde
... of his bodie already procreate and to
bloode... lineally descended of the saide
... thereto, may enjoy the title and
... Salton, in all tyme coming:
... and approven the forsaid ...
... approve of the said Alexander Fraser
him is aire of lyne and next in bloode, and
... family the title dignitie place and ranke
... that the said Alexander and the aires
... may use and enjoy the foresaid title and
... as any other Lord Abernethy of Salton
use and enjoy the same, And all the honors and
... whereof wee will and command all
our subjects to take notice. Given at our Court
... of our reigne the 22 yeir

By his Maties command
Lauderdaill

The transactions by which the ninth Lord Saltoun attempted to retrieve his fortunes, James Abernethy's unprincipled abstraction of the leaves from the register of decreets, and the subsequent events, will be there related, and need not be told here; and when the Laird of Philorth, as heir of line, became tenth Lord Saltoun, he and his son Alexander, who became Master of Saltoun, found themselves made parties to the formidable lawsuits which those proceedings had engendered.

It will also be seen that the renunciation executed by the ninth Lord Saltoun was sufficient to secure Sir Andrew Fletcher in his purchase of the estate of Saltoun, and the family of Gordon who purchased Rothiemay and other Abernethy lands, do not appear to have been very seriously disturbed in the enjoyment of those acquisitions; but the proprietorship of the estate of Balvenie, in Banffshire, was most bitterly contested.

Lord Saltoun, however, does not appear to have taken any very active part in these matters, or to have inherited any rights in the estate of Balvenie, or in any other part of the possessions of the Abernethies, for the lawsuits respecting that property were carried on almost entirely in the name of his son, the Master of Saltoun.

John, eighth Lord Saltoun, purchased Balvenie from James, Earl of Atholl, about 1609, and a few years later disponed it to Lord Ochiltree, by whom it was conveyed to Sir Robert Innes of Invermarkie, from whom, or from his heirs, it is said to have passed to Sutherland of Kinminity; but at any rate, about the middle of the century, Adam Duff of Drummuir had obtained some rights over it, proceeding from the disposition of the eighth Lord Saltoun.

The reversal of that disposition, which Sir Archibald Stewart of Blackhall succeeded in carrying out by James Abernethy's fraud, and his previous adjudication of the estates from the ninth Lord Saltoun in 1639,[1] seem to have given him command of the estate of Balvenie for a time, and he conveyed it to Alexander Fraser, younger of Philorth (afterwards the Master of Saltoun), who held it with the consent of Adam Duff of Drummuir, who seems to have been under pecuniary obligations to his father, the Laird of Philorth, as early as 1643, and this shows how the right of the Master of Saltoun arose.

[1] See Part v., Alexander, ninth Lord Saltoun.

The ninth Lord Saltoun, however, may perhaps have disponed Balvenie to Arthur Forbes of Echt, who will be seen to have obtained much influence over him; at all events the latter, as a very prominent creditor under Sir Archibald Stewart's adjudication, claimed that estate, as well as all the other Abernethy lands, and it was between him and the Master of Saltoun that litigation, embittered perhaps by Echt's failure in obtaining the succession to the title,[1] went on for many years, proving most disastrous to the interests of both.

A detailed account of a long series of lawsuits would be an infliction from which it is desirable to spare the reader, and it will be sufficient, as regards Balvenie, to say that, after many years of varying fortune, the scales of law—for justice had little to do with the whole affair—inclined in favour of Arthur Forbes, who seems for a few years to have established his title to that estate, only in 1687 to have it adjudged from him by Alexander Duff of Drummuir and Alexander Duff of Braco, the former of whom conveyed it to the latter; and it now, with many other of the old Abernethy estates, forms part of the property of Braco's descendant, the Earl of Fife.

The dull proceedings of the courts of law were, however, at times exchanged for a little violence; and it is upon record how Arthur Forbes, accompanied by James Gordon of Rothiemay, Sir John Forbes of Craigievar, Master John Forbes, Sheriff-depute of Aberdeen, Arthur Forbes of Brux, Robert Forbes, tutor of Craigievar, William Forbes of Camphoe, with many other persons, to the number of twenty-four or thirty, came to the Master of Saltoun's house at Balvenie, and called his servants and vassals to state upon oath what money they had given to the Master. The servants that were working in the house (the Master was not there) fearing an attack, left the place after "rainforcing the gates with great trees and posts of timber;" and Arthur Forbes, with his party, after trying in vain to break them open, got in by the windows of the second storey, and having done considerable damage, left the house because they did not find it tenable,—probably it was undergoing repair,—" venting a great many brags they should be there to possess it within a few moneths, who would say the contrarie," which the Master com-

[1] See Part v., Alexander, ninth Lord Saltoun.

ALEXANDER FRASER,
MASTER OF SALTOUN.
BORN CIRCA 1630.   DIED V.P. 1682.

plained so affrighted his vassals and servants, that "he cannot get them pay their dueties."

But the loss of Balvenie was not the only mischief caused by the litigation in which the Master of Saltoun was engaged, and before relating his further misfortunes, some account may be given of his more private career.

The only son of the tenth Laird of Philorth, he was born about 1630, and was educated at King's College, Aberdeen, having matriculated there in 1647. He married, on the 11th of January 1652, Lady Ann Kerr, daughter of William, Earl of Lothian, and by her had two sons, Alexander and William. She died in the course of a few years, and on the 29th of October 1660 he married a second wife, Dame Marion Cunyngham, Countess of Findlater, who lived but a short time after the marriage, for, on the 27th of June 1663, he is found a third time venturing upon matrimony, and he then espoused Lady Sophia Erskine, sister to the second and third Earls of Kellie.

This lady seems to have possessed much amiability and intelligence, and the following letter from her to the Earl of Lauderdale, in favour of her brother, the third Earl of Kellie, though in the faulty orthography of that age, is well expressed, and was probably written before her marriage :—

Petenueme, the 19 Joune.

"My Lord,—Being enformed by my brother Kellie and others tuo of your lordships gret kyendnes and seueletis to hem makes mie giue your Lordship the troubell of ther fhoue layens att thes tyem to render your lordship manay thanks for all your fauers and nobell acs of kyendnes you heau ben plesed to sheau for my brother and troulie itt dous sho a gret deal of generosetie and good neter in your lordship to heau so much kyendnes for your frends   I am houpfoull that your lordship hes ben plesed to sho hes Majestie soumvhat of the condestioune of my brother's femelie   I dout not bot your lordship knous soumtheng of itt Tho' not so much as I could wish for I knoe my brother to be of that youmer that he can hardle let hes condestioune be knoun to hes nerest relationes Tho' itt consernes hem werie much   I hear hes Majestie is a werie Gresties and kyend prens to all his soubjaks and particolerle to all Thos who hes ben soufers for hem en ther tyems and I am houpfoull hes Majestie well louk upon my brother as on of thos so my onlay desayer to your lordship is that you vold be mending his Majestie of hem and I houmblie entret your lordship laykways to giue my brother your best adues en making his adreses hem self to hes Majestie so creuing your lordship's pardoun for thes troubell I well ead no more bot that I shall euer stref to vetnes myself how much I am

                My lord
                      Your lordship's most affectionett cousing and hcumbell seruand
                                              S. ARESKINE"

"For the Earell of Latherdeall"[1]

The Master and his third wife appear to have lived together on the most affectionate terms, and at her death, which occurred in 1676, he deplored her loss in a letter to the Earl of Tweeddale that evinces much feeling.

                                        Philorth, 17th July 1676.

"MY DEAR LORD,—Your last com to me in a verie sad tyme, when my deerest and best pairtt of this world was gone to hir everlasting rest. I was not capablle to give an return then, neather now can ther com ani thing from this butt sorrow and affliction, and I doubt nott at all but your lordship and your family will hav an shair in our griffe, as having nott only lost an affectionatt kinswoman, butt the beste and trewist of freinds. O what an hairtt hav I that can call to mynd the manie sweitt conforts we hade togither, and not braik; but God Almightie, who saw how unworthie I was of what I injoyed, and how unthankful to his holy Majestie for continowing so grytt an blising with me, hes been plaised in his wisdoum to remove it. I pray him it may be in his mercie to me. I shall give your lordship no mor truble now, but I will ever be to your lordship, to my deir lady, and to all your family, my deir lord, a most faithful and humble servant,

"For the Eairlle of Twaddaille—This."[2]

[1] Lauderdale MSS., British Museum.   [2] Original Letter at Yester.

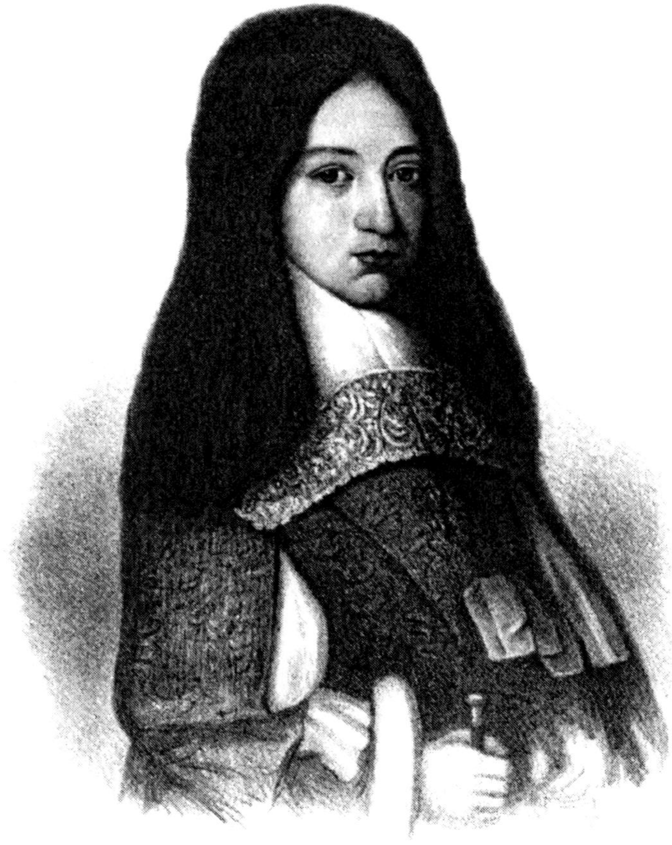

The Master of Saltoun had no issue except the two sons of his first marriage. The elder of these, Alexander, was born in 1653,[1] matriculated at King's College, Aberdeen, in 1667, and died towards the end of 1672, when about nineteen years of age;[2] and the second son, William, who was born on the 21st of November 1654, eventually succeeded his grandfather as eleventh Lord Saltoun.

The Master is described by his son William as a man of the strictest integrity and honour; but he appears to have possessed scarcely sufficient firmness of character for the troublesome times in which his lot was cast, and a somewhat facile disposition induced him to place undue confidence in pretended friends, who grossly betrayed him, but whose names are not mentioned here, as it is undesirable to re-open old animosities long since forgotten. Although his father often remonstrated strongly with him, and endeavoured to rouse him to distrust of false friends, yet in the course of the lawsuit respecting Balvenie he became more and more involved in debt to them, both on account of the expenses of litigation, and to purchase the influential support they professed to be able to procure, until at length he was obliged to pledge to them the lands of Pittullie and Pittendrum (old Fraser possessions, lying about a mile to the westward of Fraserburgh, that had been settled upon him at the time of his first marriage) in security for his liabilities; and his father had no choice but to give his consent to that measure, which he did very reluctantly.

No sooner had his pretended friends gained this point than they altogether neglected his interests, and, turning upon him, pressed for settlement of accounts; and taking every advantage that the law afforded, not only evicted those lands from him and his heirs, but left the family still under considerable liabilities to them, from which, however, it will be seen that his son, the eleventh Lord, succeeded in freeing it.

These unhappy results were therefore in a great degree due to the Master's unfortunate weakness of character; and as might be expected with a man of kindly disposition, they had a serious effect on his constitution, bringing him to a comparatively early grave, for in November 1682 he was taken

[1] Philorth Charter-room.
[2] In the records of the kirk-session of Fraserburgh the following entry is found :—

"Wednesday, December 9, 1672. Item, for the velvet mortcloth at the Laird of Saltoun's buriall, £5, 16s."

ill, and went from his own residence at Pittullie, which he seems not to have relinquished, to his father's house of Philorth, where he expired about eight days after his arrival.

Lord Saltoun being now an aged man, and having disponed all the family estates to his grandson, William, who, on his father's death, assumed the title of Master of Saltoun, appears to have passed his few remaining years in retirement, and in preparation for another and better world.

He was treated with all consideration and respect by his grandson. He had apartments in the house of Philorth and the Castle on Kinnaird Head, besides a lodging or house in the town of Fraserburgh, which he seems to have occupied when tired of company, and two men-servants were especially appointed to wait upon him.

His decease is thus quaintly recorded in the registry of the Episcopal Congregation of Fraserburgh :—

"Alexander, Lord Saltoun, came to the lodging on the 10th day of July, in the year of God 1693, and he departed out of this life the 11th day of August 1693, and was buried in his own Isle in Fraserburgh the 18th of the present month. He was of age, going in his eighty-ninth year. He was a man that was given to reading of good books, and very much in the exercise of prayer, both in his closet; and when he had occasion to meet with a minister or churchman of his own profession : He would alwise desire them to pray before they parted with him.

"He was very civil and kind to all whom he had the freedom to converse with. He was also very charitable to the poor, at all occasions, wherever he and they did meet.

"He was carried to the Seatown on the 12th day of August, at night. August began that year on Tuesday."[1]

Thus peacefully died the old Lord, nearly forty-two years after his narrow escape from a more violent fate on the bloody field of Worcester.

There is no record of the death of his second wife, but he in all probability long survived her.

By his first wife he had a daughter—

Janet, married to Alexander Fraser of Techmuiry.

[1] Register of the Episcopal Congregation, Fraserburgh.

By his second wife he had an only son—

Alexander, afterwards Master of Saltoun, who, as has been mentioned, predeceased him, leaving an only surviving son, William, who succeeded his grandfather.

And it is probable that by one or the other of his marriages he had a second daughter, for a passage in the History of the Troubles of Scotland says, " And Patrick Leslie that samen night, about ten hours at even, rode through the old toun, about 20 horss, to his son's marriage with Philorthe's daughter, which he preferred to that charge, albeit he was ane arch covenanter."[1]

"That charge" was an order from the Rev. Andrew Cant, minister at Aberdeen, delivered from the pulpit on the 18th of May 1645, for all to make ready to assist Baillie against Montrose.

Mr. Anderson, at page 112 of his History of the Family of Fraser, quoting MSS. of Frasers, Advocates' Library, p. 395, makes the following statement :—
" In February 1665, Lord Lovat paid a visit to the king at London. Sir Alexander Fraser of Philorth introduced him to his Majesty as his Chief."

It is painful to be obliged to expose, not a mistake, nor even a *suppressio veri*, but an absolute falsification of evidence which he quotes, on the part of Mr. Anderson; but it is necessary, and without further comment the passages in the MS., which is still in the Advocates' Library, are here given. Page 393 : " In February 1665, Lord Lovat, being then past twenty one years of age, set out with a noble Retinue to wait of ye King at London. He was conveyed South by his two Uncles, the Tutor and Beaufort, and several others of his Clan, who took leave of him at Edin[r], and was attended through England only by Alexander Fraser, younger of Philorth. . . . He had not bein above two days at London when his Lordship, Alex[r] Fraser, younger of Philorth, and Sir Ralph de la Ville, were introduced to the King by Sir Alexander Fraser of Dores, one of his Majesty's Physicians." Page 395 : " Sir Alexander Fraser gave him a Coach, and 4 stately Horses, and, being inferior to his son, Sir Peter Fraser, in pride, acknowledged Lord Lovat as his Chief, and introduced him to the King as such."[2]

This Sir Alexander Fraser of Dores or Durris had acquired that estate by

---

[1] History of Troubles, vol. ii. p. 477.
[2] The MS. is very clearly written, and is almost as legible as print.

purchase, but his descent from the old family of that name and designation is very doubtful.

In the year 1672, after his succession to the title, the tenth Lord Saltoun's armorial bearings were thus blazoned by Sir Charles Erskine (or as he writes his name, "Araskine") of Cambo, Baronet, Lyon king-of-arms. "Alexander, Lord Saltone, for his achievement and ensigne armoriall, bears three coats quarterlie, first and last, Saphire three fraises pearle; second, Rubie ane lyon rampant pearle; third, Pearle three piles palewayes rubie."[1]

This was bad heraldry, and the Lyon was as careless as the Herald who a few years previously, in 1663, copied the "five fraises placed salterwayes" from the shield of the Lords Yester, termed them the arms of "Lord Fraser of old," and assigned them to Lord Lovat.[2]

The true bearings of Fraser of Philorth were quarterly, 1st and 4th, Saphire three rosettes pearl for Fraser; 2d and 3d, Ruby three lions rampant pearl for Ross; though these last had through mistake been reduced to one lion during the sixteenth century.

The true bearings of Abernethy Lord Saltoun were quarterly, 1st and 4th, Topaz a lion rampant ruby, surmounted with a bend dexter diamond for Abernethy; 2d and 3d, Pearl three piles paleways ruby for Wishart; and when these two coats were impaled by the marriage of Alexander Fraser of Philorth and Margaret de Abernethy, and borne by their son, Alexander Fraser, tenth Lord Saltoun, the correct blazoning would have been, Quarterly, 1st, Saphire three rosettes pearl; 2d, Topaz a lion rampant ruby, surmounted with a bend dexter diamond; 3d, Ruby three lions rampant pearl; 4th, Pearl three piles paleways ruby. If any of these quarterings could have been properly omitted, it would only have been that of Wishart, and certainly not that of Fraser, the family name; nor that of Ross, by which came the estate of Philorth; nor that of Abernethy, which was identified with the title of Saltoun.

[1] Saphire = Azure. Pearl = Argent.
Ruby = Gules. Topaz = Or.
Diamond = Sable. [2] See account of Margaret Fraser in Part II.

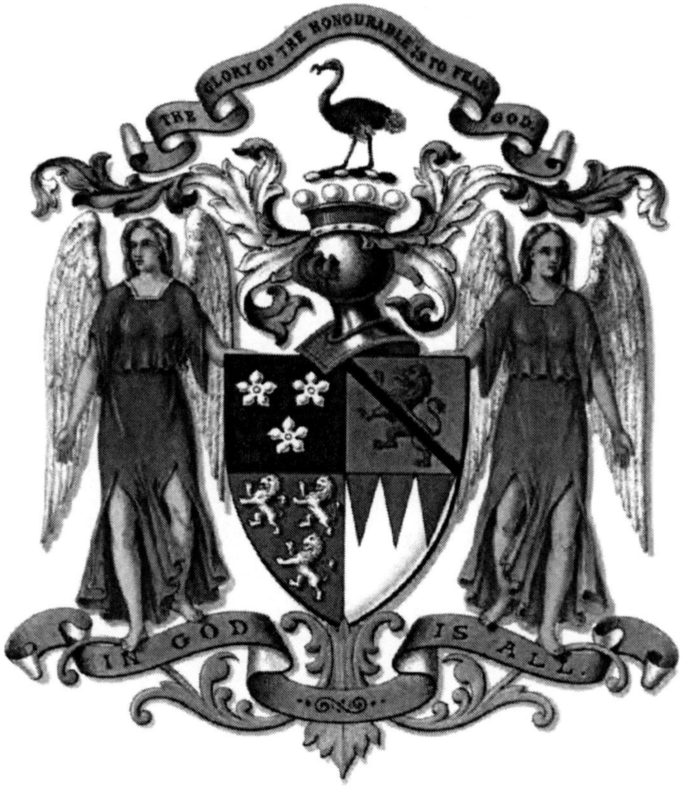
THE GLORY OF THE HONOURABLE IS TO FEAR GOD.
IN GOD IS ALL.

WILLIAM FRASER,
ELEVENTH LORD SALTOUN.
BORN 1654, DIED 1715.

WILLIAM FRASER,	MARGARET,
ELEVENTH OF PHILORTH AND ELEVENTH LORD SALTOUN.	DAUGHTER OF JAMES SHARPE, ARCHBISHOP OF ST. ANDREWS.

WILLIAM FRASER, second son of Alexander Fraser, afterwards Master of Saltoun, and the Lady Ann Kerr, was born on the 21st November 1654,[1] and with his elder brother, Alexander, was educated at King's College, Aberdeen, their names appearing together as having matriculated there in 1667.[2]

At the decease of his elder brother in 1672, he became heir-apparent to his father, and very shortly afterwards was deeply engaged with him in those lawsuits to which allusion has been made in the latter part of the life of the tenth Lord.

Though powerless to save his grandfather and father from the misfortunes which overwhelmed them, he appears to have had much common sense and prudence, which prevented his own utter ruin; and he held fast the reversion of the estates, to which he had become entitled by a deed of disposition, which their necessities had compelled them to execute in his favour in 1676, and in which he had prudently obtained infeftment by royal charter.[3]

He was often, however, very hardly pressed in reference to his pecuniary affairs, and in 1679 was forced to go abroad to France, where he remained for about a year in great distress, returning to Scotland in September 1680, at the request of his grandfather.[4]

In November 1681 he obtained from the Duke of York the command of a company of foot, and his father dying in 1682, he assumed the title of Master of Saltoun, as heir-apparent to his grandfather.[5]

On the 11th October 1683, at Scotscraig, in Fife, he married Margaret, daughter of the venerable James Sharpe, Archbishop of St. Andrews,[6] who was so barbarously murdered at Magus Moor, in Fife, on the 3d of May 1679, by a party of Covenanters, headed by Balfour of Burley and Hackstoun of Rathillet. It was the sister of Margaret Sharpe, who was with the good

---

[1] Philorth Charter-room.
[2] Fasti Aberdon., p. 485.
[3] Philorth Charter-room.
[4] Memorandum by himself in Philorth Charter-room.
[5] Ibid.
[6] Ibid.

prelate when the crime was committed, and who was wounded by the assassins.

With Margaret Sharpe the Master of Saltoun obtained a dowry of 40,000 merks, a large sum in those days, and having, as above noticed, been put in possession of the family estates during the latter years of his grandfather's life, he immediately commenced his efforts to repair the fortunes of the family, in which, aided by his excellent wife, he persevered steadily with the happiest results.

In 1689 he sold, to John Fraser, the estate of Memsie, burdened with a feu-duty of 100 merks yearly; and in the following year he sold, absolutely, to Alexander and Margaret Crawford, that part of the lands of Rathen which had been leased to their ancestor, Alexander Crawford, in 1613, by the then Sir Alexander Fraser of Philorth.

In 1695, and the next year or two after his succession as Lord Saltoun, he was engaged in litigation respecting the lands of Pittullie and Pittendrum. He however failed in recovering those estates, but succeeded in freeing himself from all further responsibility for his grandfather's and father's obligations, to meet which the sacrifice of those properties had been made.

The litigation of various kinds that had lasted for nearly half a century, and had brought the family of Philorth to the verge of ruin, here terminated.

Most of the northern Abernethy estates fell into the hands of Duff of Braco, and are now the property of his descendant the Earl of Fife; and the lands of Pittullie and Pittendrum, after passing through the hands of various proprietors, now belong to Lord Clinton, by his marriage with the heiress of Sir John Stuart Forbes, their late possessor.

William Fraser wrote a long narrative of his own and his father's share in these transactions, from which in a great degree the above brief account of them has been extracted.[1]

In the year 1693 he succeeded to the title of Lord Saltoun, upon the death of his grandfather, the tenth Lord, and on 9th May 1695, he took his seat in Parliament and the oath of allegiance.[2]

In 1697, a curious transaction occurred in which he was concerned, and

---

[1] Philorth Charter-room.
[2] Acts of the Parliaments of Scotland, vol. ix. pp. 347, 350.

Sir Peter Lely pinx.t

**JAMES SHARPE, ARCHBISHOP OF S.T ANDREWS,
FATHER OF MARGARET, WIFE OF WILLIAM FRASER, ELEVENTH LORD SALTOUN.
BORN 1613. — MURDERED 1679.**

which strongly exemplifies the very slight authority of the law in the Highlands at that period.

Hugh Fraser, Lord Lovat, in 1685 married the Lady Amelia Murray, daughter of John, first Marquis of Athole, and, dying in 1696, left no surviving male issue, but four daughters.

By his marriage-contract, in default of male heirs by that or any other marriage, he had settled his lordship and barony of Lovat, and his other estates, upon his eldest heir-female, without division, contingently upon her marrying a gentleman of the name of Fraser; but he appears, in March 1696, not six months before his decease, to have altered this destination, and to have disponed his property to his grand-uncle, Thomas Fraser of Beaufort, and his heirs-male, though it is questionable whether he had the power of legally doing so in the face of the settlement under his marriage-contract.

The eldest of these four daughters bore the same name as her mother, Amelia; and the Marquis of Athole, in 1697, when she was not above eleven years of age, arranged a contract of marriage between her and Lord Saltoun's eldest son, the Master of Saltoun, then a boy of about thirteen.

This gave great umbrage to some of the other branches of the Fraser name, and Thomas Fraser of Beaufort, with his eldest surviving son, Simon (afterwards the notorious Lord Lovat, executed in 1747), who were the nearest male heirs to the late Lord Lovat, determined to prevent the match taking place, and for that purpose entered into a confederation with Charles, Lord Fraser.

It is difficult to understand what induced Lord Fraser, whose interests were not affected, and whose estates were situated in Aberdeenshire, to interfere in the affair, and it is not improbable that his motives in doing so were political. He was an ardent Jacobite, and very possibly apprehended that Lord Saltoun, who was not disposed to rebel against the reigning monarch, would use the power which the contemplated alliance would have given him in a manner unfavourable to the designs of that party for the restoration of the Stewart family to the throne.

Beaufort and his son Simon having assembled a good many of the leading men of the clan at a place called Essick, about four miles from Inverness, on the road to Stratherrick, Lord Fraser there met them, and made a speech, telling them how severe a master Lord Saltoun would prove to be if his son should marry the heiress of Lovat, and thanking them for their readiness to support the pretensions of the Frasers of Beaufort to the succession.[1]

After Lord Fraser's return home to Aberdeenshire he received a letter from Thomas Fraser of Beaufort, and some of his party, about twenty-six in number, containing a peremptory warning which he was to convey to Lord Saltoun, not to come into that part of the country without their leave and invitation, which he accordingly intimated to him.[2]

Lord Saltoun, however, disregarded this threat, and in October 1697, having visited the dowager Lady Lovat at Castle Downie, near Beauly, was returning to Inverness, accompanied by Lord Mungo Murray, and with only the usual attendants of gentlemen travelling, when they were met in the wood of Bunchrew by Beaufort and his son Simon, at the head of above fifty armed men, who attacked them, made them prisoners, dismounted them from their horses, and putting them on country garrons, led them to Finellan House, where they were imprisoned in separate rooms, and remained for about five days, during which time Beaufort and his son, having assembled a force of several hundred men, erected a gallows before the house, upon which they threatened to hang their prisoners, unless Lord Saltoun engaged to proceed no further with the marriage of his son to the heiress of Lovat.

From Finellan Lord Saltoun and Lord Mungo Murray were taken to the rocky island of Aigas, in the Beauly river, and thence brought to Castle Downie, of which Beaufort and his son had taken possession, where they were at length released, John Fraser of Crechie, according to his own deposition, having been instrumental in saving their lives.[3]

The atrocious conduct of Simon Fraser of Beaufort towards the dowager Lady Lovat, who fell into his hands at Castle Downie, may be passed over in silence (the young heiress, happily for her, had been placed in safety under the care of the Marquis of Athole). It may be briefly mentioned that troops being sent against Beaufort and his adherents, they were dispersed, and his son Simon, not venturing to appear and stand his trial, was, in his absence, with nineteen of his associates, sentenced to death on the 5th September 1698, for the outrages they had committed. He afterwards had interest enough to

[1] Depositions at the trial of Simon Fraser, March 1698.   [2] *Ibid.*   [3] *Ibid.*

procure the royal pardon for these crimes, and to obtain from the Court of Session a decision in favour of his claim to the title of Lord Lovat.[1]

The effect of the violent opposition of the Frasers of Beaufort, however, was to break off the match between the Master of Saltoun and the heiress of Lovat, and the young lady in 1702, married Alexander Mackenzie of Prestonhall; while the Master of Saltoun, in 1707, espoused the Lady Mary Gordon, daughter of the first Earl of Aberdeen, whose fortune of 18,000 merks was paid to Lord Saltoun in consequence of settlements made by him in favour of the young couple.

As already mentioned, Lord Saltoun laboured earnestly to retrieve the fortunes of the family, and his success was very great.

In 1676, by the disposition already referred to, he had become the nominal proprietor of the estates, but he does not appear to have had the real management of them until after his father's death in 1682.

He was, to a certain degree, assisted by the dowries of his own wife, and of his son's, both of which he received; but without going into particulars, suffice it to say that he redeemed above eighty wadsets or mortgages upon the property, and besides thus removing incumbrances, was enabled at his death to dispose of a sum of ready money, the accumulations of a life of frugality and good management, nearly as large as the amount of the debt which he had to face upon his accession, and which he had cleared off.[2]

Of this sum of ready money, he left about half between his eldest son, the Master of Saltoun, and his eldest grandson, the Master's child; and divided the other half between his widow and six younger sons and daughters.

He appears to have taken considerable interest in the mercantile projects of the age, and to have been a promoter of the Indian and African Company, and other attempts to extend the commerce of the kingdom.

He was frequent in attendance to his duties in the Scottish Parliament, and in 1706 was one of the Peers who strongly opposed the union with England,—a proof how little many of the shrewdest and most sensible men of

---

[1] The present noble family of Lovat are not descended from this clever but unworthy member of the race, but from Thomas Fraser, second son of Alexander, Lord Lovat, 1544-1557.

[2] Philorth Charter-room.

that day were able to foresee the incalculable benefits which were to result to their country from that measure, though if his opposition was caused by the injustice done to the Peers of Scotland in their exclusion as a body from sitting and voting in the House of Lords—an injustice still unredressed—his motives for it should be approved of by them.

His health began to decline some months before his death, and, after a long illness, he died on the 18th of March 1715, and was buried in the family vault at Fraserburgh.[1]

In politics he seems to have been a steady supporter of the reigning family, and never to have joined the Jacobite party, from which indeed his treatment by Lord Fraser, and Fraser of Beaufort, must have severed him, if he ever had any leaning towards it.

By his wife, Margaret Sharpe, who died in 1734, he left issue three sons and four daughters:—

Alexander, who succeeded him in the title and estates.

William.[2]

James.

Helen, in 1709, married to James Gordon, eldest son of Sir John Gordon of Park, in Banffshire.

Henrietta, in 1718, married to John Gordon of Kinellar, son to Sir James Gordon of Lesmoir, died at Fraserburgh, February 26, 1751.

Mary, married William Dalmahoy of Ravelrig.

Isabella, married before 1732 to Mr. David Browne, minister of the Gospel at Belhelvie.

ALEXANDER FRASER,
TWELFTH OF PHILORTH AND TWELFTH LORD SALTOUN.

LADY MARY GORDON,
DAUGHTER OF FIRST EARL OF ABERDEEN.

His father's marriage having taken place in October 1683, Alexander Fraser, the eldest son of it, was probably born in 1684, or the following year.

---

[1] Philorth Charter-room.

[2] William and James Fraser, sons of William, Lord Saltoun, were admitted honorary burgesses of guild of the city of Aberdeen, April 7, 1707. See Appendix.

ALEXANDER FRASER,
TWELFTH LORD SALTOUN.
BORN CIRCA 1684.   DIED 1748.

He finished his education at the University of Oxford, to which he went in 1703; and in a letter from Sir Robert Sibbald to Mr. Lhuyd, on the 10th July of that year, it is said of him, "The youth is ingenuous and well natured, and I hope shall be an honour to his country."[1]

His engagement of marriage, when a boy of about thirteen years old, to the young heiress of Lovat, and the events which caused that match to be broken off, have been already narrated in the account of his father; and in 1707, as also already mentioned, he married Lady Mary Gordon, daughter of the Earl of Aberdeen.

In 1715, at the decease of his father, he succeeded to the title and estates, and also to a part of the personal property by his father's will; but as his acceptance of this bequest rendered him liable to make good any deficit in the portions assigned to his brothers and sisters, and to his own eldest son, and as the money left by his father was almost all lent to various persons upon bonds, and many of those persons were ruined by the bursting, in 1721, of the South Sea and other bubble schemes, he appears not only to have received no benefit from that bequest, but to have incurred a very heavy responsibility, and, indeed, he was forced to pay the legacy left to his own eldest son, for which his brother, the Honourable William Fraser of Fraserfield, was trustee, and the portion of his youngest sister, Isabella, out of his own funds.

Lord Saltoun appears to have taken an active part in politics, and to have frequently attended the elections of Representative Peers.

At the election of 1721, he entered a protest against the precedency of the Lord Forbes, who had been ranked in the Union Roll premier baron of Scotland, Lord Saltoun being placed second; and at the same election he objected to Mr. John Campbell, second son of the Earl of Breadalbane, assuming his father's title, on the ground of his elder brother, Lord Ormelie, having left a son, to which objection it was replied by the Earl of Findlater, that the patent created the dignity in favour of John Campbell and his heirs-male, and, in his option, any of his younger children that he should nominate to succeed him by a writ under his hand, and so it was that the late Earl of Breadalbane did appoint the present Earl to succeed him.

[1] Douglas Peerage, vol. ii. p. 477.

In 1722 there was a general election of the sixteen Representative Peers. Thirty-two candidates, of whom Lord Saltoun was one, came forward, and though unsuccessful, he had twenty-two votes in his favour.

At this election he protested against the reception of the proxy of Simon, Lord Lovat, in the following terms:—

"I do protest that no person, in prejudice of the undoubted right of Lady Amelia Fraser, Baroness Lovat, may or shall pretend to vote in the election of the sixteen Peers to represent the Peers of North Britain, in regard the honours and dignity of Lovat are by no patent or deed limited to the heirs-male of the late Hugh, Lord Lovat, last deceased, but that dignity did descend, and is legally vested in the person of Amelia, Lady Baroness Lovat, as heir of line, and eldest daughter of the said Hugh, last Lord Lovat, deceased, for that by a decreet of the Lords of Session, dated the 2d day of December 1702 years, it is adjudged and declared that the honours and dignity of Lovat were in the person of the said Amelia, Lady Baroness of Lovat, which decreet stands unreversed, and never any appeal entered against it.

"Therefore, and for several other reasons to be given to the Most Honourable the House of Lords, I do protest against any persons claiming a right to vote as Lord Lovat in this present election, and I hereby take instruments in the hands of you . . . clerks to the meeting of the Peers, and require you to give authentic extracts of this my protest, taken in name and behalf of said Lady Lovat by me, and such other noble Peers who shall please to adhere to this my protestation.   SALTOUN."

The Duke of Athole Lady Lovat's uncle, and the Earl of Cromartie her brother-in-law, adhered to this protest, and at the election of 1727 the Earl of Dunmore also protested in similar terms against the reception of the vote of Simon Fraser as Lord Lovat.[1]

It was, perhaps, this opposition to his vote that caused Simon Fraser to engage in litigation with Hugh Fraser, son of the Lady Lovat, and Alexander Mackenzie of Prestonhall, who had taken the name of Fraser and designation of Fraserdale, in which he obtained, in 1730, a decision of the Court of Session favourable to his claim,[2] which he also fortified by other measures and com-

[1] Robertson's Proceedings of Scottish Peers.
[2] Records of the Court of Session in Register Office, Edinburgh.

promises with Hugh Fraser; and no further objection was offered to his assuming the title of Lord Lovat, although there was still such uncertainty as to his right, that when brought to his last trial for high treason in 1747, it was matter for deliberation as to how he should be tried, lest if impeached as a Peer he might claim to be a commoner, and if as a commoner, assert himself a Peer. Ultimately he was tried, and sentenced as a Peer, which, without being absolute proof of the justice of his claim, yet affirms the last decision of the Court of Session upon the question in 1730.[1]

At the general election of 1734, Lord Saltoun was one of the twenty Peers who adhered to the protest made by the Duke of Hamilton and Brandon against the undue influence of the ministry of the day in the election of Representative Peers, but he declared that in signing the protest he did not include the names of the Marquis of Lothian and the Earl of Balcarres in the list therein mentioned.

Another protest against the election of the sixteen Representative Peers on the same grounds was signed by the same twenty Peers, and a petition to the House of Lords followed; but the petitioners being required to name the persons they accused, and declining to do so, the petition was dismissed.[2]

Lord Saltoun seems, upon the whole, to have been a consistent supporter of the established Government and reigning royal family; the only evidence of his ever having in any way approached the Jacobite party is found in a letter from Simon, Lord Lovat.

Lord Lovat thus writes, in 1741, from Edinburgh to a cousin of his own, but his well-known duplicity renders any statement of his doubtful, and it may have been only an attempt to implicate one he regarded as an enemy:—[3]

"At the same time that I received your letter I had the honor to receive a most gracious and most obligding letter from my Lord Saltoun. No Stratherrick man could write to me in more kindly terms. He begs my advice in the present criticall situation of affairs.

"I took the libertie to show his letter and yours to the Earl of Aberdeen

[1] State Trials.   [2] Spalding Club Miscellany, vol. ii. p.
[3] Robertson's Proceedings of Scottish Peers. 23.

who spoke most kindly of you, and laughed heartily at your postscript; but he is very much afraid that my Lord Saltoun may be led astray, and he instructed me to write to you that, when you see my Lord Saltoun, you may speak strongly to him, that he should take care not to bring a disgrace and stigma upon his noble family that was always loyall to their king and country, by abandoning now the interest of his country and the noble familys that stand up for it, and that for a pitiful pension that perhaps he would never receive a sixpence of. I am resolved to write all this to my Lord Saltoun myself, which I will do, and send at the same time with your letter."

It does not appear, however, that any overtures that may have been made to him were successful in inducing Lord Saltoun to join the Jacobites, and he certainly did not take part in the rising of 1745, and in 1746 was on the Government side, as the following letter, which is taken from the diary of the Rev. John Bisset, a clergyman of Aberdeen, will show:—January 8, 1746.—"I hear it likewise said, but I believe it is a story, that one in the habit of a gentleman came in the Kinghorn boat to Fraserburgh, asking about Lord Strichen, and was told he was then at Philorth, Lord Saltoun's, whereupon he immediately went thither. The Jacobites in Fraserburgh, repenting they had let him out of their grips, came to Philorth, would have the stranger, who, seeing that, called Lord Strichen to another room, gave him despatches, returning to where they were, gave his watch and money to Lord Strichen, then gave himself up to the Fraserburghers, who made him their prisoner, but finding nothing about him, could have been content they had not made him their prisoner.

"Immediately Lord Strichen horsed for London.

"I write you such stories as an amusement for lack of news, but I have seen the day when the Fraserburghers would not have dared to surround Lord Saltoun's house. It was a pity they did not carry the two Lords with them prisoners also."[1]

Although his sympathies seem to have been on the side of the established Government during the rising, yet he is not found to have taken any active part at the time, and this may have been due to failing health, for his last

[1] Spalding Club Miscellany, vol. i. p. 368.

ALEXANDER FRASER,
THIRTEENTH LORD SALTOUN.
BORN CIRCA 1710. DIED S.P. 1751.

attendance at the elections of Representative Peers was in 1742, and on the 24th of July 1748 he died, when about 64 years of age.[1]

He left issue—

Alexander, Master of Saltoun, who succeeded him.

William, who died unmarried, 22d November 1748, soon after his father.

George, who afterwards succeeded his brother Alexander.

Ann, died unmarried, 18th April 1807, at Fraserburgh.

Sophia, died unmarried, 4th April 1784, at Fraserburgh.

ALEXANDER FRASER,

THIRTEENTH OF PHILORTH, AND THIRTEENTH LORD SALTOUN.

THE birth of Alexander Fraser, eldest son of the twelfth Lord Saltoun, took place in 1710,[2] and he is mentioned by name in his grandfather's will in 1714. It is doubtful where he was educated; but there are extant some memoranda of a considerable tour abroad made by him while Master of Saltoun, during the years 1729, 1730, and 1731, in the course of which he visited Paris, Orleans, Angers, Bordeaux, Toulouse, and other principal towns in Europe; but the details of his journey are not of much interest, consisting chiefly of the expenditure on his account by Mr. William Garioch, the tutor who accompanied him. While in Paris, the Master and his tutor appear to have led a pleasant life. They gave suppers to their countrymen, and in January 1730, they entertained at supper the Duke of Kingston at an expense of £38, 13s., and on the same occasion the Duke's servants received £24.

His uncle, the Honourable William Fraser of Fraserfield, had been appointed trustee for the provision in his favour by his grandfather's will, and took care to enforce payment of it, so that, upon coming of age, the Master of Saltoun found himself in possession of an independent income during his father's lifetime, and this may have been one reason for his having been so little at home before his succession to the title, and for his having, as tradition asserts,

---

[1] Philorth Charter-room. [2] *Ibid.*

spent a somewhat gay and extravagant life abroad, and in London, which tastes and associations may, however, have prevented his being involved in the troubles of 1745-6.

His father dying in July 1748, he succeeded to the title and estates, and in October of that year was served heir to him, and also to his grandfather, the eleventh Lord.

Only one attendance on his part at an election of Representative Peers is recorded in 1750;[1] and his tenure of the family property was but brief, for he died on the 10th of October 1751.[2]

He never married, and was succeeded by his only surviving brother—George Fraser.

GEORGE FRASER, ELEANOR GORDON.
FOURTEENTH OF PHILORTH, AND FOURTEENTH LORD SALTOUN.

GEORGE FRASER, the third son of the twelfth Lord Saltoun, was ten years younger than the brother to whom he succeeded, having been born on the 13th July 1720.[3]

An anecdote is related of him, during his early years, that shows him to have been endowed with a certain amount of dry humour.

When he had reached an age to form some idea of what his future career should be, his father took an opportunity of saying, "George, you are growing a big fellow now, and you must not be an idle man, so I should like to hear what profession you think of following; take a few days to consider of it, and let me know." In about a week his father returned to the subject, and said to him, "Well, have you thought over the matter, and made up your mind as to what you would like to be?"

"Yes, I have, sir," said George, "and I think I should like to be a tanner."

"A tanner! what on earth do you mean?"

[1] Robertson's Proceedings of Scottish Peers.
[2] Philorth Charter-room.   [3] *Ibid.*

By Martin

GEORGE FRASER,
FOURTEENTH LORD SALTOUN.
BORN 1720, DIED 1781.

"Why, sir," replied George, "it's a very thriving trade, and it requires so little capital; you see I should only want three hides, yours and my two brothers', and then I should be set up, you know!"

Tradition says that the joke tickled the old Lord's fancy so much, that he forgave George his impudence for the sake of his fun.

George chose the life of a soldier, and obtained a commission in the Royal Marines; but from the absence of all record of individual services until a later period, no trace can be found of his connection with that corps, in which he is said to have risen to the rank of lieutenant.

His name appears enrolled among the honorary burgesses of Aberdeen in October 1747, and on the 10th October 1751 he succeeded the thirteenth Lord in the title and entailed estates (having become his heir on the decease of their intermediate brother, William, in November 1748), and, in the phraseology of his boyish days, obtained the last of the three hides which he had then estimated as his capital.

He also succeeded his brother, the thirteenth Lord, in some unentailed lands, viz., Cairness, with part of Invernorth, and Cairnbulg, which their father had repurchased; but as this last acquisition made him liable for his brother's debts, he gained but little advantage from it, and had to sell a large portion of them for the benefit of the creditors.[1]

He married his first cousin, Eleanor Gordon, daughter of his aunt, Henrietta Fraser, and her husband, John Gordon of Kinellar, on the 30th of May 1756. She was born at Kinnaird Head on the 4th of August 1731.

After his succession he seems to have taken a certain amount of interest in public affairs, and he voted pretty constantly at the elections of Representative Peers by proxy or signed list, though his personal attendances were not numerous.

In 1778, Mr. Munro Ross of Pitcalnie, as heir-male of Hugh de Ross of Rarichies, brother to William, the Earl of Ross in 1370, presented a petition to the Crown, claiming the title of Earl of Ross.

The petition was referred to the House of Lords, but the claim was not followed up by the petitioner. Lord Saltoun, as an heir of the ancient Earls of Ross, does not appear to have taken any steps to oppose these pretensions.

[1] Philorth Charter-room.

They may not have reached the stage at which opposition was requisite, or he may have been unaware of his own right, for if the annexation of the Earldom of Ross to the Crown, which took place in 1476, were annulled, and the title restored to be borne by a subject other than one of the Royal Family, it ought in justice to devolve, by the charter of David II., granted in 1370, under which it passed through five successions, upon the legitimate heirs of John, Earl of Ross and Lord of the Isles (from whom it was taken), the great-grandson of Euphémia, Countess of Ross, elder daughter and heiress of William, the Earl of Ross to whom that charter was given; and failing them, upon the legitimate heirs of Lady Johanna de Ross, the Earl's second daughter, who were the Frasers Lords Saltoun. But the title of Earl of Ross could in no way rightfully appertain to any descendant of Hugh de Ross of Rarichies, the Earl's brother, until the legitimate descendants of Euphemia and Johanna became extinct.

Lord Saltoun appears to have led a quiet and rather secluded life at Philorth, occupied in the management of his estate and the education of his family, until 1781, when he died there on the 30th of August, shortly after the completion of his sixty-first year.[1]

By his wife, Eleanor Gordon, who survived him and died in 1800, he had seven children, of whom five were living at his decease—

Alexander, his successor.

George, born 12th June, died 4th October 1759.

John, born 18th January 1762, died 6th June 1772.

George, born 29th March 1763, served in 42d and 60th Regiments, became captain in the 59th, died at Nevis, in the West Indies, unmarried, 8th January 1799.

Henrietta, born 20th July 1757, died unmarried, 1826.

Mary, born 27th October 1760, died unmarried, 1809.

Eleanora, born 29th March 1766, married, 1st, in 1786, Sir George Ramsay, Baronet, of Banff, who died 1790; and, 2d, in 1792, Mr., afterwards Lieutenant-General, Campbell of Lochnell, but had no issue by either husband.

[1] Philorth Charter-room.

By West from a Miniature

ALEXANDER FRASER,
FIFTEENTH LORD SALTOUN.
BORN 1758, DIED 1793.

MARJORY FRASER, LADY SALTOUN:
WIFE OF THE FIFTEENTH LORD: ÆTAT. INTER 80 - 90.
DIED NOV: 15TH 1851, ÆTAT. 97.

ALEXANDER FRASER, MARGERY FRASER.
FIFTEENTH OF PHILORTH, AND FIFTEENTH
LORD SALTOUN.

ALEXANDER, eldest son of George, fourteenth Lord Saltoun, was born at Philorth on the 27th of June 1758.[1]

He received a liberal education, with a view to his adopting the legal profession, and in 1780, when about twenty-two years of age, he was admitted to the Scottish Bar, according to the following extract :—

"Mr. Swinton in the chair.

"The Hon[ble] Alexander Fraser, son of the Right Hon[ble] George, Lord Saltoun, was publicly examined on Tit. VIII. Lib. xliii. Pand. ne quid in loco publico vel itinere fiat; and was found sufficiently qualified, and was recommended to the Dean, to assign him a case out of the said title, for subject of his discourse to the Lords and Faculty.   JOHN SWINTON, V.D."[2]

His career at the Bar was, however, a very short one, if, indeed, he ever obtained any practice; for in little more than a year he succeeded to the family title and estates, in consequence of the death of his father, on the 30th August 1781.[3]

In the various arrangements which this event rendered necessary, his character shows to advantage. He was generous and kind to his brother and sisters; and towards his mother, who appears to have been clever, but somewhat imperious and exacting, he used such a mixture of gentleness and firmness, highly commendable in so young a man, that he preserved unimpaired the good feeling and affection which ought to exist between such relations.

After settling these affairs, he appears to have gone abroad about January 1782, and travelled on the Continent for some time, but he returned before the election of Representative Peers on the 24th July of that year, at which he was present; and at the following election, on the 8th May 1784, he was one of the candidates, and, though unsuccessful, had fifteen votes in his favour.

[1] Philorth Charter-room.
[2] Minutes of Faculty, 1751-1788, p. 475.
[3] Philorth Charter-room.

At the same election, upon Lord Saltoun being called to give his vote, Sir Walter Montgomery Cunningham of Corsehill, Baronet, taking the designation of Lord Lyle, gave in the following protest :—

"I, Walter, Lord Lyle, do hereby require you, Alexander Orme and George Home, deputes to the Lord Register for Scotland, and clerks officiating at the election of sixteen Peers to represent the Scotch Peerage in the Parliament of Great Britain, to receive my vote as a Peer of Scotland for the Peers following, viz., the Duke of Queensberry, Earls of Glencairn, Eglintoune, Casilis, Kellie, Lauderdale, Drumfries, Dalhousie, Dysart, and Selkirk, Viscount Stormont, Lords Saltoun, Cathcart, Elphinstone, Cranstoun, and Kinnaird; and I protest that if the same shall be refused, my votes in the present election shall nevertheless be as valid and effectual as if my name had stood on the Roll, commonly called the Union Roll; and I had been regularly called to give my said votes on the present occasion, and had given the same accordingly. LYLE."

"Holyrood House,
"At Edinburgh, the 8th May 1784."

Lord Saltoun does not seem to have disputed Lord Lyle's claim to be considered a Scottish Peer, but he in turn protested against him for precedency, to which protest Lord Cathcart adhered.

His protest was in these words :—

"We, Alexander, Lord Saltoun, do protest, for myself, and in the name of all the other Peers who shall adhere to this my protestation, that Baron Lord Lyle cannot be admitted to vote in this election of Peers next in order to Lord Forbes, because—

"1st, The title of Lord Saltoun is more ancient than that of Lord Lyle; and

"2dly, By the judgment of the Court of Session in 1606, settling the precedency of the Peers of Scotland, and by the Roll of the Union Parliament Lord Saltoun is ranked, and has an established right to precedency, next in order to Lord Forbes."

Lord Cathcart immediately afterwards protested against Lord Saltoun being called before him, to which protest the latter probably returned a similar reply.[1]

At the election of Representative Peers on the 28th of March 1787 he attended, and supported the protest by the Earl of Selkirk against the votes of Peers, created British Peers since the Union, being received, which protest also received the adherence of seventeen other Peers of Scotland.[2]

On the 9th June 1784, Lord Saltoun married Margery, daughter, and ultimately heiress, of Simon Fraser, Esq. of Ness Castle, in consequence of which alliance his son and successor acquired a considerable increase of property, in addition to obtaining the inestimable blessing of one of the best of mothers.[3]

Her father, Simon Fraser, was a member of the Highland clan of that name, and his progenitors were settled in the district of Stratherrick, in the county of Inverness.

Born in 1727, he speedily raised himself from obscurity by his talent and industry, and at the time of his daughter's marriage he was the head of a West India mercantile firm in the city of London, and a very wealthy man.

His character, as evinced in such of his correspondence as is extant, shows great capacity for business, joined to a kind disposition and warm heart; and he was remarkable for his readiness to lend a helping hand to the deserving young men of his native country who were striving to push their fortune, as he himself had once done.

When at Gibraltar he had married Miss Wilson (whose sister married John Markett, Esq. of Meponcourt Lodge, in the county of Kent, then a captain in the 3d Buffs), and his family consisted of two children, a daughter, Lady Saltoun, and a son, who bore the same name as himself, Simon, but who caused him much anxiety and trouble.

Young Simon Fraser's failings, however, seem to have been more those of the head than the heart, and he does not appear to have indulged in any serious vice; but he had an inaptitude for business, and wished to enjoy at once the advantages which a share in the mercantile house, as his father's

---

[1] Robertson's Proceedings of Scottish Peers.
[2] Ibid.
[3] Register of St. Stephen's, Coleman Street, London.

heir, would give him, while the old gentleman was no less resolved that he should enter it as an ordinary clerk, and thoroughly learn his business by undergoing the hard work that he himself had experienced; and hence the differences that arose between them, which were again and again renewed until the year 1790, when, upon young Simon positively refusing to take a subordinate place in the office, his father proposed to send him to the West Indies, to look after some of the estates belonging to the firm in those islands.

He sailed for that destination about the end of that year, and died soon after his arrival there.

A letter from him to Lord Saltoun, just before his departure, shows them to have been excellent friends, and that his brother-in-law had often endeavoured, by good advice, to check him in his somewhat headstrong career.[1]

Upon the decease of her brother, Lady Saltoun became heiress of her father. He had purchased some of the lands near Inverness, forfeited after the Rebellion of 1745, and sold by Government, viz., Borlum, Kinchyle, etc., which formed the estate of Ness Castle; and, after his son's death, he employed some of his surplus funds in buying back a considerable amount of property, viz., the lands of Tyrie and Cardno, etc., which had been sold by former proprietors of Philorth, and entailing them upon his daughter's descendants.

He preserved his energies almost unimpaired until the year 1808, when failing health caused him to withdraw from the mercantile house of which he had so long been the head; and about two years later he died, on the 19th of May 1810, at eighty-three years of age.

After enjoying a tour on the Continent, Lord and Lady Saltoun took up their residence at Philorth, and Lord Saltoun soon began to employ his active mind in the affairs of the country, to which he joined literary pursuits and careful supervision of the management of his property; but though he did all in his power as a good landlord, making many improvements, and planting considerably, the time had not arrived for the extraordinary advance in the agriculture of the north-eastern district of Scotland which distinguished the first half of the present century, and is still going on.

[1] Letters in Philorth Charter-room.

SIMON FRASER, ESQRE
OF NESS CASTLE.
BORN 1737 – DIED 1810.

In the summer of 1785, while posting from London to Philorth, he noticed the fact that the charge for the hire of post-horses north of the Firth of Forth was much in excess of that in the southern districts of Scotland and in England; and the following circular letter, which he wrote to the respective conveners of the counties of Perth, Forfar, Fife, Kincardine, Banff, Moray, Inverness, Nairn, Kinross, and Aberdeen, will give an account of his proceedings in the matter. From all he received replies acknowledging the great benefit conferred upon the public by attention being called to it:—

"September 1786.

"Sir,—As the publick at large are much interested in the matter I am now to state to you, I hope you will lay the same before the Noblemen and Gentlemen of your County at the ensuing Michaelmas Head Court, not doubting but they will be disposed to pay all due attention to it.

"Having occasion last summer to post from London in a carriage of my own, which required four horses, I was uniformly charged on the English roads, and to the south of Queen's ferry, no more than one shilling and seven pence sterling per mile, made up of 9^d for the shaft horses, 6^d for the leaders, and 4^d of King's duty: But when I came to Kinross, a demand was made of $1^s/10^d$ per mile, and the same at every stage all the way to Aberdeen. I refused to pay, and did not in fact pay, more than $1^s/7^d$ till I reached Stonehaven, where the landlord would not furnish me with horses till I complied with his demand of $1^s/10^d$ per mile.

"I raised a prosecution of him, before the Sheriff of Kincardine, for restitution of the overcharge, in which I prevailed: but the defendant, having got all his brethren betwixt and the north ferry to join him, brought the matter before the Court of Session by bill of suspension. Their Lordships declared their sentiments of the impropriety of the charge, but, in respect of the former usage, passed the bill, and suggested that it belonged to the Justices of Peace to correct the abuse, recommending to them to make a general regulation in the northern counties, fixing the like rates for post horses with those paid on the south side of the Forth, as they saw no reason for any increase of charge to the northward, and that the present usage evidently appeared to be a gross abuse, and imposition upon the public.

"In this light I flatter myself the Noblemen and Gentlemen of your County will view it, and will, of course, take the necessary measures to enforce the recommendation of the Supreme Court, which I think it my duty in this manner to submit to their consideration.

"I have the honour to be, etc.,

"SALTOUN."

The above letter is inserted not as being of any present importance, but as containing a curious record of the expense of travelling nearly a hundred years ago, which, however, at a later period was almost doubled, 1s. 6d. being the charge per mile for each pair of horses, until the iron steed increased the rapidity and diminished the cost of transit from one part of the country to another.

Lord Saltoun did not generally keep copies of his own letters, but he preserved many of those written to him by his friends, from which some extracts may be of interest.

In October 1785, Mr. Alexander Fraser of Staples Inn, London, writes the following account of Irish affairs:—[1]

"It seems determined that Parliament shall not meet till the latter end of January, and in the meantime the Irish will meet, and the shop-tax be carried into execution. I am told many semi-proselytes have been made in Ireland of late, and by the meeting of Parliament your Lordship will find a new light thrown upon the propositions, by weighty arguments no doubt. One specious, and indeed most convincing argument of any, and one is founded upon a report now industriously circulated (and not without some reason too), of the Roman Catholic families, who were forfeited in Queen Elizabeth's time, and since, keeping exact records, both at home and in convents abroad, of the property so forfeited, and regularly serving, or at least making regular entries of the lawful descendants of such persons, in hope of being some day in condition to recover them in the same strong-hand manner in which they were evicted. The Catholicks are as seven to one, and many Protestants were forfeited at the Revolution. The present proprietors hold their lands by virtue of English declaratory laws, yet the Irish want a

[1] Prior to the Irish Union in 1801.

declaratory law of their own, 'That this country had not, nor has not any jurisdiction over them, nor any powers to bind them by any laws whatsoever.'[1] In case of their separation from this country, France would naturally support the Catholicks in their demands of restitution. Possession would then be weak against force, accompanied by such claims. Catholicks are good casuists and bad civilians; they could easily say to the present holders, 'semel malus semper malus, et quod initio vitiosum est, tractu temporis non convalescet.' But be this as it will, it is a notorious fact that an officer in the French service did lately offer 1000 Louis to a poor man near Cork, for his claims on the great Shannon estate, whereof his grandfather's great-grandfather was deprived. But the sons of the man would not assign their birthright as they call it. This may all turn out a ministerial manœuvre."

Among Lord Saltoun's papers is the following analysis of the Aberdeenshire election of 28th February 1786, when a keen contest took place between Mr. Skene of Skene and Mr. Ferguson of Pitfour, in which the former was victorious; and it is considered worthy of preservation, as a record of the constituency of the county at that date:—

"Aberdeenshire Election, February 28th 1786.

Disqualified by office, . . 1
    Alexander Udny of Udny.
Did not attend, . . . 8
    James Farquharson of Invercauld.
    Alex^r Ogilvie of Auchirries.
    Alex^r Bisset of Lessendrum.
    Genl Robert Fullerton of Dudwick.
    Col^l Harry Gordon of Knockespack.
    Francis Farquharson of Finzean.
    John Ramsey of Barra.
    Wm Gerard of Midstrath.
Present, but did not vote, . . 1
    John Gordon of Craig.

[1] Home Rule seems to be no new invention in Ireland.

THE FRASERS OF PHILORTH, LORDS SALTOUN.

Expunged the Roll, . . . 1
 Col¹ Henry Knight of Pittodrie.
Paired off for Skene, . . . 2
 John Turner of Turnerhall.
 Robert Turner of Menie.
Paired off for Pitfour, . . 2
 John Gordon of Balmoor.
 Sir William Forbes of Pitsligo.

"*N.B.*—Amongst the number of nominal voters are included three heirs apparent; two for Pitfour.
 William Fraser, younger of Inverallochie, and
 Alex' Leith of Glenkindy.
 One for Skene.—Peter Gordon, younger of Abergeldie."

"Real Proprietors for Mr. Skene.		Real Proprietors for Mr. Ferguson.	
John Ross of Arnage.		Charles Fraser of Inverallochie.	
Gen¹ Benjamin Gordon of Balbithan.		William Dingwall of Brucklaw.	
Andrew Skene of Dyce.		Alex' Leith of Freefield.	
Gen¹ Robert Horn Elphistone of Westhall.		Hugh Forbes of Schivas.	
Keith Urquhart of Meldrum.	5	Alex' Morison of Bognie.	5
William Fraser of Fraserfield.		Sir Archibald Grant of Monymusk.	
James Ligertwood of Tillery.		Wᵐ Brebner of Lairnie.	
Charles Gordon of Abergeldie.		Honᵇˡᵉ Gen¹ Wᵐ Gordon of Fyvie.	
William Duff of Corsindae.		Robert Gordon of Hallhead.	
Andrew Robertson of Foveran.	10	Alex' Fraser of Strichen.	10
William Wemyss of Craighall.		James Ferguson of Pitfour.	
Alexander Innes of Breda.		William Urquhart of Craigston.	
John Duff of Hatton.		John Gordon of Lenturk.	
John Paton of Grandhome.		John Lumsden of Cushnie.	
James, Earl of Fife.	15	Dʳ Alex' Hay of Cocklaw.	15
Alex' Russell of Old Deer.		Robert Stevens of Broadland.	
Alex' Dirom of Muiresk.		Arthur Dingwall Fordyce of Culsh.	
Sir Ernest Gordon of Cobairdie.		Thomas Buchan of Auchmacoy.	
Lewis Innes of Balnacraig.		Charles Gordon of Wardhouse.	
Honᵇˡᵉ Alexander Duff of Echt.	20	William Farquharson of Bruxie.	20
Thomas Gordon of Premnay.		John Dingwall of Ranniston.	

Dr Alexr Bannerman of Kirkhill.
Admiral Robert Duff of Logie.
Sir William Forbes of Craigievar.
Duncan Forbes Mitchell of Thainston. 25
James Jopp of Cotton.
George Leith of Overhall.
George Skene of Skene.
Col Alexr Leith of Leith-hall.
Sir Robert Burnett of Leys. 30
John Burnett of Elrick.
George Robinson of Gask.
John Gordon Cumine of Pitlurg. 33

Alexr Irvine of Drum.
William Forbes Leith of Whitehaugh.
Alexr Anderson of Cundacraig.
Alexr Burnett of Kemnay. 25
Dr James Anderson of Moonie.
John Dyce of Tillygreig.
Francis Garden Lord Gardenston.
William Cumine of Pitullie.
. . . Cumine of Auchry. 30
James Moir of Invernettie.
Alexr Farquharson of Haughton.
. . . Fergusson of Kinmundie.
John Taylor of Portertoun. 34

"Claims refused by the Meeting—
   Coll Charles Gordon of Shilogreen.
   John Byron Gordon of Gight.
   . . . Maitland of Pitrichie.

"Electors present, ... 114
For Skene—Real, . . . 33
        Nominal, . . . 29
                      — 62

For Pitfour—Real, . . . 34
        Nominal, . . 18
                      — 52

Majority for Skene, . . . 10."

In the year 1786, Lord Saltoun's attention was called to the practice of the Dutch and other foreign fishing vessels pursuing their occupation in British waters, a practice which probably affected the interests of the inhabitants of his town of Fraserburgh, in common with the other seaports of the east coast; and he had some correspondence upon the subject with the Treasury, and with Mr. Hunter Blair, then Lord Provost of Edinburgh, from the latter of whom he received the following reply:—

"MY LORD,—On receiving the honor of your Lordship's letter of the 15th instant, I communicated it to the Secretary of the Trustees of the Fisheries. I also mentioned it to a sensible, intelligent officer at the Custom-house, but neither of them can discover any law which prohibits the boats you mention from plying or fishing upon the coast. I am glad that your Lordship has written to the Treasury, because they may be better acquainted than we are in laws of treaties respecting nations mutually fishing on their respective coasts. The country is certainly much obliged to your Lordship's attentions.

"I have the honor to be, with esteem and regard,

"My Lord,

"Your Lordship's most obedient and most humble servant,

"J. HUNTER BLAIR."

"Edinburgh, 25th May 1786."

Endorsed in Lord Saltoun's hand : " Respecting the Dutch fishing on the coast of Scotland."

Amongst other local affairs in 1787, Lord Saltoun interested himself in a question concerning the minister's glebe at Strichen, a village about eight miles from Philorth, which came before the General Assembly in that year, and he was induced to do so by his friendship for Alexander Fraser, then Laird of Strichen, great-grandfather of the present Lord Lovat, on whose behalf he wrote to the famous Henry Erskine, the celebrated Scottish barrister and wit, whose reply is here inserted :—

"Edinburgh, May 11th 1787.

"MY DEAR LORD,—I should immediately have acknowledged the honor of your Lordship's very friendly letter of the 5th current, had I not delayed until I should have an opportunity of seeing Mr. James Fraser.

"From what I have seen of that case, I am clear the zeal of the Rev^d gentleman has a very different source from that of regard for the interest of the church, which can at best be very little affected by the issue of the question.

"I shall give Mr. Fraser of Strichen professionally the best advice in my power as to this business, and the conduct thereof. I am very happy to think that, from the view I now take of it, I shall be able in my place as member of Assembly to resist the application of the funds of the church to defray the expense of disputing a transaction that has now nearly run the course of prescription, and that, whether originally perfectly even or not, exhibits no marks of collusion or unfairness, and on the faith of which the family of Strichen has so long afforded the incumbent the free run of thirteen acres of ground, for which, were the excambion now to be set aside, they would have no equivalent.

"Be assured, my dear Lord, that I shall ever with the greatest pleasure embrace any opportunity of showing my sense of your friendship, and the real respect and regard with which

"I am your most faithful and obedient servant,

"HENRY ERSKINE."

In 1787, Lord Saltoun entered into an excambion or agreement of exchange with his feuars of Fraserburgh, by which the latter relinquished certain rights of property, commonty, and servitude, which they enjoyed over various portions of the estates, in return for some lands granted to them by him, which were situated in closer proximity to the town; and this agreement, which was to the advantage of both parties, was formally ratified in the succeeding year.

His early studies had probably given a direction to his literary labours, and in 1788 he published a work, intituled "Thoughts on the Disqualification of the eldest sons of the Peers of Scotland to sit from that country in Parliament; with observations on the civil polity of the Kingdom." In his observations he displayed considerable historical research and legal knowledge, and the book was highly commended by some of his friends; but did not treat of a subject in which the general public were much interested, though now the disqualification has long been a thing of the past, and, from a passage in the Earl of Buchan's letter of 31st October 1791, given further on, would seem to have been removed within three years after the publication of Lord Saltoun's work.

In a letter of the 31st July, William Fraser, younger of Fraserfield, says, in reference to the subject, "The case I put, however, and have not heard answered in a satisfactory way, is of Lord Huntly, and his brother Lord Alexander. The one is heir to an immense estate, the other may be serving the king as a captain or cornet; which is to be supposed most attentive to the landed interest of the country?" And Lord Gardenstone also writes: "I take this occasion to thank your Lordship for the present of your book, which I value very much, both for the matter and composition."

A sad event occurred in the spring of 1790, which brought great sorrow to Lord Saltoun and his family. This was the death of Sir George Ramsay, his brother-in-law, who was mortally wounded in a duel with Captain Macrae, on the 14th April, and died on the 16th. The quarrel was altogether of Macrae's seeking, who is called "that madman Macrae" in one of the letters written at the time, and appears to have been of a turbulent and vindictive disposition. He had some dispute, at the door of the theatre in Edinburgh, with a footman in Sir George's service. Macrae used personal violence to the servant, and though neither Sir George nor any of his family were concerned in the affair, Macrae demanded that the servant should be dismissed, which demand, however, was refused, Sir George saying that he could not see how the servant had been much in fault, and that he would not dismiss him until it should appear that he had acted improperly. The servant, however, a day or two afterwards, summoned Macrae before the Magistrates for the assault, and upon this Macrae wrote an insolent letter to Sir George, reiterating his demand for the dismissal of the man, upon the ground of his having commenced this prosecution. Sir George in his answer stated that he was ignorant of the prosecution until the receipt of Macrae's letter, that it had no encouragement from him, but that he did not think it incumbent on him to interfere in any way. This produced another note from Captain Macrae, insisting on the dismissal of the servant, and saying that it was sent by the hands of his friend Mr. Amory, who, in the event of noncompliance, was commissioned to inform Sir George of the opinion of his conduct entertained by Captain Macrae, and who accordingly did so in no measured language, and the result was the meeting at Musselburgh on the 14th, at which Sir William Maxwell, who was second to Sir George, and Mr. Amory, endeavoured to accommodate matters, but were unable to do so. It was matter of much regret that it was not the person who provoked the duel that was the victim of it, instead of the innocent Sir George Ramsay.

In a letter from Mr. Fraser of Gortuleg to Lord Saltoun, of the 15th April, after mentioning the unavailing attempts of the seconds at reconciliation, he says:—"By all accounts nothing could be more insolent and improper than the conduct of Macrae, and nothing more composed, and at the same time more determined and manly, than Sir George's conduct throughout; and his friend Sir William Maxwell is uncommonly good-humoured and conciliatory. All this, however, is but a melancholy kind of consolation to the worthy man's relations and friends, if he falls a sacrifice to the pride and insolence of so strange a person, who seems to have little other employment than to pick up quarrels in that manner. Indeed he has been so conspicuous in that way, that it will be strange if he escapes punishment, should the consequences prove so fatal as is dreaded."

Lord Saltoun did all in his power to comfort his sister in her distress, and in 1792 she married Mr., afterwards Lieutenant-General, Duncan Campbell of Lochnell, in the county of Argyll.

In 1791 Lord Saltoun took much interest in a project for obtaining a good map of the counties of Aberdeen and Banff, which was also warmly supported by several other gentlemen; and having written to the celebrated Jean, Duchess of Gordon, on the subject, the reply of her Grace is here given:—

"Gordon Castle, Monday.

"You do me much honor, My Good Lord, in wishing my name at the List you mention: Such a Map as you propose will be most useful; but, independent of that, you may at all times command my subscription to any paper patronised by your Lordship. Upon our return we talked of nothing but the joys of the Banff meeting. I hope you are of our opinion, that nothing could be more pleasant, every body seemed willing to please, and be pleased. As to the effects of the Chair, you have no reason to regret them; I wish I were to be as agreeably placed this day. I beg my best wishes to Lady Saltoun, in which all this family beg leave to join, and have the honor to be

"Yours, etc.,

"J. GORDON."

Endorsed in Lord Saltoun's hand:
"Dutchess of Gordon, Nov. 1791."

In the early part of the year Lord Saltoun had contributed a letter to the "Morning Chronicle," on the subject of the Corn Bill, which was thus acknowledged by the editor, Mr. Perry:—

"My Lord,—I had the honor of your Lordship's letter, and beg that you accept my best thanks for the communication you were so good as to make me.

"Your Lordship will see that I lost no time in presenting your valuable thoughts on the Corn Bill, which I observe has excited very serious alarm in every part of Scotland. I am so much disposed to give my feeble aid to every measure intended for the good of that country, that no apology is necessary for the length of any letter, and you may be assured that every thing which I have the honour to receive from your Lordship shall be held in the most sacred confidence.

"I have the honor to be, with respect,

"My Lord, your Lordship's most obliged and obed^t servant,

"JA. PERRY.

"Great Shire Street, 12th Feby."

Endorsed in Lord Saltoun's hand :

"Mr. Perry, Editor Morng. Chronicle, 12th Feby. 1791."

During this and the following year, Lord Saltoun had some correspondence with David, sixth Earl of Buchan, the friend of Burns, and a great patron of literature, whose Countess, Margaret Fraser, was his cousin, being the daughter of William Fraser of Fraserfield. Three letters from the Earl are so characteristic that they seem worthy of a place here :—

"Dryburgh Abbey, Septr 16th, 1791.

"MY DEAR LORD,—The strange situation of Europe, and the wretched state of Britain with respect to political sentiment, has made me avoid writing to my old friends, who think as I do, till my indignation should subside.

"That miserable madman Burke will I hope do good as Filmer did, but I am sorry to think no very essential good can be done in consequence of the people having their eyes opened, without operations of a very different nature from those in France, where fortunately having no house to inhabit, they had the choice of their plan and situation.

"I am busy promoting the introduction of an improved breed of sheep to our hill-land here, instead of the coarse-woolled black snouts, and with a

Spanish Ram, and picked Herefordshire Ewes, I expect next year to have Lambs to begin a new race. I have been likewise amusing myself with literary pursuits, and have put lately into a bookseller's hands a Life of Andrew Fletcher of Salton, to be prefixed to an Edition of his works that remains unsold !

"This Life is of no great extent, as I do not enter into any account of his writings, which sufficiently speak for themselves. I have likewise bestowed a leisure hour now and then on writing some light pieces for Dr. Anderson's Bee, which promises of late to be an useful miscellany. But my great employment has been the furthering the new road to Glasgow thro' my West Lothian property, and the Tweed Navigation, the estimate for which amounting only to £14,000, we have now on our Table.

"It will give me great pleasure to hear that your political fervor is no wise abated, and that, notwithstanding, you turn yourself to agriculture and political economy in your own country and district.

"I have always entertained the sincerest friendship for you, mixt with the best opinion of your integrity and merit, and will rejoice in every circumstance that shall tend to make you more and more usefull, and consequently more and more situated to your own satisfaction. Lady Buchan joins in kind wishes and respects to your Lordship, to Lady Saltoun, and your whole family, and I remain with continued regard and esteem,

"My dear Lord,
"Y^r Lo^{ps} most faithful and obed^t serv^t,
"BUCHAN.

"Major-General Stuart, M.P., Edin^r, will forward letters to the Abbey, when you give me the pleasure of y^r correspondence."

Endorsed in Lord Saltoun's hand :

"Sent the Albanian Duan, Pictish houses in Buchan, etc."

"Dryburgh Abbey, October 31st, 1791.

"MY DEAR LORD,—Sincerely congratulating you on the safe and happy time of Lady Saltoun, and the birth of another son, I must at the same time felicitate you on the respectable and useful employment of your time, by which you overleap the ordinary bounds of nobility, and render yourself interesting to society.

"I am glad the Scotch Lords' eldest sons have regained their Citizenship, but I shall be better pleased to see this same Citizenship extended to every man who possesses soil, whether as a free, copy, or lease holder, without which we may talk of a Constitution as we please, but we shall be no better than Goths.

"Your remarks on the Duan I have sent to Pinkerton, who is now busy with his history of Scotland from the period where he left off, to the accession of James VI. to the Crowns of England and Ireland.

"He prepares likewise, to be published this winter, the residue of primæval Scottish poems, ending, I think, with the Ballantyne Excerpts, which I caused to be transcribed for him in the Advocates' Library. Next comes Wintoun's Chronicle, hitherto inedited, and with this he closes his labours as an Editor. He is a very extraordinary man, but a valetudinarian, and not blessed with the best temper in the world, as I have sometimes experienced.

"You may depend upon my friendship to you and yours, if ever I can get upon high enough ground to look at your interests and theirs with any sort of advantage; but at present I fear there must be rough work before anything can be done to saddle the people with whom I am most immediately connected in principle. Some people think it might have been as well for Britain if Charles II. had lived and gained his point, so that we might have had clear foundations to build upon; and I am not much disposed to deny the proposition, or at least to enter into the controversy; by and bye we shall see what is to be the upshot.

"I approve highly of your idea about the Scottish Latin writers, but I fear 250 people would hardly be found to espouse the undertaking. Lady Buchan joins in affectionate services to Lady Saltoun and your household, and I allways am, with sincere regard,

"Yr. Lops. faithfull humble serv[t],

"BUCHAN."

The third letter is more than a year later.

"MY DEAR LORD,—I have mentioned Findlater to Anderson for Daviott.

"I see a Findlater his correspondent on agriculture in the Bee; perhaps he is already connected with him thro' his cousin. I think Anderson an honest industrious man, and have thrown him crumbs for the Bee, yet I can hardly pretend to move him otherwise than on the merits, which I'm glad to see, by your respectable opinion, is a relevant argument.

"I rejoice to find you still attached to the res domi, the best way to prevent them from becoming angustæ.

"Party men and party politics are now rang in, all Europe over, except in Britain and Spain, and there the days will be but few and evil during which they will prevail.

"The empire of delusion is at an end!

"I'm sorry for the g^t grandson of the Earl of Portland, but old Bentinck was but a page of the Prince of Orange, and his descendant will make nothing by his sing-song about old glorious.

"Fox himself sinks with the people on his Westminster Bore, and nothing will go down now but real common sense to the utter discomfiture of modern Patriotism. I hear our foolish people have gone so deep with Calonne, as agent for Vienna and the Malcontents, that we run a risque of breaking with Prussia, notwithstanding the dear Lady with the little shoe!

"'Fortunatus ille deos qui novit agrestes,'

for I am apt to believe, before another year goes about, there will be trouble to agitators.

"Lady Buchan and Miss Fraser join in kind respects to Lady Saltoun, and I am, my dear Lord,

"With great esteem, y^r Lop^s affect^e h. serv^t,

"BUCHAN."

"*P.S.*—I had a visit from John Miller and his wife this summer, and found him, in politics 'Sequens fratrem passibus æquis.'

"Dryburgh Abbey, Novr 4th, 1792."

In the June of the same year Lord Saltoun received from the eminent Dr. John Skinner, Bishop of Aberdeen, an account of the passing of the Act for the relief of Scottish Episcopalians, and the excellent prelate thanked him warmly for the assistance he had rendered in obtaining the measure, and the letters to the Duke of Portland, Lords Kellie, Lauderdale, Selkirk, and Stormont, and to Sir Thomas Dundas, with which he had furnished him.

About the same time occurs a letter from Sir William Forbes, Bart., of Craigievar, in which is the following curious passage :—" I approve highly of the printed Principles of the Friends of the People, and believe they will sooner or later prevail, and I think the conduct of those in power is such as will bring matters to a crisis in a very short time.

"A mighty fine proclamation! Should a diligent magistrate see this letter, I may have an answer from the Secretary of State."

And another from Mr. Wilbraham Bootle, afterwards first Lord Skelmersdale, shows that Lord Saltoun practised the duties of hospitality at home, and had friends in all parts of the country :—

"MY LORD,—The great civilities which I received from your Lordship when in Scotland have encouraged me to take the liberty of recommending my brother, Mr. Wilbraham (who has already the honor of being acquainted with Lady Saltoun), and Mr. Augustus Legge, son of Lord Dartmouth, to your notice, as they propose making nearly the same tour in the North that I did. I shall feel extremely obliged to your Lordship if you would show them the kindness which you did to me, in putting them in the way of seeing whatever is most worthy of observation in your part of the country.

"I have only to regret that my absence from Great Britain will prevent me from having the pleasure of assuring you in person this summer how much I am,

"Your Lordship's most obliged and obedient humble serv^t,

"EDW^D. WILBRAHAM BOOTLE.

"Copenhagan, June 17th, 1792."

In the flower of his age, possessed of more than average abilities, which the activity of his disposition kept in constant exercise, deservedly esteemed by, and popular with, a large circle of friends of all shades of political opinion, blessed with an amiable and devoted wife, and a family of promising children, Lord Saltoun might have looked forward to a long and happy life, and to the attainment of any position within the scope of honourable ambition, but Providence had otherwise decreed.

During the summer of 1793 he and Lady Saltoun, with their children, paid a visit to her parents, then residing at Baldwins, in Kent; and there, in the early part of September, gout, from which he had been for some time suffering, attacked his stomach, and sinking under the disease, he died on the 13th of that month, not long after the completion of his thirty-sixth year.

The following extracts from two letters written by Mr. Fraser and Lady Saltoun to his aunt, the Honourable Miss Fraser, give some account of his last moments, and evince how much they felt their loss :—

"London, September 13th, 1793.

"DEAR MADAM,—You may believe it distresses me in the extreme to inform you of the distracted state of my family, from the death of our much lamented friend your nephew, and the best of men, Lord Saltoun.

"Having the gout flying about him for some weeks past, it at last fixed in his stomach, and carried him off at seven this morning, regretted by all who knew him.

"It is impossible to acquaint you of my daughter's distress at losing the best of husbands. All I shall say is, May the Almighty support us all under such trials."

Lady Saltoun some time afterwards, and in reply to a letter from Miss Fraser, wrote :—

"I can form some idea how you feel, for he was attentive to you, and it was easily seen how much you loved him; and he deserved to be beloved, for he did good to all who had any concern with him. My loss is not to be said. His death was not violent; the same placid temper attended him to the last. He did not think himself in danger till within six hours; I thought it on Thursday forenoon, but Dr. Latham did not till towards evening. He never gave a single groan. He told me to take some rest on Thursday night at ten o'clock, and I went out of the room. He sent for me soon after twelve, and told me he was going. He then swallowed very well, and took all I offered him. My mother sent to speak to me, and he said, 'May, don't stay long away.' I did not go; and he said while he could, 'Farewell, May,' and expired a few minutes after seven on Friday morning. So little was danger expected, that my father went to town on Thursday after dinner. He was to bring Farquhar out as soon as he could find him, but as a satisfactory step, rather than one of absolute necessity; but the Almighty Father thought proper to bring things to a very speedy conclusion, and I have now only to pray to Him to assist me in the recovery of my lost happiness."

Lord Saltoun's remains were conveyed to Philorth, and interred in the family tomb at Fraserburgh.

He left three sons and two daughters—

Alexander George, his successor.

Simon, born 31st July 1787, died unmarried, 10th February 1811.

William, born 12th October 1791.

Margaret, born 29th August 1789, died unmarried, 14th August 1845.

Eleanora, born 13th June 1793, married, 5th December 1825, William Macdowall Grant, Esq. of Arndilly, county Banff, and died 26th September 1852, leaving issue two daughters.

ALEXANDER GEORGE FRASER, SIXTEENTH OF PHILORTH, AND SIXTEENTH LORD SALTOUN.

CATHERINE, DAUGHTER OF LORD CHANCELLOR THURLOW.

By the early and unexpected death of the fifteenth Lord, on the 13th of September 1793, his eldest son, Alexander George Fraser, who was born on the 22d of April 1785, succeeded when between eight and nine years of age; and though he was thus deprived of the natural guardian and protector of his early years, the loss was efficiently repaired by the ability of his mother, for whom he ever retained the fondest affection, and who was ably assisted in the care of her young family by the advice and support of her father, Mr. Fraser, until his decease in 1810.

Indeed, Lady Saltoun was one in a thousand. Of short and slight, but graceful figure, the energy and intelligence of her countenance, the good sense and firmness that guided her actions, together with her goodness of heart and amiable disposition, reflected in her kind and courteous manner, received, without appearing to claim, the respect of all, and the warm affection of those more intimately acquainted with her.

LIEUTENANT GENERAL ALEXANDER GEORGE FRASER, K.T.G.C.B.G.C.H.
SIXTEENTH LORD SALTOUN.
BORN 1785. DIED 1853.

She preserved her health, her intellect, and her capacity for the business or enjoyment of life unimpaired, except some failure in memory during the last three years, until her death at the great age of ninety-seven. She had been out in the carriage the day before her decease, and had passed the evening as usual; next morning, feeling rather weak, she did not rise for breakfast according to her custom, and about one o'clock she ate a cup of arrowroot, and handing the cup back, said, "Thank you, that is very nice," sank back on the pillow, and died in less than a minute, without a struggle or a groan.[1]

Such a mother would not only take care that her son received an education fitting him for the position he was destined to occupy, but would, in his infancy, inculcate those sentiments of honour and feelings of duty that distinguished his after career.

At the proper age he was sent to Eton, where, being endowed with great strength and activity, he became noted among his schoolfellows for deeds of daring.

The late Sir Richard Simeon, Bart., told the writer of these pages that Lord Saltoun was the first Etonian that jumped into the Thames from the parapet of the centre arch of Windsor Bridge, Sir Richard himself immediately following him on that occasion; and the late Colonel Challoner, who was also his contemporary, though two or three years junior, said that he remembered, upon first going to Eton, that the whole school was ringing with a fight that had just taken place between Lord Saltoun and a champion of the bargemen, or bargees as they were termed, in which the former was victorious.

In another encounter with the bargees he had a very narrow escape, for, tripped up by the prostrate body of a schoolfellow, whom a stone had brought to the ground, he fell on his back, while fighting in retreat, when one of the

---

[1] The evening before the funeral of Margery, Lady Saltoun, the writer of this memoir accompanied Lord Saltoun to look at the coffin containing her remains. Upon the plate the age of the deceased was inscribed as ninety-two. Lord Saltoun said, "Ninety-two! but I have reason to know, from some papers I have seen since her death, that my mother was at least five years older than that." To the suggestion that the inscription might be altered, as there was time for that to be done, he replied, "No! it does not matter, ninety-two is old enough!"

bargees stabbed at him with a pitchfork, and the crowd passed over him; however, on a rally being made, and the enemy driven back, he was found stunned by the fall and the blow, but happily otherwise uninjured, the two prongs having passed, one on each side of his neck, deep into the ground, in which the pitchfork remained standing, his assailant having been forced to let it go by the rush of the crowd.

These rough schoolboy encounters formed no bad prelude to the more important events in which he had to bear his part, where the qualities of courage, self-reliance, and common sense were of more avail than mere book learning, a fact too much ignored in the present days of competitive examinations.

In 1802, when about seventeen years old, Lord Saltoun entered the army, receiving his commission of ensign in the 35th regiment, from which he was put on half-pay, and then obtained a lieutenancy in the 42d Highlanders, remaining in that regiment until he attained the rank of captain in 1804, when, on the 23d of November in that year, he exchanged into the First Regiment of Guards, and was posted to the first battalion, but in January 1805 transferred to the third, in which he went abroad on active service in 1806, it forming, with the first battalion, a portion of the reinforcements sent to the island of Sicily.

The brigade of Guards embarked at Ramsgate about the 26th of July, and after a detention of nearly eight weeks in the Downs, proceeded to Plymouth, where it was landed, and encamped on Bickleigh Down for about a fortnight, until the whole of the troops having been got together, all embarked on the 13th, and sailed on the 24th September for their destination.

The passage was tedious, and the Guards did not arrive at Messina until the 2d of December, when they were ordered to proceed to Catania, and disembark there. Lord Saltoun's impression of the island is graphically told in a letter which, though written at a later date, might equally well have been penned at the time, and it may be given in his own words:[1]—

"The whole of the island of Sicily is mountainous, with the exception of a plain at the base of Etna, to the south, called the plain of Catania, which extends from that town to Augusta and Syracuse, a distance of about 25 miles,

[1] Letter to Lieutenant-Colonel Charles Ellis.

of which the 12 miles nearest Syracuse is rocky and hilly, but not mountain. From Catania on the north-east to Messina is about 60 miles; all lava near the town for about 10 miles, and the rest of the way all mountains. Catania is at the base of Etna, which rises at once from it on the north side of the town. The said town of Catania, which was our headquarters, is surrounded with lava, the stream on the south side being about 2 miles wide, and the one on the north-east, as I said before, about 10 miles. The superstition that prevails there is that when the great eruption took place, Santa Agatha came and spread her veil before the stream of lava, which divided into two, and the town was saved; she is therefore the great lady here, and on her day they have a grand Festa, and the priests pass a veil of some prepared stuff through the fire, and as it does not burn, the natives are convinced it is the identical veil that turned the lava; and a very abrupt and well pronounced hill, that lies to the north of the town, and did actually turn the lava in the two directions, gets no credit at all. . . . We reached Sicily about the middle of December 1806, having coasted along the whole island, from the little island of Marstino to the town of Messina at the head of the strait of that name, having sailed along a most beautiful mountainous country, in many places, particularly near Messina, studded with villas, having Etna in view the whole time; and one of the finest sights was to see the sun strike the top of Etna on rising, which it did about five minutes before you saw it, and lit the mountains down by degrees till you were aware that the sun was up, also the snow on the top, when first struck by the sun, looking like an immense ball of fire.

"We were not permitted to land at Messina, but sent at once to our respective quarters, which were as follow:—The Flank Battalion to Syracuse; the right wing 3rd Battalion Augusta; the 1st Battalion and the left wing of the 3rd at Catania; and the left wing of the 3rd was afterwards sent to Contessa, a small village near Messina. . . . So the Guards occupied the whole coast from Messina to Syracuse, a distance of about 100 miles."

Although there was no actual fighting during the eight or nine months that the battalion remained in Sicily, yet the enemy being on the other side of the strait of Messina, a strict watch had to be kept upon their movements, and all to be in readiness to repel any attempt to cross over into the island.

An incident occurred at this time of which Lord Saltoun made a memorandum, and which, to use his own words, shows "how little attention your English soldier pays to anything, unless long service and severe experience has driven something like observation into him."

The memorandum is as follows:—"We had been some months at Contessa, when the French, who since the battle of Maida had remained in upper Calabria, suddenly marched a large force down to the straits of Messina, commenced a sort of siege of the Castle of Scilla, where we had a garrison, and taking possession of Regio, a town on the coast, nearly opposite our cantonments, began collecting boats and making preparations to invade Sicily. A party of an officer and 30 men was established at a place called Milia, about six miles from our cantonments, in order to give the alarm should any landing take place about there; and we communicated by small posts of a corporal and three men at certain distances all along the line, to a particular point from which it was about 3 miles to Milia, which post was visited every night by the captain on duty, and a patrol of a corporal and file of dragoons went from Messina to Milia twice during the night.

"It had rained most of the evening, and I had started a little later than usual to go my rounds, and I had met the first patrol on its return from Milia, a little before I came to the great fiumara or watercourse, which ran from the mountains into the strait; in summer this was in general dry, or at most very small, but in heavy rains often impassable, and on the Milia side of this fiumara was situated our extreme corporal's picquet on the right, our left one communicating with the Citadel of Messina.

"When I crossed the fiumara it was running a strong stream, but nothing dangerous. I proceeded on to Milia and visited the post there, stayed a short time, and smoked a cigar with the officer. According to the time of the patrol, I ought to have met it between the fiumara and Milia, but I did not, and when I came to the fiumara I at once saw that it was utterly impassable; it was raging with a force that would have carried away an elephant, and in the current of the burn, from the stones it covered at the sides, must have been more than ten feet deep. I made no doubt but that the patrol finding it in this state had returned.

"This ford was about 200 yards above the junction of the fiumara with the sea, which is so deep, close to land all along that part of the straits of Messina, that a man-of-war could tack with its bowsprit over the land.

"As I had no inclination to stay there in the rain I coasted the torrent down to its junction with the sea, and being an excellent swimmer myself, as well as in the constant habit at that time of swimming my horse, I at once put him into the deep water, and without any difficulty reached the other side, and proceeded on my rounds. I found that the patrol had visited all the posts on its way out as usual, and on reaching the cavalry post at Messina, as I was obliged to mention in my report the circumstance of my not having met the patrol, I inquired of the officer about it, and found that it had not returned. I mentioned my fears for it to the officer, but as it was possible that they had taken some shelter to wait till the fiumara should run off, a sergeant was sent to look for them and bring them back, but they were never heard of afterwards, and as desertion was impracticable, at least with their horses, and moreover a crime not at all prevailing in the English part of the army at that time, there can be no doubt but they were carried away in trying to ford the fiumara."

Another memorandum gives an interesting account of the way in which Lord Saltoun and some of his brother officers at times relieved the tedium of the severe and harassing service in which they were engaged, without the excitement of actually meeting the enemy in the field, and affords some characteristic traits of the country people of that part of Sicily, and evidence of the corruption prevalent amongst the Sicilian officials :—

"Amongst other things that occurred to me in Sicily, was forming an acquaintance with a set of people who lived principally in the mountains. Ostensibly the occupation of these people was that of shepherds, and carriers of ice from the mountains to Messina; but in the country they generally went by the name of Ladrones, not that they ever committed robberies in the character of ice-sellers, but they certainly did at times commit pretty heavy depredations upon their own countrymen; but during the time I was in that country, I never heard of any English officer being plundered, probably (for we had gone there as friends) from some such sort of feeling as prevailed through Spain, when there was hardly an instance of an Englishman being ill treated by the inhabitants.

"The man who left ice at my quarters told me if I would go into the mountains I could get excellent shooting, and he would speak to the Capitano (a name which applied as well to the head shepherd as to the robber). Accordingly, a brother officer and myself proceeded up the mountains, and found everything prepared for us—good beds of dry fern, and a supper of kid and milk and fruit, etc. etc. In the morning we proceeded to shoot; several men had been sent off to find where the birds were, by their calling, and then drive them into the ravines. We were stationed on the top of the banks, and the rest of the men beat up the ravines, and the sport was very good, consisting of partridge, hare, and a sort of pigeon. Before beating up any ravine the Capitano hailed the scout with, 'O Juan' (or whatever his name might be), 'cantaro?' and on being answered, 'Si cantaro aqui,' the ravine was beat up; if not, we proceeded to another station. We stayed two days, and I made an arrangement with the Captain to furnish a goat with milk every week, for a Mrs. Villiers, wife of a commissary who lived near where we were quartered, and found it almost impossible at that time of the year to get any milk for her children. We made several of these trips, taking care not to have more money with us than we meant to leave amongst them. On one of these occasions, as we were taking our luncheon before going down, the Capitano told me that I should be back there that night, and on my saying it was impossible, he replied, 'si, si, voi mismo,' and told me that our troops were to surround the mountain on our side that night, and that a body were to do the same on the Milazo side, which body had already marched for that purpose, and we were to meet at the top for the purpose of making them prisoners, and that in consequence they were to shift their quarters immediately, but that the goat would be sent to the Signora Inglese just as usual, and we should find them there again, when an olive branch was left with the ice.

"We came down, told our story at mess, and were well laughed at for believing it; but a little before dark, an order came to fall in, and under the direction of certain guides we marched up the mountain, and got to the top about daylight, found no Ladrones, but met our friends from Milazo, and after some cigars, etc. etc., returned home again.

"I thought it my duty to report this to Sir John Moore, the Commander-in-chief; for as the surprise had been undertaken at the request of the Sicilian authorities, it was clear that the Ladrones had some better friends in that body than we had."

In a letter of the 18th March 1807, addressed to his mother, Lord Saltoun gives an amusing account of a tour through a considerable part of the island, in which he mentions the ruins of the temple of Jupiter Olympus, near Girgenti,—the ancient Agrigentum,—as very magnificent. He says:—"The columns were of a gigantic size, and the fluting of them large enough to contain a man. From what remains, the enormous size of the pillars is clearly to be perceived; two capitals, which are the only remains of them, are broken into four pieces, and in the small part of the pillar, still attached to one of them, Montgomery, who is rather a thin man, could get into the flute with all ease. What an immense block of stone it must have been to allow such cutting away from it, and afterwards to support a capital of such size, one quarter of which only, lying on the ground, hid six of us behind it, so as not to be perceived by a person on the other side."

He also relates a curious story or tradition respecting a peculiarity in the great church at Girgenti:—"There is also another singular circumstance, which is, that a person getting up above the altar, can hear anything said at the other end of the church, even in a whisper. This is said to have been discovered in the following manner:—A carpenter was up there one day mending the figure of a dragon, and saw his wife come into the church to confess. He was surprised at so plainly hearing the priest speak to her, and therefore listened, and heard the whole of her confession. On returning home he gave her wholesome correction for what he had overheard, and made a regular practice of mending the dragon whenever any rich person went to confess, by which means he got together a good deal of money."

After remaining about ten months in the island, the brigade of Guards returned home, and in the above-mentioned letter, to an old brother officer, Lord Saltoun says: "We left Sicily in the autumn of 1807, forming part of a force of 10,000 men, with Sir John Moore. Our first instructions were to take Ceuta, but they thought it too strong. We were then (in the event of the King of Portugal submitting to the French) to have gone to the Brazils, and taken that; but as the King of Portugal abandoned his kingdom, and went to the Brazils himself, Sir John Moore brought us to England."

From his mother having resided at Dartmouth House, Blackheath, probably in order to be near her father, Lord Saltoun's earlier years had been passed in England, and it is doubtful whether he had ever, since his succession to the title, visited his paternal estates until the year 1808, when in the autumn he proceeded to Philorth and Fraserburgh, and made acquaintance with his feudal vassals and tenantry there, from whom his handsome and manly appearance, and his frank and engaging manner, coupled with straightforward good sense, won golden opinions, and established amongst them an esteem and affection for him, which increased and deepened during his whole life. He also made a tour through the north of Scotland, visiting many of his friends and acquaintances, and everywhere winning the regard of high and low; and of this evidence is found in letters written by his brother Simon to their mother, while visiting Philorth, and making a similar tour during the succeeding autumn of 1809.

He wrote:—"Saltoun is adored round Fraserburgh; every one talks of him and his affability, when he was down last year, incessantly. I do not think I should have written to-day were it not to have told you this, well knowing how grateful it will be to you to be informed how much Saltoun is looked up to by his tenants. Indeed, were I to tell all that they have said to me about him and yourself, it would raise you at least half-a-foot higher. I shall therefore only remark, that the manner in which the old tenants who could remember you spoke of you, brought tears of delight into my eyes, and they are all as anxious to see you as my brother."

And in another letter:—"The gamekeeper at Kinrara spoke to me a good deal about Saltoun's keenness and abilities for a sportsman, and mentioned how liberally he had acted always to him, not only in making him a handsome present, but also, which seemed to flatter him more, in allowing him to take his shot in fair play; in short, Saltoun is a great favourite with everybody who has spoken to me about him. . . . It will be pleasing to you to know that it is not confined to his own estate or tenants to respect and love him."

The life of Simon Fraser, who thus wrote of his brother in terms of pride

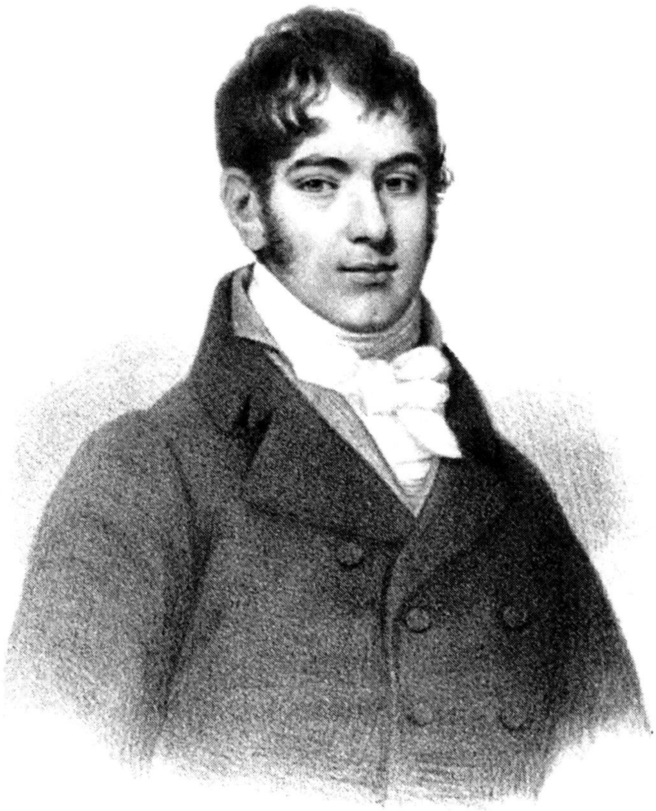

and affection, was unfortunately cut short, and his death, on the 10th February 1811, prevented the fulfilment of the promise afforded by the talents and good qualities of which his youth had given evidence.

In those stirring times a fortunate soldier was not long idle, and in 1808 Lord Saltoun was again upon active service, the third battalion, to which he belonged, with the first, forming part of the army in Spain, under Sir John Moore, and of the division commanded by Sir David Baird, which, landing at Corunna in October, reached Astorga, in Leon, about the 24th of November, and effected a junction with the main army, under Sir John Moore, which had come from Lisbon, at Mayorga, on the 20th of December.

The British army now numbered about 25,000 men, with sixty guns, and advanced against Soult in the valley of the Carrion. The brilliant combinations by which Napoleon rescued his marshal, concentrated 70,000 men and 100 guns to oppose Moore, and forced him to an immediate retreat on Corunna, by the route which Baird had lately followed from that place, are matters of general history.

During this retreat the Guards and Reserve in a great degree maintained discipline, and did not share in the disorganisation and misconduct that prevailed among a large portion of the army, which, according to the report of their general, had abandoned every military virtue except the redeeming one of courage and ardour for battle.[1]

After several weeks of severe hardship and privation, and many encounters with the pursuing enemy, the army under Sir John Moore reached the seaport of Corunna, where the Guards had landed scarce three months before, and there turning to bay, fought and won the severe battle of that name, on

---

[1] Extract of despatch from Sir John Moore, 13th January 1809:—

"I am sorry to say that the army, whose conduct I had much reason to extol on the march through Portugal, and on its arrival in Spain, has totally changed its character since it began to retreat. I can say nothing in its favour, except that when there was a prospect of fighting the enemy, the men were then orderly, and seemed pleased, and determined to do their duty."

Napier, comparing Sir John Moore's retreat with that of Wellington from Burgos in 1812, says, vol. v. p. 375:—"The reserve and the foot guards in Moore's campaign, the light division and the foot guards in Wellington's, gave signal proof that it was negligence of discipline, not hardships, though the latter were severe in both armies, that caused the losses. Not that I would be understood to say that those regiments only preserved order — it is certain that many others were eminently well conducted—but those were the troops named as exceptions at the time."

the 16th of January 1809, repulsing with a force reduced to less than 15,000 men the vastly superior numbers of the French led by Soult, and secured an undisturbed embarkation, though the victory was dearly purchased by the death of their gallant general, whose left shoulder was carried away by a cannon-ball, and who died that evening, and was buried the same night on the ramparts of Corunna.

On the night of the 16th, and during the 17th, the British army embarked in the fleet that had appeared on the 15th, and set sail for England, where, in spite of a storm that dispersed the ships and wrecked some of them, the transports conveying the brigade of Guards arrived safely, and the two battalions landed at Portsmouth on the 25th, and marched to Chatham.

About six months later Lord Saltoun was again on active service; for in the summer of 1809 the Government of the day resolved to send a force to the coast of Holland, to capture the fortified city of Antwerp, where Napoleon had established large arsenals, and to destroy the shipping in the river Scheldt.

This project, which is known as the Walcheren Expedition, might have led to important and glorious results, but from mismanagement unfortunately resulted in complete failure.

A force of about 30,000 men, of which the first and third battalions of the First Guards, with detachments from the Coldstream and Scots Fusilier Guards, formed a part, embarked under the command of the Earl of Chatham, in numerous transports, and escorted by a very powerful fleet, under Admiral Sir Richard Strachan, sailed on the 28th, 29th, and 30th of July.

Sir John Hope's division, which included the brigade of Guards, formed the advance, and landing upon the north shore of the island of South Beveland on the 1st and 2d of August, obtained considerable success during the ensuing week, advancing as far towards Antwerp as Fort Batz, which it captured; and the other divisions of the army also operated successfully in the island of Walcheren, reducing the town of Flushing and other places of strength.

But the over-caution and consequent delay of the general and admiral commanding-in-chief lost precious moments. The French and Dutch strained every nerve to assemble a superior force for the protection of

Antwerp. Sickness of a most fatal description broke out in the British ranks, and the opinion of the seven lieutenant-generals of the army having been taken towards the end of August, further progress was decided to be impracticable.

The bulk of the expedition therefore re-embarked before the 4th of September, and returned to England, leaving a small force to hold the island of Walcheren, which, in its turn, decimated by disease, was before Christmas ordered to abandon that post and to return home.

While serving in this unfortunate and—by the commanders-in-chief—ill-conducted campaign, Lord Saltoun did not escape the terrible Walcheren fever, caused by malaria, that proved fatal to so many, from the effects of which even his iron constitution suffered in no slight degree during future years.[1]

The dilatory proceedings of the military and naval commanders-in-chief of this unfortunate expedition were commemorated in the well-known epigram:—

> "The Earl of Chatham, with his sword drawn,
> Was waiting for Sir Richard Strachan:
> Sir Richard, longing to be at 'em,
> Was waiting for the Earl of Chatham!"

In the spring of 1811 Lord Saltoun again went abroad on active service with the third battalion, which formed part of the garrison of Cadiz, and in a letter from Isla de Leon, written 22d September 1811, he related an instance of that jealousy and misconduct on the part of the Spanish authorities which so often impeded the operations of the English commanders throughout the whole war:—"You say I do not send you any politics, the fact is there is nothing going on here but the old story; the Spaniards make no efforts themselves and lay all their losses to the fault of the English government and generals. Mutual dissatisfaction had been brewing a long time, but did not openly break out till after the battle of Barrosa, in which, notwithstanding it was clearly proved that the English army saved the whole of the Spanish

---

[1] "In the whole army no less than 67 officers and 4000 men died of the fever, and at the date of the report in February (1810), above 200 officers and 11,000 men were still in hospital."—History of the Grenadier Guards, by Lieut.-Gen. Sir F. W. Hamilton, K.C.B.

army and the Isla de Leon; notwithstanding that two of their own generals, namely, Sayis and Ladizabal, were so convinced that we had gained a complete victory, that they repeatedly urged La Peña to advance on Chiclana; although General Graham offered to advance on Chiclana if they would support him, which they declined; yet the Spanish government countenanced a false account of the action, which was published by General Lacy, the head of their staff (a runaway rascal who had been turned out of the French service), in which he gives the whole merit of the action to the Spanish army, denies General Graham's statement, and attributes the failure of the general plan to the ill-judged attack (as he calls it) that the English made. This produced a correspondence between them, and General Graham obliged him to eat his words. Lacy had been put under arrest after the battle of Barrosa, but, soon after this statement made its appearance, was reinstated in his rank and command; this of course created an open rupture between our heads of departments and the Spanish government, which is likely to continue, at least as long as things go on in their present style. The mass of the people and the army are with us, and if we were to offer them our pay we might revolutionise the place in three days; but that is not our system. So much do the Spanish government fear this, that false accounts are circulated, in order that the people may not be acquainted with the extent of their obligations to the British, and to excite, if possible, a jealousy between the two nations. They yesterday ordered away four thousand men, against which our Minister remonstrated very strongly. Some of the troops, however, marched yesterday evening. Whether they will embark or not I know not, but if they do, our force will not be sufficient to defend the place, as our works are now become very extensive; but we must do the best we can, and I do not think the French will attack."

Lord Saltoun remained with his battalion in Cadiz until August 1812, when just before the raising of the siege by the French, consequent on Lord Wellington's movements in the centre of Spain, it marched with the force under General Cruz Mourgeon and Colonel Skerrit to join Hill's division, which was operating to the southward of Lord Wellington's advance upon Madrid.

From a journal kept by him at this time it appears that they embarked at Cadiz on the 9th August, and reached Huelva at eleven P.M. on the 13th, and after resting two days, during which the remainder of the troops, stores, etc., were landed, the whole force proceeded on the 16th by Trigeras, Nuebla, Palma, and Villa Abba, to Manzanilla, where it arrived on the 19th, and in the vicinity of that place first fell in with the enemy, for after a halt of four days, the following memorandum appears in the journal:—

"24th.—Marched with a detachment at eleven at night, and attacked the enemy's outposts at San Lucar le Major, and drove them in with little loss on their side, and none on ours; distance four leagues.

"25th.—Fell back one league; took post near a river in the rear of San Lucar.

"26th.—Marched at five in the morning with the hussars to make a reconnoisance; the troops joined us next morning.

"27th.—Marched with the whole of the force towards Seville, fell in with the enemy at his advanced posts at Castellega, one league from Seville, drove them in, and about seven in the morning advanced to the attack of that place; distance of march four and a half leagues. The British column advanced for more than two miles at double-quick, and were just in time to drive the enemy from the bridge with the bayonet, as they were trying to cut it; at ten we were in complete possession of the place. The French force was eight battalions infantry and two regiments of cavalry, commanded by Victor; ours consisted of 3500 Spaniards under Cruz Mourgeon, and 1500 British, with three six-pounders, under Colonel Skerrit, and the place was only carried by the rapidity of the British advance, which terrified the enemy."

The army remained in or near Seville until the 30th September, when, after leaving a garrison in that place, it renewed its long march, and by way of Truxillo, Talavera, and Toledo, effected its junction with Hill's corps at Aranjuez on the 26th October.

"26th.—To the park at Aranjuez, four leagues, there had been an alarm during the night, and General Hill had ordered the bridge to be destroyed. Bivouacked. The park very fine; a number of trees planted in avenues, but marshy.

"27th.—Halt; the enemy made his appearance in front of Aranjuez.

"*28th.*—The enemy occupied the town and gardens of the palace, on the opposite side of the Tagus.

"*29th.*—Retired at one in the morning over the Jarama river, and took post on the Madrid road, in rear of the Puente Larga, which we were preparing to destroy. In the evening marched to Cien Pozuelos, one league.

"*30th.*—The enemy attacked Puente Larga, the mine of which failed, and were repulsed with loss by the 47th regiment.

"Joined headquarters as orderly officer."

Wellington's retreat from Burgos obliged Hill also to retire, and while with the headquarters Lord Saltoun accompanied them to Aravaca, the Escurial, Espinar, Lavajos, and Villa Nueva de Gomez, where on the 5th November he rejoined his battalion, which retired to Fonte-viros.

The retreat continued, and on the 9th the battalion reached Salamanca.

"*9th.*—Marched in the afternoon to Salamanca, and were quartered in a convent. The first time we had been under cover, except at Cien Pozuelos, since we left Añover on the 26th October. Distance marched from Huelva 636 miles. Joined Lord Wellington's army, which had retired here from Burgos."

With Lord Wellington's army the battalion retreated through Ciudad Rodrigo, Gallegos, and past Fuentes d'Honore, until the 8th of December, when the troops went into cantonments, and the Guards were quartered in Viseu, Mondeo, and Spraida. "Had at this place marched from Huelva 800 miles, computing the Spanish league at four English miles."

The British army, after its retreat from Burgos, remained in cantonments during the winter, and about this time Lord Saltoun was elected one of the Representative Peers of Scotland.

In a letter to his mother of the 26th December, he wrote that it must depend upon whether operations are begun early in the following year or not as to whether he can return to take his seat in the House of Lords.

On the 8th of February he mentioned the severe sickness which had attacked the troops, especially the brigade of Guards; and in the same letter, alluding to the censure passed by Lord Wellington upon the conduct of the army during the retreat, he made the following sensible observations:—

"I am very sorry, but not surprised, at a certain letter having crossed the Atlantic; it should never have gone beyond the orderly books of the army, ... and it is foolish for a General to abuse his army for disorders arising from the want of a proper commissariat, which Frederic the Great says it is his first duty to provide. It is no excuse for him that there is no wood in a country, but it is a very great one for a soldier pulling down a house to cook his provisions with the materials; and in everything, when one disorder is permitted, another will soon creep in upon the heels of it. I do not mean to say that the army was not in a very bad state, but every man knows, who has ever seen an army, that such must be the case, if that army be ill supplied with bread; and the saddle should always be put on the right horse. To say nothing of the hardships of the first part of the retreat, which were tolerably severe, the commissary might, and ought to have been at San Muños with a supply of bread for the army; we should then have had ample means of carrying the wounded and those men who were unable to march from fatigue, and their number would also have been very much lessened by the seasonable arrival of the bread, which would have enabled many to go through the very severe march we had from that place, for an extra half pound of over-driven beef is a very poor substitute for a pound and a half of bread, especially when that is issued for three days running."

These remarks evince that he, in common with many other good officers, resented Lord Wellington's censure, from the feeling that it was unjust to blame the soldiers for the disorder caused by the failure of the commissariat, which feeling, however, in no degree impaired the alacrity and devotion with which they served under their great commander.

Soon afterwards Lord Saltoun obtained leave of absence, and returned to England, where, however, he remained only a few weeks, and sailed about the 11th of April from Falmouth to rejoin the army in Spain; but this visit was productive of an important event in his life, as he then made the acquaintance of his future wife, Catherine, daughter of the Lord Chancellor Thurlow.

He arrived at Lisbon, from Falmouth, about the 20th April, and on the 2d May started, by way of Mafra and Cintra, for Oporto, to which place the brigade of Guards had moved during his absence.

The general orders for the march of the *corps d'armée* under Sir Thomas

Graham, which was to advance on a line to the northward of that pursued by the force under the immediate command of Lord Wellington, were issued about the middle of May; but owing to the terrible loss sustained by the Guards from sickness, it was decided to leave their first brigade at Oporto for some time longer.

On the 14th May Lord Saltoun wrote: "Lord Wellington has, however, determined not to move *us* for the present, and they say it will be a month before we begin our march. We are certainly much better, and the men begin to look something like soldiers again, but it is shocking to think that since the month of December last we have buried 800 out of 2000."

After a delay of six weeks the welcome order came for the first brigade of Guards to join the main army, which after the glorious battle of Vittoria had advanced to the Pyrenees, and on the 29th of June the brigade left Oporto, and passing up the right bank of the Douro to Toro, from thence through Palencia and Durada, came up to the front on the 18th of August, and were encamped near Irun, to cover the siege of St. Sebastian, which was carried on by the fifth division.

In a letter of the 2d September Lord Saltoun gave the following account of the fall of that place, and other operations :—

"The place was carried by storm at 12 in the day, on the 31st. Our loss was very great; they rate it, as well as it can now be got at, to be about 1500 men. The place was stormed by detachments from different divisions of the army, and by the fifth division, under the command of Sir J. Leith, who is wounded. We sent a detachment of one lt.-colonel, two captains, four subalterns, and 200 men, fifty of whom have returned. Of the officers, Burrard was mortally wounded, and died yesterday; he is son to Sir H. Burrard, the second he has lost in action in the regiment. Ensign Bridgeman slightly wounded, and Chaplin, who belongs to the Coldstream Guards, severely; he is shot in the breast, and his thigh broken so high that they cannot amputate.

" On the morning of the storm Soult made a general attack on our line, with an intention to relieve the place. The ground in our front is very strong, and defended by the Spaniards of the Gallician army under General Frere.

" The French attacked an hour before daylight, and carried a small height, which they surprised. This enabled them to establish a bridge over the Bidassoa, and at eight in the morning they had passed over about 10,000 men, and made a regular attempt to carry the hill occupied by the Spaniards, without which they could not with safety pass any great force of artillery. The Spaniards defended it with great obstinacy, and about two, when the French had carried the hill, made a very splendid charge, and with the bayonet drove them fairly to the bottom again.

"Towards evening the French made another attempt, but a very feeble one, and on the Spaniards giving three cheers on being informed of the fall of St. Sebastian, they retired, and during the night took away the bridge, and have not since troubled us. I have just come from the field, and from the number of dead lying there I should think the loss on both sides must be about 5000 men, of which number the Spaniards certainly lost the most. The French made an attack more on the right, and were met by the seventh division British, and repulsed with great loss. The castle of St. Sebastian still holds out, and will cost some more men; we are at present pounding away at it at a great rate."

On the 27th September, having obtained a few days' leave, Lord Saltoun paid a visit to Sir Rowland Hill, then in command upon the right of the line, near Roncesvalles, and in this trip visited the scenes of the recent actions in the Pyrenees, which he characterises as "the finest ever yet fought by the British;" but returned to his battalion in time to take part in the passage of the Bidassoa, which he thus described in a letter of the 9th October:—

"On the night of the 6th we got our orders at twelve to attack the next morning, and at three on the morning of the 7th marched to our points to reach them before daylight, so that the enemy might not observe our movements, and at a quarter before eight, it being then low-water, forded the Bidassoa in five columns, and advanced against their positions. The enemy made but little resistance, being partly surprised, and our plan of attack was so well combined, that his position was turned, and attacked hill after hill, nearly at the same moment. He ought, however, to have defended his position, which is a very strong one, with greater obstinacy. Our loss was small,—between 300 and 400 men I should guess. At twelve we had gained our present position, just above the town of Urogne, which is now the French advance, and before dark were quietly encamped upon it. During the time that this operation was going on the light division debouched by the pass of Wora, and attacked the hill of Urogne, which is a high mountain on the right of our present line, and carried it in good form."

On the 30th of October he wrote from the camp above Urogne:—

"We have a great deal of duty; our light infantry do the advanced duty and no other. I am on every fourth day; and the posts are so close, our advanced sentries at night standing within thirty yards of each other, that both parties are tolerably alert; indeed the Germans, who take that duty with us, and who have been all their lives on that species of service, say they never saw posts so close, without a ravine or brook, or something of the kind, between them, which is not the case here."

The continuance of wet weather prevented any general advance for some weeks, but at length Lord Wellington was able to make a forward movement; and after the action at the passage of the Nivelles river, the Guards were engaged in the three days' fighting, from the 9th to the 12th December, in front of Bayonne, of which Lord Saltoun wrote the following account in a letter of the 13th from the camp near Bidart:—

"We are again under canvas, and have had some sharp work for three or four days; we have had two officers killed and wounded. Colonel Martin and Captain Thompson are killed, and Captain Streatfield and Ensign Latour wounded, the latter severely. We have lost 150 men.

"Old Soult has been manœuvring, and trying to deceive Lord Wellington by showing a large force at different points of our line. On the 9th we advanced, and attacked in front of this place, and drove the enemy into his strong ground in front of Bayonne. In the meantime Sir R. Hill crossed the Nive at Ustaritz, and rested his right flank on the Adour, so as to interrupt Soult's supplies, which he received from Pau and Oleron by that river. This obliged Soult to make some decided movement, and on the 10th he attacked us, but was repulsed by the fifth division. On the 11th he again attacked us, and got a hill in our front that covered his movements. That night we took the outpost duty, and on the 12th he appeared in force, and manœuvred under a very sharp affair of tirailleurs, but finding us well prepared at all points he recrossed the Nive during the night, and on the 13th made three desperate attacks on Sir R. Hill, and was defeated and driven into Bayonne with great loss."

On the 10th January 1814 he again wrote from St. Jean de Luz :—

"Since I wrote last nothing has taken place with us in the fighting line, but for all that we have not been perfectly quiet. It pleased Soult to cross the Adour in force on the 3d, above the right of our army, and, accordingly, on the 4th we were all put in motion, and both armies continued manœuvring until the 8th, when Soult retired across the river, and resumed his old position, and to-day we have followed his example and taken up our old cantonments. At one time on the 7th he had very nearly put his foot in it, and Lord Wellington would have attacked him on the 8th, but he found it out in time, and was off during the night. We have fortunately not had a great deal of rain, but it is very cold lying out at this time of year."

Lord Saltoun had obtained his promotion to the rank of captain and lieutenant-colonel upon the 25th of December 1813, but he does not seem to have been aware of his having been gazetted for some weeks, as on the 6th of February he wrote as follows to Miss Thurlow :—

"You, of course, before this time know of my promotion, and perhaps are among the number that expect me home; but if so you will be disappointed, at least for the present, for I have accepted the command of the light companies, in which I have always served, and mean to remain with this army till the thing is decided, which must be the case, one way or the other, in a very few months. . . . This is not any sudden idea of mine, for I had settled in my own mind, when I left England, if I got my promotion not to go home. I never mentioned it to my mother or you, because although I knew it to be perfectly right in me to do so, I should have had some difficulty in persuading you of that. Now, however, that it is past altering, I think I could persuade you that it is correct for me not only to serve with a good grace when ordered, but, at the present time especially, to show that I am willing and ready to serve without being compelled to do so; and I have accordingly made an offer of my services to the commanding officer of the brigade, who has been pleased to accept of the same, not but what I would give a good deal for one fortnight in London, though the fog were ever so thick."

His promotion had caused him to be transferred to the second battalion, then at home, but in consequence of this offer, so creditable to him, the light companies of the first brigade of Guards were placed under his orders, a command which he retained to the end of the war.

The first division, composed of the two brigades of Guards and one of Germans, together with the fifth division, marched on the 15th of February to the heights above Anglet, preparatory to forcing the passage of the river Adour, which they accomplished on the 23d and 24th. Sir John Hope, who was in command, at once proceeded to invest the Citadel of Bayonne, and the brigade of the First Guards, having driven the enemy out of the village of St. Etienne, formed the right of the besieging line, the Convent of St. Bernard, overlooking the Adour, being made into a strong post and occupied by Lord Saltoun and his light companies, as it protected the bridge of boats over the river. This part of the army was thus employed in the important service of blockading Bayonne, while Wellington, with his other forces, pursued his victorious career in the south of France.

On the 14th of April the French garrison made a vigorous effort to destroy the lines of the besieging force, in which they were for a time successful, but were soon driven back again, though not without severe loss on both sides; and in a letter of the 15th Lord Saltoun thus told of the encounter :—

"Since I wrote last we have had a very sharp affair, and one that has fallen very severely on the Guards. The enemy made a most desperate sortie on the morning of the 14th, about 3 o'clock, and were not driven in without very great loss on our side. They got through the piquet line near the Bordeaux road, and the night was so dark that it was impossible to tell friends from foes. Sir John Hope very imprudently rode to the front during the dark, met with a party of the French, whom he mistook for Germans, and in endeavouring to get away, his horse was shot, and himself wounded in two places and taken prisoner. He was endeavouring to rally a piquet that had given way, which would have been a very proper place for a Lieut.-Colonel, but was a very improper one for a Commander-in-Chief. General Hay was killed, General Stopford wounded, poor Sir Henry Sulivan and Captain Crofton killed; Captains White and Shifner dead of their wounds; Colonel Collier, Captains Burroughs and Woburn very severely wounded, and in all about sixteen officers of the Guards and Colonel Townshend taken prisoner, and I believe wounded, but am not certain. What makes the loss the more provoking is that we had heard of the abdication of Bonaparte the day before the sortie took place. We expect that a suspension of hostilities will take place to-day or to-morrow, as we have sent in the confirmation of the news to the Governor of the place."

This was the last action of the war in which the Guards were engaged, and peace being declared, Lord Saltoun proceeded to visit Thoulouse, from whence he returned to Bordeaux, and in writing to Miss Thurlow from there on the 22d May, said :—"We have had a most delightful trip from Thoulouse to this place, by way of Montauban and Ajen, along the course of the Garonne, through the most beautiful country. We passed through the whole of Soult's army, which were cantoned on that side of the Garonne. The behaviour of the troops, although perfectly respectful towards us as officers, clearly showed that they were not by any means well satisfied with the new order of things, and that they considered it as forced upon them."

In the same letter he gives a sad reminiscence of the fatal sortie from Bayonne :—" I much fear our letters have not been sent as they ought to have been, which is a melancholy thing for the friends of our poor fellows who were wounded in the sortie, as no less than nine have died of their wounds, and their friends will hear of their death before they have the least idea of their danger."

After attending a levee held by the Duke D'Angoulême, and a grand ball given in honour of that prince, Lord Saltoun resigned his temporary command of the light companies; and proceeding to Tours, and thence to Paris, in a few weeks reached England, where he was welcomed by his family and friends, and ere long he made proposals in due form for the hand of the lady to whom he was attached, of which the acceptance is apparent from a letter of his in August of that year, commencing, "My dear Catherine," instead of the more formal, "My dear Miss Thurlow," with which his numerous letters had hitherto begun.

In after years the writer of this memoir heard Lord Saltoun relate various adventures that had befallen him in his long and active military service, and some of these which must have occurred during the Peninsular campaigns may prove of interest, and may here be told in his own words, although the date and locality of each cannot be given, for the facts themselves were impressed upon the memory of one who was a boy at the time when he heard them far more strongly than, what were then to him, minor details.

There is, however, good reason to believe that it was in 1812, in the long march from Cadiz to join Sir Rowland Hill at Aranjuez, or in the subsequent retreat, until winter quarters near Viseu, in Portugal, were reached, that the two following events occurred, one of which shows the good feeling that existed between the private soldiers and their officers, and the other affords a rather absurd illustration of the occasional accidents and hardships of a bivouac :—

"We had been marching through difficult country, and on very bad roads, when, upon the halt for the night being ordered, we officers of the light company had the unwelcome intelligence conveyed to us that although the rations for the men had arrived all right, our mule, with all our supplies, had broken down some miles to the rear, and that we were in consequence supperless.

"As we were very hungry this was far from agreeable, and we sat down under a tree in no very cheery humour; but after a while were roused by the approach of the senior private of the company. He carried a mess tin in each hand, which prevented him from saluting; but his words were very much to the point. 'Gentlemen, the men are very sorry to hear as how your mule has broke down and you ain't got no supper, so, says we, let's each give a little bit of our own, and it's in these here tins, and we hope you'll take it, gentlemen.' Take it! we were only too glad to get it, and capital it was; but the circumstance showed what care soldiers will take of their officers if they like them, and I especially noticed that the oldest private was the spokesman, and that none of the non-commissioned officers were asked to interfere in what was an affair of kindly feeling, and not of duty."

"When on a march, I generally carried a large and strong umbrella. It served for a walking-stick, and as I had coated it with oil varnish, it was waterproof, and many a wetting it saved me.

"Upon one occasion, however, it took revenge for all its previous benefits.

We had halted after dark in ploughed land, on the steep slope of a hill, and tired as we all were, it was impossible in the dark to attempt to better our position. The men settled themselves to rest as best they could. It was raining heavily, and blowing hard; but, fortunately, the drift was down the slope of the hill, and I therefore sat down, with the umbrella over my shoulders, to pass the night. A brother officer sat down between my knees, and another took a similar position between his knees, all three more or less sheltered by the umbrella. After moodily chatting a while we dropped off to sleep, but how long we slept I cannot say, I only know that I was suddenly roused by the most unpleasant hip bath I ever got: the rain water descending the hill side had been dammed up in the furrow, above where we sat, by the edge of the umbrella resting on the ground; some movement of mine, in my sleep, must have raised it, and the water rushed down upon us, drenching me and the one next to me up to the waist, but our friend below did not escape even so well; in his sleep he lay down, and the rush of water took him in the nape of the neck, and went right through him from head to foot. Three such miserable wretches, as we were till morning broke, were never seen."

The next adventure probably occurred towards the end of the war, when the outposts of the contending armies were very near each other, as described in Lord Saltoun's letter of the 30th October, from camp above Urogne:—

"Upon one occasion, when I was in command of the outposts of our brigade, I was going my rounds with a small escort very early in the morning. Our sentries and those of the enemy were at no great distance from one another, and I noticed that one of the French sentries, who was posted on a rising ground affording some view of the country beyond, appeared to be asleep. I determined to surprise him if possible, and obtain a look at what might be the scene of our own operations in a few days.

"Taking one of the escort with me, and leaving the others to watch, he and I crept, as if deer-stalking, towards the sentry, and managed to reach him without awakening him. He reclined with his back to a tree, against which he had leant his musket, and of this I quickly made myself master; then, while my companion kept guard over the still sleeping sentry, I examined the country beyond with my glass, and got a good deal of information as to its nature, the disposition of the enemy's troops, etc. etc.

"I intended at first to go back without wakening the Frenchman, and to take his musket with me; but reflecting on the severe punishment, perhaps even death, that would await him if discovered by his own officers in that state, and without his arms, and noticing that he was a young soldier, I could not find it in my heart to do so, and we therefore awakened him. His surprise and horror may be more easily imagined than described, and if we had not held him down and stopped his mouth, he would have bolted shouting an alarm. When he became a little calmer, I said to him, 'My friend, it is far better for you that I have caught you asleep than that one of your own officers should have done so; now, no one will know of it unless you tell, be more careful in future, and keep better watch; I return you your musket, and shall trust to your honour not to fire at us as we retire.' However, not to depend too much on his honour, I took out the flint, and shook the powder out of the pan before giving it back to him. He seemed very grateful, and thanked me most warmly, and then we rejoined our party. A few nights after this I was again in command of the outposts, and wishing to visit another post at some distance, I set off on horseback alone. The night was pitch dark, and I lost my way, and got close to the cordon of French sentries, when my horse, crashing through a slight hedge, half scrambled, half fell into a hollow road; and at the same instant came a challenge from the top of the opposite bank, 'Qui v'là?' and I heard the ring of a firelock brought to the ready. I sang out, 'Officier de la poste Anglaise,' and explained that I had lost my way in the dark. The French sentry asked if I was hurt by the fall; and on my replying, 'No,' that I was all right, he most civilly directed me how to get within our lines again; and as we parted said, 'I am happy to be of this service to you; we have all heard of the kindness of one of your officers the other day to a young sentry of ours that he caught asleep.' I told him that I was the officer in question. 'Ah!' he said, 'that makes me doubly happy, that is the way brave enemies should always treat one another;' and so we parted excellent friends, and I found my way by the directions he had given me."

Although the following anecdote does not relate to Lord Saltoun personally, yet as he used to tell it of his old brother officer and intimate friend, the late Lieutenant-colonel Charles Ellis, and as it shows great presence of mind and cool observation in a young officer under difficult circumstances, it is worthy of being placed on record.

"You know Charley Ellis. He is not very big now, and when a young man he was still smaller; but he is the pluckiest fellow I ever met, and I don't think he knows what fear means.

"We were skirmishing in a thickly-wooded bit of country, and Charley had somehow got separated from his men, and lost his way for a time. Trying to rejoin them, he dived through an opening in the bushes, and found himself in a little clearing, just as a tall French soldier entered it through a similar opening on the opposite side, about twenty paces from him. Charley was staggered for an instant, but his eyes and wits were as keen as ever, and he noticed that the hammer of the Frenchman's musket was down, and the pan open. Rushing at him with his sword drawn, he cried in French, 'Down with your arms, and surrender! My men are all round, in a moment you'll be cut to pieces!' The soldier, taken by surprise, threw down his musket. 'Now, off with your cartouch-pouch,' cried Charley. The man obeyed; and Charley, before his adversary had time to think, had loaded the weapon. 'Now,' said he, 'I don't know where my men are any more than you do, but I know the way to find them, so you march on quietly before me, if you try to escape, I'll blow your brains out.' When he appeared with the Frenchman, some six foot two or three in height, before him, the men all cheered him; and when they heard how the capture had been made, they were still more pleased, for he was a general favourite with them, from his kindness to them, and from his invincible courage joined to so small a frame."

During the autumn of 1814, Lord Saltoun passed some time at his family seat of Philorth, from which he had been so long absent, and also visited some of his numerous friends in Scotland.

On the 6th of March 1815 he was married to Miss Thurlow, and he and his bride proceeded to pass the honeymoon at Worthing House, which they had hired for the purpose, situated in the small watering-place of that name, a few miles west of Brighton, where they might hope to remain undisturbed for some time, as although Napoleon's escape from Elba, and his subsequent proceedings had roused Europe once more to arms, yet recent changes and promotions in the regiment had transferred Lord Saltoun back to the third battalion; and as the first battalion was ordered on the 1st of April to proceed abroad to join the second in Belgium, there appeared no chance of his being soon engaged in active service. But their anticipations of quiet life were rudely dispelled; certain circumstances caused the order of the 1st April to be countermanded on the 2d, the third battalion was sent abroad instead of the first, and a few weeks after his wedding, he was called upon to leave his bride, don harness, and take part in a struggle far fiercer, and for a time more doubtful, than any in which he had yet been engaged.

The third battalion embarked at Ramsgate on the 9th of April, reached Ostend the next day, and marched, *viâ* Bruges and Ghent, to Enghien, where it found the second battalion; and the two, formed into the first brigade of Guards, were quartered in that town and the neighbouring villages of Marq, Hove, etc. Lord Saltoun joined on the 26th of April, and on the 15th of May he was again put in command of the light companies of the brigade, as he had been towards the close of the war in Spain, and was quartered at Hove.

While at Hove he kept up a constant correspondence with his wife, but, as might be expected, the letters related chiefly to domestic details. In one, written 7th May, however, he mentioned a short trip that he had made to visit Antwerp, and the fortress of Bergen-op-Zoom; and on the 18th of the same month he wrote:—"The Duke of Wellington has been for some days back riding a good deal, and we used to say in Spain that whenever 'the Beau,' meaning the Duke, took to riding, it was time to look out. However, I believe this time he is only looking at his troops, which have been much increased lately by several battalions of Hanoverian Landwehr, who are tolerably good-looking men in general. . . . The spirit which the French call *morale* is very good in them, and they are pleased at acting with the British, whom they consider as countrymen. John Bull, however, does not admit them by any means to that honourable distinction, but calls them 'rid Jarmins,' from their being dressed in red." And again, on the 31st:—"I have just returned from a grand review by our royal commander, the Prince of Orange. Our performance was very good; and those spectators who were good judges have complimented us most highly, as well as the Prince, who was pleased to say that, although he had been many years with the British army, he never before had seen so perfect a body of men. This brings me to your having heard that the Duke was not satisfied with his infantry. He never had so good before, for the Hanoverians are much better than the Portuguese, and John Bull has not, I should think, altered much in a year. Never believe any humbugging stories of that sort until we are well beaten and afraid to meet our enemy, which, beaten or not beaten, will never be the case."

In succeeding letters he gave accounts of reviews, balls, cricket matches, and other amusements by which the tedium of a life in somewhat dull quarters was relieved; and in a letter of the 14th of June is the following passage :—" Our grand cricket match did not take place, for the day turned out to be a very rainy one, so that it stands over till next Saturday, when the Duke of Richmond is to come over for the purpose." Before that Saturday morning dawned the cricketers were engaged in a far more desperate match, and were playing a game in which the balls used were of a different description.

The story of the battles of Quatre Bras and Waterloo, and of the heroic defence of the Château and Orchard of Hougomont, the key of the British position in the latter action, has been so often told and retold, that nothing can be added to the general account of those eventful days.

The share of the First Guards in those glorious achievements, which earned for the regiment the honourable title of "Grenadier Guards," in consequence of it having defeated the Grenadiers of Napoleon's famous Imperial Old Guard, is admirably related in the following extracts from the interesting and ably written history of that regiment by Lieutenant-General Sir F. W. Hamilton, K.C.B., in which the name of Lord Saltoun is mentioned in a way that shows how he bore himself in those well-fought fields, while passages from his letters to Lady Saltoun, after the victory had been won, and during the march on Paris, afford some details that are worthy of preservation :—[1] " On the morning of the 15th the Duke had given directions for the first Division to assemble at Ath, but when, at a late hour of that day, the news of the French advance reached Brussels, he issued an order, dated ten o'clock at night, directing, amongst other things, that the first Division should move from Enghien to Braine-le-Comte. This order reached Enghien

[1] History of the Grenadier Guards, vol. iii. p. 15.

at half-past one in the morning of the 16th. The drums immediately beat to arms, and at two the Guards, having assembled at Hove, were ready to move off. At four o'clock they commenced their march, the First Brigade leading, preceded by its light companies under Lord Saltoun. Their route led them over the position of Steinkirk, rendered famous, 123 years earlier, by the gallant conduct of their predecessors in 1692, and they reached Braine-le-Comte at nine in the morning, having been joined on the march by the second Brigade under Byng. The first Division, after experiencing some delay in marching through this town owing to its crowded state, halted for a few hours on its eastern side, while General Cooke, commanding the Division, made a reconnaissance to the southward. On his return at midday he took upon himself the responsibility of continuing the march of the Division towards Nivelles, ten miles further, though the heat of the day was excessive, and the men were suffering from the weight of their packs. The Division of Guards were therefore again *en route*, and in due course arrived at three o'clock at a position within half a mile of Nivelles, where they expected to rest from their day's march, but they had not halted many minutes and piled arms, before an aide-de-camp brought an order to advance immediately. The Division was again under arms, and as it was supposed, from the firing having become very heavy and apparently very close, that the enemy was entering Nivelles on the other side, it moved off at the double down the hill to encounter them. After passing through the town unopposed, the march was continued to Hautain Caroll, where the artillery was allowed to pass to the front, thence along the chaussée leading to Namur. During this part of the march many wounded were passed going to the rear, and a wounded officer of the 44th regiment that was met, urged the quick advance of the division, as things he said were going on badly for the Allies. As the march continued, more and more wounded were met on the road side, telling of the seriousness of the work going on in front; at last, about five o'clock in the afternoon, the leading companies of the First Guards, viz., the Light Infantry under Lord Saltoun, arrived at a critical moment at the north-western extremity of a wood called the Bois de Bossu, about three-quarters of a mile long and 300 yards broad, which lay to their right, on the south side of the chaussée, near Quatre Bras."

[1] "A sharply-contested action raged during the whole afternoon as the several regiments of the 5th Division, the troops under the Duke of Brunswick, and the contingent of Nassau successively reached the scene of action. The French, superior in Infantry, and possessing nearly double the force of Cavalry, made repeated attacks upon the hard-pressed lines of the allies. At length the French light troops succeeded in driving the Dutch-Belgian infantry out of the Bois-de-Bossu, while some of them almost cleared the space between that wood and the high road, thus rendering the issue of the day very doubtful. Picton's 5th Division was already very much reduced, and it had become not only impracticable to make any offensive movement, but it was with difficulty that the Allies were even maintaining their own ground, when, at this critical juncture, the opportune arrival of the leading Brigade of Guards, after a march of twenty-six miles, changed the aspect of affairs, and caused the French skirmishers to pause in their onward career.

"The Prince of Orange, who had galloped along the road to meet the British Guards, ordered the light companies of the First Regiment, under Lord Saltoun, to advance into the wood to the right of the road, and drive the enemy out of it. Lord Saltoun, not perceiving the enemy at the moment, as they were mostly concealed from view, asked the Prince where they were? The Prince, mistaking this for hesitation on the part of the officer, replied in a hurried, hasty manner, 'Sir, if you don't like to undertake it, I'll find some one.' Saltoun quietly repeated his question; and on its being pointed out to him that they were in the wood, formed his line of skirmishers, and led the attack. A small stream runs north and south, through the centre of this wood, and at its eastern extremity, furthest from where the Guards approached, is a hollow way, affording protection to troops who may occupy it. As the leading battalion companies of the Second Battalion, under Colonel Askew, came up, they were also ordered by the Prince to enter the wood, two companies at a time, and, though wearied with a fifteen hours' march, the men received the order with a cheer, and with fixed bayonets pushed forward after their comrades. Once in the wood, the leading companies had nothing to guide them but the sound of the enemy's firing; but in vain did the thick

[1] History of the Grenadier Guards, vol. iii. p. 17.

trees impede their progress; for although the enemy made a resolute defence, they were driven back on every side, and the loud sharp rattle of musketry, which was heard gradually but steadily advancing, told plainly how successful was the progress of the British Guards, and, that even in this quarter, where the enemy had hitherto been most successful, he was encountering a most vigorous and determined resistance. The French skirmishers attempted to take advantage of the rivulet, which crosses the wood, to form up, and arrest the further progress of the attack; but their stand was only momentary, for the First Guards, forcing their way across, charged, and, with a cheer, drove everything before them, till they debouched on the other side. During this manœuvre, the Light Companies sustained considerable additional loss from the hasty and hurried manner in which the Battalion companies were ordered forward by the Prince of Orange, to support Lord Saltoun, for, upon entering the wood, and hearing a heavy fire in their front, these imagined it was the enemy, and commenced firing, and although Lord Saltoun's subaltern, Charles Ellis, was sent back to explain, it was impossible to stop the firing till they emerged from the wood, at the other end. From the spot where the Guards came into the open, they observed the 33d Regiment lying sheltered, behind a low hedge, about 150 yards to their left rear, while on their right was the deep ravine or hollow way before referred to, and the Guards had no sooner reached this spot than they became exposed to the direct fire of the enemy's artillery and reserve infantry. The thickness of the underwood had thrown the line into some confusion; and as it continued to be exposed to the galling fire of artillery, to which no return could be made, it was deemed advisable to draw back to the stream in the wood, which was more out of range; but even here, under the comparative shelter of the trees, some men were killed or maimed by the artillery fire that the French continued to direct upon them.

"The Third Battalion of the First Guards, under Colonel Hon. William Stuart, had now come up, and the Regiment, after a few moments' repose, again advanced, being ordered to form line outside, and to the left, of the wood; which was at once commenced. As the companies had got mixed in advancing through the tangled thicket, the men formed up in succession to the right as they came into the open; and men of other Regiments who had been engaged before the First Division arrived, gallantly left its cover and fell in, taking the opportunity of renewing the fight with the Guards. Their right now rested on the trees, while their left extended through the fields of standing corn, towards the chaussée leading from Brussels to Charleroi. In this formation General Maitland again and again led forward the First Guards to the attack, and as frequently drove the enemy back, but could never get beyond a certain point. The Commanding Officers of both Battalions, Askew and Stuart, were wounded and put *hors de combat* in these repeated encounters, and were succeeded by Colonels Edward Stables and Francis D'Oyly. Though the Guards could not break the enemy's line, they stood steadily pouring a withering fire into the French columns, as these attempted gradually to deploy; while the French Cavalry continually moved about, seeking for an opportunity to charge. When the Brigade had emerged from the wood to form line, a battalion of Brunswickers followed it into the open, and was in the act of moving, so as to form up on the Guards' left, when the French Cavalry came suddenly down upon the left flank of the Second Battalion, forcing it back towards the wood; and it being impossible to form square in presence of the enemy, owing to the previous irregular formation of the line, the men intuitively made for the protection offered to them by the hollow way above referred to. Here the line was immediately re-formed, protected from any further Cavalry attacks, and again the men commenced pouring upon their assailants a fire so destructive as nearly to annihilate them. Nothing perhaps could have better tested the perfect discipline of the Battalions of Guards than the celerity with which, after having been temporarily put in confusion by a sudden charge of cavalry, they rallied, re-formed, and becoming themselves the assailants, repelled the enemy. The Brunswickers, whose front became exposed when the Guards were forced into the wood, formed square, and opening fire upon the advancing Cavalry, materially assisted in their destruction. Many Frenchmen were here taken prisoners, and several of their horses which fled riderless were appropriated as fresh chargers by the Field Officers of the Guards. The firing was kept up as long as daylight lasted, when General Maitland led the Third Battalion forward beyond the outskirts of the wood, for which the enemy no longer contended, and throwing out a line of picquets in his front for the night, showing thereby undisputed possession of the battle-field, he directed Colonel Stables, who brought the Second Battalion out of action, to move his men to the chaussée at the end of the wood, where they enjoyed a well-merited short repose before the labours of another day commenced."

It was probably during the attack of cavalry just mentioned that James Lord Hay, eldest son of the Earl of Erroll, who was aide-de-camp to General Maitland, fell. He had been acting for the moment as adjutant to Lord Saltoun, who used to say that, seeing him mounted on a well-bred horse, he advised him to go down a narrow path leading into the wood, before the French cavalry came too near, as he had often known highly-bred horses refuse awkward places if put suddenly at them, but that Lord Hay said there was no fear, as the horse was such a perfect hunter; that, however, when the time came for them both to go down, the horse did refuse, reared, and tried to turn round, and that, as Lord Saltoun went down the path, a man's body fell across his horse's neck, and rolled off. He called out, "Who's that?" and one of his men answered, "It's Lord Hay; but I shot the man that shot him." The momentary delay caused by his horse refusing had enabled one of the cavalry to fire at him with fatal effect. Sir F. W. Hamilton mentions this occurrence in a note.[1]

To resume the extracts from his valuable work, passing to the next day, the 17th:—

[2] "Upon the order being given for the allied army to retire from the neighbourhood of Quatre Bras, the First Division of Guards left their ground a little after eleven o'clock, and moved along the chaussée leading to Brussels. The day was excessively hot, with indications of a coming storm.... After a march of about eight miles, the First Division quitted the high road and moved to its left along a cart track that soon brought it behind the château and farm of Hougomont, with its garden, orchard, and wood, all of which became for ever memorable on the following day. Here the Division was halted, and the men were preparing their bivouac for the night, when an order came to move to the right and take up a position on the next rise, along the south-west side of the chaussée leading from Nivelles to Mont St. Jean. Scarcely had the several battalions moved to their new position than the storm of rain

[1] History of the Grenadier Guards, vol. iii. p. 22.   [2] Ibid. p. 26.

that had long been threatening came down, and continued throughout the greater part of the night, deluging the men to the skin.

"About six o'clock in the evening the four Light Companies of the Division were suddenly ordered to take possession of the farm-house and grounds of Hougomont; the two light companies of the First Guards, under Lord Saltoun and Ellison, occupied the orchard and wood, while the two of the Second Brigade occupied the farm-house and garden, which was surrounded by a wall. The night and the following morning were spent by the Light Companies in making this position as strong as their means would allow them, barricading the gates, and otherwise rendering the buildings as defensible as possible, and, at Saltoun's suggestion, loop-holing the garden wall. During the first part of the night the French brought up their advanced posts close to the line of picquets of the First Guards in the wood and orchard, though without attempting to molest them; but about two in the morning, as their tirailleurs were advancing too near, Lieutenant-colonel Ellison, who was picquet officer for the night, was ordered from the orchard into the wood to drive them out. This he accomplished; and the wood being an open grove without underwood, and easily traversed in every direction, the advanced files of the picquets could keep up the communication with each other without difficulty."

[1] "The several Battalions of the Guards were posted on the rising ground above Hougomont in the following order. The Third Battalion First Guards on the extreme left, on the crest of the ridge, in quarter distance column of companies, at deploying distance from the right of Halkett's Brigade; the Second Battalion First Guards, in the same formation, was to the right rear of the Third Battalion, on the reverse slope, and immediately under the crest of the hill. The Second Brigade, under Byng, stood on the crest of the ridge between the right of the First Brigade and the Nivelles road, completely commanding the château and grounds of Hougomont, and thus forming a support to the troops stationed there.

"It has generally been understood that the Light Companies of the First Brigade of Guards under Saltoun remained permanently in the orchard and wood from the previous night till relieved in the course of the action of the

[1] History of the Grenadier Guards, vol. iii. p. 29.

18th. Such was not the case, for in the early morning, just before dawn, a staff Officer conducted to the post a Battalion of Nassauers, one company of Hanoverian riflemen, and 100 Lüneburghers, and handed to Lord Saltoun an order to deliver up the charge of the orchard to the Officer commanding them, and to retire with his own men to join his Brigade, posted on the hill in rear of Hougomont. After taking the Nassau officer over the orchard, and showing him all the plans and preparations for defence, Saltoun was marching towards the First Guards' Brigade on the ridge behind Hougomont, when about half way, in the early grey of the morning, he met the Duke of Wellington and Lord Fitzroy Somerset. The Duke called out, 'Hallo, who are you? Where are you going?' Saltoun immediately halted, ordered arms, directed his men to lie down, according to an invariable custom; and on advancing to the Duke, explained to him the orders he had received. The Duke was surprised, and said, ' Well, I was not aware of such an order; but, however, don't join the brigade yet; remain quiet here where you are until further orders from me,' and then he rode away.[1] Saltoun remained here several hours, when, just as the battle was beginning, an aide-de-camp rode up and said he was to follow out his former orders and join his Brigade, on reaching which he gave up his temporary command, and resumed that of his company, in rear of his own battalion. Lord Saltoun had no sooner done this and ordered arms, when a shout came up, ' Light infantry to the front,' and a cry arose of, ' The Nassauers are driven out of the orchard;' and such proved to be the case, for the French had attacked, and in spite of the gallant defence that was made, had swept them clear and clean out of it. No time was to be lost; Saltoun was again put in command of the light companies of the First Guards, and went down the hill to attack the French. The first duty, therefore, that these Light Companies had to perform that day was to retake the orchard, not to resist an attack upon it; and that made a great difference in the work to be performed so far as these companies were concerned; for when they had re-occupied the wood, which they were not long in doing, they found nearly all the preparations they had made for defence completely

---

[1] In relating this occurrence, Lord Saltoun used to say that upon his ordering the men to lie down, the Duke turned to his companion and said, "That don't look like running away, Fitzroy," and that it was a false rumour of the desertion of large bodies of the troops that had caused the Duke to ride about at that early hour to ascertain the truth.

destroyed, and during the action they had to trust to sheer hard fighting, often hand to hand, to maintain their ground.[1]

"Shortly before the action commenced, the Duke of Wellington visited the advanced position of Hougomont occupied by the second Brigade of Guards under Byng; and on riding off to another part of the field, left as his parting injunctions to that General, that it was to be defended to the last extremity, and nobly were those injunctions responded to by the British Guards.

"The battle commenced shortly after eleven o'clock with an attack upon this, the key of the allied position, by the infantry of Prince Jerome's corps, preceded by a cloud of skirmishers, while from 200 guns the French artillery opened fire along their whole line against the allied forces.

"As the French skirmishers advanced upon Hougomont, they were twice checked by the direct fire of the British artillery from the rising ground above, but they at length succeeded in effecting an entrance to the wood, and in driving back the Nassauers and Hanoverians who had occupied it, when the direct fire could no longer be continued. But the further advance of the French was soon checked by some shells from a howitzer battery, which the Duke sent for, and by the return of the light companies of the First Guards, under Lord Saltoun, now again ordered to the front. The companies of the Second Brigade at the same time rushed gallantly forward to relieve the foreign troops, and the four Light Companies of the two Guards' Brigades together eventually cleared the wood for a time of the French skirmishers, who retired into the fields beyond.

"While Wellington had recognised this as the key of the allied position, Napoleon had also felt the necessity of securing it before he could make any impression upon the centre of the Allies. Jerome's skirmishers were accordingly reinforced, and in conjunction with General Foy's infantry on their

---

[1] In 1871 the writer of the present work, in conversation with some old officers, mentioned having heard from Lord Saltoun the fact of the light companies of the First Guards having been relieved by the Nassau troops, and afterwards having to retake the orchard, thus related by Sir F. W. Hamilton, when General Sir John Blomfield, R.H.A., who was one of the party, said, "To be sure it was so; I remember perfectly seeing the Nassauers retiring in skirmishing order from the orchard, up the hill towards us, not running away, but retiring steadily, fighting in good order, and very fine and picturesque they looked."

right, renewed the attack with great vigour. The British Guards of both brigades offered a desperate resistance, retiring from tree to tree, and frequently making a bold and resolute stand, but a superiority of numbers forced them at length to return to their original positions; the First Guards' Light Companies on the left falling back to their position in the orchard, the Second Brigade Companies retiring to the shelter offered by the château itself and by a haystack standing outside. The French skirmishers, believing all opposition to have ceased, now rapidly advanced through the wood towards the building and garden. A hedge forming the northern boundary of the wood, towards which they were approaching, appeared to them to form also the enclosure of the garden beyond, and, in full confidence that they were about to become masters of it, they rushed forward *au pas de charge*, but were soon fatally undeceived; the loop-holed garden-wall stood thirty yards behind the hedge, running parallel to it, behind which stood the Coldstreams and Third Guards, and a deadly musketry fire bursting forth from the loopholes, suddenly brought them up surprised and staggered by so unexpected a reception, which laid low their foremost ranks. As the French could not hope to succeed in storming this little fortress by any direct attack, they had recourse to the shelter of the hedge and surrounding trees, from which they kept up for some time an unequal fire against the garrison who had so well protected themselves.

"As the French battalions in support were rapidly pushed forward, the British artillery recommenced its fire upon them, causing much confusion in their ranks, of which the garrison and light companies First Guards at once took advantage, and, sallying forth from the flanks, soon regained possession of a considerable portion of the wood. On the advance of the Guards the British artillery ceased firing, whereupon the French recovering themselves, and receiving further reinforcements, again advanced with such determination as to force the Guards to return, the Second Brigade to the flanks of the château, the First Brigade to the left of the garden-wall. The Coldstream and Third Guards companies, after having for some time resisted very superior forces, at length retired within the buildings, barricading the entrance-gate with every available object, and manning the garden-walls, so as to be prepared to resist the enemy at every point, while the companies of the First Guards retired as far as the hedge on their left of the garden-wall, where Saltoun continued to maintain himself. The French in the wood finding a direct attack against the garden-wall of no avail, endeavoured to come round its left flank through the orchard. Here Saltoun was prepared to meet them, and as they were debouching through a gap from the wood into the orchard, he seized the opportunity, charged the head of the column with the First Guards' light companies, and drove the enemy back into the wood.

"Another attempt was shortly made by a considerable body of the enemy's light troops to turn the left flank of the grounds of Hougomont, by advancing along the eastern hedge of the farm enclosures; while a simultaneous attack was made through the wood and the orchard occupied by Lord Saltoun. He had already lost many men, and was once again obliged to withdraw, retiring from tree to tree till he reached the shelter of the hollow way in the rear face of the enclosure, where he awaited reinforcements before he could renew any forward movement. The Duke, from the height above, observing how matters were progressing, directed Byng to send down reinforcements from his Brigade, and shortly afterwards two companies of the Third Guards were seen advancing along the eastern enclosure to meet the enemy; when Lord Saltoun, being thus reinforced on his left, and the advance of the French skirmishers in his front having exposed them to the flanking fire from the eastern garden-wall, resumed the offensive, cleared the orchard of the enemy, and re-occupied its front hedge.

"Lord Saltoun relates that the several attacks against the front of his post were at the time attended with more or less partial success, but that in the end the French were always repulsed; that in one of these attacks, when he had been driven from the front hedge of the orchard to the hollow way in rear of it, the enemy occupied the front hedge with infantry, and brought up a gun to bear upon him, which he endeavoured to seize. He failed in that attempt, but regained possession of the hedge, where he firmly established himself."

[1] "About two o'clock, after Byng had reinforced Hougomont with two companies of the Third Guards, he perceived that these renewed attempts of the enemy upon the orchard were constantly reducing the numbers of those entrusted with its defence; acting, therefore, upon the directions

[1] History of the Grenadier Guards, vol. iii. p. 34.

given to him by the Duke, to relieve the men as often as he found it necessary, but to keep the post to the last moment, he desired Colonel Hepburn to move the remainder of his Second Battalion Third Guards down the slope, as a further reinforcement to that position. Hepburn on reaching the hollow way found it occupied by very few men, viz., the survivors of the two light companies of the First Guards, under Saltoun, who (his own subaltern, Charles Ellis, being wounded) was left with scarce an effective man with whom to continue the gallant defence, which he had been maintaining with varied success for nearly four hours in the wood and orchard in front of the Château. Lord Saltoun, therefore, gave over to Hepburn the charge of that part of Hougomont, and at three o'clock rejoined his own battalion, the Third, on the heights above.

"General Maitland said, with reference to the two light companies of the First Guards, that they were detached with the other brigade, and that General Byng spoke in the highest terms of the conduct of Lord Saltoun, and of all the officers and men on this occasion, saying of Lord Saltoun, that 'his conduct was admirable.'

"The battalion of Coldstreams, under Colonel Alexander Woodford (with the exception of two companies left on the ridge in charge of the colours), was also subsequently sent forward to assist in the defence of Hougomont, which, at a later period, sustained another still more determined attack, but thanks to the opportune arrival of these comparatively fresh battalions of Guards, the enemy's efforts were as unavailing as before.

"The value that Napoleon attached to the possession of this post may be estimated by the fact that eight thousand of his troops were placed *hors de combat* in these several unsuccessful attempts to carry it, and when evening and defeat came to him, the burning ruins were still in possession of its gallant defenders."[1]

[2]"It was now about four o'clock, and the cannonade was very heavy during the interval of the Cavalry charges. The two commanding officers of battalions, D'Oyly and Stables, were both wounded, and placed *hors de combat*,

---

[1] These defenders, from first to last, numbered under 2000 men, of whom, for the first four hours, not more than one-third were engaged in the defence.

[2] History of the Grenadier Guards, vol. iii. p. 37.

when the command of the 3rd Battalion devolved upon Lord Saltoun, who had lately joined from Hougomont, and that of the second upon Lieutenant-Colonel Reeve. The two wounded Colonels were carried off the field, and Colonel Stables died the following morning, to the great regret of all his brother officers."

[1]"The Prussians at length began to make their appearance on the field near Planchenoit, to the right and right rear of the French, and Napoleon was now pressed by them on that flank. In vain had he endeavoured with his cavalry to shake the British squares; in vain had he stormed again and again the stronghold of Hougomont on the British right; in vain had he attempted to force Picton on their left. Most of his troops had been baffled, but there still remained to him one more chance of retrieving the fortunes of the day; he still fondly hoped that the hour of his triumph was at hand, and that he should be able once more to grasp as firmly as ever the sceptre of Imperial France. He resolved to organise the columns of Grenadiers and Chasseurs of his Imperial Guards, and hurl them against the centre of the allied position, where stood firmly as a rock Maitland's 1st brigade of British Guards.

"The following anecdote, referring to this period, is recorded of Lord Saltoun by an intimate friend, and his former Adjutant. During a lull, just after the repulse of one attack, and before the final one, the Duke was on his horse close to the 1st Brigade, and after looking carefully with his glass along the whole of the French position, turned to those of his staff near him, saying, 'Well, I think they are pretty well told out now.' Saltoun immediately said to one of the staff officers, 'I don't know; when I was outside the wood at Hougomont, this morning, before the action began, I watched a column of men, as far as I can guess about 5000 or 6000, go into a hollow opposite; I have kept my eye on this spot all day, and have never seen them come out yet.' Upon this being repeated to the Duke, he turned his glass in that direction, and after a moment's pause exclaimed, 'By God, he is right! they are coming out now;' and it is said that the Duke was so much struck with the coolness and power of observation exhibited by Lord Saltoun under such circumstances, that he ever afterwards spoke of him as a thorough soldier."

[1] History of the Grenadier Guards, vol. iii. p. 39.

[1]"For an hour before carrying out his plan, Napoleon directed a furious concentrated fire from the whole of his artillery, upon that portion of the allied position lying between the farm of Hougomont and La Haye Sainte. Fortunately there ran along this part of the field of battle a cart road, on one side of which was a ditch and bank. In and under cover of these, the 1st Brigade of Guards sheltered themselves during this terrific cannonade, which lasted about three-quarters of an hour, and without its protection the two battalions must have been annihilated. Napoleon probably calculated on such an effect, but he had yet to learn the extent of British fortitude and endurance.

"The Duke was well aware of the enemy's intention, and being at this time close to the two battalions of the First Guards, which at first were in squares, and with which he remained during the subsequent attack, he desired General Maitland to form them into line four deep, as he thought it possible that Napoleon would support the attack with his cavalry. Maitland immediately carried out the Duke's order, covering his change of formation with a line of skirmishers under Swinburn, who only rejoined his battalion a few moments before the enemy was upon them. The formation into line, instead of being made by deployment, was effected by simply wheeling up to the front the four-deep flank faces of the square, the rear faces forming the extremities of each battalion, so that the grenadier companies were in the centre, and the men could more readily form square again, should circumstances require it. The whole brigade as it now stood, four deep, occupied only the length of one battalion in line."

[2]"The above formation was scarcely completed, and the men ordered to lie down again, when, at a quarter past seven, the furious cannonade suddenly ceased. As the smoke gradually cleared away, under cover of which Napoleon had been organising his attack, near La Belle Alliance, a superb sight opened upon the brigade. Close columns of regiments of the Old Imperial Guard, 5000 strong, directed by Napoleon himself, and led by Ney, on foot (for his horse had been shot under him), were seen advancing up the slope *au pas de charge* direct upon them, with shouts of ' *Vive l'Empereur!*'

"These columns were composed of the 2nd, 3rd, and 4th regiments

[1] History of the Grenadier Guards, vol. iii. p. 40.   [2] *Ibid.* p. 41.

of grenadiers of the Old Imperial Guard, under the command respectively of Generals Christiani, Poret, and Harlet, all in line of battalion close columns, forming a front of three companies. The 1st regiment of grenadiers of the Guard, 1300 strong, remained in reserve on the heights of La Belle Alliance, and General Count Friant, the colonel and commander-in-chief of the Old Guard, remained with this regiment on the heights.

"As the leading columns, apparently as regularly formed as for a field-day, began to ascend the incline on the top of which the British First Guards were posted, they became exposed to the concentrated artillery fire of the right wing of the allies, by which they suffered much. Notwithstanding this they continued their advance in admirable order, and with the greatest enthusiasm, preceded by a cloud of skirmishers; but these were soon driven back upon their main body by a fire of canister, grape, and shrapnel shells, delivered at a distance of less than 100 yards. At first, to their astonishment, these columns met no enemy to offer any obstruction to their further progress, when, after arriving within from twenty to thirty yards of the position occupied by the First Guards, they suddenly saw rise up before them what proved to be to them an impenetrable barrier.

"The Duke now gave directions to Maitland, saying, 'Now, Maitland, now's your time,' and immediately the men were ordered to rise. They had already been warned to reserve their fire till the enemy should arrive within a very short distance. It was, as Siborne relates, a moment of thrilling excitement. The First Guards springing up so suddenly, in a most compact four-deep line, appeared to the enemy as starting out of the ground. The Imperial Guard, with their high bonnets, as they crowned the summit of the ridge, appeared to the British, through the smoky haze of the battle-field, like a corps of giants advancing upon them.

"The British Guards instantly opened their fire with a tremendous volley, thrown in with great coolness and precision, and the enemy were then so close upon them, some only fifteen yards, that the men would fire without putting their muskets to the shoulder, while to accelerate the subsequent file-firing the rear ranks passed their loaded muskets to the front. An oblique fire was also poured in upon the right flank of the advancing column by the 33d and and 69th British regiments, which had been promptly pushed forward by

Halket on the left of the Guards. The head of the column, surprised at this sudden apparition, halted, and the entire mass staggered under the effect of the murderous fire poured into them at such close quarters. In less than a minute, more than three hundred of the 'Vieille Garde' fell to rise no more; but the high spirit and innate valour of the Imperial Guard were not to be subdued by a first repulse; their officers, placing themselves in the front and on the flanks, called aloud, waved their swords, and by words and gestures attempted a deployment into line, in order to acquire a more extended front; but the head of the column being continually shattered and driven back by the well-sustained fire of the Guards within so limited a space, the attempt was fruitless. The confusion into which the enemy's columns were now thrown became every moment more manifest, and the Duke, seizing the opportunity, ordered Maitland to charge, which order was instantly obeyed. At the same time Saltoun, equally alive to the real state of the enemy's columns, shouted to his battalion, 'Now's the time, my boys.' The brigade answered with a cheer, and led by Maitland, Saltoun, Reeve, and Gunthorpe, who placed themselves in front, sprang forward to the charge, and as they continued down the hill in pursuit of the Imperial Guard, they passed over a hedge of dead and dying bodies that lay in front of the position they had so gloriously defended." . . . .

"As the brigade continued its pursuit down the slope, in the direction of La Belle Alliance, its right flank became exposed to a second column, the Chasseurs of the Imperial Guard, who were advancing, but too late, from a point nearer to the enclosure of Hougomont, to the support of their brethren of the first column. Maitland perceiving this, and seeing that his right flank might be turned, halted, and ordered the right wing of the second battalion to be thrown back, so as to be parallel with the line of advance of the French column. In the midst of this manœuvre the third battalion, mistaking the word of command, '*halt, front, form up*,' for '*form square*,' commenced that formation, expecting the enemy's cavalry to be down upon them. The mistake, however, was soon rectified, and in a few moments the brigade was again near its former position, in a four-deep line, with its left thrown a little forward, ready to repel this second attacking column of the Imperial Guards. Meanwhile Adams, having brought his brigade to the ground formerly occupied by the second brigade of Guards, had formed his line, throwing forward his right shoulder, the second battalion 95th on the left, then the 52nd and the 71st on the right, extending towards Hougomont. As the second column of the Chasseurs of the Imperial Guard advanced up the slope in similar formation to the First, it was received by Adams' Brigade, which poured a destructive fire into its left flank, and was met in front by the direct fire of the First Guards, who had thrown forward their left, to be more directly opposed to the advancing columns. This flank fire of Adams' Brigade mainly contributed to the final overthrow of the second column, and as the Duke of Wellington saw it begin to waver, he ordered a general advance of the whole line; Adams' Brigade followed this second column, while the First Guards, under Maitland, followed the track of the first column, until it reached the Charleroi road, near La Belle Alliance. Here the first regiment of Grenadiers of the old French Imperial Guards, that had been left in reserve, attempted, after forming square, to stem the flying torrent and its pursuers; but to no avail; it shared the fate of the other regiments, broke, and nought remained of the army of Imperial France but a confused mass of soldiery, which during the following night continued a disorderly retreat, pursued by the avenging Prussians.

"As for the supposed historical reply of the French Guard, '*La Garde meurt mais ne se rend pas!*' General Cambronne, who commanded part of it, did surrender, and was made prisoner by the British Guards; and it was Lord Saltoun himself who, at the moment of his surrender, gave him in charge to a tall grenadier, named Kent, who conducted him to Brussels.

"The First Guards, having pursued as far as the Charleroi road, formed into column, and continued their advance along the chaussée, through the whole depth of the late French position, and bivouacked for the night in the fields on the right, two miles in advance of the position of WATERLOO, a name which their bravery and discipline, as well as devotedness to their sovereign and their country, had this day so much contributed to render immortal."

The above extracts speak for themselves, and show the opinion of Lord Saltoun's conduct during those eventful days, formed by those well able to judge of how a soldier did his duty; and his letters to his wife, while they say little or nothing of his own personal adventures, breathe a spirit of honest exultation at the success of his country's arms, of cheerfulness and resolute contentment as regarded himself, and of much feeling for the loss of comrades and the sorrows of others. The first of these letters was written the day after the battle, and consists of a few hurried lines to relieve the anxiety of those at home :—

"Field of battle, near Waterlude,
"June 19th.

"I have only just time to tell you that I have lived through two of the sharpest actions ever fought by men. We have defeated the French at all points, and they are in full retreat. Our loss has been prodigious, and many of my best and oldest friends are gone, but these things must tarry,—my favourite little horse was shot under me, and at present I have only one, but I must get another here. I have no time to write more at length, as, if I do, I fear I shall be too late for the Staff Officer who is to take this. So God bless you, my dear love, and believe me ever your affectionate

"SALTOUN."

He did not find time to write again until the 22d, when he gave his wife the following simple account of the events in which he had been engaged :—

"Camp near Gomini (Gourmignies),
"22 June 1815.

"I wrote you a few lines from the field of battle on the 19th, but I have just heard that letters are to go immediately to England. I take this opportunity of telling you what has taken place since I wrote last from Hove on the 15th. A few hours after my letter was gone, we got the alarm that Boneparte had attacked the Prussians, and we were ordered to march at a moment's notice, and on the morning of the 16th, at 3, we marched from Hove, through Braine and Nivelles, to a place called Quatre-bras, which place we reached about 5 in the afternoon, and were immediately very hotly engaged in the Bois de Bossu, and at nightfall we had succeeded in taking the wood from the enemy, but not without very great loss. My old friends Grose and Miller fell in the affair, with many others, and about five hundred men of the Regiment. During this time Boney had attacked the Prussians at Fleurus, and had gained some advantages, so as to oblige them to retreat. Our position of Quatre-bras being in consequence exposed on the left, we were obliged to fall back, and accordingly, on the 17th, retired, and took post in position at Water-leud. On the 18th Napoleon attacked us with the whole of his army. The action was extremely severe, and our loss much greater than in any of the battles in the Peninsula. . . . The infantry formed squares, and about five o'clock had completely repulsed and destroyed the finest cavalry by their steadiness in square, and the excellence of their fire. About half-past six Napoleon made his last desperate attack, at the head of his Old Imperial Guards, upon our brigade. It was a thing I always wished for, and the result was what I have often said it would be; to do them justice they came on like men, but our boys went at them like Britons, and drove them off the field in less than ten minutes.

"From that moment the day was our own, and the French were completely routed, and fled, leaving their artillery, stores, baggage, and an immense number of prisoners. The Prussians are in hot pursuit, and have taken a great many prisoners.

"On the 19th we marched to Nivelles, 20th to a village near Binche, yesterday to Bavay, and to-day we are bivouacked here. Our baggage is a long way in the rear, and I do not know when I shall get a clean shirt, I have got my tooth-brush, so I am not quite a beast.

"I am sure you will be very sorry for poor Stables, he was killed on the 18th.

"In short, we have lost in the First Regiment twelve officers killed and twenty-two wounded. I was in great luck again, as I had two horses killed under me, and a ball through my cap, but the head remains as good as ever. I have been very much applauded, and so forth, and been reported for good conduct, and every one says that I am sure of a medal. I am so glad England had the first of it, I was always certain of the event, if he and the Duke ever met, and now we consider the whole thing as over."

On the 25th he wrote :—" I like your quizzing about our soldiers. . . . We have tolerable proof now of what they are worth, and the oldest French soldiers say they never saw such a battle as the one at Water-leud. I think I told you that our Reg^t and Napoleon's Guards came in contact, and I can assure you we handled them most handsomely."

And again, on the 29th:—"I suppose people in England are half mad, we hear of illuminations, etc. etc., to be sure the Victory is the greatest that ever was gained, not only by us, but by any people, but it was at the same time very dearly bought, the Gazette does not contain one-fifth of the officers who have suffered in this business. I send you that of our Reg^t, as you may hear them asked for.

"Killed—

"Lt.-Colonel Stables.	Captain Grose.	Ensign Pardoe.
„ F. D'Oyly.	„ Chambers	„ Lord Hay.
„ Thomas.	„ Cameron.	„ Barrington.
„ Miller.	„ Brown.	
„ Milnes.		

"Wounded—

"Colonel Askew.	Lt.-Colonel Townshend.	Captain Adair.	Ensign Batty.
„ Stuart.	„ Cooke.	„ Streatfield.	„ Barton.
	„ H. D'Oyly.	„ Clements.	„ Bruce.
	„ Bradford.	„ Bridgeman.	„ Fludyer.
	„ Hardinge.	„ Ellis.	„ Lascelles.
	„ Lord F. Somerset.	„ Simpson.	„ Mure.
		„ Luttrell.	„ Croft.
		„ Burgess.	

"We had 82 officers of the regiment in the field, of which 34 have been killed or wounded;[1] so shot, you will perceive, did not fly very thin that morning. I should have mentioned Stables in my first letter, but I did not know what had been his fate. I saw him fall, and the next morning when I wrote, I did not know what sort of a wound he had received, and I did not like sending a false report of his death, although, from the way he fell, I was much afraid of him."

In these letters Lord Saltoun mentions having had two horses killed under him; when each fell the saddle was, of course, ungirthed, and with the cloak rolled up across the pommel, was placed upon another horse. After the battle, when his bâtman unrolled the cloak, no less than seventeen musket-balls were found in it, many of which must have been fatal had they not been stopped by the cloak. It is said that the bâtman, who had previ-

[1] The above list is not quite correct, though very nearly so; the name of Lieutenant-colonel George Fead slightly wounded, being omitted, which makes thirty-six killed and wounded out of the eighty-two officers in the field. Lord Saltoun, in the hurry of writing, says thirty-four, though he names thirty-five in his list.

ously been a very foul-tongued man, was so struck with this, that no oath or bad language was ever heard to proceed from his mouth again.

In his letter of the 25th, begun at Camp near Serain, Lord Saltoun says, "Yesterday we marched from Gourmignies to a place called Boussiers short of Cateau, to-day we marched through Cateau" (Le Cateau Cambresis) "to this place. The weather is most horrible, and resembles more a winter than a summer campaign; for it has rained almost every day since the action, and the roads—for as yet we have been marching by the crossroads, and not the chaussées, to avoid the strong places—are up to the men's knees in mud. The old King came up to us yesterday, and to-day remains at Cateau. I am sorry to say poor Hughes" (his servant) "is in a bad way. I have been obliged to leave him in the village where we halted last night, for from violent rheumatics he was unable to sit on his horse; and the number of our wounded is so great, added to the confusion that took place in the rear, owing to the false alarm the day of the Battle, that our carts for carrying sick men have never come up, so I do not know whether I shall ever see him again, indeed I much fear I shall not; this, added to the very disagreeable task, which I have just got through, of writing to the families of all our poor officers who fell an account of their death, which as Commanding Officer I am obliged to do, the loss in action having given me the temporary command of the second Battalion, has made me very melancholy."

Lord Saltoun appears, however, to have been superseded in his command of the battalion by some senior officer, for in the next service performed by the First Regiment of Guards, for the description of which a reference must again be made to Sir F. W. Hamilton's pages, he is found once more in command of the light companies of the brigade. This service was the capture of the maiden fortress of Peronne.

[1] "On the morning of the 26th of June, as Sir John Byng" (who was now temporarily commanding the first *corps d'armée*, consisting of the first and third infantry divisions) "was passing the village of Vermand, where the main body of the Duke's army lay, he learnt that the Duke himself was there, and waited on him. The Duke at once exclaimed, 'You are the very person

[1] History of the Grenadier Guards, vol. iii. p. 55.

I wish to see; I want you to take Peronne; you may as well take with you the Brigade of Guards and a Dutch-Belgian brigade. I shall be there almost as soon as yourself.' Peronne was distant about eleven miles from the Guards' then position. Byng having given the necessary instructions to Maitland's Brigade of First Guards and to a Dutch-Belgian brigade, the former marched off at once, and reached Peronne at the same time as the Duke, who immediately summoned the garrison, and proceeded to reconnoitre the fortress in person. Perceiving that it might be taken by storm, he gave orders to prepare for an assault, and directed the attack to be made upon a hornwork which covers the suburbs on the left bank of the Somme. To the Third Battalion First Guards, preceded by the light companies of the First Brigade under Lord Saltoun, was given the task of assaulting the place, while the Second Battalion carried the fascines for their comrades. As the Guards advanced they separated into two columns of attack, the left one destined to scale the left face of the right demi-bastion; the right one to force an entrance by the ravelin and through the gate, which was blown open by the Engineers who assisted in the operation. Saltoun immediately rushed to the assault with his light companies, which experienced some slight loss as they crossed the ditch, while Saltoun himself was struck by a grape-shot as he was mounting the scaling-ladder, but fortunately the shot striking a purse full of coins, in his pocket, lessened the blow, so that it inflicted but slight injury, and he refused to report himself wounded. The hornwork was carried with little loss, and a Dutch brigade of four 9-pounders being brought up and established to the east of the town, to take in reverse the face to be attacked, a few shots were exchanged; while a brigade of four field-pieces was placed so as to command the front of the hornwork itself. After a short interval General Byng sent forward Lieutenant-Colonel Stanhope, his acting Quartermaster General, with a flag of truce, upon which the garrison capitulated, and the maiden fortress surrendered to the Guards, on condition of the men being allowed to go to their homes. As General Byng was returning to Vermand to report to the Duke the capture of the fortress, he met about halfway the Dutch-Belgian brigade, which had been ordered at the same time as the Guards to proceed to the front."

In writing to his wife of this affair, on the 27th, in continuation of his letter begun on the 25th, Lord Saltoun said :—" I am now, my dear love, quite out of the blue devils; for yesterday, on the march from Serain to Caulaincourt, we were halted at Vermand, and our brigade sent to the right to attack Peronne, which we stormed yesterday evening with very little loss. I have heard an old saying that everything is made for some purpose; but I do not suspect you had the least idea, when you made my little purse, that it would ever be put to the use that it was. Yesterday, during the storm of Peronne, a grape-shot hit me full in the thigh. Fortunately, I had the little purse in that pocket, full of small gold pieces called ducats, which so stopped the ball, that, although it knocked me down, it lodged in the purse, and has given me a slight bruise, not half so bad as a blow from a stick. Had it not been for the purse it would have been very near a finish. So you see, my dear Kate, I owe you something. The purse is cut right open by the ball, but I shall not have it mended until it comes into your hands. What is rather odd, the little heart I had in it is the only thing not hurt, for all the gold pieces are bent and twisted about properly. I write this, first, because I promised to write exactly what happened; and next, because they are so fond of killing people in reports, especially if they have been hit in the slightest manner possible."[1]

In reply to this letter, Lady Saltoun wrote on the 3d of July :—

"I this morning received your dear letter of the 25th and 27th. I am most thankful your life has been spared, but the many narrow escapes quite horrify me. I had hoped, from your letter of the 22d, all the fighting was

[1] Although he had many narrow escapes, this was the only occasion upon which Lord Saltoun was hit during his long service. He made light of the matter to his wife, describing the bruise as slight, and, doubtless to remove all apprehension, said that he told her exactly what happened; but the blow was, in reality, much more severe. The purse and its contents were driven into the groin, from which the surgeon, having cut the pocket away from the trousers, and gathering its edges together, pulled out the whole mass, when a pledget and some plaister put all to rights. The purse, the gold coins, and heart were long preserved by Lady Saltoun, and after her death by himself. At his decease they were given to Mrs. Brown, wife of General Samuel Brown, and Lady Saltoun's sister, who had expressed a wish to have them. They were kept by her, together with Lord Saltoun's letter of the 27th June, and Lady Saltoun's reply of the 3d July, relating to the affair, from which the above extracts have been made. When Mrs. Brown died, the purse and the letters were missed, probably stolen by some unprincipled person for the sake of the gold. The letters were picked up on the high road, near Ipswich, during the time of some races near that town, and were forwarded to the writer of this narrative by the finder; but the purse and gold pieces have never been recovered.

over, not that I shall, or can, feel really happy till you are returned safe; this last escape is quite frightful to think of, and most miraculous that your valuable life should hang on such a trifling thing as that little purse; lucky indeed it was you had it in your pocket. I shall value it ever more; pray don't part with any of the gold coins that were in it if you can help it, they will be invaluable to me. I want words to express all I feel at your repeated kindness and attention in writing so often, and such long letters too, when you must have a thousand other things to do and to think of; they do afford me great comfort, and as much consolation as I can receive in your absence. I immediately communicate to your mother and sisters the heads of your letters, so that they are never kept in suspense about you. . . . I am very sorry for poor Hughes, I read that part of the letter to your mother and sisters, so that they will use their discretion in telling his wife; she seems to love him so sincerely, that I pity her from the bottom of my heart. I trust you do not give up all hopes of his coming home safe at last, poor man! The chance is but small, I fear. I heard you were promoted, but have yet to learn what it is. . . . I heard of your word of command being given through the whole line, to follow your example, and that it was the Duke who ordered them to follow the example of the Guards. I hope and trust he knew it was you who commanded them at the moment, for I long for you to have all the honours due to you; I am sure they would be pretty numerous. . . . You seem to have but a scanty quantity of comforts just now with these quick movements, but you always make the best of everything."

In another letter, in answer to one from his wife, he writes on the 15th July, upon the same subject of his having been hit at Peronne:—

"As to being returned wounded at Peronne, it is all fiddlesticks. I do not intend that my military reputation, if ever I get any, shall have so hollow a foundation."

He continues in the letter of the 27th June:—

"The headquarters are to-day at Nesle, where a deputation has arrived from Paris to wait upon the Duke. I hope he will receive no terms till he dictates them from the Tuilleries, and I rather think he will be of my way of thinking in that particular."

On the 29th he writes from the camp at Choisi :—

"The Prussians had an affair two days ago with Soult at Compeigne, in which Soult was beat, and suffered considerably; they say to-day that Boneparte has left Paris and gone to Havre, with an intention of embarking for America, it is the best thing he can do now, for if he is taken, I do not know what the Allies will do with him, but I should think they would hang him.

"We have to-day fallen into the line of a column of Prussians, who have been plundering at such a rate that all the villages are entirely deserted, and I may almost say destroyed. To be sure they are only paying off old scores, but it is rather a bore for us, as we have great difficulty in purchasing any articles of provision, for the people are afraid of returning to their houses, as they do not know that they will be protected by us."

On the 2d July, from Le Bourjet :—

"I wrote you last on the 29th, on the 30th we marched to La Chapelle, about two miles beyond Senlis; and yesterday we came to this place, which is about two miles beyond Gonesse, on the left of St. Denis, and nearly parallel with it; and we have taken our position on this ground, our right resting on the Seine, opposed to St. Denis, where the French are strong, our centre in this town, which is immediately opposite to Mont Martre, and our left resting on the canal de l'Ourcq, to the left of the road that runs through this place to Paris, which is about four miles distant; and I rather think we shall remain in this position till the Russians and Austrians come up. The Prussian army, on our arrival yesterday, made a movement to the right, crossed the Seine at the bridge of St. Germain, and are to take post on that side of Paris, at Malmaison, St. Cloud, and Versailles. . . .

"We were yesterday on the advance posts with the Prussians, supporting them, until Lord Hill's corps came up, when we took our front of the line, and they told us they took the whole of Vandame's baggage, as well as Napoleon's. One of their officers of light cavalry fell in with his jewels, and had his pocket full of diamonds. I wish I had had the same luck, I would have put them to good account, besides the *éclat* of the thing. If I fall in with him again, I will try and buy some of them, but yesterday I was not very full of cash, as the baggage had not come up; he wanted to buy a horse, but mine had such a devil of a sore back that it would not go down, even with a Prussian. They have the greatest confidence in us. They say that the French used to tell them that we were good for nothing on land, of which, however, they had doubts; but they say they had not the least idea our troops were so good as they are. All their troops formed and cheered us as we passed them, which we answered; and as the French posts were quite within hearing, the effect on them could not have been very animating."

"Bourjet, 4th July 1815.

"I am at this moment on the advance posts, and we have just heard that we are to occupy Paris to-morrow, and the French army is to retire behind the Loire, and make as good terms with the King as they can. Our army is to encamp in the Bois de Boulogne."

"Villette, 6th July 1815.

"I this morning received yours of the 29th, and I did not intend to have written before to-morrow, as I was in hopes that we should have marched through Paris with laurels in our caps, as we deserve to do, but the Heads think otherwise, and we are therefore to go to-morrow to the Bois de Boulogne to encamp. . . . It does not suit my taste sneaking round a Capital in this manner. I almost regret that they did not defend the heights of Mont Martre: to be sure we should have lost 2 or 3 thousand men in taking them, but then we should have burned the town, and that would have been some satisfaction, for I hate these rascals almost as much as I love you, and that is more than they can be hated by any other. Poor Grose and myself were brothers in that hatred, and if the brave fellow were alive, he would have gone half mad to suppose that we came victorious to the gates of Paris, and did not show the natives that we were so. So much for national indignation! Our chief has probably good reasons; for my part I would not give a straw to march through it when the Russians come up. As to your getting what you call a detailed account of the action of Waterloo from the Duke, you will get no other than the one you have got already. It is rather unfortunate, and the army are sorry for it, that my name was not mentioned, and but for a mistake, which I will explain when we meet, I know that it would have been; but I have been so handsomely reported by the Prince of Orange, Generals Byng and Maitland, to the Dukes of Wellington and York, that I am perfectly satisfied, and some day I shall lead a division, perhaps a victorious army; so your moralising preamble must be postponed *sine die*, as it is the only point I think you will never gain with me. To tell the truth, I do not think you remember we always agreed that a dead lion was better than a living dog.[1]

"We came here yesterday. This is, if I may use the term, part of Paris, as much so as Connaught Place is of London, for it is the same distance from the Barriere as that is from Tyburn. Lord Castlereagh has arrived: I saw him as he passed by here, but I understand he has not gone into the town, but has gone to the Duke's headquarters. Party is running very high in the town, but I think we shall have no more fighting.

"I have no doubt myself that Napoleon is with the army, *incog.*, but his chance gets more and more desperate as the allies come up, and he will probably start for America, for the army will never give him up to us; at least if they do, they will lose with me that little respect I still have for them. Your story of ears and noses is quite morning post. They had something else to do about that time, but the Prussians treat them much as if their noses and ears had been cut off, and I suspect that the Russians are not far off, for the people have come in to-day from the country, saying that the pillage is still going on: they are perfectly thunderstruck at our men not doing the same, as their own troops plunder them, and how we prevent our men from doing it perfectly astonishes them."

"Paris, 10th July 1815.

"Here we are well established, and the old King as regularly crammed down their throats as anything could possibly be. He made his *entrée* yesterday at the head of the National Guards, and all the Eagles are upset, and the Fleur de Lys everywhere; not but what there is a very strong party against him, but I do not think they lean towards Boney, they are rather for a Republick.

"I was at the Opera last night, and the people had Vive Henri Quatre

---

[1] Evidently in reply to a suggestion that he should leave the service.

played over and over again, and a great deal of hollaing, and so forth; but I am told they did just the same when Napoleon came: if so, it all goes for nothing. They say that the army have sent deputies to make submission: if so, the game is over, for this time at least. . . . At present we are encamped in Bois de Boulogne, and I suppose we shall remain there. I am in a house half way between the Bois and the Barriere de Roule: the distance is not above two miles, so it is nothing on horseback; not that there is much to see here since I saw it last, but one rides in to dinner, as the *traiteurs* here are rather superior to our soldier cooks. . . . The people here, I mean the gentlemen, are inclined to be particularly civil to us; indeed, they are much struck with the strict discipline we preserve, so totally different from continental armies now-a-days, and which gives us such a decided advantage over them; and lucky for them it is so, for if our army were permitted to plunder and destroy as the Prussians and others are, they would first of all get drunk, and then they would burn down the town, or commit some horrible massacre or other. . . .

"I have as yet heard nothing of poor Hughes. I mean to send a man back to the village to inquire about him, for it is rather out of the direct road. He was perfectly well in health when he was left, and therefore I am not afraid of him,—at least the surgeon is not,—yet I think he ought to have turned up before now."

"Paris, 12 July 1815.

"I forget if I told you in my last that the Kings and Emperors were arrived. They are however come, and, what is worse, we have to mount guard over them, which, in our present reduced state of Lt.-colonels, comes rather sharp; and what I am most afraid of is, that when our draft comes, they may, in consequence, take it into their gracious heads to refuse me leave, which will be rather a bore, as it will fix me here till the end of the chapter. Now, if that event takes place, and they refuse me leave, you shall, if you like, come here, for, as Mahomet observed (and he is very good authority), if the mountain would not come to him he must go to the mountain. My only reason, next to seeing you, for wanting to go home, is that I wish to go to Scotland: now, if I can't go there, I see no reason why you should not see France. . . . I think all the fighting over, but if anything else should blow up before these grand continental matters are settled, you can only return. I do not think these things will be settled under three or four months, and if you were here, I don't care if they take as many years to debate it, for the country is a very good one to live in. . . . No one knows anything certain about Napoleon, and nobody seems to care anything about him. Paris is just the same as when I was here last, and the rascals are calling Vive le Roi now, as lustily as they last week cried Vive l'Empereur. . . . Hughes came up yesterday, his rheumatism has left him, but he is very thin, as he got very little to eat on the road."

"Paris, 15th July 1815.

"You may see by the paper I am not at home. The fact is, I am on guard over H.M. the Emperor of all the Russias, and as he gives nothing but long paper, I am obliged to manœuvre it as well as I possibly can. We have just done dinner, six o'clock, about an hour before you are thinking about dressing for yours; it is very well this hour for His Majesty's household, who can go out and walk in the cool of the evening, but for us, who have to remain here, rather too early. However, I will do him the justice to say that the dinner was a very good one, and by a fortunate accident we had a clean table-cloth, for the waiter, a regular ruffian of a fellow, had put such a beastly thing on the table that it was even too much for us, who of late days have not been much used to luxury. However, I had the satisfaction to make the most unfortunate mistake in the world, just as he put some wine down, by breaking a bottle of it, which so sluiced the table-cloth that we were perforce obliged to have another, which was clean. Some of the Emperor's household dined with us, and they were tolerably genteel fellows, and spoke very good French, and some little English, indeed most of the Russians are good linguists. . . . About Gazettes, as if 500 others were not exactly in the same situation as I am, and as if I do not know that it has been the only outcry against the Duke of W. ever since he commanded an army, that he seldom or never mentioned people, excepting Generals and others high up in the army. . . . I rather suspect you will have to come here, for General Vivian has gone to England for the same purpose, to bring his wife, and if any person could have got leave, I think he might. Besides, if they only give a month, it will not be worth while, so you may, if you feel inclined, make up your mind to soldier a little. . . . No news of any kind, and nothing as yet known of what the remains of Boney's army mean to do. They have not as yet made submission, nor will they, I suspect, as long as they can get any thing to plunder where they are. I hope the king will cut off a good many heads, but I am told he will not, and the consequence will be that he will be deposed in less than two years, and France a Republick."

"Paris, 22nd July 1815.

". . . To-day we had a review of a division of the Prussian Guards, 13,000 strong; the finest body of men I ever saw in my life, the only horrid thing is the French have licked them like sacks. On Monday next, at 10 o'clock, the Duke of Wellington's army is to be reviewed. We shall be about 65,000, and it will take up nearly the whole day marching past. We shall not be able to show such fine men as these Emperors and Kings have, but yesterday, as the Prussians etc. were marching by, Lord Wellington said to Lady Kinnaird, 'On Monday I will show you some men that will lick those fellows.'

"The remains of the French army, under Davoust, have not as yet made submission, they say they will acknowledge the king if he will retain them as an army; but the king says they shall be disbanded, and they are at issue on that point. I think probably the end of it will be that we shall send some troops against them, and give them a good licking: that army will never have the king. It is a curious fact, that during his short reign before Boney came back, the soldiers, in telling off from the right, never mentioned the number eighteen, but said, 'dixsept, gros cochon, dixneuf,' and so on; and whatever man it fell to to be 18, he was the butt for the day; that shows how little they cared for him, and he now ought to hang every twentieth man by lot, and then, such slaves are these rascals, that he would be very much respected, and thought a very good king."

"Paris, 28th July 1815.

". . . I have put off writing from day to day, in hopes of being able to say something about leave. Yesterday I was ordered to send in my reasons in writing, so I went this morning to Barnes, the Adjutant-general, and told him that my reason was not one that could well be sent upon paper, but I would be much obliged to him to tell the Duke that I had been married a fortnight, and I wished to go home to bring you out here. I am to have my final answer to-morrow, and I shall then either write you how to proceed, or shall forthwith proceed to England, as the case may be.

"We expect that the army will shortly move into Normandy, as we begin to be short of forage for the cavalry, but they say the first division is to remain in Paris, or near it; however, if I get my leave, that will make no difference to us. Hughes, I told you in one of my letters, has turned up, and he is now quite well again, and the horses consequently begin to show the improvement."

Here the letters end, for Lord Saltoun immediately afterwards obtained the leave he requested upon so reasonable a plea, and proceeded to England, from which country he soon returned, accompanied by his wife, and, excepting temporary leave of absence in each year, served in France with the army of occupation until November 1818, being quartered with his battalion at Cambray from 16th February 1816 to that period, during which time his mother, the Dowager Lady Saltoun, with his sisters Eleanor and Margaret, joined him, and resided for some time with him, and he also received flying visits from his brother William, who was a partner in a West Indian mercantile house in the city of London.

An anecdote, related to the writer by Lord Saltoun, of a circumstance which occurred during this period, although not part of his own history, is yet worth insertion, as affording a characteristic trait of "the Duke," as all his old soldiers loved to style His Grace of Wellington, *par excellence.*

"There was a good deal of heartburning and jealousy amongst the disbanded officers of the old French army, and many of them sought to revenge their ill success in the war by insulting British officers, and forcing them to fight duels, in which, from the more practical swordsmanship of the Frenchmen, they were often severely wounded, and in one or two instances killed outright. A very stringent order was therefore issued from headquarters against duels and brawls of all sorts, and a court-martial was threatened against any officer inculpated in an affair of the kind. It so happened that a young officer was one night returning home to his quarters, when he was attacked by two men armed with swords. Being in uniform, and having his sword by his side, he defended himself with such success, that he speedily killed one of his assailants, and severely wounded the other. The noise of the combat brought up the watch, when it was found that they were two disbanded French officers; the affair became public, he was put under arrest, and the whole matter reported to headquarters. The poor young fellow was very anxious about the result; if he had been brought to a court-martial, it would have been difficult for him to prove that he acted only in self defence, for the wounded man refused to give any evidence; and as I knew the officer who was Adjutant-general to our portion of the forces very well, I tried to learn the decision of the Duke in the matter as soon as possible, in order to ease his mind. At length it arrived; the Duke, taking the common-sense view that one man would not be the assailant of two, and rightly interpreting the refusal of the wounded man to give evidence, ordered the young officer's release from arrest, and said, 'I only wish that every officer in the army would constantly wear his sword when in uniform' (which too many neglected to do), 'and upon just occasion use it as boldly and skilfully as this young gentleman appears to have done.'"

Upon the return of the battalion to England in 1818, Lord Saltoun was enabled to enjoy for a more lengthened period the blessings of peace and tranquillity; which for many years had fallen to the lot of himself and his brave fellow-soldiers only at rare and long distant intervals; and to occupy and adorn the position in which Providence had placed him; and in which the frankness of his manner, and the integrity of his conduct, together with his unfailing generosity and goodness of heart, gained the love and respect of all who knew him.

As his military duties required much of his time to be passed in London, he fixed his residence there, at No. 1 Great Cumberland Street, which house he retained until his death; but the periods of leave of absence were generally spent in Scotland, where he rented for many years the extensive grouse moors of Coignafearn, in the heart of the Monadhliadh Mountains, in Inverness-shire. His house of Philorth also welcomed many a joyous assemblage of his friends, and his ancestral lands were the scene of many a cheerful shooting party. Salmon-fishing and fox-hunting were also among his recreations; bringing to the pursuit of every sport the same energy that he had evinced in the more serious game of war, he excelled in each and all, and amply justified the predictions of the old gamekeeper at Kinrara, mentioned in his brother Simon's letter to their mother, years before.

Nor was he neglectful of more intellectual pursuits. Fond of reading, well informed, and well versed in the literature of the day, he was an accomplished and agreeable member of society; but, above all, his chief delight was in music. He was a constant patron of the Opera, and a member of the Madrigal Society, the Catch Club, and other festive and musical reunions; and he also belonged to the once famous, but now extinct, Beefsteak Club.[1]

While in Spain he had learned to play on the guitar, and at his house in Great Cumberland Street many of the best public performers, both vocal and instrumental, frequently attended, and assisted in the afternoon concerts which he gave, in which he always took a part with his guitar, though its notes were often altogether lost amid those of the more powerful instruments.

But music with him was a passion, and on one of these occasions a lady, somewhat maliciously, saying to him, "Lord Saltoun, I can't hear your guitar at all," he replied, "Oh! that doesn't matter; I hear it myself, and that's enough for my pleasure."

He was also a member of the Scottish Hospital of London, the Highland and Agricultural Society, and the Caledonian Asylum; and his hand was always open to assist any really charitable institution.

The above general description applies to his whole life, after the termination of the great war, for except when broken into, as hereafter related, by the calls of duty, which he never neglected, such was the tenour of an existence, always energetic and active, whether in the more serious work of life, or in recreation and amusement.

Shortly after the return of the Grenadier Guards from France, an amusing incident occurred, which is worth recording as an illustration of the eccentricities of soldiers, and which is here given as related by Lord Saltoun.

---

[1] On the dissolution of the Beefsteak Club in 1869, the writer of these memoirs purchased the chair used by Lord Saltoun at the meetings of that celebrated community, and it is now at Philorth. It is a plain oak chair bearing his crest, coronet, and cypher, S, with the famous gridiron of the club, and around them the motto, "Beef and Liberty."

"There used to be a sentry placed at Storey's Gate, between Birdcage Walk and Great George Street, Westminster.

"About noon, on a hot summer's day, the sentry then on that post saw a round-about, ruddy little man carefully examining his sentry-box, and, though it was against orders, entered into conversation with him, which turned on the merits of the said article.

"'Lord bless me!' said the little man, 'I never saw anything so nice and convenient. When I'm at home I lives out to the east, and has a little garden right down to the river, and I'm blowed if I don't have one like it made, and put a seat in it, and then when work's done, I can sit of evenings and smoke my pipe in it, and look at the ships going by.' 'Why,' said the sentry, 'why should you go to the expense of having a new one made, which will cost you a matter of three or four pounds, when you can have this one for a guinea.' 'How can I have this one?' exclaimed the little man. 'Why, what day is this?' 'It's his gracious Majesty's birthday, God bless him! to be sure, and that's the reason I'm out for a holiday.' 'Well, that's just it' (taking a confidential tone). 'We soldiers is treated very hard, you see; but we has our privileges, and one is that we has new sentry-boxes every year, and they are changed every king's birthday, and the man that's on sentry in them at the end of that day has a right to sell the old one. Now, what o'clock is it?'

"'Close upon twelve o'clock,' says the little man. 'That's it! and I shall be on sentry here again to-night at twelve o'clock, so it's my right to sell the box; now it's your's for a guinea; say done!'

"'Done!' said the little fellow, and paid his guinea; 'but how am I to get it away?'

"'I'll tell you all that. You see, there's a rule that the old boxes stand till noon the next day, and that then they may be taken away; but if they are not taken away before twelve that night they go on for another year, and the Government is so shocking mean and stingy that they always runs the chance of our not selling them, and won't put another down till the first is gone; but I'm up to their tricks, and ain't going to be done by them. So you just be here any time after twelve to-morrow with a cart and ropes and carry it off. No one will stop you, and there'll be a new one put down directly.'

"So they parted good friends, on this understanding; and about one o'clock the next day the little man came with a horse and cart, and a friend or two to help him, and without ceremony began to lay violent hands upon the sentry-box, and to pull it down, in order to put it on the cart. A considerable row was the result of these high-handed proceedings, which ended in the dispersion of the little man's friends at the point of the bayonet, and his own capture by the sentry then on duty at the post, by whom he was penned up in his much-coveted sentry-box, while the guard was alarmed, and a party being sent from it, he was brought in a prisoner. I happened to be there at the time, and he came before me, and on being questioned unfolded his pitiful tale of how he had been duped and done by the unscrupulous sentry of the day before.

"None of those present could refrain from shouts of laughter as he went on; but I soon got the guard report, and seeing in it who was the sentry on that post at twelve o'clock, ordered him to be sent for from the barracks.

"In a short time he arrived, and was brought in to answer the charge. When the complainant had again told his story, 'Now,' I asked, 'what have you got to say in answer to this?' 'Well, my Lord,' he replied, 'I'm very sorry; but, first of all, I'm willing to give him back his guinea—there it is,' laying it on the table. 'Thank God I hadn't time to spend it! and, my Lord, you knows me; I haven't been a bad soldier; you've seen me in Spain and at Waterloo, and I hope you'll look over it; but— he was such a d—d fool I couldn't help it!'

"The last plea was acknowledged in all our hearts to be a valid one, and with a good wigging he got off; but I really believe he would have considered it a tempting of Providence had he failed to use the opportunity which meeting such an inconceivable idiot threw in his way."[1]

Lord Saltoun became a major in the Guards, and full colonel in the army, on the 17th of November 1825, and succeeded to the command of the third battalion of his regiment, which he held until the 12th of February, when,

---

[1] Some years ago the writer met the late General Sir James Simpson at a friend's house in Norfolk, and happening to tell the above story of the man selling his sentry-box, Sir James said that he recollected the circumstance well, as at that time he was adjutant, and was present, and that the name of the sentry was "Stephen Gagin."

in consequence of certain changes and promotions, he became senior major, and was transferred to the first battalion, which he continued to command while he remained in the regiment.

In February 1826, when marching into the barracks at Windsor, a very severe accident befell him. He was mounted upon a young and spirited horse, which, on passing through the gate, was so startled by the guard presenting arms, that it plunged violently, and slipping on the causeway, fell upon its side, crushing its rider's right leg between its body and the curbstone of the foot-pavement.

The fracture was very serious; the bones were broken in five places between the knee and the ankle, but they were set, and for eight weeks Lord Saltoun was confined to his room. At the expiry of this period he drove as far as the long walk in Windsor Park, and there tried how he could use the limb; after a while, however, feeling much pain, he returned home and sent for the best advice from London. On the arrival of the surgeons summoned, a consultation was held, at which it was decided to rebreak the leg, and set it anew, which was done, and he was condemned to a further imprisonment in his room of nine weeks' duration, when he was well enough to return to London, though for several weeks longer he was obliged to use crutches, and a slight shortening of the leg ensued, which however only caused him to limp a little when tired in walking, but was not otherwise perceptible.

It is only right to mention here with proper gratitude the kindness of His Majesty George IV. to Lord Saltoun upon this occasion.

Not content with frequently sending to inquire how he was going on, the King interested himself in his comfort, and presented him with a table and reading-desk of then novel construction, adapted for a sick-bed, which His Majesty had himself used when suffering from illness.

In July of the same year Lord Saltoun went to Scotland, but on the journey thither a severe domestic affliction overtook him.

Lady Saltoun was suddenly attacked by illness at Bramby Moor Inn, in Leicestershire, and after short but severe suffering, died there upon the 9th of that month, their married life having lasted little above eleven years. Her remains were conveyed to Edinburgh, and interred in Holyrood Chapel, from whence in the year 1853 they were removed, and laid beside those of her husband in the mausoleum at Fraserburgh.

Lord Saltoun had been elected one of the Representative Peers of Scotland in 1812, and was from time to time re-elected during the remainder of his life. He however did not take any prominent part in the debates of the House of Lords, but contented himself with giving a consistent support to the Tory, or, as it is now called, Conservative party, to which he belonged. On the 4th of February 1830 he seconded the address in reply to the speech from the throne at the opening of Parliament, and his speech on that occasion, as reported in the pages of Hansard, shows that he had brought his sound common sense and good judgment to the consideration of the questions in agitation at that time; but action was far more to his taste than speaking, and with the exception of a few words now and then upon any question which particularly interested him, he did not take much share in Parliamentary debates.

In 1831, shortly after the accession of William IV., the Whig party, which was then in office, brought in the Reform Bill, which passed through the House of Commons, but was thrown out in the House of Lords by a majority of forty-one, among whom was Lord Saltoun; and in the succeeding year, when it was again brought in, and passed the House of Lords by a majority of nine, he was one of the minority who voted against it, and was also one of the seventy-three Peers who subscribed the protest against the passing of the Bill, that was entered on the journals of the House by the Duke of Wellington.

He also voted against the Bill to abolish subscription to the Thirty-nine Articles as a preliminary to admission into the Universities; against that for the repeal of the Corn Laws in 1846, being one of the eighty-nine Peers who signed the protest against the third reading; and in 1848 against the repeal of the Jewish Disabilities; but this short notice is all that is necessary of his conduct as a member of the Legislature, and shows him to have adhered to the political views of his party.

The course of promotion in the army advanced him to the rank of major-general on the 10th January 1837, and this put an end to his connection with the gallant regiment in which he had seen so much service, and which he never ceased to regard with pride and affection.

A few years later he was once more summoned to active service. War with China had been going on for a year or two, and a considerable force had been sent from India under the command of Sir Hugh Gough, afterwards Viscount Gough. In 1841 it was determined that reinforcements, under a major-general, should proceed from England to join him. Lord Saltoun was selected for this duty, and the following letters passed between Lord Hill, then commanding-in-chief, and him :—

Horse Guards, 3d November 1841.

My dear Saltoun,—The Government having called upon me to nominate a major-general for service in China, to act of course under Lt.-General Sir Hugh Gough, who is in command of the expedition, I have considered that I could not do better than select you for that duty, and I shall be happy to nominate you for it, if it be agreeable to you, as soon as I receive your answer to this letter.

Believe me to be,
My dear Saltoun, very faithfully yours,
HILL.

Major-General The Lord Saltoun, G.C.H., etc. etc. etc.

Nesbit House, Dunse, 5th November 1841.

My dear Lord Hill,—I have just received your Lordship's letter.

I shall be happy to serve on any active service which your Lordship may nominate me for; but, if I might be permitted, I should like to make a stipulation on this occasion, which is that, the service being concluded, I am not to be considered as belonging to the army in India, but to be permitted to return home, as I have no wish to carry on the ordinary duties of colonial service.

I remain,
Dear Lord Hill, yours very sincerely,
SALTOUN.

General the Lord Hill, etc. etc. etc.

P.S.—I shall be in London on Monday or Tuesday, when I hope to see your Lordship, at your usual hour, at the Horse Guards.

Having accepted the duty for which he had thus been chosen, Lord Saltoun had but a short time in which to make preparation for a lengthened absence from home, as the reinforcements were ordered to sail with as little loss of time as possible; and one of the arrangements most important to his comfort was to secure the services of a faithful valet and a trustworthy groom.

The conduct at this time of the two servants who accompanied him in these situations deserves mention, as an evidence of their feeling towards their master.

The valet, Thomas Phillips, had been a private in the Grenadier Guards, and his valet for many years, having remained in that situation after obtaining his discharge from the army. A short time previously, however, he had married, and quitting service, had set up a small shop; but on hearing that his old master was again going on foreign service, he at once said, "It is impossible that my Lord can do without me," and offered to give up his business and return to his valet's situation, which offer was gladly accepted. The groom, a man of the name of Shean, had also been a Guardsman, and was still in the service of Lord Saltoun, who at first did not think of taking him abroad, imagining that he would not like to go; but on sending for him, and saying, "Well, Shean, you know I am going to China," the reply was, "Yes, my Lord, I hear we've got the route, so when are we to march?" Both these faithful servants returned home with Lord Saltoun, and remained in his service until his death.

The reinforcements under his command sailed from Plymouth on the 29th of December 1841, in H.M.S. Belle-isle, Captain Kingcombe, and the Sapphire and Apollo troop-ships; the headquarters' staff, the 98th regiment, commanded by the well-known Colin Campbell, afterwards so renowned as Lord Clyde, and some artillery, being on board the Belle-isle.

Lord Saltoun had selected Lieutenant-Colonel Hope Grant (the late General Sir Hope Grant, K.C.B.) for his brigade-major, and Captain Cunynghame (now Lieutenant-General Sir Arthur Cunynghame, K.C.B.) for his first aide-de-camp, the rules of the service requiring that his second aide-de-camp should be taken from some regiment serving in the country to which he was going.

[1] They had a favourable but somewhat tedious voyage, passing the island of Madeira on the 28th, and reaching Teneriffe on the 30th of December; after replenishing the supply of water, they sailed again for Rio Janeiro on the 1st of January 1842. They crossed the line on the 17th of that month, and had the usual visit from Neptune, productive, as is customary, of much fun and some roughish horse-play; and without further incident, except the loss of a man of the 98th regiment, who jumped overboard on the 19th, arrived at Rio Janeiro on the 3d of February, where they remained until the 8th, when they again sailed, and anchored in Simon's Bay, at the Cape of Good Hope, on the 14th of March.

During the passage from Rio to the Cape, Mr. Craven, an officer in the navy, son of Mr. Fuller Craven, was lost, having fallen overboard from the Apollo during his watch. He did not belong to that vessel, but was a passenger going out to join his ship in China, and, as is often the case, had taken part in carrying on the duty of the vessel in which he was for the time.

Lord Saltoun and his staff having bought three horses at the Cape, and passed a few days there, the ships sailed again on the 22d March, but in a gale on the 24th and 25th, the Belle-isle lost sight of both her consorts, and proceeded on her way to Singapore, which place she reached on the 13th of May, without having again seen them.

On the 17th, just as the Belle-isle was weighing anchor, the two missing ships came in sight, but leaving them to follow, she sailed for Hong-Kong, where she arrived on the 2d of June.

At Hong-Kong Lord Saltoun had an interview with Sir Henry Pottinger, of whom he appears to have formed a favourable opinion, and whom he characterises in a letter as "a quiet, sensible, strong-minded man, quite used to the business he has to transact."

In the same letter Lord Saltoun gives a very graphic sketch of the state of affairs at that time; he says, "It is impossible to say what effect this great display of force we are making may have when it comes to be known by the great Emperor, but as yet nothing whatever has been done in coming to a settlement, and in point of fact things are exactly in the same state they

---

[1] The account of his stay abroad is extracted from a journal kept by Lord Saltoun, and numerous letters from him to various friends and relatives.

were in when he (Sir H. Pottinger) came here. When we get up, which I suppose we shall do in ten days from this, Sir H. Gough will have an efficient force of from 8000 to 10,000 men, at least they say so here. Now whether he has the head to seize such a position, and maintain himself in it, as will really be felt by the said great man, remains to be proved. As yet anything that has been done has been a sort of marauding warfare, taking a town one day and giving it up the next, and so forth; but that is not the way to conquer a great and obstinate people. We must take and hold such a position as, by cutting their resources off, will be felt by those at the head of the Government. Such a position is to be found (I think) in the Yan-tze-Kan river, and we are certainly going there in the first instance."

While at Hong-Kong they heard the news of the conflict with the Manchu Tartars, after the capture of the town of Chapoo, and of Colonel Tomlinson and twenty men having been killed, and seventy wounded, before the enemy were defeated.

On the 7th June the Belle-isle left Hong-Kong (the Apollo and Sapphire, which had come in there two days after her, followed on the 8th) for Chusan, where she arrived on the 17th, and on reaching that place Lord Saltoun found a letter from Sir Hugh Gough, who was then in the Yang-tse-kiang river, telling him of his plans, and requesting him to join him there as soon as possible; and, accordingly, on the evening of the same day, the Belle-isle was again under weigh, attended by the Venus steamer, and on the morning of the 19th anchored at Amherst rocks, near the mouth of the Yang-tse-kiang, which she entered on the 21st, and Lord Saltoun, with the first instalment of the troops he had brought from England, joined the army, just six months and one day after sailing from Plymouth.

Two days before his arrival the small town of Woosung, and that of Shanghai, further up the river, had been taken, and he gives in a letter an amusing account of some of these operations, and also his idea of what it would be requisite to do. He says, "After taking this place, Woosung, the ships went up the river to Shanghai, with half the troops, the other half, with four guns, marched, and a very severe march it was. They (the Chinese) had a battery of fifty guns about four miles below the town, which they fired as the ships passed, and immediately ran away. The marching column found no resistance, but when our force was about four miles from the town it was abandoned by the authorities and better classes, and forthwith pillaged by the lower orders, and pretty regularly sacked before the troops reached it. This seems to be the regular practice, and these wags always begin by plundering the pawnbrokers' shops, on the principle, I suppose, of getting their own things back first of all. . . . This sort of passive resistance is the most extraordinary way of making war that ever was, and no one can guess when it will end. Since Sir H. Pottinger came out last year we have taken Amoy, Chusan, Chinghai, the town of Ningpo, where they wintered, and were abundantly supplied with everything. This summer we have taken Chapoo, and where we are now, and yet no sort of communication has taken place between him and any Chinese person in authority. The only thing is that, after we have taken any of these places, an order comes out in the Pekin Gazette, ordering the general and his army to drive the red-headed barbarians into the sea, which they obey by giving up the next place attacked, without hardly firing a shot for it. . . . We have still about 2500 men to come up, and I conclude we shall stay here till they join us. In the meantime the surveyors are examining the river Yan-tze-Kan, which, in my opinion, we must go up, and establish ourselves in some position, which will bring those matters to a climax, or at all events give us entire military possession of all the south and richest part of China, and having by so doing cut off their means of sending their effects to the north, we can levy contributions at our leisure."

The plan thus roughly sketched was that decided upon, and when all the troops had arrived, the force was divided into three brigades, of which the right brigade, numbering about 2200 men, and comprising the 26th and 98th British Regiments, the Bengal Volunteers, and the flank companies of the 41st Madras Native Infantry, was placed under Lord Saltoun's immediate command.

The expedition then proceeded up the river Yang-tse-kiang in five divisions, and in the following order of sailing:—

1st. Sir Henry Pottinger and Sir Hugh Gough, with the Headquarters, Engineers, and Sappers, under charge of the Admiral Sir Wm. Parker's flagship, the Cornwallis.

2d. Lord Saltoun's brigade, in eleven vessels, under charge of H.M.S. Belle-isle.

3d. General Schoedde's Brigade, under charge of H.M.S. Blonde.

4th. General Bartley's Brigade, under charge of H.M.S. Endymion.

5th. The Artillery, with the powder ships, under the command of Lieutenant-Colonel Montgomery, Madras Artillery, together with the stores, etc., of which division H.M.S. Dido had the charge.

They sailed on the 6th July, with the intention of reaching the point where the Yang-tse-kiang is cut by the great canal, and on the 19th and 20th arrived before the town of Chin-kiang-foo, situated at that spot, which they found strongly fortified and full of Chinese and Tartar troops, of which latter there was also a large camp, at a short distance from the town.

Orders were issued for the army to land on the following morning, the 21st, at four o'clock, and Lord Saltoun received instructions from Sir Hugh Gough to attack the Tartar camp with his brigade, while the remainder of the forces were to assault the town.

After a toilsome march of some miles, over a difficult and marshy country, Lord Saltoun found the enemy posted in a very strong position on a rising ground, with a marshy bottom in front, their right covered by some houses, and their left occupying, in considerable numbers, a high hill, which inclined round, so as to completely outflank the right of any force attacking the centre.

On the British troops arriving within 700 yards, the Tartars opened a heavy fire from their jingalls, firing in salvos, and shouting and roaring after each discharge; but their fire did no execution, and Lord Saltoun, detaching two companies of the Bengal Volunteers against their right flank, and two other companies of the same corps against their left flank on the hill, advanced with the 98th regiment, two companies of the Madras Native Infantry, and three three-pounder guns, until about 300 yards from the main body, when he sent the light company of the 98th, supported by the remainder of that regiment, and the two companies of the 41st Madras Native Infantry, against the centre, covering their advance by the fire of the guns.

The battle was neither long nor severely contested, and to the old soldier of the Peninsula and Waterloo, must have offered a great contrast to former stern encounters. In a letter he says, "They stood a few shots from the flank parties, but before the guns had fired six rounds, and long before we got within reach of them, they broke and dispersed in the greatest confusion, and scampered away over the hills in their rear, and we saw no more of them, having only three men of the Bengal Volunteers wounded; but the sun was the worst enemy, for thirteen men out of the 98th died on the ground, from the heat."

While the brigade under Lord Saltoun's command had been achieving this decisive, though easy, victory, the remainder of the army had attacked and taken the town of Chin-kiang-foo, though not without some loss, several officers, and about 150 men having been killed or wounded. The whole of the operations were, however, successful, and Chin-kiang-foo, said to be one of the strongest places in China, was in the hands of the British.

The troops re-embarked on the 29th of July, leaving General Schoedde's brigade to hold possession of Chin-kiang-foo, and on the 3d August the expedition sailed for Nankin, where it arrived on the 5th and two following days, and the forces were landed for the purpose of investing that city; but negotiations having been opened between Sir Henry Pottinger and the Chinese commissioner, Elipoo, a suspension of hostilities was agreed to, and, after some delays, peace was finally concluded, and a treaty signed on board the admiral's ship, upon the 29th of the same month.

The object for which the expedition had been undertaken was thus happily accomplished, and its retirement from the Yang-tse-kiang river commenced in the early part of September, not one instant too soon, for disease of the most fatal description had broken out among the troops, and especially in the 98th regiment, which was almost entirely destroyed by its ravages.

Upon the retirement of the expedition from the river, Sir Hugh Gough, according to his instructions, prepared to return to India with part of the forces, leaving Lord Saltoun in command of the army of occupation, which was to hold certain posts, until the stipulations of the treaty were fulfilled; and the island of Hong-Kong being the appointed headquarters of that army, he arrived there on the 29th of October, and assumed the command on the departure of Sir Hugh Gough, upon the 20th December.

A good description of the state of military affairs on the island is given in a report from Lord Saltoun to the Duke of Wellington, which was written in January of the succeeding year, 1843.[1]

"I conclude that your Grace has received a report from Lt.-general Sir Hugh Gough on his leaving this place to return to India.

"On the 20th of last month Sir Hugh Gough sailed from this place, leaving me in command of the troops left for the occupation of certain parts of this country; but as Sir Hugh Gough left me no sort of instructions as to what authority I was to report to, I having been sent from England to this country, have the honour of reporting direct to your Grace, sending a copy of the same to H.E. the Commander-in-chief of India.

"In the margin I send your Grace the strength and distribution of the troops left for this service, and although the force is not large, I believe it to be sufficient for the purposes intended.

"This island, Hong-Kong, is composed of a succession of high steep mountains, having narrow spurs running out towards the sea-side, and small vallies between them; and there is no place whatever on this, the town side of the island at least (and I believe the whole island to be of the same character), that is at all favourable for a fortified place, all these spurs being commanded by the high hill behind them, and more or less by each other.

"One place exists where a very fair *place d'armes* might be made, and it would also have been a very favourable situation for barracks, hospital, etc., but unfortunately, from the manner in which land was originally granted here, it has become the property of individuals, who are building their houses upon it.

"There are other points where a *place d'armes* might be constructed, but in my humble opinion the expense of doing so would be greater than any advantage gained from it would warrant.

"The principal inconvenience that we suffer from at present is want of cover of any kind for the troops, and also for the immense quantity of commissariat stores which have been landed here, and which are placed in mat buildings, and, consequently, very much exposed to danger arising from fire.

"I have proposed to H.E. the Plenipotentiary, who in his capacity of Chief Commissioner of trade is Governor here, to hire godowns for these

[1] From copy retained by Lord Saltoun.

commissariat stores, until buildings can be erected for them, and I have sent in plans and estimates of the said buildings.

"We have a temporary barrack here, called Cantonment Hill, originally constructed partly for European and partly for Native troops; in this I have placed the Royal Artillery, the Gun Lascars, the Sappers and Miners, and the hospital for the troops.

"We have barracks for Native troops, in which, by adding some buildings, I can put up the wing of the 41st Madras Native Infantry.

"At West Point, a place about a mile from the end of the town, there is a temporary barrack for about 250 men, with an hospital; part of H.M. 55th Regiment occupy this, the rest of them are on the other side of the island, at a place called Chuck Choo, and some recruits that have just arrived for this regiment remain on board.

"The place built for the General Hospital, capable of holding twenty men, is at present occupied by the sick of the 98th, and the rest of that regiment remains on board the Belle-isle, but as another barrack at Chuck Choo will shortly be completed, it will then be able to hold 300 men, and it is my intention to land the 98th Regiment and put them into these quarters, principally on account of the sickly state in which they have been on board; and the 55th, whom they will relieve at Chuck Choo, must go on board when they return here.

"Under these circumstances I have sent in to H.E. the Plenipotentiary plans and estimates for two permanent barracks, one to be built here for 400 men, and the other at Chuck Choo, which is stated to be the most healthy part of the island, for 600 men; these barracks to be built on a plan, that they may be added to when the temporary barracks decay, in the event of its being advisable to keep here a larger force than 1000 infantry.

"The magazine is now finished, and the powder placed in it; a large quantity of powder must, however, still remain on board, as the magazine is a very small one.

"I am happy to be able to report to your Grace that since the wet weather set in, the health of the troops has very much improved, and I trust in future they will not be more sickly than is usual in tropical climates; and also, that I have every reason to be satisfied with the good and orderly conduct of the men and officers of this Garrison.

"I have received a report from Major-General Schoedde, commanding at Chusan, equally satisfactory on the score of the health of the troops, and stating that in a very few days all the barracks at that place will be completed.

"I have received a report from Major Cooper, 12th Regiment, commanding at . . . in which he states that the fever and ague still continue amongst the troops, but that it is of a milder character."

The above report gives some idea of the deficiency in provision for the accommodation of the army of occupation at Hong-Kong, and the following memorandum, addressed by Lord Saltoun at a prior date to Sir Henry Pottinger, the Plenipotentiary, respecting the arrangements necessary at Chusan, only a portion of what was to be his command, will further illustrate the multiplicity of subjects that claimed his attention and occupied his time.

[1] "Memoranda for his Excellency Sir H. Pottinger regarding the force to be left at Chusan.

"1*st*. Provisions for the troops.

"1. How are they to be supplied?

"2. In the event of a short supply, or none at all, what steps are to be taken by the officer commanding?

"2*d*. Administration of justice.

"1. How are disputes to be settled that may take place between the troops and the inhabitants?

"2. How are evil-disposed English or other Europeans, who may come here in other ships, and consequently are not followers of the army, to be dealt with?

"3*d*. Quartering of the troops.

"1. How are the houses proper for this purpose to be taken? and in the event of the owners or inhabitants objecting to give them up without remuneration, through what authorities is this question to be settled?

"4*th*. Steam communication should be placed at the disposal of the Military Officer, for the purpose of sending urgent despatches.

"I suspect this can only be ordered by the authority of your Excellency.

[1] From copy retained by Lord Saltoun.

"5th. The Commissary should be authorised to issue fuel, not only for cooking, but also for warmth, as the cold weather comes on.

"It would be advisable that warm clothing should be issued to the Native Troops, if any of this force are kept on that station.

"6th. If any Revenue is to be collected, either by, or on account of China, your Excellency will see the necessity of that being put on a proper footing.

"7th. A competent Interpreter must also be left to assist the Officer in command.

"8th. It would be highly advisable that some ponies should be sent to Chusan, to form a mounted Police, similar to what Major-General Schoedde has organised at Chin Kan foo, as some such force will be absolutely required at Chusan.

"SALTOUN, M.-Genl."

Lord Saltoun, after the active operations were over, lost no time in reminding the authorities at home of the promise that he should be recalled as soon as possible after their termination, but the exigencies of the service did not allow of the appointment of a successor to him at once, and for a year he was obliged to retain his command, during which time he vigorously exerted himself in getting affairs into better order, and in taking measures for combating the sickness which still to a great extent prevailed amongst the troops, in which he was to a considerable degree successful; but in the month of March 1843 his labours suffered a temporary interruption, in consequence of a severe accident which befell him, and which is thus described by himself:—

"*7th April.*—On Wednesday the 29th the pony Ruskin ran away with me, just as I mounted, at the top of the hill on which the house stands. He left the road, and ran for the precipice. I turned him, and got him back to the road, and just as we got there, he gave a short turn, I lost my seat, and he kicked me over his head; a heavy fall down hill. I broke a rib, which is doing well, but the bruises are not yet quite well; nor are they certain whether the collar-bone is broke or not."

It turned out that not only was the collar-bone broken, but the shoulder-blade was split, and the utmost quiet was necessary for a time, to enable the fractured parts to unite properly; but notwithstanding these severe injuries, the natural strength of his constitution, and the good courage and cheerful temper that he always brought to bear against every accident or misfortune, assisted his recovery, and by the middle or end of May he was again able to resume his ordinary mode of life.

In the beginning of June he had the gratification of receiving the notification of the thanks of Parliament, which, on the 14th of February, had been moved in the House of Lords by the Duke of Wellington, and in the House of Commons by Lord Stanley (the late Earl of Derby), and unanimously voted by both Houses to the army and navy employed in the expedition, and to the general officers and the admiral by name.

On the 26th June he was present at the exchange of the ratified treaties between Sir Henry Pottinger and the Chinese chief commissioner, Key Ing, and his colleagues, which ceremony took place at the Government House, Macao, and was attended with much festivity, the Chinese commissioners, Key Ing, Hayling, and Whang, dining with the Plenipotentiary, and proving themselves boon companions when off duty.

Lord Saltoun received, on the 4th August, the medal presented to the Knights of the Order of Maria Theresa by the Emperor of Austria, on the occasion of the Archduke Charles' fiftieth anniversary as Grand Master of that Order. He had obtained the knighthood of Maria Theresa of Austria, as well as that of St. George of Russia, at the close of the campaign of 1815.

In the summer of this year some difference of opinion seems to have occurred between Lord Saltoun and Sir Henry Pottinger as to certain measures. It is unnecessary to inquire what these may have been, but the official correspondence caused some misunderstanding and consequent temporary interruption of the friendly relations which had hitherto subsisted between them, which Lord Saltoun rectified by a manly and straightforward letter, of which the following is an extract:—

"Victoria, Hong-Kong,
"31 August 1843.

"MY DEAR SIR HENRY,—I wish to put an end to this disagreeable correspondence. I see no reason why two gentlemen, whose only object was the good of their country, should, because they have got into a disagreeable official correspondence, make that a reason for a personal disagreement, and I trust you are of the same opinion; for as my stay here is not likely now to be very long, I should be sorry, when we meet hereafter in our own country, it should be otherwise than as friends. You have taken up, and, by your official letter received this morning, still entertain a false impression of my letters, and I cannot help it. I cannot have the slightest objection to your sending the correspondence home.

"Except the usual monthly returns, and forwarding, without any remarks of my own, General Schoedde's letter to the Duke of Wellington, I have never sent a single line home to the Government;[1] indeed, my authority here being purely military, nothing has occurred to make this necessary, and if they require any explanation of anything I have written to you, I shall be as ready to give it to them as I am to yourself."

To this characteristic letter Sir Henry made a reply, of which an extract of the portion bearing on the subject is here given:—

"Macao, 2 September 1843.

"MY DEAR LORD SALTOUN,—Your very kind note of the 31st August I received this morning, and it has given me sincere gratification.

"I most unfeignedly assure you that the idea of having had any difference of opinion or coolness with you has preyed on my mind amidst my late severe trials, and that I have several times thought of writing to you, to say that, if any one impartial person would declare that I had taken a wrong view of your letter, I would acknowledge I had made a mistake, and would withdraw my share of the correspondence."

Thus terminated this slight misunderstanding, in a manner equally creditable to both of the eminent men between whom it had occurred.

In June, Lord Saltoun had made a visit of a week's duration to Amoy and Canton; and upon the 4th December he sailed for Manilla, in the Cornwallis, the flag-ship of the Admiral, who had offered to take him to that

---

[1] This refers, of course, to non-military subjects, his report to the Duke of Wellington, on assuming command of the army of occupation, being a purely military one.

place, where he landed on the 13th December, and remained until the 1st January, visiting many parts of those beautiful islands. He returned to Hong-Kong in H.M.S. Dido, Captain Hon. Henry (now Admiral Hon. Sir Henry) Keppel, arriving on the 7th January, and found, to his great delight, that Major-General D'Aguilar had come from England to relieve him.

Having given over his command to that General, as from the 1st of January, he sailed on the 31st for Calcutta, and upon his departure the following general order was issued :—

"General Orders.

"30th January 1844.

"Major-General Lord Saltoun, K.C.B. and G.C.H., will embark for England on board H.M. Ship Dido to-morrow, at four o'clock.

"His Lordship carries with him the respect and regret of every branch of the troops that have had the honour to serve under his orders; and the Officers of the Garrison, together with the Staff and Heads of Departments, are requested to attend at the Commissariat Wharf, to pay to his Lordship their last tribute of respect on his departure.

"A Guard of Honour, consisting of the Grenadiers of the 41st Regiment Madras Native Infantry, will form at the point of embarkation, and a salute of eleven guns will be fired on his Lordship entering the boat that carries him from Hong-Kong, with the best wishes of his fellow-soldiers for his prosperity and welfare.

"By order,

"L. M. EDWARDS, Captain,
"Ass^t Adj^t-Genl."

On his voyage home Lord Saltoun went as far as Calcutta in H.M.S. Dido, arriving there on the 10th February, having touched at Macao and Pulo Penang, remained a day or two at the latter place, and having visited the Marquis of Tweeddale, then commanding at Madras. On the 15th February he went on board the Bentinck steamer, and stopping for a day at the island of Ceylon, and at Aden, reached Suez on the 13th April, and crossed the desert to Cairo, where on the 14th he had an interview with Mahomet Pacha, who, in the course of a conversation lasting about forty minutes, asked him many questions respecting China, and whom he describes as a small but fine looking old man.

After a day spent in a visit to the Pyramids, etc., he left Cairo on the 16th, and passing some days at Alexandria, where he visited the docks, the Vice-Admiral Mahomet Bey's flag-ship, and the field of the battle of 1801, at which Sir Ralph Abercromby was killed, sailed on the 24th in the P. and O. steamer for England, arrived at the Mother-bank on the 10th of May, and after a few days to complete the quarantine, landed at Southampton.

It need scarcely be said that he received a warm welcome from all his numerous friends; and at the Waterloo banquet of that year the Duke of Wellington proposed his health in the most flattering terms.

But, perhaps, as warm a reception, and certainly the most curious in some respects, was that which he obtained from the tenantry of his estates, on his return to Philorth in the autumn.

The tenantry resolved to entertain him at a grand dinner in Fraserburgh, on the 22d October, and the fishermen of the village of Broadsea, not to be behind the others in their demonstrations of affection and respect, determined to provide a triumphal car of a novel description for his public entry into the town upon that occasion. What this was will be seen from the following letter, which is worth insertion:—

"Seatown of Broadsea, 10 Oct. 1844.

"To the Right Honble. Lord Saltoun.

"MY LORD,—The Fishermen on your Lordship's Estate here being anxouse to pay all the esteem in their power to your Honour, came to the Resolution, if your Lordship should accept of it, to draw you and your friends from your seat at Philorth to the entry of the town of Fraserburgh, on the day of the dinner to your Lordship from the Farmers, in a Boat mounted on four wheels, and acquiped for the purpose; your Lordship may depend that the utmost decorum will be observed, and a slow peass kept, in order to prevent the least chance of any accident.

"I have the honor to be, my Lord,
"Your Lordship's most obedient servant,
"JAMES NOBLE, *Preses*."

TOWN HALL AND MARKET CROSS.
FRASERBURGH.

The offer having been accepted in the same spirit that prompted it, the whole affair went off most satisfactorily; the boat, one of those used in the herring fishery, was painted white and ornamented with gilding, and dressed out with laurels and evergreens, the sternmost portion was handsomely carpeted and cushioned, and surrounded with an ornamental railing, and there were three masts, bearing numerous flags with appropriate mottoes. It was manned by four stalwart oarsmen, who when it moved went through the motions of rowing, and being placed on wheels, it was drawn by some fifty or sixty fishermen, with shoulder-bands fastened to a rope attached to the under carriage. Lord Saltoun and some of his friends, among whom was Captain Cunynghame, his aide-de-camp in China, having taken their seats, the procession moved off, his Lordship steering the boat, moving the tiller, and answering "Starboard it is," or "Port it is," etc., in accordance with the orders shouted back through a speaking-trumpet by the master mariner, standing at the bow, who conned the vessel at each turn of the road. Thus they proceeded from Philorth, escorted by a cheering crowd of some two or three thousand people, to a pavilion erected in front of the Saltoun Arms Hotel, near the Town Cross of Fraserburgh; and many gentlemen of the neighbourhood having accepted invitations, a large party, numbering about 250, sat down to dinner on the occasion of this public expression of the good feeling that existed between Lord Saltoun and his tenantry, their admiration of his public career, and their esteem and affection for him in his more private capacity of their landlord.

After his return from China, Lord Saltoun resumed the usual tenor of his life, passing the Parliamentary season in London, and enjoying the sports of flood and field during the recess with as keen a zest as ever. His lease of the extensive shootings of Coignafearn, in the Monadhliadh, having come to an end about 1846, he did not seek to renew it, finding that ground too steep and high for his advancing years, but took a moor near the village of Rothes, on the bank of the Spey, where he also rented a considerable extent of salmon-fishing. He resided during August and September of each year at the beautifully situated shooting-lodge of Auchinroth in that vicinity, and towards the end of the latter month paid his annual visit to Philorth, where he entertained a party of his friends during October, and then betook himself to his hunting-quarters, which for some years he shared with his brother-in-law, William Macdowall Grant of Arndilly, who had married his sister Eleanor. These hunting-quarters had been at Dunse, in Berwickshire, but after his return in 1844, they rented the house of Lees, near Coldstream, during the minority of the proprietor of that estate, Sir John Marjoribanks, Bart., where they hunted usually with the celebrated pack of hounds belonging to Lord Elcho (now the Earl Wemyss), an old and valued friend, and occasionally were able to meet the Duke of Buccleuch's pack.

This arrangement lasted until the death of Mr. Macdowall Grant, which occurred from cholera on the 29th of January 1849, and Lord Saltoun, after that sad event, gave up the house of Lees, and took a lodging in the town of Coldstream, where, however, his residence was scarcely more than nominal, as he was, during the hunting season, a constant and welcome guest at the hospitable mansion of Ladykirk, about four miles from Coldstream. His frank and open-hearted manner, the kindness of his disposition, and the geniality of his conversation and intercourse with all, whether in the hunting-field or at the social board, made him a general favourite, and many an expression of esteem and affection for him, and of regret for his loss, has the writer of this history heard from his associates of those days. He invariably left his hunting-quarters for some weeks at the end of the year, to eat his Christmas dinner with an old brother officer, Colonel Charles Ellis, who had been his subaltern at Quatre-bras and Waterloo, and this custom was continued until the death of the latter, after which he often passed Christmas with another old brother Guardsman, Colonel Samuel Long.

On the 9th of November 1846, Lord Saltoun attained to the rank of Lieutenant-general in the army. He had been appointed, 23d February of that year, colonel of the 55th Regiment, and on the 7th August he had been transferred to the colonelcy of the 2d, or Queen's Royal Regiment, which very considerable advancement was regarded by all as preparatory to his obtaining the colonelcy of one of the regiments of Foot Guards, had he survived until a vacancy occurred in the Household Brigade.

On the 25th March 1852, Her Majesty was pleased to invest him with the Order of the Thistle, the highest of Scottish distinctions, and the following correspondence, so highly honourable to all concerned, conveyed the announcement of Her Majesty's gracious intention to him:—

LORD JOHN RUSSELL (NOW EARL RUSSELL) TO LORD FITZROY SOMERSET
(THE LATE LORD RAGLAN).

"Pembroke Lodge, August 13, 1851.

"MY DEAR LORD FITZROY,—As you kindly consented to transmit my message to Lord Saltoun, I write to tell you what I wish to be said.

"It is my opinion that the orders of knighthood should not be exclusively confined to the friends and adherents of the existing ministry, but should embrace men of distinguished service in the military and civil departments, whatever may be their political opinions.

"The vacancy in the Order of the Thistle, caused by the death of the late Lord Melville, enables me to recommend to the Queen a Knight of that Order.

"The military services of Lord Saltoun, so long and so distinguished, make me desirous of placing his name before the Queen, as deserving of a mark of honour, which belongs to the Scotch Peerage.

"Of course I do not wish to influence in any way his political conduct, and I am quite aware that I could not hope for his support.

"May I beg you to obtain an answer for me.

"I remain, yours very truly,

"J. RUSSELL."

LORD FITZROY SOMERSET TO LORD SALTOUN.

"Horse Guards, August 14, 1851.

"MY DEAR SALTOUN,—Happening to meet Lord John Russell at Buckingham Palace a week ago, where I attended an investiture of the Bath, he asked me whether I should be willing to convey to you the expression of his desire to recommend you to the Queen for the Order of the Thistle, as a recognition of your distinguished military services, and apart from every political consideration.

"I readily undertook to comply with his request, as soon as I should hear from him on the subject, feeling happy to be the channel of a communication so honourable to Lord John Russell and yourself; and I have now the satisfaction to send you a letter I received from him this morning.

"In this you will observe he states his opinion that the orders of knighthood should not be exclusively confined to the friends and adherents of the existing ministry, but should embrace men of distinguished service in the military and civil departments of the country, whatever might be their political sentiments; and on these grounds he expresses his desire to lay your name before Her Majesty for a mark of honour, which belongs to the peerage of Scotland, without any wish to influence your political conduct, and without any hope of your support.

"I have thought it right to show Lord John's letter to the Duke of Wellington, who is highly gratified to learn that your services are so properly appreciated.

"I will take care to forward your answer to Lord John as soon as I receive it.

"Believe me, very faithfully yours,

"FITZROY SOMERSET."

LORD SALTOUN TO LORD FITZROY SOMERSET.

"Auchinroth, Rothes,
"Fochabers, 16 August 1851.

"MY DEAR LORD FITZROY,—I this morning received your kind and most unexpected letter, enclosing one from Lord John Russell to your Lordship, proposing to lay my name before Her Majesty, for the purpose of conferring upon me the high honour of being made a Knight of the Thistle.

"Permit me, in the first place, to thank your Lordship for the very kind and complimentary manner in which you have made this communication to me, as also for your kindness in informing the Duke of Wellington of Lord John Russell's intention.

"I have to request that you will convey to Lord John Russell my most sincere thanks for the honour his Lordship proposes to confer upon me, and express to him how highly I appreciate his kindness in not expecting any change in my political conduct.

"I remain, my dear Lord,
"Your sincere and faithful servant,
"SALTOUN."

LORD JOHN RUSSELL TO LORD SALTOUN.

"Pembroke Lodge, August 23d, 1851.

"MY LORD,—The Queen has been pleased to declare her gracious intention of conferring upon your Lordship the Order of the Thistle.

"Your many and distinguished services in Her Majesty's army have rightly earned for you this honourable distinction.

"It gives me great pleasure to be the organ of conveying to you the notification of Her Majesty's commands.

"I have the honour to be, my Lord,
"Your Lordship's most obedient servant,
"J. RUSSELL."

LORD SALTOUN TO LORD JOHN RUSSELL.

"Auchinroth, Fochabers, 30th August 1851.

"MY LORD,—I have the honour to acknowledge the receipt of your Lordship's letter of the 23d inst., informing me of Her Majesty's gracious intention to confer upon me the Order of the Thistle for my services in the army.

"I am quite aware that it is the favourable consideration of that service by your Lordship which has induced your Lordship to recommend me for this high mark of distinction, and I beg to convey to your Lordship my grateful acknowledgments and thanks for your kindness on this occasion.

"I have the honour to be, my Lord,
"Your Lordship's most obedient servant,
"SALTOUN."

Lord Saltoun thus received the highest Scottish honour on the recommendation of the leader of the party which he opposed in politics, and solely on account of his distinguished career in the army; and as he had already long been a Knight Commander of the Bath, a Knight Grand Cross of Hanover, and a Knight of the foreign orders of Maria Theresa of Austria, and St. George of Russia, these decorations, with his Waterloo, Peninsular, and China medals, worthily adorned the breast of the gallant soldier, who had won them by long and arduous service and heroic deeds on many a battle-field.

Until the year 1845, with the exception of his brother Simon, whose decease in 1811 has been already mentioned, the family circle, of which Lord Saltoun was head, had been unbroken; but during the next few years the hand of death was very busy, and he was eventually left the sole survivor of his generation.

His brother William died on the 21st of March 1845, and but a few months after was followed by his sister Margaret, who died on the 14th of August of the same year.

In January 1849, as above noticed, he lost his brother-in-law, Mr. Macdowall Grant of Arndilly, whose death caused him sorrow proportionate to the sincere and ardent affection that had long existed between them; and on the 15th November 1851, his mother, the Dowager Lady Saltoun, departed this life, having enjoyed, during an existence extended far beyond the natural limit, the happiness of seeing her favourite son achieve honour and distinction in the career for which her sedulous attention to his early education had prepared him.

Not quite a year after his mother's death, his sister Eleanor (Mrs. Macdowall Grant of Arndilly) died on the 26th September 1852, and he then remained the sole survivor of his generation in the family.

The fatigues and hardships of his early campaigns, the poison of the Walcheren fever yet lurking in his system, and the effects of the unhealthy climate in which his last active service had been performed, at length began to tell upon even his iron frame and constitution; and, doubtless, upon one of so warm-hearted and affectionate a disposition, the loss of so many dearly-loved relatives, in so short a period of time, had a very depressing effect, and during the winter of 1852-3, and the following spring, his health began perceptibly to decline.

But the indomitable courage and energy of his character prevented his believing that he was really ill, or yielding to the illness which he felt; and making no change in his manner of life, he passed the Parliamentary season of 1853 in London, after which he went north to his shooting lodge of Auchinroth, where, on the 18th of August in that year, he died of a rapid dropsy, consequent upon the failure of his weakened system to throw out an attack of gout, to which malady he had been subject during the latter part of his life.

His remains were conveyed to Philorth, from whence, on the 25th of August, a solemn procession of the tenantry of his estates and the feuars of the town of Fraserburgh, accompanied by the Duke of Richmond, Sir John Bayley, Baronet, Mr. Lyttleton H. Bayley, the writer of this history, his brother, then Captain D. Fraser, R.H.A., and many of the gentlemen of the county, attended them to their resting-place in the family mausoleum at Fraserburgh.

Such, in his sixty-ninth year, was the end of this eminent man, who had held the family dignities and possessions for a period of very nearly sixty years, during which the improvement, both in the country and in the town of Fraserburgh, had been very remarkable; the former, in common with a great part of Aberdeenshire, having been changed by the energy and industry of the farming population, assisted by the liberality of their landlords, from barren moors and mosses, with areas of cultivation here and there, into valuable agricultural lands; and the latter having been considerably enriched by the increase of trade, and its public buildings and harbour greatly extended and improved.

Although the preceding account of his career affords sufficient evidence as to what manner of man he was, the following brief but just summary of the character of the sixteenth Lord Saltoun may here be made.

Endowed with high personal courage and unflinching integrity, he was intolerant of anything in the shape of cowardice and deceit, but tender and gentle to unmerited misfortune or suffering, and to the infirmity or weakness of old age or childhood; and though his manner and voice were somewhat stern and abrupt, they but veiled the kind heart that beat beneath.

His distinguishing qualities were energy and activity of mind and body, a cheerful and contented disposition, that laughed at hardship, sound common sense, great moral courage, and inflexible resolution in what he considered right. A strong sense of duty led him to sacrifice any personal comfort or advantage that might interfere with its demands; and in all matters, whether important or trivial, his promise, once given, was performed to the fullest extent, at whatever cost to himself.

While he attained to high honour in the profession that he had chosen, and in his public career received the approbation of his sovereign and of all entitled to judge his conduct, it was acknowledged by those who knew him in private life that he uniformly sustained the still more excellent part of a thoroughly true and good man.[1]

It is beyond the scope of this work to give any detailed account of individuals belonging to the present generation; but a brief notice of the course of succession down to the present time is necessary, for the sixteenth Lord Saltoun left no issue, and his next brother, the Honourable Simon Fraser, died unmarried.

The Honourable William Fraser, third son of the fifteenth Lord Saltoun, was born on the 12th of October 1791. He was educated at Harrow, and although his own wish was to enter the army, in which his eldest brother was then beginning his distinguished career, the advantages of a partnership in a West Indian mercantile house, offered for his acceptance, were so apparent, that he reluctantly consented to abandon his own inclinations, and become one of the time-honoured merchants of the city of London.

For many years the firm was prosperous, and in process of time he became the senior partner, trading under the appellation of the Honourable William Fraser, Neilson, and Co.; and in a well-written and amusing series of papers, called "The World of London," which appeared in Blackwood's Magazine in 1841, there is the following passage:—"We have seen with pleasure the name of the Honourable Mr. Fraser figuring upon a brass plate on the door of an eminent mercantile house in the city; and we are vulgar enough to imagine the scion of a noble house looks quite as much to advantage in that place as on the steps of Crockford's, or in the profligate society of the saloon."[2]

The mercantile house of which he was the head, however, shared the ruin brought upon many similar establishments by the enactment of the abolition of slavery in the West Indian islands and dependencies, which the compensation of twenty millions granted by Parliament was but as a drop in the ocean to avert.

[1] His character, in very similar terms, is given by Sir F. W. Hamilton, History of the Grenadier Guards, vol. iii. p. 143.   [2] Blackwood's Magazine, vol. 50, p. 777.

THE HONOURABLE WILLIAM FRASER
THIRD SON OF ALEXANDER 15TH LORD SALTOUN.
BORN 1791. DIED 1845.

However right in the abstract, it is very doubtful whether that measure has proved as beneficial to the negroes themselves as its promoters anticipated and desired, or whether a more gradual change might not have produced better effects upon their protégés, and less ruinous consequences to some of their fellow-countrymen; but these pages are not the proper place in which to discuss that question.

The struggles of William Fraser against the adverse circumstances which he had to encounter, and the destruction of his expectations of wealth and independence, seriously affected his health, and after the failure of the firm he retired from business, and passed the last two years of his life in Scotland. In the spring of 1845 he went to London on a visit to his brother, Lord Saltoun, but a few days after his arrival, either from the fatigue of the journey, or from having taken cold, he became very unwell, and after a short but severe illness he died at his brother's house on the 21st of March in that year, aged 53.

His character may be given in a very few words. He never made an enemy. Robust and active, he delighted in field sports and athletic exercises, while the kindness of his disposition and geniality of his temper made him a very general favourite. A good husband and father, and a warm friend, there were many that sorrowed for his comparatively early death.

On the 9th of April 1818 he married Elizabeth Graham, second daughter of David Macdowall Grant, Esq. of Arndilly, in the county of Banff, and by her, who died on the 5th of May 1853, he had a numerous family, of whom, although their names will be found in the Pedigree, it is, as above mentioned, beyond the scope of this history to give any more detailed account. The eldest son, Alexander, succeeded as seventeenth Lord Saltoun on the decease of his uncle 18th August 1853.

END OF THE FIRST VOLUME.

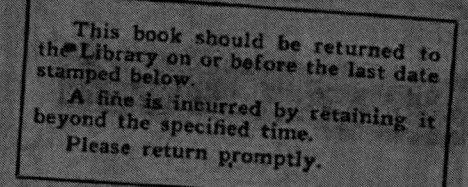

This book should be returned to the Library on or before the last date stamped below.

A fine is incurred by retaining it beyond the specified time.

Please return promptly.

Lightning Source UK Ltd.
Milton Keynes UK
173949UK00004B/29/P